THE PAPERS OF
James Madison

VOLUME I
16 March 1751—16 December 1779

Volume I of this definitive edition of the papers of James Madison begins with the record of birth and baptism of James Madison, Jr., on March 16, 1751. Youthful jottings in his Commonplace Book, his "Collegiate Doggerel," and letters to and from his father and friends show us the young Madison as he was being educated at private school and at the College of New Jersey (Princeton).

From 1774 on, the documents reveal Madison's steadily increasing involvement in public affairs, first as a member of the Orange County Committee of Safety and then as county delegate to the Virginia Convention. In 1776, as a member of this convention, he persuaded his colleagues to include in the Declaration of Rights of Virginia a guarantee of religious freedom rather than merely of religious toleration. In 1778 and 1779 he served as a member of the Council of State of Virginia under governors Patrick Henry and Thomas Jefferson.

This volume ends on December 16, 1779, when Madison accepted his election by the General Assembly as a delegate from Virginia to the Continental Congress, where he was so soon to play a leading role.

THE PAPERS OF

James Madison

SPONSORED BY

The University of Chicago

AND

The University of Virginia

JAMES MADISON

THE PAPERS OF
James Madison

VOLUME 1

16 MARCH 1751—16 DECEMBER 1779

EDITED BY

WILLIAM T. HUTCHINSON AND WILLIAM M. E. RACHAL

EDITORIAL STAFF

JEAN SCHNEIDER   ROBERT L. SCRIBNER
RALPH L. KETCHAM   DONALD O. DEWEY

THE UNIVERSITY OF CHICAGO PRESS

Library of Congress Catalog Card Number: 62-9114

The University of Chicago Press, Chicago & London
The University of Toronto Press, Toronto 5, Canada

© *1962 by The University of Chicago. All rights re-*
served. Published 1962. Composed and printed by The
University of Chicago Press, Chicago, Illinois, U.S.A.

To

LEONARD D. WHITE

1891–1958

CONTENTS

CONTENTS

1771

1771–1774

1772

1773

1774

1775

1776

1777

CONTENTS

1778

1779

ILLUSTRATIONS

xiii

ILLUSTRATIONS

INTRODUCTION

On 9 June 1835, after reminding James Madison that his papers "must possess a higher interest with your Countrymen, than those of any of y'r contemporaries," Edward Everett asked permission to edit selections from these manuscripts and also to use them later in preparing "a history of the Constitution . . . or a history of Constitutional Liberty in the U.S. in a broad philosophical sense." Madison declined for the reason that he wished to reserve his papers for posthumous publication.[1] With his death on 28 June of the next year, the tangled story of the dispersal and partial publication of his manuscripts properly begins.

During the last fifty-five years of his life, Madison tried to collect a documentary file on his public career. From the beginning of his service in the Continental Congress in March 1780, he kept much of the correspondence addressed to him although he rarely retained full copies of his own letters. He also made a careful summary of some of the debates in that Congress as well as a more complete record of those in the Constitutional Convention of 1787. At the same time, he complicated the task of editing his papers by including among them many undated sheets of various sizes bearing his rough notes on letters received or to be sent, on his reading of unspecified books and pamphlets, and on speeches delivered or in preparation.

During nearly twenty years in retirement following the close of his presidency in 1817, he was more careful than before to preserve drafts of his own letters. Trying also to regain those which he had written earlier in his career, he recovered many sent by him to his fellow Virginians, Thomas Jefferson, Joseph Jones, James Monroe, Edmund Pendleton, Edmund Randolph, and George Washington.

Madison evidently assumed that only correspondence and other papers relating to public affairs were worth saving. He eliminated documents which, in his opinion, had no historical importance, including many bearing upon his family and his plantation.[2] Besides destroying some of these manuscripts, he and Mrs. Madison scattered others among their kinsfolk, friends, and autograph collectors. Thus by the

[1] Massachusetts Historical Society: Edward Everett Papers.

[2] Dolley P. Madison to Edward Everett, 25 February 1840, Massachusetts Historical Society: Edward Everett Papers.

time of his death, his files contained a much more ample documentation of his public career than of his private life.

As early as 1788, and occasionally thereafter, he apparently had in mind writing an account of the Revolutionary epoch, or at least of the formation and adoption of the federal Constitution.[3] With much more persistence, however, he arranged and edited, with a view to their appearance in print after his death, his notes on the debates of the 1780's and many of his letters and other papers bearing upon public affairs during that decade. By doing this he hoped to benefit historical scholarship, to enhance American patriotism, to justify his early public career and that of his friends, to enjoy the reminiscences stimulated by rereading what he had written long before, and to assure the payment of $12,000 in legacies, made contingent upon the income expected from the posthumous publication of his notes taken in the Constitutional Convention of 1787. His views about history and the role of the historian were well summarized in his letter of 19 March 1823 to Edward Everett:

It has been the misfortune of history that a personal knowledge and an impartial judgment of things, can rarely meet in the historian. The best history of our country therefore must be the fruit of contributions bequeathed by co-temporary actors and witnesses, to successors who will make an unbiassed use of them. And if the abundance and authenticity of the materials which still exist in private as well as in public repositories among us should descend to hands capable of doing justice to them, then American History may be expected to contain more truth, and lessons certainly not less valuable, than that of any Country or age whatever.[4]

Madison's efforts during his years in retirement to assist the future editor of his papers and the future historian of his country were not altogether to their advantage. Besides excluding his private correspondence from the material eligible for publication, he designated for that purpose only portions of his own letters dealing with political matters; furthermore, he or someone else at his bidding wrote many explanatory comments, recopied some documents, and clarified a word or revised a sentence or paragraph in others. In most instances at least, these emendations are readily identifiable because of his changed penmanship and his use of a different ink, or because the handwriting is clearly not his own. His principal copyists were his wife, her son, and, above all, his wife's brother, John Coles Payne, who lived not far from

[3] JM to Thomas Jefferson, 8 December 1788, and to Edmund Pendleton, 4 April 1790, LC: Madison Papers; JM to Noah Webster, 12 October 1804, LC: William C. Rives Papers.

[4] Massachusetts Historical Society: Edward Everett Papers.

Montpelier and wrote in a distinctive hand. Dolley Madison's statement to an unknown correspondent on 16 March 1839 is not wholly reassuring. She wrote:

I consider my husband's writings Sacred, and no more to be infringed or altered than his last will. He desired me to read them over and if any letter —line—or word struck me as being calculated to injure the feelings of any one or wrong in themselves that I would withdraw them or it.... The slight corrections therefore are consonant to his wishes and directions, and made with my concurrence.[5]

The sources agree that Dolley Madison was a devoted wife with an unusually attractive personality, but they also permit no doubt that she was not qualified to be an unbiased editor of her husband's papers.

The task of organizing and correcting the material chosen for publication was well advanced toward completion by the time of Madison's death. Immediately thereafter, the making of two copies for submission to book publishers in the United States, and a third copy for possible use in bringing out a European edition, was vigorously pressed forward. Payne's daughter informed a friend on 16 July 1836 that at Montpelier there were "three clerks finishing copies of Uncle M's manuscripts."[6] Before the end of that year, however, this tedious labor seemed to have been all for naught. In Mrs. Madison's judgment, no publisher had made a sufficiently remunerative offer.[7]

Under these circumstances, several of her influential friends in Washington easily persuaded her to seek from the federal government a proposal to purchase some of her husband's papers. Accepting Congress' offer of $30,000, although she had first thought $100,000 not too high a price, she arranged for the delivery to the Department of State, on 6 April 1837, of the original and one copy of Madison's notes taken in the Constitutional Convention of 1787, together with his notes made on the debates "in the Congress of the Confederation in 1782, '83, & '87 . . . and selections made by himself & prepared under his eye from his letters, narrating the proceedings of that Body during the periods of his service in it."[8]

[5] Stan. V. Henkels, Jr., Catalogue No. 1478 (Philadelphia, 13 October 1933).

[6] Anna C. Payne to Mrs. Frances D. Lear, LC: J. Henley Smith Papers.

[7] John C. Payne to Edward Coles, 6 and 18 July, 3 August, 25 September, 2 and 27 November 1836; Anna C. Payne to Edward Coles, 23 October 1836, Princeton University Library: Edward Coles Papers.

[8] Dolley P. Madison to Andrew Jackson, 15 November 1836, LC: Madison Papers; Virgil Maxcy to John Payne Todd, 25 March, and John Forsyth to Dolley P. Madison, 30 March 1837, McGregor Library, University of Virginia; William C. Rives to Dolley P. Madison, 20 February and 28 March 1837, Rosenbach Founda-

In 1838, Congress appointed Henry Dilworth Gilpin, solicitor of the United States Treasury, to oversee the publication of these documents and cautioned him against altering their text, except by correcting "a few slight and evident clerical errors." Two years later, after he had become the Attorney General of the United States, Gilpin received from the press of Langtree and O'Sullivan of Washington the three volumes, entitled *The Papers of James Madison, purchased by order of Congress; being his correspondence and reports of debates during the Congress of the Confederation and His Reports of Debates in the Federal Convention; now published from the original manuscripts, deposited in the Department of State, by direction of the Joint Library Committee of Congress, under the Superintendence of Henry D. Gilpin.* During the next four years, these volumes were reprinted at least three times, by J. and H. G. Langley in New York at an unspecified date, and by Allston Mygatt in Mobile in 1842 and in Boston in 1844.

With the exception of the brief foreword and most of the footnotes, prepared by Gilpin with much help from Jared Sparks, these volumes had really been edited by James Madison.[9] All, or almost all, the selections, revisions, and omissions had been determined by him or by members of his family working under his direction. Whether these emendations were merely stylistic, or significantly altered what he or others had actually said or written during the Constitutional Convention of 1787, was a question asked by George Gibbs in his *Memoirs of the Administrations of Washington and John Adams, edited from the Papers of Oliver Wolcott, Secretary of the Treasury.*[10] All papers in the first two volumes of the present edition date too early to be an issue in this controversy.

Even before the purchase by Congress in early 1837, John C. Payne had supervised at Montpelier the arranging and copying of enough additional Madison manuscripts, dating before 1801, to fill two volumes. Not long thereafter, selections of Madison's correspondence about foreign affairs while he was Secretary of State and President were

---

tion, Philadelphia; Dolley P. Madison to William C. Rives, 27 February 1837, LC: Rives Papers; Dolley P. Madison to Richard Smith, 1 April 1837 (with Secretary of State John Forsyth's note of 6 April appended to it, showing that the "box of ms" was to be delivered to his office on that day), Historical Society of Pennsylvania.

[9] Dolley P. Madison to Edward Coles, 15 June 1837, Princeton University Library: Edward Coles Papers; Henry D. Gilpin to Jared Sparks, 7 May, 17 July, and 16 October 1839, Harvard University Library: Jared Sparks Papers.

[10] (2 vols.; New York, 1846), II, 290–91.

grouped together to make a third volume.[11] Payne and Mrs. Madison interpreted the action of Congress to mean that the purchased documents would soon be published under its aegis. Since these were almost entirely on constitutional subjects, their appearance might create a market for more of Madison's writings of a similar nature. With this expectation, Payne and Mrs. Madison brought together sufficient documents on constitutional matters to make another volume in addition to the three manuscript volumes mentioned above.[12] As early as the summer of 1837, or nearly three years before the "Gilpin edition" came off the press, Mrs. Madison gave Harper and Brothers of New York City an option to print the four manuscript volumes. Although she strongly hoped that the fourth of these would be published simultaneously with the volumes to be brought out under government auspices, she was less concerned about making available to the public, at an early date, the other three and a projected two or three more to follow the "fourth."[13]

Why Harper and Brothers did not publish the "fourth" volume, or, for that matter, the first three volumes, remains a mystery—a mystery only deepened by Dolley Madison's remark in an undated letter to her son "ab't the Vol Harper lost." In the spring of 1842 this "fourth" volume was in page proof. Almost two years later it was ready to be released as soon as its "Preface and Title Page" had been prepared.[14] There is no evidence that this front material was ever written, or that Harper published the volume under its imprint. In some manner, however, James C. McGuire of Washington, D.C., acquired the stereo-

[11] John C. Payne to Edward Coles, 28 February and 15 March 1837, Princeton University Library: Edward Coles Papers.

[12] Dolley P. Madison to Edward Coles, 15 June 1837, Princeton University Library: Edward Coles Papers; Andrew Stevenson to John Payne Todd, 12 November 1838, LC: Madison Papers; Dolley P. Madison to Richard D. Cutts, 20 April 184[0?], MS owned by Mr. and Mrs. George B. Cutts, Brookline, Mass.; "Prospectus of Writings of James Madison," undated, but probably prepared by Anna Payne in 1839 or 1840, University of Virginia Library.

[13] Dolley P. Madison to Edward Coles, 15 June 1837, Princeton University Library: Edward Coles Papers; Dolley P. Madison to Charles J. Ingersoll, 15 June 1838, MS owned by R. Sturgis Ingersoll, Philadelphia.

[14] Notes of Richard Rush on the page proof, 26 April 1842, Historical Society of Pennsylvania; Edward Coles to Dolley P. Madison, 6 May 1842, Illinois State Historical Society; Dolley P. Madison to Richard Rush, May 1842, Princeton University Library; Dolley P. Madison's undated letter to John Payne Todd, probably written late in 1842 or 1843, LC: Dolley P. Madison Papers; James K. Paulding to Dolley P. Madison, 4 January 1844, American Art Association Catalogue, "President Madison's Correspondence from . . . the Notable Collection of . . . Frederick B. McGuire" (26 February 1917), item no. 113.

type plates of this "lost" volume and used them as the basis of his edition, "exclusively for private distribution," which appeared in that city in 1853 under the title *Selections from the Private Correspondence of James Madison from 1813 to 1836.*[15]

During the early years of the vicissitudes of this "fourth volume," the first three manuscript volumes experienced an equally unhappy history. When it became clear that neither Harper nor any other publisher was much interested in these compilations, Mrs. Madison deposited them in a bank vault in Washington. The originals of these copies, as well as most of the rest of Madison's papers, were from time to time in the precarious and sole custody of her son, John Payne Todd, at Montpelier or at his own bachelor quarters called "Toddsberthe" not far away. Sometimes with her consent, but often without her knowledge, he sold portions of his stepfather's papers in order to satisfy the claims of his insistent creditors. Partly because of her son's extravagant style of living, and partly because of her own naïveté about business matters, Mrs. Madison by 1840 needed money—a need which became more and more acute during the next seven years.[16]

Early in 1844, she and her son agreed "to offer the entire writings of Mr. Madison to Congress including the 4th volume—this seems the only mode left for me to pursue, with my unabated wishes to place them before the world."[17] This decision, reached in the same month when Harper was finally ready to publish "the 4th volume," perhaps induced that firm to shelve the project. Lack of primary evidence permits no certain answer.

After Congress adjourned in mid-June without making an offer, her son, acting as her attorney, formally signed on 24 September 1844 a second, and what proved to be another abortive contract with Harper and Brothers, giving it the exclusive right "to print and publish, from Stereotype Plates owned and furnished for the purpose by Mrs. D. P. Madison, the Correspondence and other Writings of James Madison."[18]

[15] Richard Rush's seven sheets of notes on the Harper's page proof, mentioned above, list page references corresponding exactly with the pagination of McGuire's volume; see also William C. Rives to Edward Coles, 18 March 1858, Princeton University Library: Edward Coles Papers.

[16] Dolley P. Madison to Edward Coles, 3 March 1840, and 26 September 1842, Princeton University Library: Edward Coles Papers; Dolley P. Madison to Richard D. Cutts, 12 May 1840, and to John Payne Todd, 22 January 1844, both letters owned by Mr. and Mrs. George B. Cutts, Brookline, Mass.

[17] Dolley P. Madison to James K. Paulding, 10 January 1844, Boston Public Library.

[18] Handwritten and witnessed "Article of Agreement," 24 September 1844, Harper & Brothers, New York City.

Congress may have presented these plates to Dolley Madison after Langtree and O'Sullivan published the first "Gilpin" edition four years before.[19] Since many sets of this printing had been destroyed by fire in Langtree and O'Sullivan's shop, Harper perhaps believed that the issuance of additional copies would be financially feasible.[20]

Although her economic situation became increasingly critical, Mrs. Madison was obliged to wait four more years before President James K. Polk, on 31 May 1848, signed a bill to pay her $25,000 for "all the unpublished papers of the said James Madison, belonging to [her], and in her possession."[21] To receive this sum she had to agree to use up to a maximum of $5,000 of it to pay her more pressing debts, and to permit the balance to be entrusted to three men in order to keep it out of her son's control. The trustees pledged to remit to her the semiannual interest on the balance of about $20,000 and to turn over the principal to her heirs after her death.[22]

Congress had delayed its purchase much too long to acquire "all the unpublished papers" of Madison. When his widow delivered four trunks full of them to Secretary of State James Buchanan on 8 June 1848, she evidently believed that her obligation under the contract of purchase had been completely fulfilled. Unknown to her, John Payne Todd had rifled the collection of some of its most valuable manuscripts and held back others which should have been sent to the Department of State in 1848.[23] From his standpoint, Todd's anger over the mistrust of him shown by the terms of purchase is understandable.[24] In justice to him, at least some of his raids into his stepfather's archives should probably be called deceptive rather than dishonest, since his mother on several occasions had either made him her attorney for the disposal of

[19] By its contract with Congress' Joint Committee on the Library, Langtree and O'Sullivan acknowledged that the stereotype plates would be the property of Congress (Senate Doc. 145, 25th Cong., 3d sess. [1838–39]; Nicholas P. Trist to Dolley Madison, 27 September 1836 and 12 and 14 October 1836, Virginia Historical Society: Nicholas P. Trist Album Book).

[20] Senate Doc. 442, 26th Cong., 1st sess. (1839–40).

[21] John Bassett Moore, ed., *The Works of James Buchanan* (12 vols.; Philadelphia, 1908–11), VIII, 85–87.

[22] Copy of a witnessed agreement signed by Mrs. Madison on 13 December 1847, LC: Madison Papers.

[23] Dolley P. Madison to John Payne Todd, 21 May 1848, LC: Dolley P. Madison Papers; Edward Coles to William C. Rives, 3 February 1857, LC: William C. Rives Papers.

[24] Dolley P. Madison to John Payne Todd, 29 June 1848, LC: Dolley P. Madison Papers.

the papers or had less formally extended him a free hand to do whatever he wished with them and with many valuable books and pamphlets in Madison's library.[25] However this may be, the United States government received much less in 1848 than it had contracted to buy. Until his death in 1851, Todd continued to levy upon this treasury of manuscripts for funds with which to pay his gambling and liquor debts. James C. McGuire, his heaviest creditor, appears to have been chief among the presumably innocent purchasers.

Following Mrs. Madison's death on 12 July 1849, Todd, as executor of her will, had McGuire appointed as its administrator. In partial or full payment of Todd's debts to him, McGuire then transferred from Montpelier to his own home in Washington "papers and other valuables" found "packed in trunks and in the drawers of an old bureau."[26] In an undated memoir, now owned by Mr. and Mrs. George B. Cutts of Brookline, Massachusetts, Mary E. Cutts remarked that although these manuscripts were mostly the "private letters and papers of Mr. and Mrs. Madison," they also included some letters to Madison from Washington and other correspondents. Nearly three thousand letters, comprising most of the James C. McGuire collection, were sold at auction to a large number of buyers in 1892.[27] The Library of Congress eventually retrieved many of these manuscripts. Other sales between 1892 and 1933, notably those of the James H. Causten, Frederick B. McGuire, and Dolley P. Madison collections, scattered additional hundreds of items which originally had been in Madison's files.[28] Except when one or another of these papers comes to rest in a university or historical society library, they continue to circulate frequently in the manuscript market. "Papers" of an unspecified nature, given to Anna C. Payne by Dolley Madison shortly before her death, were evi-

[25] Edward Coles to John C. Payne, 21 September 1836, Princeton University Library: Edward Coles Papers; two deeds of gift, dated 16 and 17 July 1844, respectively, of furniture and books at Montpelier by Dolley P. Madison to her son, McGregor Library, University of Virginia; John Payne Todd to his mother, [October 1844?], and 10 April 1846, LC: Dolley P. Madison Papers; Ambrose Madison to James H. Causten, 19 December 1852, LC: Madison Papers; William Wertenbaker to William C. Rives, 18 May 1857, LC: William C. Rives Papers.

[26] Frederick B. McGuire to Henry A. Willard, 22 December 1888, Wisconsin State Historical Society: Lyman C. Draper Papers.

[27] Stan. V. Henkels Catalogue No. 694 (6–7 December 1892).

[28] Stan. V. Henkels Catalogue No. 686 (11–12 May 1892) and Catalogue No. 821, Part VI (9 May 1899); American Art Association Catalogue, "President Madison's Correspondence from . . . the Notable Collection of . . . Frederick B. McGuire" (26 February 1917); Stan. V. Henkels, Jr., Catalogue No. 1478 (13 October 1933).

dently burned in 1903 by Anna's daughter Mary Kunkel, thus belatedly carrying out Dolley's wishes as expressed to Anna.[29]

Even the Madison papers purchased by Congress in 1848 did not remain safely in the archives of the Department of State. Immediately after Madison's death, his widow had been eager to have his "life and times" written by someone of literary prominence, such as George Tucker, James Kirke Paulding, or Jared Sparks.[30] Here, too, as with the publication of her husband's papers, she experienced keen disappointment. During the last years of her life she had some reason to hope that Senator William Cabell Rives, her friend and counselor, whose Castle Hill plantation was not far from Montpelier, would eventually undertake the biography.[31] His appointment in 1849 as minister to France obliged him to postpone indefinitely any further consideration of the matter. In 1856, three years after his return to the United States and shortly after the Virginia Historical and Philosophical Society had urged him to write a life of Madison, Congress invited him to edit for publication the Madison papers which it had purchased eight years before. Upon noting the "chaos & confusion" of these manuscripts, he hesitated to accept the assignment, but eventually did so after being assured that he would be paid a $3,000 honorarium and could move the documents from the State Department archives to his plantation.[32]

Having so much primary source material conveniently at hand and supplementing it by borrowing other manuscripts from James C. McGuire, Rives decided to write the biography while he prepared the government-owned documents for publication.[33] In early 1859, when the first volume of the "Life and Times" was ready for press and the

[29] Anthony Morris to Anna C. Payne, 7 October 1849, with marginal notes signed "M. C. K.," Dolley Madison Memorial Association, Guilford College, N.C.

[30] John C. Payne to Edward Coles, 18 July 1836, Princeton University Library: Edward Coles Papers.

[31] Charles C. Lee to Lyman C. Draper, 4 May 1846, Wisconsin State Historical Society: Lyman C. Draper Papers; Edward Coles to William C. Rives, 21 January 1856, Princeton University Library: Edward Coles Papers.

[32] Copy of James A. Pearce to William C. Rives, 27 August 1856, University of Virginia Library; Conway Robinson to William C. Rives, 27 July 1855, William C. Rives to James A. Pearce, 15 September 1856, William C. Rives to Alfred Rives, 12 December 1856, copy of receipt signed by William C. Rives, 7 January 1857, for three trunks full of Madison papers from the State Department, all in LC: William C. Rives Papers. The "Society" later dropped "and Philosophical" from its name.

[33] William C. Rives to James C. McGuire, 10 June and 8 July 1857, and memorandum of Rives, 17 June 1857, McGregor Library, University of Virginia.

editing assignment was almost completed, he gained permission to keep the manuscripts in his possession until Congress asked for their return.[34] His *History of the Life and Times of James Madison*, published in three volumes by Little, Brown and Company of Boston between 1859 and 1868, portrays the career of Madison only until his retirement from the House of Representatives in 1797.

Before the opening of the Civil War, during which Rives aligned himself with the Southern cause, he delivered a copy of the edited documents to Congress. The original manuscripts remained at Castle Hill throughout the war. While it was in progress, Philip R. Fendall of Washington, with the co-operation of James C. McGuire, added enough material to what Rives had sent in to make four volumes of about equal size. Under contract with Congress, J. B. Lippincott and Company of Philadelphia published them in August 1865 with the title, *Letters and Other Writings of James Madison Fourth President of the United States*.[35] A new printing appeared in 1884. The title pages of these volumes, usually called the "Congressional edition," make no mention of Rives and Fendall as editors. At the request of Congress, Rives returned two trunks full of Madison papers to the State Department on 16 March 1866.[36] By then, however, he had mixed many Madison documents with his own papers. Approximately seventy-five years went by before these, or at least about nine hundred of them, came again into the possession of the federal government as a part of Rives's own papers acquired by the Library of Congress.

Between 1900 and 1910, G. P. Putnam's Sons of New York published, under the editorship of Gaillard Hunt of the Department of State, nine volumes of *The Writings of James Madison, Comprising His Public Papers and His Private Correspondence*. Besides reprinting almost all the documents in the Gilpin, McGuire, and Congressional editions, Hunt added about three hundred other government-owned items and a few which were in private hands. Together these four editions provide the reader with about 1,020 papers by Madison and 49 addressed to him. These are approximately one-sixth of the extant documents by him and an insignificant fraction of the fifteen thousand or so extant letters addressed to him. Furthermore, the items in these

[34] William C. Rives to John A. Pearce, 18 February 1859, and to William C. Rives, Jr., 16 April 1859, LC: William C. Rives Papers.

[35] Philip R. Fendall to William C. Rives, 27 November 1865, Yale University Library.

[36] Timothy O. Howe to William C. Rives, 18 January 1866; William H. Seward to William C. Rives, 16 March 1866, LC: William C. Rives Papers.

editions often are not printed in full and are documented lightly, if at all. As a rule, letters to Madison are represented only by brief extracts.

Nearly a quarter of a century ago these shortcomings led John Cook Wyllie and Francis L. Berkeley, Jr., of the University of Virginia Library to begin an inventory of the writings of James Madison. They established a card file designed to record the whereabouts of each extant paper written by or to him. This check list grew to include some fifteen thousand items. For some years these items increased in number more rapidly than the momentum needed to launch an editorial project. In 1952, Philip M. Hamer, executive director of the reorganized National Historical Publications Commission, joined with a Virginia committee, comprising Mr. Berkeley, Lyman H. Butterfield, David J. Mays, and William J. Van Schreeven, in an effort to discover a means whereby the Madison Papers could be published. Colgate W. Darden, Jr., president of the University of Virginia, lent his influential support to this enterprise. By the close of 1952 six volumes of the *Papers of Thomas Jefferson*, edited by Julian P. Boyd, were available to serve as a model for the guidance of any group undertaking a similar task. Financial support and an editorial staff, with an adequate office, remained to be provided.

Several years later, Leonard D. White of the Department of Political Science, University of Chicago, became interested in editing the papers of Madison. Upon hearing of the preparations already under way at the University of Virginia, Chancellor Lawrence A. Kimpton of the University of Chicago joined with Mr. White and President Darden in arranging for the two institutions to sponsor the project and to seek funds for its support. Their efforts led to the opening of the headquarters of the "Papers of James Madison" in the Social Sciences Research Building of the University of Chicago on 1 October 1956. At the same time, the University of Virginia office was established at Richmond, with William M. E. Rachal as its head. Until Mr. White's death on 23 February 1958, he was Chief Editor and devised the project's methods of operation in the areas of manuscript search, office management, and editorial procedures. Most fittingly, therefore, and with a continuing sense of loss, the editors dedicate the first two volumes to his memory.

Liberal subventions from the Ford Foundation and the Rockefeller Foundation provide for most of the project's editorial expenses. Highly gratifying, also, has been the biennial appropriation by the General Assembly of the Commonwealth of Virginia. The Virginia Historical Society generously permitted Mr. Rachal, the editor of its quarterly, to devote whatever time he needed in order to represent the University of Virginia as an editor of the Madison Papers and afforded him space in the Society's headquarters for that purpose. The University of Chicago Press has fostered the enterprise since its inception. By their generosity, these institutions and the University of Chicago have manifested their confidence in the value of Madison's papers. The editorial staff shares their confidence and greatly appreciates their financial aid in making these writings available in printed form.

The Advisory Board of the "Papers of James Madison," listed on page vi, has assisted the editors whenever they have called upon it for advice. Mention will be made later of several of its members who individually have often helped the editors with special problems connected with their work.

Although Ralph L. Ketcham is no longer a member of the staff of the "Papers of James Madison," he contributed much to the editing of the first two volumes. During his tenure in the Chicago office, from its opening until February 1960, he led in the field search for manuscripts and shared importantly in preparing some of them for publication. William H. Gaines, Jr., now on the staff of the Virginia State Library, helped the project as its assistant editor for five months during its first year.

Many of the papers to be published in this edition are from the eleven thousand or more manuscripts written by or to Madison, and now in the Library of Congress. This repository also houses the papers of several hundred of his correspondents. Chief among these were Thomas Jefferson, James Monroe, and George Washington. In the National Archives are many of Madison's official documents in various collections, such as the papers of the Continental Congress, of the House of Representatives, and of the Department of State. And yet a large number of letters from or to Madison, including considerable portions of his correspondence with his kinsfolk, with John Beckley, William Bradford, David Jameson, Joseph Jones, and Edmund Pendleton, have apparently been irretrievably lost.

Madison papers, besides those in the Library of Congress and the National Archives, are widely scattered among the collateral descendants of James or Dolley Madison; among private collectors of manuscripts and autographs; and among semiprivate endowed libraries. They have also been found in the libraries of states, counties, cities, and religious denominations; of patriotic, historical, and other learned societies; and of academies, institutes, museums, memorial foundations, seminaries, preparatory schools, colleges, and universities. The files of the

"Papers of James Madison" include photocopies of manuscripts from approximately 250 different sources.

ACKNOWLEDGMENTS

The assembling of the papers of Madison, including the letters written to him, depended for its success upon the willingness of their many owners to have the documents photocopied and published. The editors gratefully acknowledge the extending of this favor by Mrs. Aimee McCormick King of Alabama; Harry Ackerman, Mrs. Stuart Chevalier, Judge Elmer E. Robinson, and Justin G. Turner of California; Mrs. Theodore P. Dixon, Jr., and Henry N. Flynt of Connecticut; Jasper E. Crane of Delaware; Mrs. John W. Davidge, Mrs. Harry Hull, and Mrs. John W. Stenhouse of the District of Columbia; Mrs. D. Mercer Sherman and R. Carter Pittman of Georgia; Roger W. Barrett, Dr. Joseph E. Fields, Richard J. Hooker, Ralph G. Newman, Dr. Charles W. Olsen, Charles N. Owen, Mr. and Mrs. Philip D. Sang, Nathan H. Schwartz, Dr. Max Thorek, and Joseph Z. Willner of Illinois; J. William Goodwin and Warren A. Reeder, Jr., of Indiana; G. Davis Buckner, Miss Henrietta Clay, and Mr. and Mrs. Walter Ferguson of Kentucky; Mrs. Howard Campbell, Mrs. Laurence R. Carton, Mrs. E. H. Cohn, Mrs. James Madison Cutts III, Jacob E. Engelbrecht, Richard Helms, Mrs. James F. Jordan, Dr. Herbert E. Klingelhofer, J. William Middendorf, Jr., and Mr. and Mrs. Edmund L. R. Smith of Maryland; Miss Frances G. Colt, Mrs. Thomas Jefferson Coolidge, Jr., Mr. and Mrs. George B. Cutts, Henry L. Seaver, Charles M. Storey, and Craig Wylie of Massachusetts; Charles E. Feinberg of Michigan; Allyn K. Ford and Alvin R. Witt of Minnesota; Frank Glenn of Missouri; William C. Coles, Jr., Walter N. Eastburn, W. Parsons Todd, and Alexander D. Wainwright of New Jersey; Mrs. Richard M. C. Aldrich, John E. Boos, Phillips Bradley, Raymond E. Burdick, Hugh F. Dangler, Dr. Frederick M. Dearborn, Stephen Decatur, Joseph J. Frank, the Reverend Cornelius Greenway, Carl Haverlin, Mr. and Mrs. Richard Maass, Charles J. Nourse, Mrs. Henry M. Sage, Nathaniel E. Stein, Norman H. Strouse, and Ray Trautman of New York; Colonel Roy G. Fitzgerald of Ohio; J. Hampton Barnes, Charles J. Biddle, Herman Blum, Ralph Earle, R. Sturgis Ingersoll, William Kennard, Mrs. Arthur Loeb, Gilbert S. McClintock, Frederick W. Nicolls, John F. Reed, and Miss Virginia G. Stair of Pennsylvania; the Reverend David H. Coblentz, John A. May, and John T. Walker of South Carolina; Stanley F. Horn of Tennessee; William C. Breckinridge, Robert F. Kennedy, Mrs. John S. Thornton, and Albert C. Wilkerson of Virginia; and Louis St. John de Crèvecoeur of France.

The complete roster of institutions that have furnished photoreproductions of their manuscripts to the editors is too long to list here. The two largest of these collections, other than the repositories of the federal government, are the nearly 400 official documents in the Virginia State Library relating to Madison's career, and the approximately 475 unofficial ones in the Library of the University of Virginia. Other major groups are the James Bowdoin Papers in the Bowdoin College Library; the Jonathan Russell Papers in the Brown University Library; the David Erskine Papers in the Public Archives of Canada; the De-Witt Clinton Papers in the Columbia University Library; the Jared Sparks Papers in the Harvard University Library; the Wallace-Bradford, William Jones, Lafayette, Daniel Parker, and Richard Rush papers of the Historical Society of Pennsylvania; the A. J. Dallas and William Eaton papers in the Henry E. Huntington Library; the John G. Jackson and Lafayette papers in the Indiana University Library; the DuPont de Nemours Papers in Longwood Library, Kennett Square, Pennsylvania; miscellaneous Madison papers in the Hall of Records of Maryland; the William Pinkney and David B. Warden papers of the Maryland Historical Society; the Thomas Jefferson, Edward Everett, and Adams Family papers of the Massachusetts Historical Society; miscellaneous Madison papers in the William L. Clements Library of the University of Michigan; the William C. C. Claiborne Papers in the Mississippi Department of Archives and History and in the Louisiana State University Library; the Frederick Bates Papers of the Missouri Historical Society; miscellaneous Madison papers of the New Hampshire Historical Society; the Albert Gallatin, Rufus King, and Robert R. Livingston papers of the New-York Historical Society; the Madison, James Monroe, and other collections in the New York Public Library; the Elkanah Watson and other collections in the New York State Library; the Thomas McKean and Simon Snyder papers in the Pennsylvania Historical and Museum Commission collections at Harrisburg; the Lafayette, Henry Wheaton, and other papers in the Pierpont Morgan Library of New York City; the J. B. Shane and other papers of the Presbyterian Historical Society Library in Philadelphia; the Edward Coles Papers of the Chicago Historical Society and on deposit in the Princeton University Library; the William C. Rives and other papers of the Rosenbach Foundation in Philadelphia; the Nicholas P. Trist and other papers of the Virginia Historical Society; and miscellaneous Madison papers in the libraries of the College of William and Mary and of Yale University. The few Madison items in each of many other institutions sometimes include a "fugitive" document, apparently unknown to earlier scholars, which especially rewards the searcher because it clears up a puzzling matter that otherwise would remain a mystery.

Large collections of autographs are another important source of Madison material. Those which contain a dozen or more of his papers are the Chamberlain Collection in the Boston Public Library, the Roberts Collection of Haverford College, the Fogg Collection of the Maine Historical Society, the Lloyd W. Smith Collection at the Morristown National Historical Park, the Emmet Collection in the New York Public Library, the Gratz and Dreer collections of the Historical Society of Pennsylvania, and the De Coppet Collection in the Princeton University Library.

By far the biggest concentrations of Madison papers are in two repositories of the United States government. Their custodians, Wayne C. Grover, Archivist of the United States, and David C. Mearns, Chief of the Manuscript Division, Library of Congress, opened these resources to the use of the project and often lightened the task of hunting through many additional collections in their charge. In connection with this search, as well as with more particular matters, the editors are indebted to Mrs. Dorothy S. Eaton, Robert H. Land, Donald H. Mugridge, and Fred Shelley of the Library of Congress staff, and H. B. Fant, W. Neil Franklin, Thad Page, Buford Rowland, and Miss F. Helen Beach, Miss Maude E. Lyles, and Mrs. Marian Tinling of the National Archives staff.

For a special resolution of the United States House of Representatives permitting photocopies to be made of Madison material in the archives of that body, the editors are especially indebted to Congressmen Barratt O'Hara and Sidney R. Yates of Illinois, Congressman John W. McCormack of Massachusetts, and the Honorable Ralph R. Roberts, Clerk of the House of Representatives.

Many individuals affiliated with institutions have frequently manifested a helpful interest in the project. The editors gratefully recall the assistance extended by Herbert C. Schulz and Miss Norma Cuthbert of the Henry E. Huntington Library and Art Gallery; Robert C. Sale, State Librarian of Connecticut; Clyde C. Walton of the Illinois State Historical Library; Stanley Pargellis and Mrs. Ruth Lapham Butler of Newberry Library; Robert Rosenthal of the University of Chicago Library; James W. Foster and Francis C. Haber of the Maryland Historical Society; Nelson J. Molter of the Maryland State Library;

Walter Muir Whitehill of the Boston Athenaeum; Clarence S. Brigham and Clifford K. Shipton of the American Antiquarian Society; Malcolm Freiberg and Stephen T. Riley of the Massachusetts Historical Society; I. Albert Matkov of the Massachusetts State Library; Alexander P. Clark of the Princeton University Library; Herbert Cahoon of the Pierpont Morgan Library in New York City; Robert W. Hill and Edward B. Morrison of the New York Public Library; James J. Heslin and Wilmer Leach of the New-York Historical Society; H. G. Jones of the North Carolina Department of Archives and History, Raleigh, North Carolina; Whitfield J. Bell, Jr., and Miss Gertrude D. Hess of the American Philosophical Society; Miss Sarah A. G. Smith and Nicholas B. Wainwright of the Historical Society of Pennsylvania; John Cook Wyllie, Francis L. Berkeley, Jr., William H. Runge, Jr., and Robert E. Stocking of the University of Virginia Library; John M. Jennings and Howson W. Cole of the Virginia Historical Society; William J. Van Schreeven and John Dudley of the Virginia State Library; James A. Servies and Herbert Ganter of the College of William and Mary Library; Edward M. Riley of Colonial Williamsburg, Inc.; and Admiral E. M. Eller, Director of Naval History, United States Department of the Navy.

Personal friends of one or another of the editors have aided the project in special ways. They and other scholars engaged in research or editing have kept the Madison staff informed of Madison material in manuscript collections or other primary sources bearing upon their special subjects. For such courtesies the editors wish to thank Douglass Adair of the Claremont Colleges; Harry Ammon of Southern Illinois University; Keith M. Berwick of the University of California at Los Angeles; Aaron Boom of Memphis State University; Lester J. Cappon of the Institute of Early American History and Culture; Henry E. Cheaney of Kentucky State College; Thomas D. Clark of the University of Kentucky; Ronald S. Crane of the University of Chicago; Jack Cross of the University of Arizona; William W. Crosskey of the University of Chicago; Anthony G. Dietz of Silver Spring, Maryland; L. Ethan Ellis of Rutgers, the State University of New Jersey; Miss Margareta A. Faissler of Baltimore; Louis Gottschalk of the University of Chicago; J. Wesley Hoffmann of the University of Tennessee; E. Harold Hugo of Meriden, Connecticut; Miss Margaret Maddox and Mitford M. Mathews of the University of Chicago; John A. Munroe of the University of Delaware; Mrs. Granville T. Prior of the South Carolina Historical Society; Mr. and Mrs. William Rogers Quynn of Frederick, Maryland; John Reardon of Loyola University

(Chicago); Miss Rae E. Rips of the Detroit Public Library; Harry R. Stevens of Ohio University; Karl J. Weintraub and Warner A. Wick of the University of Chicago; Gordon R. Williams of the Midwest Inter-Library Center (Chicago); Lyman H. Butterfield and Leonard C. Faber of the "Adams Papers"; W. Edwin Hemphill and Robert L. Meriwether of the "Papers of John C. Calhoun"; James F. Hopkins of the "Papers of Henry Clay"; Leonard W. Labaree of the "Papers of Benjamin Franklin"; Harold C. Syrett and Mr. and Mrs. Jacob E. Cooke of the "Papers of Alexander Hamilton"; Leroy P. Graff of the "Papers of Andrew Johnson"; and Julian P. Boyd of the "Papers of Thomas Jefferson."

Julian Boyd's association with the "Papers of James Madison" has been unusually close ever since the project was in its planning stage. As a member of its Advisory Board, as an editor whose volumes have set a standard of excellence which other editors of historical manuscripts use as their gauge, and as a scholar whose knowledge of the writings of Madison's closest friend is unrivaled, Mr. Boyd has been the best of guides on many occasions.

The editors also have had the good fortune to enjoy the friendship of Irving Brant, author of the authoritative and comprehensive biography of James Madison. They have often benefited from his readiness to share with them his vast fund of Madison lore.

Philip M. Hamer, executive director of the National Historical Publications Commission, helped to launch the "Papers of James Madison" and continues to be one of its mainstays. During the last six years his counsel, his generosity in supplying photocopies of documents in the National Archives, and his leadership in maintaining liaison between the projects engaged in editing the papers of "the Fathers" have been of outstanding service.

The editors are also happy to record their thanks to the Misses Jane Hobson, Alice Karpen, Muriel Porter, and Ellen Thro, and to David McKeith, Keith Neilson, Albert Romasco, and Thomas White. As stenographers or research assistants for periods of varying length during the last five years, they brought a fine spirit and interest as well as efficiency to their tasks.

EDITORIAL METHOD

The present edition includes all extant writings of Madison which appear to have been wholly or in large degree the product of his mind. This standard of selection justifies the omission of some papers in his handwriting. Examples of these are a few notes by him, devoid of personal comments and merely a record of what he read in a book or heard in a lecture, and clerk-like copies of letters or legislative proceedings in no way reflecting his own thought. On the other hand, this same standard is not so rigidly applied as to exclude the publication of certain items, such as his speeches in Congress or almost contemporaneous accounts of his conversations, recorded by someone who heard him. Included also are letters and other papers, addressed to him and known to have received his careful attention.

In applying this test of "careful attention," the editors assume that Madison accorded it to all writings directed to him except during the years 1801–1817, when he was successively the Secretary of State and President. Of the thousands of dispatches reaching his office during that sixteen-year span, only those are printed in full which can be shown to have been read by him, or which demonstrably influenced his thought or action. Wholly excluded are the many routine reports made to him by his subordinates in the executive branch of the government. Unless the precise language of a dispatch from a territorial governor, minister, consul, or other official is needed to make Madison's reply clear, the content of a paper of this kind is merely summarized. Entirely omitted, except for one sample of each, are the thousands of land patents, warrants, circulars, form letters, passports, ships' papers, civil and military commissions, and kindred documents signed by him as Secretary of State or President. Without eliminating, summarizing, or sampling in this way, the quantity of incoming correspondence and routine outgoing papers between 1801 and 1817 becomes unmanageable. If all were printed in full, the volumes covering those years would be only incidentally the writings of Madison.

Foremost among special problems are the various types of documents related to his legislative career. Bills and resolutions, with their amendments, if any, introduced in bodies of which he was a member, are included only when there is evidence of his major share in determining their form or substance. For example, the amended version of the clause about religious freedom in the Virginia Declaration of Rights of 1776 is given, but the Virginia constitution of that year is not, even though a partial copy of it exists in his hand. Motions or amendments to motions made by Madison are included; his secondings of motions generally are not. Any report delivered by him as chairman of a legislative committee is reproduced, unless he was merely its voice rather than its author or co-author. Recommendations by a committee of which he was not chairman are printed only when he appears to have been their draftsman or mainly responsible for their content. His speeches are given in whole or in summary, depending upon the form in which they survive. Variations between the extant texts are noted if they are at all significant. Madison's votes as a legislator are not automatically included but find frequent mention in footnotes.

Accounts by contemporaries of what they wrote to him or he to them, when the letters themselves have disappeared, are printed, provided that they have the ring of authenticity and add knowledge of his career. As a case in point, the record in William Bradford's diary of what he told Madison in a lost letter of 20 May 1776 is shown, but vague or commonplace information, such as a statement in a letter that "Mr. Madison argued against the constitutionality of the bank," is not ordinarily reproduced. Madison's anonymous essays in newspapers, and speeches or letters apparently by other persons but in reality prepared by him, are included, or at least his contributions to such writings appear in condensed form. Illustrative of these are his share in composing George Washington's First Inaugural Address; his draft of a letter from Robert Smith to William Pinkney dated 23 November 1809; an "editorial" in the *National Intelligencer* on 13 May 1813; and an unsigned letter defending Jefferson's conduct during the presidential election controversy in 1801, printed in the Philadelphia *National Gazette* on 25 January 1831.

Letters and documents signed by him, or which were sent to him, as one of a group of persons, are usually reproduced. The frequent dispatches to and from Madison and the other delegates of Virginia in the Continental Congress represent this type of paper. On the other hand, because there is no convincing evidence that Madison as a member of the Council of State of Virginia composed, or shared in composing, any document signed by the governor "in Council," only samples of its journals and many letters, showing the types of matters engaging Madison's attention, are printed. Communications addressed to persons other than Madison, but obviously or inferentially intended mainly for him, appear either in full or in summary in connection with some related document. Most petitions signed by him, whether or not he was their author, are included, but the signatures, if they make a roster of unwieldy length, are not. A petition addressed to a legislative or other committee of which he was a member, or to him alone as Secretary of State or President, is not printed unless the document was obviously of special interest to him.

Documents witnessed or countersigned by Madison are also omitted unless his presence as a signer was more than a routine matter. In that case the content of the document is summarized. Bills of sale, powers of attorney, indentures, leases, purchase orders, financial records, and similar documents relating to his private affairs are included, at least in abbreviated form. On the other hand, entries of money paid to, or received from, him in the accounts of other persons are omitted except for mentions of them in the editorial notes.

Each of the above canons is broken whenever fidelity to its spirit appears clearly to warrant a departure from the letter of the rule. In a further assertion of discretionary power, the editors reserve the right to reproduce a few entries, of which the first one in this volume is an example, that obviously are neither from nor to Madison, but clearly merit a place in a comprehensive edition of his papers. After these volumes reach 15 September 1794, the date of Madison's marriage to Dolley Payne Todd, they will also include letters from and to her which throw light upon her husband's career.

DOCUMENTS

Position. The documents are presented in chronological order. Letters which cannot be dated specifically are given inclusive dates and placed at the end of the first month or the first year when they *may* have been written (e.g., a letter dated [July–December 1780] is printed after the last item specifically dated in July 1780, and a letter dated [1780–1783] will be found after the last item definitely known to have been written in 1780). Letters so elusive as to defy any dating whatsoever will be grouped at the close of the series' final volume.

Several letters written on one day, as increasingly was the case as Madison gained in prestige, are alphabetized by the last names of his correspondents. If he wrote to a person on the same day that person wrote to him, the letters are arranged, if possible, in their exact time sequence; if this is unknown, Madison's letter precedes the other. Documents of the Continental Congress are placed among the "C's" and those of the Virginia General Assembly among the "V's."

Available information about the content of a missing letter appears at the chronological place in the volume where the letter would appear if it were available. If nothing but the date of this stray is known, it is mentioned only in the footnotes of another letter written at approximately the same time.

Presentation. The reproduction of each paper as closely resembles the form of the original as is feasible without creating unusual typographical difficulties or confusion on the part of the reader. With certain exceptions, noted below, the original spelling, grammar, capitalization, and punctuation remain unaltered.

The words which Madison and his correspondents actually wrote are scrupulously retained, even when these words are misspelled or abbreviated. However, when obsolete usages, a flagrantly misspelled word, or slips of the pen might mislead the reader, the editors either insert letters within brackets or explain the word in a footnote. For instance, the abbreviation "Cee." is printed "C[ommitt]ee." A question mark placed before the closing bracket indicates that the writer's meaning is uncertain.

Each writer's capitalization is also closely followed. In some cases, however, letters are halfway between a capital and a lower-case in size. The editors resolve this ambiguity by either adopting the form which the writer customarily employed or, if this is unknown, by resorting to modern usage.

Short gaps in the original document are indicated by similar blanks in the printed text, if they are relevant to an understanding of the document (e.g., "Your letter of the   was received on the   of   "). If the editors are able to supply what the writer clearly intended to put into these spaces, they do so in a footnote. Longer omissions, caused by tears in the manuscript, by the editors' inability to decipher badly faded words, by sections in inexplicable code or shorthand, or by the writer's evident desire to leave space for later remarks which he never inserted, are also mentioned in footnotes.

When several copies of a letter survive, including the recipient's copy, it is selected for reproduction, but variant readings of the text appear in the footnotes if these deviations have significance. Letters in a foreign language are printed as written, followed by a translation. The only letters in a foreign language in Volumes I and II are in French and Italian.

Although the editors seek to present as faithful a transcription of the original document as possible, they are obliged to make a few changes for the sake of clarity and typographical convenience. When the author repeated a word, obviously through a slip of the pen, the word is not printed twice. Superscript letters, used frequently in the late eighteenth century at the end of abbreviations (e.g., "Philad.ª" and "com.ᵉᵉ"), are printed on the line with the other letters. Another frequent device employed in abbreviations was a tilde to indicate letters omitted from the middle of a word (e.g., "Com̃rs"). This appears most often when one "m" of a double "m" was omitted. In this case, the word is printed with a double "m"; otherwise, the word is printed as an abbreviation and the tilde ignored. Because the press is less facile than the pen, an exact representation of symbols for weights and measures and currency is not always possible. The editors adhere as closely as is typographically convenient to the symbols as originally written.

Words in cipher or in shorthand in the original are decoded when possible and are printed in italics. Minor addenda made by the writer, either in the margins or above the line, are incorporated into the text without comment, unless the fact that a remark was an afterthought seems to be worthy of note. Longer insertions are duly footnoted. Ordinarily, words or phrases struck out by the writer are omitted without comment. In some cases, however, the deleted words appear in the footnotes. In a few highly important documents, where the development of Madison's ideas is indicated by the words he chose and the words he changed, strikeouts and insertions are presented in as close an approach to the original document as is typographically possible. In these cases, his deletions have a horizontal line printed through them. Changes which the editors believe that Madison made in later life, while looking back over his papers, are given in footnotes.

Four deviations from the original punctuation appear to be warranted. The dashes frequently used in the eighteenth century to end a sentence are converted into periods. Extraneous dashes following periods are omitted. A paragraph is indented whenever a writer aligned its beginning with the left-hand margin of his message. Bracketed punctuation is occasionally added to assist the reader.

The format of the original documents is altered in three respects. In all letters and other papers closing with a dateline, it is moved to the beginning of the document. Dates are inserted in brackets at the top of undated manuscripts. When a letter's complimentary close spreads over a considerable space, it is consolidated into one or two lines.

xxxvii

Annotation. Documents other than letters are given a title briefly describing their content. Letters are preceded by the name of the recipient, if written by Madison, or by that of the sender, if written to Madison. When Madison was a member of a group dispatching or receiving a letter, both the recipients' and the senders' names are shown in the title (e.g., Virginia Delegates in Congress to Thomas Jefferson).

The repository or other source where a document is to be found is named in a brief headnote to the document. Since a letter in private possession tends to pass from one collector to another, and therefore its present location may be unknown to the editors, its headnote mentions the year when they obtained a photocopy of it. Whenever there are several manuscript copies of an item, the location of each is listed in the headnote, beginning with the one from which the printed text was taken. If the condition of a manuscript and notations on its docket or cover add to an understanding of its context or its text, they, too, are commented upon in the headnote.

Where a more general background is needed to clarify the main subject of a paper or several interrelated papers, an editorial note on that topic precedes the earliest of these documents.

Lengthy inclosures often accompanied the dispatches dating from Madison's years as Secretary of State or President. If any of these inclosures is of prime importance to an understanding of the main letter or of Madison's reply, it is reproduced in full. Otherwise a footnote briefly summarizes the content of the inclosure and tells where, if anywhere, it has appeared in print.

Most of the documentation identifies persons, places, events, and literary allusions, provided that they are not generally well known. In a number of instances, however, the footnotes necessarily read "unknown" or "known only as . . ." when referring to obscure individuals who apparently left no other written trace in history. A person is usually identified the first time his name appears in a document. This particular reference is shown in boldface type under the individual's name in the index of the volume, unless he is mentioned only once in it. The editors expect to append to *The Papers of James Madison* a consolidated index volume for the entire series.

Since a sketch of each member of the Continental Congress is readily available in the *Biographical Directory of the American Congress*, he is ordinarily not identified in the present series beyond a footnote mentioning the state he represented. When an article on a person is in the *Dictionary of American Biography* or in any of its major American, British, or French counterparts, the source of the editors' information about him is not cited unless they borrow interpretative material from one or another of these compilations.

If an annotation of one document includes a reference to another Madison paper not yet published in the present edition, the book or periodical containing a printed version of this second document, or the repository where it may be found, is mentioned rather than the photocopy in the office of the "Papers of James Madison."

ABBREVIATIONS

FC File copy. Any version of a letter or other document retained by the sender for his own files and differing little if at all from the completed version. A draft, on the other hand, is a preliminary sketch, often incomplete and varying frequently in expression from the finished version.

JM James Madison

LC Library of Congress.

MS Manuscript. A catchall term describing numerous reports and other papers written by Madison, as well as items sent to him which were not letters.

NA National Archives.

PCC Papers of the Continental Congress, a collection in the National Archives.

RC Recipient's copy. The copy of a letter intended to be read by the addressee. If its handwriting is not that of the sender, this fact is mentioned in the headnote.

Tr Transcript. A copy of a manuscript, or a copy of that copy, usually handwritten, made considerably later than the date of the manuscript and ordinarily not by its author or by the person to whom the original was addressed. The "Force Transcripts," made under the direction of Peter Force in the mid-nineteenth century, are those most frequently used in the present series.

SHORT TITLES FOR BOOKS

Only those books used very frequently, and a few whose titles are so long as to necessitate an abbreviation, have been given short titles. This list applies only to Volume I; succeeding volumes will contain lists of titles abbreviated in them.

Alexander, *Princeton College*. Samuel Davies Alexander, *Princeton College during the Eighteenth Century* (New York, 1872).

Boyd, *Papers of Jefferson*. Julian P. Boyd *et al.*, eds., *The Papers of Thomas Jefferson* (16 vols. to date; Princeton, N.J., 1950——).

Brant, *Madison*. Irving Brant, *James Madison* (6 vols.; Indianapolis and New York, 1941–61).

Doniol, *Histoire*. Henri Doniol, *Histoire de la participation de la France à l'établissement des États-Unis d'Amérique* (5 vols.; Paris, 1886–92).

Fitzpatrick, *Writings of Washington*. John C. Fitzpatrick, ed., *The Writings of George Washington, from the Original Sources, 1745–1799* (39 vols.; Washington, D.C., 1931–44).

Force, *American Archives*. Peter Force, ed., *American Archives*, 4th ser. (6 vols.; Washington, D.C., 1837–46).

Hening, *Statutes*. William Waller Hening, ed., *The Statutes at Large; being a Collection of all the Laws of Virginia, from the First Session of the Legislature, in the Year 1619* (13 vols.; Richmond and Philadelphia, 1819–23).

Journal of the House of Delegates. *Journal of the House of Delegates of the Commonwealth of Virginia; Begun and Held At the Capitol, in the City of Williamsburg*. Beginning in 1780, the portion after the semicolon reads, *Begun and Held in the Town of Richmond. In the County of Henrico*. The Journal for each session has its own title page and is individually paginated. The edition used, unless otherwise noted, is the one in which the journals for 1777–1781 are brought together in one volume, with each journal published in Richmond in 1827 or 1828, and often called the "Thomas W. White reprint."

Madison, *Letters* (Cong. ed.). [William C. Rives and Philip R. Fendall, eds.], *Letters and Other Writings of James Madison* (published by order of Congress; 4 vols.; Philadelphia, 1865).

Madison, *Writings* (Hunt ed.). Gaillard Hunt, ed., *The Writings of James Madison* (9 vols.; New York, 1900–1910).

New Jersey Archives. William A. Whitehead *et al.*, eds., *Documents Relating to the Colonial History of the State of New Jersey* (1st ser., 42 vols.; Newark, Trenton, Paterson, 1880–1949).

Pennsylvania Archives. Samuel Hazard *et al.*, eds., *Pennsylvania Archives* (9 ser., 138 vols.; Philadelphia and Harrisburg, 1852–1949).

Sprague, *Annals*. William B. Sprague, *Annals of the American Pulpit* (9 vols.; New York, 1857–69).

Wharton, *Revolutionary Diplomatic Correspondence*. Francis Wharton, ed., *The Revolutionary Diplomatic Correspondence of the United States* (6 vols.; Washington, D.C., 1889).

MADISON CHRONOLOGY

1751 (16 March)	Born at Port Conway on Rappahannock River, King George County, Va., at home of his maternal grandmother.
1762–1767	Attended Donald Robertson School, King and Queen County, Va.
1767–1769	Tutored at Montpelier by the Reverend Thomas Martin.
1769 (August)–1772 (April)	Studied at College of New Jersey, Princeton, N.J.
1771 (29 September)	Received baccalaureate degree from College of New Jersey.
1772–1776	At home at Montpelier, Orange County, Va., engaging in miscellaneous studies and suffering frequently from poor health.
1774 (May–June)	Took trip through Pennsylvania and New York.
1774 (2 December)	Elected to Orange County Committee of Safety, of which his father was chairman.
1775 (9 May)	Address to Captain Patrick Henry and the Gentlemen Independents of Hanover (probably written by Madison).
1776 (May–December)	Orange County delegate to Virginia Convention and General Assembly meeting in Williamsburg.
1776 (June)	Secured substitution of liberty of conscience provision for religious toleration provision in Virginia Declaration of Rights.
1777 (24 April)	Defeated for re-election to House of Delegates.

1777 (15 November)	Elected by General Assembly to Virginia Council of State.
1778 (14 January)– 1779 ([16?] December)	Served as member of Virginia Council of State under Governors Patrick Henry and Thomas Jefferson.
1778 (27 May)	Election to House of Delegates rejected because he was serving on Council of State.
1779 (16 June)	Declined election by General Assembly as a delegate to the Continental Congress.
1779 (14 December)	Elected a Virginia delegate to the Continental Congress.

THE PAPERS OF
James Madison

Record of Birth and Baptism of
James Madison, Jr.

MS (Princeton University Library). The complete title of the
Madison Family Bible reads, *Holy Bible, containing the Old
and New Testaments newly translated out of the Original
Tongues; and with the former Translations diligently compared
and revised with the Apocrypha* (London: Thomas Baskett,
1759). Following "The End of the Apocrypha," the seventh
entry, given below, is in the hand of James Madison, Sr. He
appears to have owned a second copy of the same edition of
the Bible. This volume, now designated by the name of JM's
sister, Sarah Catlett Macon, is in the Virginia Historical Society. The record of JM's birth and baptism, as written in this
book, is virtually identical with the one given below (Patricia
P. Clark, ed., "Madison Family Bible Records," *Virginia Magazine of History and Biography*, LXVI [1958], 80–84).

[16 March 1751]

James Madison junr. was born on Tuesday Night at 12 o'Clock it
being the last of the 5th. & begining of the 6th. day of March 1750–1[1]
& was Baptized by the Revd. Mr. Wm. Davis, Mar. 31. 1751 and had
for God-Fathers Mr. John Moore & Mr. Jonatn. Gibson & for God-
Mothers Mrs. Rebecca Moore, Miss Judith Catlett and Miss Elizabeth
Catlett.[2]

---

[1] The 1759 publication date of the Bible indicates that this record was written at
least eight years after the birth of JM. In the British colonies the switch from the
Julian to the Gregorian calendar was made in 1752. By the Julian calendar each
year ended on 24 March rather than on 31 December. The new or Gregorian
calendar also advanced the date eleven days. This change was effected by having
2 September 1752 followed immediately by 14 September 1752. The net effect of
these two changes was that two periods were omitted from the chronology—3 September 1752 to 13 September 1752 and 1 January 1752 to 24 March 1752. Hence, JM
was born on 5 March 1750, old style, or 16 March 1751, new style. In like manner
his baptismal dates were Sunday, 20 March 1750, old style, or Sunday, 31 March 1751,
new style.

[2] JM was born at the home of his maternal grandmother, Mrs. John Moore (d.
1760), the former Mrs. Rebecca Catlett Conway, and of her second husband, John
Moore (d. 1759). This was in King George County, opposite Port Royal, Va., on the
Rappahannock River and about fifty-five miles east of the Madison plantation of
Montpelier. The Reverend William Davis was rector until 1758 of the Hanover
parish church which the Moores attended (Edward Lewis Goodwin, *The Colonial
Church in Virginia* [Milwaukee, 1927], p. 263). Jonathan Gibson (d. 1791) was a
large landowner in several Virginia counties. His wife, Mary Catlett Gibson, was an
aunt of JM's mother. Through the marriage of his daughter to George Taylor,
Gibson was also related to JM's father. The Misses Judith (d. 1798) and Elizabeth

Catlett were also aunts of Nelly Conway Madison (Dr. and Mrs. William Carter Stubbs, comps., *A History of Two Virginia Families Transplanted from County Kent, England* [New Orleans, 1918], pp. 13–21; Frederick Adams Virkus, ed., *The Abridged Compendium of American Genealogy* [7 vols.; Chicago, 1925–42], I, 20; II, 320).

Commonplace Book

MS (Charles M. Storey, Boston, Mass., 1957). This twenty-four-page notebook has a rough, brown-paper cover. Over this cover is a loose paper jacket on which is written, "Extracts made by James Madison in 1759, M. E. Cutts." Mary E. Cutts, a daughter of Dolley Madison's sister, Anna, was a favorite niece of the Madisons. How she acquired the "Commonplace Book" is unknown, but it may have been given to her by Dolley Madison as a memento, following JM's death. Miss Cutts made two copies of notes from this book. Mr. Storey owns one of these copies while the other, along with additional material prepared by her for a memoir about the Madisons, is the property of Mr. and Mrs. George B. Cutts of Brookline, Massachusetts. Both Mr. Storey and Mr. Cutts are grandsons of Mary E. Cutts's brother, Richard D. Cutts. The inability of the editors to be more precise about the time when JM wrote in this copybook will be explained in the following editorial note.

EDITORIAL NOTE

This manuscript volume is in part a copybook and in part a notebook, all written by JM in his youth with the exception of the final six lines. On the one hand, there are nearly accurate transcriptions of poetry from two magazines, and, on the other, notes upon selections from three fairly difficult books, supplemented by JM's comments and other interpolations. At the top of the first page of the notes, JM wrote "Dec. 24. 1759," a date falling within his ninth year of age. Long afterward, Miss Cutts accepted this as the time when her uncle began to enter the material in his notebook. Although the present editors cannot convincingly explain why JM wrote that date, they cannot agree with her interpretation of its significance. Unwilling to charge JM with mistakenly writing "1759" for "1769," they are driven to the surmise that he was merely recording when he received the notebook as a Christmas gift.

The dating problem might be somewhat less complex if it were not for the fact that the selections show no progression from rather elementary to more difficult reading. There are, however, a few indications (cf. nn. 3 and 24, below) that JM copied at least some of his notes from rough jottings made earlier; and hence the sequence of material may not necessarily indicate the order in which he did the reading. In other words, it is entirely plausible that, as a labor of love or as an assignment for the improvement of his penmanship, a precocious youngster, eight years old, mechanically copied poetry, even though in his old age he recalled that the *Spectator* first attracted him in 1763, or when he was about at the age of twelve (n. 103, below). On the other hand, it is incredible that an eight- or twelve-year-old boy had the thorough knowledge of Latin, the comprehensive acquaintance-ship with works in that tongue, and the maturity of thought, emphasis, and selectivity exhibited by some of the comments and interpolations scattered among his notes on the more difficult reading.

Furthermore, JM apparently knew no Latin before he entered the school of Donald Robertson (1717–1792) near Dunkirk in King and Queen County, Virginia, in 1762, and was not sufficiently versed in that subject to make some of the comments in his notebook until well toward the end of his sojourn there five years later, or perhaps not until he was a student at the College of New Jersey. Besides its occasional entries of "Deo Gratia & Gloria" when bills for tuition and textbooks were paid, Robertson's "Ac-count Book," now in the Virginia Historical Society, lists many, and perhaps all, of the volumes in his library. This roster makes clear that, while under Robertson's tutelage, JM could have taken the notes on Montaigne's *Essays* and, incidentally, have gained his initial acquaintance with Montesquieu's *The Spirit of the Laws* and Locke's *An Essay Concerning Human Under-standing.* Moreover, he studied there almost all the Latin classics from which he quotes in his notebook, as well as others he found no occasion to cite. The "Account Book" reveals "Jamie" Madison buying works by Virgil, Horace, Justinian, and Cornelius Nepos, and probably also reading others by Caesar, Tacitus, Lucretius, Eutropius, and Phaedrus. With Robert-son as his mentor, JM used selections from the writings of Plutarch, He-rodotus, Thucydides, and Plato in his study of Greek. Abel Boyer's *The Compleat French Master for Ladies and Gentlemen* may have introduced JM to the French language (Robertson's "Account Book," pp. 11, 30, 65–66, 69, 72, 74, 78, 80–81, 132–37, 143). If the missing letters of Robertson to JM's father could be found, they might help to determine whether JM took any or all of his notes while in Robertson's school. These letters were appar-ently in existence as late as 1836 (statement by John C. Payne inclosed in a letter from Dolley P. Madison to John Quincy Adams, 3 August 1836, Massachusetts Historical Society). Although each of the volumes from which JM gleaned the material in his "Commonplace Book" was accessible at the College of New Jersey, only the *Spectator*, insofar as is known, was ready at hand at Montpelier (below, n. 103).

In spite of the "Dec. 24. 1759" mentioned above, the editors conclude that little if anything in the copybook is so early in its origin, and that the notes probably reflect samples of JM's reading and thought between 1762 and 1772, with the second half rather than the first half of this decade as the more likely time when he made most of the entries.

The notes are probably much more indicative of JM's intellectual inter-ests during those years than is his "A Brief System of Logick" (*q.v.*). Unlike the latter's mechanical and emotionless organization of material, this "Com-monplace Book" usually reveals what passages from hundreds of pages of text JM deemed particularly worthy of record. The notes also mirror his interest in generalizations about social and individual conduct rather than his need to accumulate factual data about some definite subject or transient problem. In this characteristic they sharply contrast with most of the jottings made by JM on his reading in later years.

The five works which he either transcribed or took notes upon in the "Commonplace Book" are all in the domain of polite literature, noteworthy for their style, their ease of expression, or their emphasis upon manners and morals. In his note-taking, JM was attracted toward the authors' epigrammatical statements about the nature of man or men and rarely toward the historical situation which elicited these comments. Being also concerned to master the art of writing well, he occasionally experimented with an epigram of his own and often refashioned the authors' sentences in an effort to heighten their clarity, precision, and conciseness. Moreover, his notes demonstrate his analytical skill, the maturity of his "asides," and his ability to discern the pith of a matter presented at length and to summarize effectively the main thought of an involved passage. Even when the author provided English translations of his Latin quotations, Madison copied the Latin into his notebook, and sometimes drew upon his memory for additional "pat" phrases in that language, and for references to ancient Roman writers not mentioned in the text.

Any assessment of the influence of this reading upon his thought and action during his public career is at best highly speculative. Perhaps, for example, it was sheer coincidence that many years later James Kirke Paulding told of often recalling the *Memoirs* of Cardinal de Retz while listening to Madison reminisce about his share in events of national moment (LC: William C. Rives Papers, p. 7 of MS entitled "Our Presidents" by Paulding). This may merely signify that Madison referred to de Retz when talking with Paulding. However this may be, the Cardinal's stress upon the need for prudence and caution when holding a public office, and upon the ruinous effect of a close union of church and state, calls to mind Madison's known outlook upon these same subjects a few years later. In like manner, the *Critical Reflections* of Abbé Du Bos may have stimulated Madison to ponder upon the meaning and sources of "national character," and how differently it expressed itself in one country as compared with another. Montesquieu's *De l'Esprit des Lois*, however, could have directed Madison's thought into a similar channel.

Finally, the notes in this "Commonplace Book" on de Retz and Du Bos, and above all those on Montaigne, and the transcriptions from the *Spectator* and the *American Magazine*, may indicate that Madison's interest in systematic and weighty discourses in the realm of political philosophy did not monopolize his student years. During that period, in other words, because he adapted much of his reading to the prevailing literary fashion and even composed Whig Society doggerels (*q.v.*) while at the College of New Jersey, he was by no means as unworldly and concentrated in his scholarly interests as tradition has pictured him. These "polite" memoirs and essays, with their frequent observations about human nature, society, citizenship, and government, may merit attention, along with the works of Montesquieu,

Locke, and their kind, as possible sources of some of Madison's views about those subjects.

In the following copy, parentheses inclose what JM bracketed in the original, while brackets designate editorial inserts.

[1759–1772]

Abstracts from the Memoirs
of the Cardinal de Retz.[1]
Dec. 24. 1759

Nothing is more Subject to Delusion than Piety. All manner of Errors creep and hide themselves under that Veil. Piety takes for sacred all her imaginations of what sort soever. My Father's predilection for his Eldest Son, & their view of the Archbishoprick of Paris[2] for me were the true Causes of his endeavouring to tye to the Church the Soul in the World perhaps the least Ecclesiastical, & yet he neither believed it nor felt it. I dare say he would ha[ve] sworn, that he was led to all this by no other motive than the Spiritual good of my Soul, & the fear of the danger to which it might be exposed in any other Profession. [I, 5–6]

Strength of Mind or Resolution is much more necessary for great actions than stoutness of Heart. Vol 1. p. 34.

Cardinal Richlieu was a Pedant in Love, but a Gentleman in every thing else. [I, 14–17][3]

The fittest Persons to be employed in Popular commotions are those whose condition is bad enough to desire a change in the administration, but not so low as to reduce them to beg in Publick. For the Rich are afraid of Changes, & known Beggars raise in other People an apprehension of being Pillaged. Vol. 1. p. 46.

Irresolute minds waver most when they are upon the point of Action. Vol. 1. p. 47

Secrecy is not so rare among Persons used to great affairs, as is believ'd. Vol. 1. p. 51.

Secrets that are discovered make a noise; but these that are kept are Silent. p.[4]

The President de Thou was in the right to say that we have no true Histories but such as have been written by Men sincere enough to speak the truth in what relates to themselves. p. 60.

A Grave Air hides many defects. p. 61

I knew a Man who had but small defects, and every one of these defects was either the product or the cause of some good Qualities in him. And it may be true too, as I once said of Card. Richlieu, that a

7

man may have not one great Qualification, but what is either the Product or Cause of some great defect in him. p. 63

Narrow Minds are full of suspicions & difficulties. p. 68.

The King of France intended the Archbishoprick of Paris for the Abbot de Retz, ever since he heard of the two adventures of Pinmaker's Niece & of Coutenau. Judge you says the Cardinal what relation those two trifling matters have with the archbishoprick of Paris. And yet this is the manner most things are brought about in. p. 71.[5]

De Retz upon promotion to the Archbishoprick preached before a great Concourse of Parisians, who had rare seen their Archbishops in the Pulpit. [I, 73]

The great Secret says he, for those that enter into employments, is at first to sieze upon Peoples fancy by an Action which some circumstances make peculiarly their own. [I, 73]

To act ill designedly is beyond comparison most criminal before God, but without doubt the wisest as to the World. For when you act in that manner, you always take some previous measures that will cover part of the ill action. p. 74. To descend to the lowest is the surest way to become a Match for the highest p. 75. communis infimis, par principibus. C. Nepos.[6]

Persecution to Persons of High Rank stands them in stead of an eminent Virtue. p. 81.

The Clergy who was always foremost in showing themselves friends to Slavery, preached it to the People under pretence of preaching obedience to them. Vol. 1. p. 88.[7]

The Coadjutor of Paris[8] having succeeded in a dispute with the D. of Orleans,[9] found that even those who had blamed him during the dispute, after his success fancied they had only pitied him. The like observation he says he has made on a thousand other occasions [I, 103]

One is oftner deciev'd by mistrusting People than by confiding in them. p. 104.

The King's and the People's rights never agree better than by not being spoken of. p. 119

Some People fall into such circumstances, as by consequence compell them to commit new Errors. This is always by their own fault: fortune has nothing to [do] with it. p. 132.

It is more unbecoming a Minister to speak foolishly than to act foolishly. [Ad]vices when they come from a Man out of favour are looked upon as Crimes. p. 141.

It is as dangerous and almost as criminal with Princes, to have the Power to [do] good, as to have the Will to do Evil. p. 144.

A Blind Rashness and an excessive timorousness cause the same Effects when the Danger is not known. p. 146. For both endeavour to persuade themselves that the Danger is not real.[10]

Flattery is dangerous to a person in fear. The desire he has of removing that fear from him makes him reject all measures that might remedy the Evil Vol. 1. 147

There is a wonderful Sympathy between some minds. Like Unisones, they are moved alike, and move one another. [I, 148]

It is much more natural for fear to consult than to determine. Vol 1 p. 149

A Citizen clapt his Musquetoon to my head, & tho he was altogether unknown to me, I thought it best to make him think otherwise, I cried to him, Ah Wretch! if thy Father saw thee! It startled him. He stopt & fancied I was his Father's best friend, tho I knew the Father as little as I knew the Son. Vol. 1. p. 152[11]

I appeased the mob without any great Pain, because Suppertime drew near. For at Paris in Popular commotions the most inflam'd are unwilling to lose a Meal. Vol. 1. p 154, 198, 291.

I have all my Life time esteem'd Men more for what they forbore to do than for what they did. Vol. p. 156.

Nothing is of greater Consequence in popular commotions, than to make the[m] believe, even when they are attacking, that they are only defending themselves. p. 161.

People are mistaken to imagine that a Party without a Head is not to be fear'd. Chiefs may arise in the night. P. 172.

In some Cases it is harder to please those of our own Party than to act against our Adversaries. p. 177.

The greatest Dangers have something pleasing in them, if even a M[is]carriage be attended with Glory. But slight dangers are horrible, if ill Success be attended with the loss of Reputation. Extremes are always dangerous; but they become wise means, when they are necessary. There is that comfort in them, that they never work by halves, but will always decide the matter one way or other. P. 178

One did purely out of fear one of the boldest Actions that has perhaps ever been spoken of. p. 179.

In some conjunctures it is even an Act of Prudence to rely on Accidents. p. 182

There is a Critical Minute in every thing, & the master-piece of Good Conduct is to perceive it and take hold of it. If it is miss'd, chiefly in revolutions of State, 'tis odds if it can be met with or percieved again. p. 195.

9

It is a Maxim necessary to Princes, To look on small Matters as Victimes only, which ought always to be sacraficed to greater Affairs. Small Articles should be observ'd even with ostentation as a Cloke to violation of Greater. p. 197.

Caution is most necessary with regard to the People, because Nothing is more unruly: but that caution is most carefully to be conceal'd from them, for nothing is more distrustful. P. 236.

Credit with the People, if long cultivated and deeply rooted, never fails to overcome Slight & accidental demonstrations of Publick Love. p. 238.

Weak Men never yield at the time they ought to yield. p 242

Nothing touches and moves the common People and even Companies who resemble them, so much as a variety of Spectacles. The Duke de Longueville first entered and offered to serve the Parlmt. under the Prince of Conti: soon after the D. of Bouillon[12] entered & in the like manner offered his Service; & lastly the Marschal de la Mothe entered & made the same compliment. These three successive Pushes determin'd the Company to confer the supreme command upon the Prince of Conti,[13] more effectually than if the three great Men had made their offers conjunctly. The thing was not accidental but concerted by a foresight of the event. p. 242.[14]

In great affairs the Head signifies nothing without the heart. p 245

Molé was a man of the greatest courage and a true Patriot, but he carried every thing to extremes, & I have observ'd that he always judged of Actions by Men, & never or seldom of Men by their Actions. p. 256. Vid. p. 339.[15]

Posterity will hardly believe, that a Princess of England, Granddaughter to Henry the Great, wanted a Faggot in the Month of January to get out of Bed, in the Louvre and in the Eyes of a French-Court.[16] We read in Histories with Horror, of Baseness less monstrous than this; & yet most People heard this with little concern. Examples of past times move Men beyond comparison more than those of their own times. We accustom ourselves to what we see; & I question whether the Consulship of Caligula's Horse would have surprized so much as we imagine. p. 262.

Companies appointed for the establishment of Tranquility can never be proper for War. They are obstinate in adhering to their Usual Forms in Affairs that are inconsistent with formality. p. 265. Dant operam ut cum ratione insaniant. Ter.[17]

I never knew but One, who never contested what he believ'd he could not[18] obtain. p. 280.

There is no greater Proof of a solid Judgment, than to be able to chuse when the Inconveniences are great on both sides. p. 285.

The properest and surest way of bringing any extraordinary matters to pass in such assemblies (as the Parliament) is to stir up the Young Counsellers against the Old. p. 286.

Tho a Private Cabal direct an Assembly, it puts a Period to the Power of the Cabal when their secret management is known. p. 291.[19]

In Disputes be quiet when Your Answer is weaker than the Objection, & exert Yourself when the O[b]jection is weaker than Your Answer. p. 289.

Popular power is never believed but when it is felt: because those in whose hands it ought naturally to lodge by reason of their Character, love to flatter themselves that they possess it still, when they have really lost it;[20] But it is often more profitable, as well as more honourable, for the Leaders of the People to have the Popular power rather believ'd than felt. p. 299

The Old Prince of Orange used to say that at the time we recieve the best News about the most important Matters, we ought then to give the greatest attention to the smallest matters in Hand. P. 310.

Credit with the People makes us answerable for all that they do even against our Consent. p. 316.

One of the greatest Inconveniences of a Civil War is, that one ought to study with greater care what is to be hid from ones Friends, than what is to be done against one's Enemies. p. 318.

The Malignity of Vulgar Souls is not always able to take away from extraordinary Men the credit which in some occasions they even deserve to lose. p 339. Vid p 256.

By means of the Parliamt. you hold the People, who are never more your's, than when you hold them by other Hands than your own. p. 342

A Desire to act cunningly, frequently prevents a Man's acting Wisely. p. 34[9]

One Inconveniency of Civil Wars is, that one is often forced to commit faults that proceed from good Conduct. p 358.

A Man shows himself greater by being capable [of] owning a fault, than by being incapable of committing it. p. 369.

It happens sometimes that a Man is not thanked if he executes an Affair, & yet blamed if he does not. p. 387.

Tis not always a sure Game to refuse Gratifications from Persons that are above us. p. 390.

What appears hazardous & is not really such fails to be a wise choice. p. 400.

Monsr. de Bouillon with the Physiognomy of an Ox had the Perspicacity of an Eagle. p. 403.

The Reputation of Power is Power. Vol. 2. p 8.[21]

There are times when some Persons are ever in the right. Mazarin by a contrary reason was ever thought in the Wrong. p. 10.[22]

Nothing serves better to persuade Persons of little Sense, than what they dont understand. p. 12.

Whatever is necessary ought not to be hazardous. p. 13.[23]

Patience works greater Effects than Activity. P. 25.

In Publick affairs Morality is not so strict as in Private ones. But that Liberty should be used with extreme caution; because nothing justifies it but Success; for which who can be answerable? p. 29.

Fear, when it is once come to a certain Pitch, causes the same Effects as Temerity. p. 42.

The imagination, while it is hot, will never yield. p. 42.

Nothing is more capable of occasioning Distrust in New Reconciliations than to show an Averseness of being obliged to those with whom we are reconciled. p. 61.[24]

We Princes, says the D. of Orleans, reckon words for nothing, but we never forget Actions. He thought it seems, that all Princes had the like Sentiments upon certain Matters. V. 3. p. 63.[25]

The Duke instead of answering me, answer'd himself; & it always happens in this case, that he, that does so, never percieves it, which makes the Conversation go on without an End. p. 70.

The Generality of Mankind are less able to distinguish the real from the Specious in the Virtue [of prudence] than in any other Virtue. p. 74[26]

In respect to Calumny, all that does not hurt the Person calumniated is advantagious to him. Vol. 3. p 92.

There is a pleasure in discovering People's Wickedness under the name of Zeal, & their impertinence under the disguise of Penetration. p. 92.

The most ordinary cause of Peoples mistakes is their being too much frigh[te]ned at the present Danger, & not enough so at that wch. is remote. p. 33.[27]

Men naturally fancy that they will amuse others by the same means that would amuse themselves. p. 24. Many vainly imagine that others have the same imperfections as themselves, & think & act in the same Circumstances as they would themselves. p. 25.

The World desires to be decieved. p. 52. Si populus vult decipi, decipiatur.[28]

To lessen Envy is the greatest of all Secrets. p. 116.

Policy, as well as Civility, requires that Persons in superiour Stations should make the first advances to Friendship. p. 117.[29]

The D. of Orleans was, of all Men I have ever seen, the most liable to fall into false steps by his fear of falling into them: being in that like unto Hares. p. 135.

There are conjunctures wherein it is impossible to act well. p. 143.

Nothing is so dangerous as Proposals that appear mysterious & are not so: for they raise Envy & defeat themselves. p. 154.

The Prince of Conde, reading a Pamphlet written against himself, said to one of his Attendants, I read this with Great Pleasure, since it tells me my faults, which none of you dare to do. p. 147.

Men are often Valued for Actions which they ought the most to be blamed for. p. 177.

Experience alone can teach Men, not to prefer a present Pleasure to what would be afterwards a much more real one. p. 180.

Enmities that are the worst grounded are the most obstinate. p. 269.

Except Religion & Good Manners every thing else is indifferent. p. 273.

The E. of Montrose was the only Man in the World that recalled in me the Ideas of some Heroes who are now to be found only [in] Plutarch's Lives. Vol 2 p. 75.[30]

One of the greatest misfortunes which the despotic Power of the Ministers of the last Age has brought upon the State, is the Custom wch. their private (but mistaken) Interest has introduced, ever to support the superiour against the Inferiour. That Maxim is one of Machiavel's, whom most of his readers do not understand, and whom others take to be a great Politician for no other reason but for having ever been Wicked. p. 78.[31]

I never knew a Man who respected truth so little as Mazarin. p. 83.

The Cardinal had no reason to complain of me, & I was unwilling to complain of him though I had reason: It is easier for those who are in this last disposition to be reconciled, than for those who complain without cause. p. 91.

We ought not to be so much offended at our Friends faults, as to give thereby an Advantage to our Enemies. p. 109.

The Talent of insinuating is more useful than that of persuading. The for[mer] is often successful, the latter very seldom. 118

In matters which in themselves are not favourable, any unnecessary Alteration becomes pernicious, because it is odious. p. 123.[32]

All Interlocutory Proceedings appear wise to irresolute Minds, because they incline to avoid (as long as possible) the coming to a final Resolution. Knowing the Duke's foible to be timorousness, I always fancied that the best way was to animate & encourage him, but Caumartin's Scheme was better, to keep his Eyes always open by moderate & Succesive fears. For Persons naturally Weak should be shown precipices on all sides, & then they go onto the first Path, which you keep open for them. ibid. [pp. 141–42][33]

Every thing possible ought to be ventured upon when one can take advantage even of want of Success. p 143.

When Persons have been for a long time in suspence about undertaking a thing, for fear of a disappointment, the impression which that fear leaves in their mind commonly makes them afterwards go on too fast in managing the same undertaking. p. 152.

It is less imprudent to act like a Master, than not to speak like a Subject. p. 153.

It is very difficult for irresolute Men to determine upon the means, tho they are determined upon the End. p. 155. This defect is one of the worst causes of the false steps which Men take. p. 168.[34]

Card. Mazarin always believed that a back door was kept open, when there was least Room for it. When you deal with Men of that Character; make them believe you intend to decieve those, whom you really intend to serve. p. 182.[35]

The averseness which most Men have to part with their Money is the cause that they never did it [in] time enough, even in conjunctures when they are most resolved to do it. Vol. 4. p. 9.[36]

In Italy the discredit of passing for a Dupe is greater than any where else. ib. p. 10.

Cardinal Barberini, whose Life was A[n]gelical, had an Oddness of Humour, that rendered him, as they say in Italy, Inamorato de l'impossibile, delectatus Impossibilitate. Vol. 4. p. 15.[37]

Hypocrisy may decieve, but it cannot do it long when able Persons undertake to unmask it. Vol. 4. p. 18.

In a short conversation he showed himself more reserved and wise (Savio col Silentio, sapiens cum silentio) than any Man I ever knew. p 21 He showed his wisdom by saying nothing.[38]

All the World is, & will be for ever decieved in things which flatter their Passions. p. 22. facile credimus quod valde volumus.[39]

It is impossible to keep one's self so much upon the Reserve, as never to discover any thing of one's Natural Temper. p. 24. A Man's being addicted to trifles discovers not only a small Genius, but a low mind. The least things are sometimes more distinguishing Marks of a Man, than the Greatest. ib.

Those, who are expecting the Papal Dignity with the greatest impatience, appear the most surprized when it comes. p. 38.

In the Conclave they are so far from suspecting any thing like those sorts of Revenges, which common errors charges the Italians with, that it is pretty common for the Cardinal elected to drink at his Dinner Wine sent him in the Morning by the excluded Cardinal. p. 44.[40]

Great Men have great weaknesses, & are not exemp[t] even from small ones. But there are some sorts of weaknesses, of which they are not capable, & I have never seen a Great Man, for example, begin his entrance into a great Employment with trifling matters. p. 49.

Pope Alexander VII's true Genius was to make use of Finisses in every thing. A Great defect, & so much the greater when it is met with in great Dignities; because in such men there is no hopes of a Reformation. For hearing no complaints from timorous Inferiours, they fancy their finesses, how palpable soever, to be always unpercieved. p. 53[41]

In great affairs especially, deny yourself the Pleasure of Raillery. This Pleasure has on many occasions cost the Pr[ince] of Condé dear. Words spoke often engage more than Actions. In great Affairs the least Words cannot be too nicely weighed. p. 62

The best man in the World at finding out Expressions the most promising & the least significant. p 63.[42]

It is an inffallible rule of acting with cunning Men, to give them such Answers as will oblige them to explain themselves p. 65.

Nothing but a Continuation of Your good Fortune can secure you most Men's friendship. (cum fueris felix &c)[43] Every body thinks he does honour to a disgraced Man [by] serving him. This borders upon Gratitude. Those who are guilty of Ingratitude, seldom percieve it, because they first lessen in their own thoughts the Obligations they have recieved from their Benefactors. p. 76. The Friends of Unfortunate Persons are a little hard to please. ib.[44]

A Prudent Man ought always to keep his natural Goodness under some restraint: And a Person of great Quality, whose Soul can never be too much inclined to Goodness, ought by his Good conduct to keep it carefully hid, & not disclose but with precaution, that he may preserve the dignity of it chiefly during his Disgraces. The Cardinal's familiarity & Generosity to his Domestics during his Prosperity enclined them still more to murmer and be dissatisfied with him in his Adversity. p. 79, 80[45]

Men by a pretended Gratitude to Some screen themselves from the imputation of being really ungrateful to others. For Mankind give but a slight attention to Ingratitudes in which they are not concerned. p. 104.

The only or at least [the best][46] Remedy agt. the uneasiness occasioned by Ingratitude, is never to do good for the sake of Good itself. ib. Nothing is greater than to bestow favours upon those who have been wanting to us: Nothing in my opinion is weaker than to recieve any from their Hands. [p. 103]

All Kings are Ravenous Beasts, said Cato. He did not see that the Roman People were as Rapacious & oppressive as any Tyrant. How could he think, that that was glorious in many Men, which was detestable in one? Hobbes.[47]

From Mont. chiefly.[48]

He may well go afoot who leads his Horse in his hand. Prov.[49]

People use Pleasures more rarely and sparingly, when they have them entirely at Command. People of Easy Circumstances are commonly most temperate. Restraint begets desire. Our Nature is Elastic. Those who have pleasure a[t] command are apt to amuse themselves with other things, keeping that as a Treasure in reserve. Others are eager to snatch the opportunity. Abundance begets satiety, & want begets an Appetite. Many People have [lived?] in London for many Years without seeing many Curiosities, which Strangers take care to see in a Week.[50]

My Thoughts sleep, if I sit still: My fancy does not go by itself; My Legs must move it: & all those who study without a Book are in the same condition.[51]

I think it more supportable to be always alone than to be never alone, Mo[nt][52]

Nunq̄m minus Solus, q̄m cum Solus. Scipio.[53]

Our passions are like Torrents which may be diverted, but not obstructed. Time is the Sovereign Physician of our Passions, & gains its End chiefly by supplying our imaginations with other & new Affairs; wearing out the Old by new Impressions. Mont.[54]

A Mathematician looks with contempt upon the Pursuits of others, as Pleasure, Title, Pomp or Money: & what are his Diagrams & Demonstrations when his Hand & Brains are for ever scattered in the Dust?[55]

Pleasure is a Quality of very little Ambition; it thinks itself rich enough of itself without any Addition of Repute; & is best pleased

16

where most obscure. Mont. And why? Is it conscious of its own weakness & asham'd to be seen? Or is it afraid of Envy & a Rival? It cannot endure another to enjoy even the sight of the Transports of the Beloved.[56]

Few will quarrel with the Liberty of my writings, who have not more to quarrel with in the licence of their own thoughts; I conform well enough to their Inclinations, but I offend their Eyes. I dare to say, what I dare to do; & the worst of my Actions & Qualities do not appear to me so foul, as I think it foul & base not to dare to own them. Every one is wary & discreet in confession but Men ought not to be so in Action. Mont.[57]

I know a Man, reputed moderate, just & devout, who is a Mortal Enemy to Auricular confession. And why? Is he conscious of some extraordinary & atrocious Qualities? or does he desire to appear much better than he really is? People who pretend to Religion cannot help confessing in general that they are Sinners; but they conceal or disown all Particulars. Why should I be so unwilling to confess even my Particular faults to men? Since they have the same faults or Equivalent. They may well admire my Sincerity or (if you will) my Impudence; but they cannot be surprized at my Wickedness. I am Humble before God, but confident before Men.[58]

Quare vitia sua nemo confitetur? quia etiam nunc in illis est. Somnium narrare vigilantis est. Sen. Epist. 53.[59]

Those who conceal their Vice from others commonly conceal it from themselves; & do not think it covered enough, if they them selves see it. Mont[60]

A Man should not delight in Praises that are not his due, nor be uneasy at Slander. The Praise or blame aim at another Person. The Object is mistaken. Socrates being told that People [spoke] ill of him, not at all, said he, there is nothing in me of what they say. Mont.[61]

People who are too tender of their Reputation, & too deeply piqued by Slander, are conscious to themselves of some inward Infirmity. I am suspicious of some guilt, when I hear the most earnest Vindications. A Reputation grounded on true Virtue is like the Sun that may be clouded, but not extinguished. Plato, being slandered, said, I shall behave so as Nobody shall believe it.[62]

Bashfulness, says Aristotle is an Orniment to Youth, but a reproach to old Age. Mont.[63]

Assurance is a Vice, if Natural, & a Virtue, if acquired.[64]

If a Man does not always his Duty, he ought at least to love & acknowledge it. Mont.[65]

17

A Woman may yield to such a Man as she would by no means have married, not only for the condition of his fortune, but the dislike of his Person. Mont. Mollia tempora. Few Men have made a Wife of a Mistress, that have not repented it. Mont.[66]

A Poem published in the American Magazine
upon the Tropes of Rhetoric.[67]

A Trope a Sovereign Pow'r o'er Language shows,
And upon words a foreign Sense bestows,
God is a Rock, & guards his Saints from ill:
Herod's a Fox, & will be cruel still.

A Metaphor compares with out the Sign*   *as, like &c.
Virtue's A Star, & shall for ever shine.

An Allegory in a length of Chain
Will the redoubling Metaphor detain.
A Vine was rescued by the Almighty's hand
From Egypt's wast[e] & Placed in Canaan's Land:
Fenced round by Heaven, the fruitful Branches grew,
Blessed the warm Sun, & drunk th' enliv'ning Dew:
But now the Trampling Bull & hungry Boar,
Wild from the Woods, the lovely Tree devour.
Fence, Clusters, Boughs, one general ruin share,
And Fire consumes what Savage Monsters spare.
Look, gracious Heaven! on this thy mourning Vine,
And let thy[68] Guardian-care attest it thine.

A Metonymy will for kindred sake
The name of one thing for another take.
Causes effects intend:—His Sin will find
Th' offender out, and rack his guilty mind[.]
Effect the cause denote:—Pale Death destroys
Gay giddy Youth, & withers all its Joys.
Subjects for Adjuncts stand:—Friends, take the Cup,
And, thankful for its blessings, drink it up.
Adjuncts the Subjects mean:—Mankind despise
Virtue alive, but wail it when it dies.

A Metalepsis throng'd with Tropes appears;   ⎫ Post aliquot
The Spikes of Corn denote the Golden Ears,   ⎪ mea regna videns
The Ears the Crop, the Crop the Summer means,   ⎬ mirabor aristas.
Summer the Year in all its various Scenes.   ⎭ Vir. Ecl. 1.[69]

18

Antonomasia for a common name
Bestows a proper.—He in virtuous fame
Is quite a Socrates.—On th' other hand,
A Proper for a common name shall stand.[70]
The Thunder of the *Orator controuls   *Cicero.
The Senates will, & vanquishes their Souls.

Synecdochè our Style diversifies,
And at her call unnumbered Bea[u]ties rise.
The Whole intends a Part:—The Silver Thames
Eager we drank, and quenched our raging Flames.
A Part denotes the Whole:—'Twas Marlborough
At Blenheim fought, & crushed the Gallic Foe.
Generals for Specials stand:—New Life proclaim
To every Creature in the Saviour's Name.
Specials a General mean: The East Wind raves,
And heave[s] th' Atlantic in ten thousand Waves.

An Irony in soft mellifluent Phrase
Strikes an invenomed Sting of Deep disgrace.
Ye are the Men of all Mankind most Wise,
And when Ye die, no doubt all Wisdom dies!

Sarcasm is Irony in its excess,
King of the Jews we humbly Thee address;
Low at thy feet, we bend submissive down;
Revere thy Reed, & hail thy thorny Crown.

Hyperbolè the Truth will oft neglect
By bold excess, or by as bold Defect.
Mark how it Rises:—Yon' tall Mountain Shrouds
Its height in Heaven, & tow'rs above the Clouds.
Again it sinks:—Shall man his Grandeur boast.
An Atom of an Atom World at most.

A Catachresis thro' the want of Words
Or the sweet Charms which Novelty affords,
Most boldly breaks Expressions wonted Fence,
And make the Reader tremble for the Sense.
For me the Wheat's fat Kidneys crown the Plains
And mine's the Blood the mellow Grape contains.
If tempted with the whistling of a name,   }
See Cromwell damn'd to everlasting Fame.   } Mr. Pope.[71]

19

Farewell! My Friend, with forc'd Praise do not damn,
But dare to Censure what is worthy blame.   Sent from London to
                                             Mr. Davis from a Co-
                                             respondent.[72]

Extracts from the Abbe de Bos's
Critical Reflections

On Poetry & Painting[73]

The Arts of Poetry & Painting are neve[r] more applauded than when they are most successful in moving us to Pity. Vol. 1. C. 1. A Tragedy is one of the Principal Entertainments for a Company assembled for their Diversion. Vol. 1. p. 2.

The Natural Pleasures of Men are always the fruits of Indigence. The most delicious Banquet without an appetite is insipid. Ch. 1.

Solitude and a Stagnation of Mind are to most if not all People, more intolerable than the toil of Business & the tumults of the Passions. ib.

Men are more addicted to Levity than Hypocrisy; & frequently they are only guilty of inconstancy, when they are charg'd with dissimulation.[74]

The Romans were fond of the Bloody Spectacles of the Amphitheatre, the Spaniards of Bull-fighting, every body to see a Duel, a Shipwreck, a Battle where the Event is dangerous, if not tragical. What is the reason of this Pleasure, which is always attended with Horror & Pity? The mere emotion of the mind, occasioned by the sight of these things, is the attracti[on]. Even Gentlemen of Sense & Honour are fond of Gaming, & chiefly of Hazard, not from Avarice, but merely from the violent Emotion of the Passions; which gives such an enchanting Pleasure, as makes them undervalue the Ruin & Poverty into which they are running. Ch. 2.[75]

It is the opinion of several, that Laziness alone prevents more wicked Actions than All the Virtues put together. ib.[76]

Of all Talents proper for raising Man to a State of Empire and Command, A Superiority of wit & knowledge is not the most effectual. 'Tis the art of moving men, as one Pleases; An Art that is acquired chiefly by a person's seeming to be moved & penetrated with those very Sentiments he intends to inspire. (si vis me flere dolendum est primum ipsi tibi).[77] At an Assembly, we take notice of those Gamesters who play highest, rather than those who play best. These affect us most, who are most affected themselves.[78] If a Rope-dancer dances on a Rope, a foot or two from the Ground, he will not move us so much as if he danced a dozen or 20 foot from the ground.[79] C. 4. It should seem that Ca[e]sar excell'd Cicero in the Art of Persuasion.[80]

Those pieces, which move our Passions, please us more, than those wch. inform the Understanding. It seems more difficult to keep up a correspondance with the mind than with the Heart. C. 8. As Heaviness (Tedium vitae) is more burthensome & disagreeable than Ignorance, we prefer the Pleasure of being moved to that of being instructed. C. 9.[81]

The mind has but an imperfect Notion of Passions wch. the Heart never felt. The Heart attains to its full strength much earlier than the Mind; & it is almost impossible, methinks, for a Man of 25 Years of Age not to have felt all those Passions, of which his constitution can be Sensible. C. 17.[82]

Major e longinquo Reverentia. Tac. Adita Visis laudamus libentius. V. Pater. Virtutem incolumen odimus; Sublatam ex oculis quaerimus invidi. Hor.[83]

No Man deserves our admiration unless he be viewed at a certain Distance. One says smartly that Heroes Valet[s] a Chambres are the greatest Enemies to the[ir] Glory. C. 20[84]

The Strongest & Soundest Minds often possess the weakest & most sickly bodies. The Knife cuts the Sheath as the French express it. Dr. Molyneux to Mr. Locke.[85]

—— says, she has had a Melancholy Christmas, having been at two Burials. Not so I judge, but from the Teeth forwards; for she heartily loves a Fuss & a Feast; & who are not glad to see others not so happy as themselves?[86]

Suppose two Men equally Ingenius & Skillful, of whom one has had a Regular Education, & the other has acquired his Skill by the dint of his own Labour; the former is more capable than the latter to communicate his Knowledge to another. Mr. Snodgrass.[87]

Poetae & equi alendi sunt, non saginandi. Charles IX of France.[88]

Nothing makes one say & commit so many Silly things as the desire of appearing witty. Ch. 24.[89]

The Passion we have for one kind of Painting or Poetry more than for another arises not from reason but from Taste, & our Taste depends on the organization of our bodies & the dispositions or situations of our Minds. When our Taste happens to change, it is not owing to Argument or Persuasion, but to some Physical Alteration in our Bodies, or to some prevailing & aspiring Passion of the mind. Ch. 49.[90]

Sometimes we impute to an unlucky or cross Accident those chagrins, whose origin is entirely in the intemperature of our humours or in some disposition of the Air that oppresses our Machine. Vol. 2. Ch. 13.

Virtutes iisdem temporibus optime ostimantur, quibus facillime gignuntur. Tac. Vit. Agric.[91]

National Characters.[92]

The Spartans & Spaniards have been noted to be of small dispatch. Mi [ven]ga la muerte di Spagna, mihi veniat mors ex Hispania. The French are wiser than they seem, & the Spaniards seem wiser than they are. Bac. Ess.[93]

Englishmen go to France for their finishing stroke of Breeding. The French are much addicted to Grimace.[94] The British Climate more than any other, requires such Entertainmts. as disperse Melancholy & put our Faculties in good humour. Spect. 179.[95] Querulus, incertum suo an Gentis vitio, said by a Dutchman of a Englishman.[96] Were an English Comedian to show so much Vivacity in his Gesture, such disquiet in his visage, such eagerness in his Countenance, such frequent Exclamations as an Italian Comedian, he would act his part very ill: because the English who ought to be his Model, have not that behaviour & Gesture. That which is sufficient to move an Italian makes no Impression upon an Englishman. An Englishman receiving Sentence of Death, appears with less agitation than an Italian condemned to a small pecuniary fine. Abbè du Bos.[97]

No Workmen in the world have a greater Beauty in the Execution, or manage their Tools better than the English. But they have not been able as yet to attain to that taste in their designs which the foreign Artists carried over with them to London; where it has never stirr'd out of their Shops. Id. The English own themselves to be more capable of improving than of inventing.[98]

The Goldsmiths Trade, whether in Large or small Work, and all those Arts whose value is raised by the design, are more perfect in France than in any other Country. Abbè du Bos.[99] A Spanish Grandee squanders his Money in Intrigues & Galantry: but a Polish Palatine's profusion consists in Wine & Brandy. The Influence of Climate is stronger than that of Origin & Blood. Abbè du Bos.[100]

Difference of Climate has a very sensible effect upon Vegetables, why not also upon the Tempers & Genius of Mankind. Fontenelle.[101]

It is easier to bear Hatred than contempt. For this reason, others, as well as Princes, forgive Injurious sooner than contemptuous Words.[102]

On Orpheus, written by Antipater[103]

No longer, Orpheus, shall thy sacred strains
Lead Stones, and Trees, and Beasts along the Plains;
No longer sooth the boisterous[104] winds to sleep,
Or still the Billows of the raging Deep.
For thou art gone, the Muses mourn'd thy Fall
In solemn strains, thy Mother most of All.
Ye Mortals, idly for your Son, ye moan
If they a Goddess could not save her own.

On Homer, by Alpheus of Mytilene

Still in our ears Andromache complains,
And still in sight the fate of Troy remains:
Still Ajax fights, still Hector's dragg'd along,
Such strange Inchantment dwells in Homer's Song;
Whose Birth could more than one poor Realm adorn,
For all the world is proud that he was born.

On Euripides, by Ion

Divine Euripides, This Tomb we see
So fair, is not a Monument for thee.
So much as thou for it, since all will own
Thy Name and lasting praise adorns the stone.

On Sophocles, by Simonides

Winde, Gentle Ever-green, to form a Shade
Around the Tomb where Sophocles is laid.
Sweet Ivy winde thy Boughs, and Intertwine
With Blushing Roses and the clustring Vine.
Thus will thy lasting leaves, with Beauty[105] hung,
Prove gratefull Emblems of the lays he sung;
Whose Soul, excelled like a God of wit
Among the Muses and the Graces writ.

On Menander, the Author unnamed

The very Bees, O sweet Menander hung
To taste the Muses spring upon thy Tongue
The very Graces made the Scenes you writ

23

Their happy point of fine expression hit.
Thus still you live, you make your Athens shine,
And raise it's Glory to the Skies in thine.

On the Author of the above who in some publication
hinted his possession of a spark of Homer—

> Gibbon & Homer how they sound
> A farthing & a thousand pound
> An atom & a brilliant star,
> A cock boat & a man of War—[106]

1 *Memoirs of the Cardinal de Retz. Containing the Particulars of his own Life, with the most Secret Transactions at the French Court during the Administration of Cardinal Mazarin, and the Civil Wars occasioned by it. To which are Added Some Other Pieces written by the Cardinal de Retz, or Explanatory to these Memoirs* (In Four Volumes. Translated from the *French* [by P. Davall]. With Notes. London: Printed for Jacob Tonson at *Shakespear's Head* in the *Strand*, 1723). In this edition the page numbers correspond with those cited by JM in his notes. Politician as well as ecclesiastic, Cardinal de Retz (Jean François Paul de Gondi, 1614–1679) shared importantly for nine years after 1643 in the intrigues of the French court in Paris. He opposed Cardinal Mazarin and was a leader of the parliamentary Fronde from 1648 until its breakup and his consequent fall from royal favor in 1652, the year after he became a cardinal. He wrote the *Memoirs* late in his life.

2 The father was partial to the eldest son, but hoped that his third son, the author of these *Memoirs*, would become Archbishop of Paris.

3 Richelieu is consistently spelled "Richlieu" in this English translation of the *Memoirs* (1723 ed.). Even though JM's note summed up much on these pages, his sentence appears in slightly altered form in *Memoirs*, II, 403. This transposition, together with that mentioned in n. 24, below, probably signifies that he sometimes devoted his "Commonplace Book" to a revised version of jottings made earlier in a rough form.

4 The statement of de Retz on p. 51 of his *Memoirs* probably suggested this comment, but, unless it was original with JM, its source is unknown.

5 The citation should have been pp. 66–68. JM inadvertently repeated "says" twice in the middle of the paragraph. De Retz used "the two adventures" not only to illustrate how "trifling matters" sometimes produce results of great consequence but also to show the importance of self-restraint in advancing a man's career. In the one instance, although he had "bought" a beautiful girl, about fourteen years of age, to be his mistress, he was so impressed by her "modest" and "godly" conduct that he at once "released" her to a convent. In the other episode, although de Retz had been grossly insulted by Captain Coutenau and could have killed him when he accidentally dropped his sword in the ensuing duel, de Retz spared his life. Thereupon Coutenau apologized and spoke in praise of de Retz to the king.

6 JM interpolated the Latin words. They are from "T. Pomponii Attici Vita ex Cornelio Nepote," chap. iii, lines 1–4 in John Clarke, trans., *Cornelii Nepotis Vitae Excellentium Imperatorium* (London, 1773), p. 222. "Hic autem sic se gerebat, ut communis infimis, par principibus videretur" (He likewise behaved so, that he seemed upon a level with the lowest, and yet equal to the greatest).

7 JM should have written 86 rather than 88. He accidentally wrote "was" twice.

8 De Retz held the office of Coadjutor of the Archbishop of Paris before becoming Archbishop.

9 The Duc d'Orléans (1608–1660), a son of Henry IV and his wife Marie de Medicis, veered from one side to the other during the wars of the Fronde until he was driven out of public life by Mazarin in 1652.

10 This sentence is JM's own reflection upon the unwise advice given to the queen at the time of the Paris riots in August 1648 by timid councilors who advocated doing nothing, and by rash ones who urged her to end the disturbance by using force. Both recommendations, being premised upon a belief that the outbreak was trivial, were wrong. By the queen's refusal to be conciliatory, as de Retz had wished, the August riots expanded in scope and time into the tumultuous years of the parliamentary Fronde.

11 De Retz mentioned this incident as an example of how a quick-witted leader could deflect an excited member of a mob from carrying out his purpose.

12 The Duc de Bouillon (1605–1652), a Frondist leader generally admired by de Retz, was a brother of Marshal Turenne (see n. 15).

13 The Prince de Condé (1621–1686), one of the ablest of French generals, sided for a time during the civil war with de Retz and the Parlement of Paris. After his defeat in the summer of 1652, Condé fled to Spain and served that power until he returned to his French allegiance eight years later. The keen observation of Condé was likened by de Retz to the wisdom of Plutarch.

14 This paragraph is JM's summary of the *Memoirs,* I, 241–43.

15 The fact that JM cross-referenced to the *Memoirs,* I, 339, where de Retz praises Marshal Turenne (1611–1675), one of the greatest of France's military leaders, suggests that he was much impressed by the ability of courageous and honest public leaders to triumph over opponents who questioned the disinterestedness of their patriotism.

16 Following the execution of Charles I of England in 1649, his widow, Queen Henrieta Maria, and her daughter, lived in Paris. Upon visiting them, de Retz was shocked to find their rooms so cold that they felt obliged to stay in bed.

17 De Retz's generalization was based upon the attention paid by the Parlement of Paris to trifling matters of punctilio even during the three months' siege of the city early in 1649. JM supplied the modified quotation from Act I, scene 1, line 16 of *Eunuchus* by the Roman dramatist Publius Terentius Afer. The passage is "nihilo plus agas, quam si des operam ut cum ratione insanias" (you would get no further than if your object was to be mad by the rules of reason). JM could have derived this quotation from his reading of Montaigne's *Essays,* Vol. III, chap. v.

18 Repetition of the four words "believ'd he could not" is in the original by JM.

19 This is JM's own observation upon the account by de Retz of how, at a critical moment when his faction covertly managed public affairs, he skilfully concealed that fact from the Parlement of Paris.

20 The words between the colon and semicolon comprise JM's own reflection upon de Retz's account of the rivalry between the Parlement and various outside leaders to direct the anti-Mazarin or popular party.

21 This aphorism by JM is based on de Retz's observation that people, when assured they can do something, generally discover they are powerful enough to accomplish it.

22 During a lull in the civil war, the Mazarinists vied with the Frondists for the favor of the Parisians. Because the Parisians generally mistrusted Cardinal Mazarin, de Retz found that they nearly always accepted as true his own pro-Frondist explanations.

23 By omitting the word "reckon'd" before "hazardous" JM weakened the force and obscured the meaning of de Retz's sentence.

24 Why JM at this point stopped taking notes on Volume II, moved to Volume III, and then turned back to noting only 120 pages more of Volume II, before extracting some observations from Volume IV, is unknown. This strange arrangement at least suggests that he read the *Memoirs* at intervals over a considerable period of time.

25 Perhaps the troubled relations between Great Britain and the thirteen colonies made the generalization in this paragraph on the opinion of rulers about what was said to them, and the comment in the preceding paragraph, seem especially noteworthy to JM.

26 "Of prudence" has been inserted by the editors to rectify what was certainly an unintentional omission by JM.

27 For the material in this and the next two paragraphs, JM reverted to earlier pages in Volume III.

28 JM added this Latin sentence, which states that if the people wish to be deceived, they will be deceived. It is an adaptation of the old proverb, "Qui vult decipi, decipiatur" (Jacques Auguste de Thou, *Historia Sui Temporis* [ed. by Pierre Dupuy and Nicolas Rigault; 5 parts; Geneva, 1620], Part I, p. 17).

29 This maxim and the comment about "Envy" were reflections by de Retz upon his elevation to a cardinalate in 1651.

30 The Earl of Montrose (1612–1650), after his unsuccessful military efforts in Scotland to aid Charles I during the English Civil War, stayed in France from 1647 until the end of 1649. While there, he and de Retz became friends. Returning to Scotland, Montrose was captured and hanged in May 1650.

31 This is the first mention of Machiavelli in JM's extant writings. De Retz was obviously much influenced by Machiavelli's views about the art of statecraft.

32 JM may have been impressed by de Retz's stress in his *Memoirs* upon inaction as frequently the least dangerous course to follow when confronted by a delicate situation.

33 In order to achieve his ambition to become a cardinal, de Retz deemed the support of the Duc d'Orléans necessary. Louis Lefevre de Caumartin (1624–1687), who was probably the closest friend and the most trusted adviser of de Retz during the years of the parliamentary Fronde, helped him gain this support.

34 JM's apparent conclusion that nothing was worth noting on pp. 156–67, which deal with a succession of boudoir intrigues, illustrates his primary interest in generalizations about human nature in relation to politics and statecraft.

35 The rest of JM's notes on the *Memoirs* all bear upon its Volume IV. The long portion of Volume III, to which he gave little or no attention, deals with de Retz's declining influence in public affairs and eventual imprisonment.

36 Volume IV begins with de Retz's journey to Rome following his escape from a French prison. He ruefully comments that he might have avoided incarceration if he had been less parsimonious.

37 JM interpolated the Latin equivalent of the Italian. Cardinal Antonio Barberini (1608–1671), of the Italian princely family of that name, was a protégé of Cardinal Mazarin and hence out of favor with the pro-Spanish-Hapsburg Pope Innocent X. Following the latter's death in 1655, Barberini supported for election as pope a cardinal who had no chance of winning—hence the comment in the *Memoirs* that he was fascinated by the impossible.

38 Here de Retz referred to Cardinal Fabio Chigi (1599–1667) who, with de Retz's help, during a conclave lasting eighty days, finally became Pope Alexander VII, successor of Innocent X. The three Italian words, except that "Silentio" should be

"Silenzio," are in the *Memoirs*. JM added the Latin equivalent, and his last sentence is an approximate translation.

[39] "We readily believe whatever we very much wish" to believe. The origin of the Latin sentence, which JM rather than de Retz supplied, has not been found. The same thought, however, was expressed by Demosthenes in his *Third Olynthiac* (348 B.C.) and by Caesar in *Commentarii de bello Gallico* (*ca.* 51 B.C.) iii. 18. In the latter, for example, Caesar remarks "quod fere libenter homines id quod volunt credunt" (the willingness of men generally to believe what they wish).

[40] This sentence and the one which precedes it refer to the extraordinarily prolonged conclave of cardinals mentioned in n. 38.

[41] This paraphrase by JM heightens the clarity of the original. JM used the word "Genius" in the sense of "bent" or "nature" rather than "talent," and the word "Dignities" in the sense of "Dignitaries."

[42] According to de Retz, Pope Alexander VII was skilful in leaving an impression of saying weighty things when, in truth, his words committed him to nothing of consequence.

[43] JM's interpolation, if he had completed it, would have been Cato's "Quum fueris felix, quae sunt adversa caveto: Non eodem cursu respondent ultima primis" (*Dionysii Catonis Disticha de moribus ad filium* i. 18). Translated it reads: "When you are enjoying prosperity, provide against adversity; the end of life will not be attended by the same train of fortunate circumstances as the beginning."

[44] This paragraph illustrates JM's ability to distil the essence from a fairly lengthy passage—in this instance a two-page discourse by de Retz about how he was persecuted by the King of France and disregarded by the Pope after helping to elect him.

[45] In this instance the "Cardinal's familiarity" was de Retz's.

[46] An editorial interpolation of what JM probably intended to write.

[47] This paragraph is an addendum by JM, not based upon any specific comment by de Retz. De Retz's account of the fickleness and oppressive measures of the Parisian populace during the civil war of the Fronde probably reminded JM of Thomas Hobbes's strictures upon Cato's remark that "a king is no better than a ravening beast that lives off the prey" ("Epistle Dedicatory of Hobbes," in Hobbes, *Philosophicall Rudiments Concerning Government and Society* [London, 1651]; W. H. D. Rouse, ed., *The Lives of Aristeides and Marcus Cato* [*by*] *Plutarch* [London, 1928], p. 82). JM may also have recalled the closing chapters of Hobbes, *Leviathan; or, the Matter, Forme, and Power of a Commonwealth, Ecclesiasticall and Civill* (London, 1651).

[48] Pages 12, 13, and 14 of JM's "Commonplace Book" contain quotations from the *Essays* of Montaigne, summaries of what he wrote, and some comments by JM. Of the three volumes of essays which Michel de Montaigne published late in his life, only the third was the source of JM's notes, insofar as they were gleaned from this author. Although JM used the Charles Cotton translation, he cited no page numbers and hence the edition which he read cannot be known. In the rest of these footnotes the page references are to *The Essays of Michael Seigneur de Montaigne, Translated into English* (the Eighth Edition, with very considerable Amendments and Improvements, From the most accurate and elegant French Edition of Peter Coste [3 vols.; London, 1776]). All of JM's extracts, with the exception of four unidentified ones, were from the essays "Of Three Commerces, i.e. Familiarities with Men, Women, and Books," "Of Diversion," and "On Some Verses of Virgil." Over half of JM's notes reflect his reading of a few pages of this last-named essay, a discursive and frank series of observations about love, passion, and marriage. His interest in these subjects is further evidence (see above, editorial note) that he probably did not take these notes as early as 1759. The un-

identified four extracts, although they bear upon subjects treated by Montaigne, may explain why JM included "chiefly" in his heading of this section of his notebook. Perhaps, however, he used this adverb merely to signify that Montaigne himself had derived several of his comments, of which JM made note, from some other author.

49 Montaigne, *Essays*, III, 50. Le Roux de Lincy in his *Le livre des proverbes français* (2 vols.; Paris, 1859), I, 163, merely dates the proverb from the sixteenth century, while Burton Stevenson, ed., *The Home Book of Proverbs, Maxims and Familiar Phrases* (New York, 1948), p. 1179, attributes it to Montaigne.

50 Montaigne, *Essays*, III, 124-27. Here the author elaborates upon the theme that restraint heightens interest in what is forbidden or difficult of attainment. JM's paragraph, although on somewhat the same subject, in no way resembles Montaigne's discussion in its style, examples, or language. Moreover, JM's mention of London suggests that either he derived his note from some other author or he recorded personal reflections upon a topic suggested by Montaigne.

51 *Ibid.*, III, 51.

52 *Ibid.*, III, 52. Montaigne wrote: "I think it somewhat more tolerable to be always alone, than never to be so."

53 "Numquam se minus otiosum esse, quam cum otiosus, nec minus solum quam cum solus esset" (Cicero *De officiis* iii. 1). Here Cicero purported to repeat what Scipio Africanus told Cato. The Latin has been translated, "He was never less idle than when he had nothing to do and never less lonely than when he was alone" (Cicero *De officiis;* with an English translation by Walter Miller [London, 1921], p. 271).

54 Montaigne, *Essays*, III, 61. JM supplied the simile at the beginning of this paragraph.

55 Here JM apparently records his own comment upon Montaigne's counsel to scholars not to become conceited because of their erudition (*ibid.*, III, 41-43).

56 The first sentence of this paragraph quotes Montaigne almost word for word (*ibid.*, III, 69); the rest seems to be JM's addendum.

57 *Ibid.*, III, 72-73. Possibly by intent but most probably by error, JM inserted "not" in the concluding sentence and thus reversed Montaigne's meaning.

58 *Ibid.*, III, 73-75. JM seems in this passage to have tried to mirror Montaigne's style and thought without using his words. Unlike his model, however, who limited "Auricular confession" to the Roman Catholic confessional, JM evidently used the words to signify a public rather than a private avowal of personal faults.

59 The full citation is Seneca's *Letters*, Book VI, Letter I, sec. 53. In Montaigne, *Essays*, III, 73, the passage is translated: "Why does no man confess his vices? Because he yet continues in them: it is for a man who is awake to tell his dream."

60 *Ibid.*, III, 73.

61 JM inadvertently repeated "is nothing" and omitted "spoke" (*ibid.*, III, 75-76). The reference to Socrates is probably to his "Apology" to the Athenians (Irwin Edman, ed., *The Works of Plato* [Modern Library Edition, New York, 1928], pp. 59 ff.).

62 Montaigne, *Essays*, III, 97. With the exception of its final sentence, taken from Montaigne, this paragraph illustrates JM's considerable skill in discerning the general principle implicit in the essayist's particular examples.

63 *Ibid.*, III, 77.

64 Although Montaigne often wrote (e.g., *ibid.*, III, 25-28) about the differences between men's natural and acquired characteristics, the source of this aphorism, unless it was JM's own, has not been found.

65 *Ibid.*, III, 84.

66 *Ibid.*, III, 84. JM's interpolation in Latin means "a favorable opportunity." Although he quoted inaccurately, he probably had in mind the "mollissima . . . tempora" of the *Aeneid*, Book IV, line 293, where Virgil tells of Aeneas' desertion of his mistress Dido.

67 *The American Magazine and Monthly Chronicle for the British Colonies* (published by a Society of Gentlemen, Philadelphia; printed and sold by William Bradford), I (July 1758), 503–5. Except as noted below, the marginalia are in the printed version.

68 Here JM miscopied "they" for "thy."

69 This 69th line of the First Eclogue of Virgil is translated by Thomas Fletcher Royds on p. 11 of his edition of *The Eclogues, Bucolics, or Pastorals of Virgil* (Oxford, 1922) as "and marvel as I gaze at a few ears of corn, my realm of old."

70 The poem, as printed, reads, "a common for a proper name shall stand."

71 In the magazine, quotation marks inclosed this couplet. JM inserted the "Mr. Pope" and might have added: " 'An Essay on Man,' Epistle IV" (Louis Kronenberger, ed., *Alexander Pope: Selected Works* [Modern Library Edition, New York, 1948], p. 134). In this edition "Or ravish'd" is used instead of "If tempted."

72 This is JM's marginal note. In the magazine, the poem is prefaced by a letter to the editors signed "Virginianus Hanoverensis," in which the poet is called simply "a worthy and ingenious gentleman in London." The editors describe the writer of the letter as "an ingenious clergyman in Virginia." JM evidently inferred from these two clues that the verses had been sent to the Reverend Samuel Davies (1723–1761). Davies may have thus cloaked his own authorship of them. This eloquent Presbyterian minister preached in Virginia, and mainly in its Hanover County, from 1747 until 1759, when he became president of the College of New Jersey (*Dictionary of American Biography*, V, 102; Robert Douthat Meade, *Patrick Henry: Patriot in the Making* [Philadelphia, 1957], pp. 70–74). JM's casual reference to "Mr. Davis" suggests that the minister, at least by reputation, was too well known to him to need a more precise designation. Even if this assumption is correct, however, the fact does not help to fix the year when JM copied the poem into his notebook.

73 *Critical Reflections on Poetry, Painting and Music. With an Inquiry into the Rise and Progress of the Theatrical Entertainments of the Ancients* (Written in French by the Abbé Du Bos, Member and perpetual Secretary of the French Academy. Translated into English by Thomas Nugent, Gent. From the fifth Edition, revised, corrected, and inlarged by the Author [3 vols.; London, 1748]). Probably this is the edition which JM used since it was the only translation prior to 1772, and his extracts are wholly in English or Latin. When he read a book written in French he customarily took some of his notes in that language. The first French edition of *Critical Reflections* appeared in 1719. Jean Baptiste Du Bos (1670–1742) was a French diplomat and historian. Although he, unlike de Retz and Montaigne, was interested in the fine arts, he shared their penchant for fashioning epigrams, for commenting upon human nature, and for ornamenting his prose with quotations from Greek and Roman classics. Du Bos's discussion of how the unique characteristics of different nationalities resulted from diversities of "air" and climate drew JM's particular attention. Like JM's extracts from the writings of de Retz and Montaigne, his notes on *Critical Reflections* reveal his maturity of thought and his pursuit of generalizations about the springs of human conduct —in this instance as illustrated in poetry, painting, drama, etc., and by men's reaction to art forms.

74 These first five selections are from the Introduction and opening chapter of *Critical Reflections*. The second and third extracts are paraphrases of what Du Bos wrote; the other three are direct quotations.

29

75 This paragraph summarizes eleven pages of Du Bos's second chapter. The notes well illustrate JM's skill in condensation without omitting the particular instances mentioned by the author to sustain his main point. JM wrote "attractive" rather than "attraction."

76 *Critical Reflections*, I, chap. ii, p. 20.

77 This quotation, lines 102–3 of Horace *De arte poetica*, was transferred by JM from *Critical Reflections*, I, chap. xli, p. 338. Edward Henry Blakeney (ed., *Horace on the Art of Poetry* [London, 1928], pp. 26, 45) translated the passage to read: "If you would have me weep, you must first of all feel grief yourself."

78 *Critical Reflections*, I, chap. iv, pp. 34–35.

79 *Ibid.*, I, chap. ii, pp. 11–12, as paraphrased by JM.

80 Du Bos did not mention Caesar and Cicero to illustrate his theme of the "art of persuasion," but the tenor of his discussion near the close of chapter iv justified JM's reference to them. In this connection Du Bos stressed Cromwell, but JM evidently preferred the two Romans as examples.

81 *Ibid.*, I, chap. viii and also pp. 52–53, 56 of chap. ix. JM added the Latin phrase.

82 *Ibid.*, I, chap. xvii, pp. 105–6. JM extracted these comments from Du Bos's denunciation of dramatists who intrude romantic love stories into their tragedies.

83 *Ibid.*, I, chap. xx, pp. 123–24. Here, as in his notes on de Retz and Montaigne, JM records the Latin from Tacitus, *Annals*, I, 47, but omits a translation of it. This passage, "majestate salva, cui major a longinquo reverentia," relates to the sons of Tiberius who would "not compromise the imperial dignity, which inspired the greatest awe at a distance" (Alfred John Church and William Jackson Brodribb, trans., *Annals of Tacitus* [London, 1895], p. 24). "We are more inclinable to commend things we have heard of, than such as we have seen ourselves" is an English version of a part of Paterculus' "nisi quod naturaliter audita visis laudamus libentius et praesentia invidia, praeterita veneratione prosequimur et his nos obrui, illis instrui credimus" (R. Ellis, ed., *Vellei Paterculi ad M. Vinicium libri duo* [Oxford, 1896], p. 105, lines 18 to 21 of section 92). Although Du Bos often quoted from Horace, he apparently failed to recall this relevant passage in the Odes, and JM supplied it. It is from Book III, Ode XXIV, lines 31–32. Philip Francis, on p. 127, Vol. I, of his edition of *Horace* (2 vols.; London, 1831), translated it:

> Though living virtue we despise,
> We follow her when dead with envious eyes.

84 *Critical Reflections*, I, chap. xx, p. 124. Above, n. 83, quotation from Tacitus. The familiar "No man is a hero to his valet-de-chambre" has been attributed to Marshal Catinat, but the general sentiment is at least as old as Plutarch's statement in his "Of Isis and Osiris."

85 Letter from Dr. Thomas Molyneux to John Locke, 20 December 1692, printed in *Some Familiar Letters between Mr. Locke, and Several of his Friends* (London, 1708), pp. 280–83. Du Bos's generalization led JM to mention this letter.

86 At the opening of this paragraph, JM wrote a woman's name, but either he or someone else inked it out so completely that it cannot now be deciphered.

87 Failing to identify "Snodgrass," the editors have only two possibilities to suggest. Snodgrass may have been a "homespun philosopher" who lived in the neighborhood of Montpelier, Robertson's school, or the College of New Jersey. At Tappahannock, not far from Robertson's school, a William Snodgrass was established as a merchant-importer (Beverley Fleet, comp., "Virginia Colonial Abstracts: Records Concerning 18th Century Persons" [mimeographed; 34 vols.; Richmond, 1937–49], XXVIII, 60). Perhaps he sold books to Donald Robertson; perhaps while doing so he became known to Robertson's pupils; perhaps he was "Ingenius" but

lacking in formal education; and perhaps he was the man to whom JM referred. In the congregation of Reverend John Witherspoon at Paisley, Scotland, before he moved to America, was a John Snodgrass (*ca.* 1740–1797) whose irreverent conduct caused Witherspoon much distress. Snodgrass later became a Presbyterian minister of considerable eminence (Varnum Lansing Collins, *President Witherspoon: A Biography* [2 vols.; Princeton, 1925], I, 59–62; II, 141). The remark by Du Bos may have reminded JM of some comment about this Snodgrass by Witherspoon in his classroom at the College of New Jersey.

88 *Critical Reflections*, II, chap. ix, pp. 76–77. In discussing why youths raised in luxury seldom became great artists, Du Bos included the Latin sentence which the editor translated: "Poets and horses . . . ought not to be fattened, but fed." Henry L. Mencken, *A New Dictionary of Quotations* (New York, 1942), p. 926, also attributes the adage to Charles IX.

89 *Critical Reflections*, I, chap. xxiv, p. 166.

90 *Ibid.*, I, chap. xlix, p. 396. Typically, JM selected the rather incidental remark by Du Bos about human nature in his detailed and technical analysis of taste.

91 *Ibid.*, II, chap. xiii, pp. 107–8. JM's "ostimantur" should be "aestimantur." Maurice Hutton translates the passage: "Virtues are best appreciated in those ages which most readily give them birth" (*Tacitus: Dialogus, Agricola, Germania* [Loeb Classical Library, London, 1914], pp. 168–71). The English translator of *Critical Reflections* had Tacitus write: "Those times which are fertile of eminent men, abound likewise in such as are capable of doing justice to their merit."

92 Here JM began a new page in his "Commonplace Book" and, for the first time in his extant writings, set about assembling, mainly from Du Bos, observations about a single subject. It is interesting, although perhaps merely coincidental, that the initial topic of his particular concentration was "National Characters."

93 This paragraph's first sentence and the six following words in Spanish are a direct quotation from Francis Bacon's essay, "Of Dispatch" (Oliphant Smeaton, ed., *The Essayes or Counsels Civill & Morall of Francis Bacon Lord Verulam* [Everyman's Library, London, 1906], p. 76). JM apparently added the Latin equivalent of the Spanish, but the full aphorism, "let my death come in Spain, for then it will be long in coming," is not given here in either language. The paragraph's last sentence is a quotation from Bacon's "Of Seeming Wise," *ibid.*, p. 78.

94 The bases for JM's observations in this sentence and the one preceding are not clear, although they may have been suggested by what Du Bos wrote in *Critical Reflections*, I, chap. xlii, pp. 342–43, and II, chap. xv, p. 196.

95 *The Spectator*, No. 179 (25 September 1711), p. 169 in Volume V of the seventh edition (1724). This citation is not given by Du Bos.

96 Not in *Critical Reflections*. JM's source is unknown. "Whether his proneness to complain reflects his own nature or that of his people is uncertain."

97 *Critical Reflections*, I, chap. xlii, p. 348.

98 The final sentence in this paragraph is JM's own comment. He took the two preceding sentences almost verbatim from Du Bos. *Ibid.*, II, chap. xiii, p. 114.

99 *Ibid.*, II, chap. xiii, p. 128.

100 *Ibid.*, II, chap. xv, pp. 190, 197. Du Bos's chapter, from which these extracts were taken, is entitled "The power of the air over our bodies proved by the different characters of nations." It is the conclusion of the author's lengthy discussion of how climate shapes personality and the characteristics of a nation.

101 From Bernard Le Bovier de Fontenelle, *Digression upon the Ancients and Moderns* (1688) quoted in *Critical Reflections*, II, chap. xiii, p. 111. JM merely summarized Du Bos's long quotation from Fontenelle's book.

102 The content of these two sentences, reminiscent of what de Retz might have written in his *Memoirs*, is not found in *Critical Reflections*.

103 JM entered "Spectator—551 Paper" in the right-hand margin of both pages of his notebook on which he copied this poetry. Appearing on 2 December 1712, it will be found on pp. 8-20 of the fifteenth volume of Joseph Addison, Richard Steele, *et al.*, *The Spectator* (16 vols.; London, printed for J. Tonson, 1724). These poems, together with three others which JM did not transcribe, embellish an essay on poetic eulogies by, and chiefly about, ancient writers. The unknown author, probably Richard Steele, remarked that his verses were "conceived in the form of Epitaphs." At least some issues of *The Spectator* were probably available for JM to read at Montpelier, because his grandmother, Mrs. Frances Madison, was billed in 1749 for two volumes of *The Guardian* and eight of *The Spectator* (invoice of Hunt and Waterman, London, 16 March 1749, in Madison Family Papers, Shane Collection, Presbyterian Historical Society). In the autobiography which he sent to James K. Paulding in 1832, JM declared that "One of the earliest books which engaged his attention was the 'Spectator,' which from his own experience, he inferred to be peculiarly adapted to inculcate in youthful minds, just sentiments, an appetite for knowledge, and a taste for the improvement of the mind and manners" (LC: William C. Rives Papers). His high and lasting regard for *The Spectator* led him on 4 January 1829 to recommend it strongly to his eleven-year-old nephew, Richard D. Cutts. In this letter JM added that he had read *The Spectator* with profit "at an age which will soon be yours." Then in his seventy-eighth year, JM sometimes failed to remember accurately the details of events long in the past. If in this instance, however, his recollection was trustworthy, he probably copied these verses about 1763, or four years later than the date written on the first page of his "Commonplace Book."

104 In the original the word is "boistrous."

105 "Beauties" in the original.

106 The basis of this jingle appears to have been a misinterpreted remark by Edward Gibbon (1737–1794) in his letter of 4 October 1788 to Lord Sheffield. This letter first appeared in print in John, Lord Sheffield, *Miscellaneous Works of Edward Gibbon, Esquire, With Memoirs of His Life and Writings Composed by Himself* (2 vols.; London, 1796), I, 192. For this reason and also because Gibbon was still inconspicuous when JM copied the poems from *The Spectator*, this verse must postdate by many years the other entries in the notebook. The verse seems to be in the hand of JM's young brother-in-law, John C. Payne, who frequently visited the Madisons after their marriage in 1794. The expression "the Author of the above" in the prefatory line must merely mean "anonymous," that is, corresponding with "the Author unnamed" of the poem "On Menander."

Notes on a Brief System of Logick

MS (LC: Madison Miscellany). One hundred and twenty-two pages of this copybook are filled with writing in JM's youthful hand. They are preceded by four almost blank pages and followed by fourteen others devoted to the drawings described in the editorial note below. JM's great-nephew, James Madison Cutts II, gave this manuscript to the Library of Congress in 1881. On the manuscript's cardboard cover is written, "Mr. James A. Garlick, King William County, Virginia." On the third of the pages in the front of the notebook is a doodle by JM consisting of a "1766" succeeded by two apparently meaningless pen marks and "6" repeated nine times. This date, if that is what it is, together with the fact that a Samuel Garlick had children in Donald Robertson's school in 1767 when JM was a pupil there, suggests that he may have taken the notes, or at least have acquired the notebook, at about that time. Moreover, although logic was not customarily taught in a preparatory school, Robertson's collegiate education in Scotland probably qualified him to offer instruction in the subject. Furthermore, if Robertson gave the course in 1767, Madison by then was amply prepared to employ the Latin and Greek words with which these notes are sprinkled. Finally, as will be pointed out in the editorial note, at least two of the drawings in the back of the copybook could have been based upon illustrations in volumes in Robertson's library.

In the opinion of the editors, however, it is more probable that JM took these notes during his junior or senior year at the College of New Jersey. Its quite inflexible curriculum included a course in "Logick or Dialectick," in all likelihood offered by the president, Reverend John Witherspoon. The intellectual level of the notes also strongly suggests what a college rather than an academy would expect of its students. Worthy of mention, although of no demonstrable significance, are the initials "h B," twice written by JM on the third of the pages preceding the notes. Assuming that these stand for the name of one of his acquaintances, they at once call to mind Hugh Brackenridge, one of JM's closest friends at the College of New Jersey. Judging from the account book of Donald Robertson, he had no pupil with those initials while JM attended his school. Then, too, unless John Locke's *An Essay Concerning Human Understanding* is considered to be a textbook in logic, no volume on that subject seems to have been in Robertson's school library. Although one section of the notes reflects this treatise, far more of them echo Isaac Watts's handbook, entitled *Logick: or, the Right Use of Reason in the Enquiry after Truth*, first published in London in 1725, and in its twelfth London edition by 1763. This volume, apparently neither among Robertson's books nor at Montpelier, was readily available, along with Locke's essay, in the College of New Jersey Library ("Donald Robertson's Account Book," pp. 132–35, MS in Virginia Historical Society; "A Catalogue of Books belonging to His Excellency Jonathan Belcher," p. 2, given to the College of New Jersey in 1755 by the Governor, and "Titles of Volumes once belonging to president Witherspoon, and bought by the college from president Smith," p. 4, MSS in Princeton University Library). Furthermore, in an autobiographical sketch sent in January 1832 to James Kirke Paulding (LC: William C. Rives Papers), JM mentions the subjects he studied in Robertson's school but does not include logic.

33

EDITORIAL NOTE

If JM had prepared an outline of his notes, it might have resembled the one which follows. The page numbers below are taken from the copybook. Wherever quotation marks are omitted, the headings or summaries have been supplied by the editors.

Part III

"Of Discourse & Syllogism"

Sec. I.   Of Discourse (pp. 50–55)
Definitions and examples of discourse or argumentation, judgment, inference, and syllogism.

Sec. II.   "Of Categorical Syllogisms" (pp. 55–84)
Analysis of a syllogism and its possible "modes"; nine "axioms"; seven "General Theorems" with example of each.

Sec. III.   "Of the Other Forms of Syllogisms" (pp. 84–94)
Hypothetical, enthymena, disjunctive, dilemma, prosyllogism, sorites, and epichirema, with example of each.

Sec. IV.   "Of the Invention of Middle Terms or Arguments of common places or Topicks" (pp. 95–112)
Definition of "middle term" and "topick"; twenty types of argument with an example of each; observations about the effects of argument upon the mind.

Sec. V.   "Of False reasonings or Sophisms" (pp. 113–22)
Three types of "parallogisms" with example of each; illustrations of seven types of fallacious syllogisms arising from "impertinence, or falsehood, or ambiguity of Premises."

One reason for presenting this outline is to make clear the traditional nature of the notes, both in their arrangement and content. Hobbes (p. 26) and Locke (p. 12) are briefly mentioned, and Part I owes more to Locke than this meager reference to him suggests. In the main, the author hews closely to a line of logic which extends back from Isaac Watts's popular textbook through the works of Peter Ramus and the scholastics, to those of Aristotle and Plato, including Plato's reports of what Socrates said. Isaac Watts's *Logick* was levied upon for the formulation of several points of logic, for a few fairly long passages, and for a goodly number of illustrative examples. Both in their allusions and examples, the notes have a pronounced classical, biblical, and Christian flavor. In a word, they lack originality both in organization and thought. They do not even suggest the personality of their author, except that he was methodical and painstaking, something of a pedant, and a devout Christian well versed in Latin and acquainted with at least a few Greek words.*

Although the notes were written by JM, they were not the product of his mind except in the sense that he may have collated the material after extracting it from a number of books. In the judgment of the editors, however, he more probably was summarizing the lectures of a teacher, or, because of his occasional cross-references to earlier pages in the copybook, transcribing rough notes taken in class. Furthermore, the many misspellings support the conclusion that he was recording oral discourse. He would hardly have erred so often in this regard if he had taken the notes from

---

* For the conclusions expressed in this paragraph the editors are much indebted to Professors Ronald Crane and Warner Wick of the University of Chicago.

printed texts. Whatever may have been their source, these notes owe to JM at the most their arrangement, and at the least the patience of his pen. Because they are not "Madison," except to this very limited extent, the editors confine their publication of the notes to four extracts, one from each of the first two main parts and two from the long concluding section.

The drawings on the final fourteen pages of the copybook run sequentially as follows: (1) design of a fort whose main feature is a hexagon separated from its inclosing twelve-sided polygon by a "Fousse, Moat, Trench or Ditch"; (2) a half-circle marked to show "the Line of Chords," "The Line of Secants," "The Line of Signs," and "The Line of Tangens"; (3) an elaborately annotated sundial, adjusted to latitude 38° north, approximately that of Montpelier; (4) "The Solar System from Copernicus," consisting of the sun at the center with six concentric circles around it—one circle for each planet marked with its time of circumsolar rotation and its distance from the sun; the outermost circle, that of Saturn; the more remote planet, Uranus, not having been discovered until 1781; (5) overlapping eastern and western hemispheres, each showing the continents and main lines of latitude and longitude; (6) "The Sphere [Earth] projected on the Plane of the Meridian," marked with the "Ecliptic or Zodiac" and degree numbers on the circumference and equator, as well as with the other lines of No. 5; (7) "The Sphere projected on the Plane of the Horizon," marked similarly with No. 6, but with the North Pole in one hemisphere and the South Pole in the other located about halfway between the center and the circumference on the left; (8) "The Sphere projected on the plane of the Equinoctial [Equator]," similar to No. 7, except for the altered projection; (9) apparently an incomplete drawing, identical with No. 8 in its projection but designed to show the altered location of the "Ecliptic or Zodiac" when, in opposite fashion to that in No. 8, the South Pole is at the center of the hemisphere on the right rather than of the one on the left; (10) a diagram showing the sun in its effect upon the moon as the latter revolves about the earth; (11) seemingly an uncompleted tryout of No. 10; (12) merely eight squares of varying sizes—apparently an unsatisfactory start toward No. 13; (13) "A Square dra[wn] in Perspective," with an indicated "Point of Sight" and "Point of Distance"; (14) "A Hexagon drawn in Perspective & Elevated [?]," with the two "points" of No. 13 also shown.

From what books, if any, JM derived these drawings or his ideas for them is not known. All of them, with the exception of No. 3, are similar to diagrams customarily found in eighteenth-century textbooks on geography, geometry, or astronomy. For this reason the subjects of the drawings, including the one of the sundial, are of but slight help in determining whether JM made them at Robertson's school, at Montpelier, or at the College of New Jersey. From their elementary nature, as compared with that of "The Brief System of Logick," they suggest exercises appropriate to Robertson's classroom; and it is known that JM studied arithmetic, algebra, geometry, and geography there. Yet only two of the sketches could have been based upon illustrations in volumes owned by the schoolmaster—if the surviving list of them is complete.* The library at the College of New Jersey, on the other hand, could readily have supplied JM with the models needed to make these diagrams in his notebook.

[1766–1772]

Aristotle[1] and after him the Scholastics have divided all Ideas into ten parts, which they call Predicaments[2] or Categories. For they say every thing imaginable or concievable is either Substance, or Quality, or Quantity, or Relation, or Action, or Passion, or Place, or Time, or situation or Cloathing.[3]

Part 1st. Sect. 2nd.
Of the Signs of Ideas[4]

A Sign in general is a thing that gives notice of something different from itself. As the cause may signifie, that is, be a sign of the effect to follow: or vice versa. The effect may be the sign of the cause; as Smoak is the sign of fire: Or Concomitants may reciprocally be the signs of one another.

The signs or external marks of our internal Ideas, with which alone we are now concernd, are either Natural or Arbitrary and artificial.

The Natural signs are such as, smiling, Laughing, the indications of Joy; Dejection of countenance, weeping, wailing, the indications of Sorrow; paleness, trembling, the signs of Fear, Blushing the sign of Shame &c.

These being the Language of Nature, have been always the same with inconsiderable variation in every person, age, & Country. And by these an Acute Man may penetrate far into the most secret sentiments and affections of others: Notwithstanding Politicians and other cunning Men of Business, by great and refin'd dissimulation, have in great measure confounded and stifled the natural Indications of their inmost thoughts.

The arbitrary signs of Ideas have been invented & instituted by Men for the communication of their thoughts to one another, & discover their not being Natural but artificial by their being in various Countries and Ages, various and changeable.

* No. 6 could have been derived from a drawing following the text of Thomas Salmon, *A New Geographical and Historical Grammar* (4th ed.; London, 1756). In like manner No. 10 might have been based upon a sketch opposite page 22 of the fourth volume of Noël Antoine Pluche, *Nature Delineated: Being a Translation of those Universally-admired Philosophical Discourses, entitled Spectacle de la Nature* (4 vols.; London, 1739). No. 4 is reproduced in Brant, *Madison*, I, opposite p. 65.

The Brute creation have nothing but the Language of Nature, which is intelligible to all those of the same species; but being given only for necessary Uses, makes their conversation and correspondence very narrow and confin'd.

Men alone have contrived a more extensive communication of thoughts by inventing several Signs; which in[?] company have agreed to use & understand commonly as expressive of the same sentiments.

These signs are partly similar to the Ideas of the mind as pictures and the most ancient Hieroglyphycks, partly dismission, as words either spoken or written; which have no manner of resemblance to the Ideas which they are intended to represent.

Speech of all these Inventions, if it be an human invention, & not rather a divine Lesson, is by far the most excellent & has contributed chiefly to exalt the human species above the Brutes.

Universal Terms may denote, either a Metaphysical, a Physycal, or a Moral Universality.[5]

A Metaphysical or Mathematical Universality, admits of no exception. As, all Circles have a Center and circumferen[ce.]

A Physical or Natural Universality admits of some accidental and Praeternatural Exceptions. As, all men use words to express their thoughts, yet dumb Persons are excepted.

A Moral universality admits of many exceptions being a sort of Hyperbole, As all men are govern'd by affecti[ons] more than by reason. The Cretes are always Lyars.[6] An universal term is sometimes taken collectively for all its particular Ideas united together; and sometimes distributively meaning each of them single and alone.

1. Collectively: as, all these Apples will fill a Busshel: all the Hours of the night are sufficient for Sleep: All the rules of Grammer overload the memory. In these Propositions it is evident, that the Predicate belongs not to the Individuals seperately, but to the whole collective Idea: for we cannot say, one Apple, or every Apple will fill a Busshel. &c. Wherefore such a Proposition is properly singular.

2. Distributively: when you may turn the word all into every: and the Predicate belongs to every Individual: which makes the Proposition truly and properly universal. As, all Men are mortal, which you may turn into every Man or any Individual Man is Mortal.

But of these Distributive Universals there are two kinds. For sometimes they include all the Individuals distributively; as, every sickness has a tendency to Death, i,e, Every individual Sickness.

Sometimes they are restricted to every Species or kind; As, every

Disease was heal'd by Christ, i,e, every kind of Disease.[7] The first of these is call'd by Logicians the Distribution of an universal in Singula generum, and the second in genera Singulorum.

Propositions are either Single or compound. Single Propositions are the same as categorical which have been explained already Vide. P. 37 &c.[8]

A compound Proposition is made up of two or more Subjects or Predicates, or both: and contains two or more single Propositions, explicit or implicit.

Of compound Propositions we shall recken up Eleven different sorts. In the first six, the composition is plain and express'd, in the others only implyed.

There[9] is yet another Method of arguing remaining; call'd the Socratic from the celebrated Socrates, who employ'd it for the instruction of Scholars & company, & for the entrapping & confutation of the Sophists of his time. This manner was, when he intended to confute or convince any one, to introduce some Topick suitable to his Design, never to declare his own opinion but to ask Questions as if he desir'd instruction, having his mainpart in view, & wheeling the Stream of the Discourse Slyly to his Purpose; till at last by a sudden turn he surpriz'd his Opponent into sudden conviction or an absurdity. This is a very captitious & insiduous Method: for when you are [ac?]costed[?] in this manner, having no suspicion of an attack, or [at] least not knowing where the Push is to be made, you may expose yourself unwarily, & make such concessions as the Adversary will not fail to turn to his advantage. I own this Method may do very well between a Master & his Scholars: and so it was us'd among the Philosophers, whom their Scholars heard with reverence, and bore to be confuted without being offended. But to interrogate others in this manner is not well taken; and probably help'd to kindle & blow up that hatred against Socrates, which put a violent Period to his Life[.]

To exemplify this Method let us suppose a Dialogue between a Theist and an Atheist: imagine the Atheist to have returnd from his Travels & the Theist to accost him in the Socratic way as follows.

Theist. I would gladly know, Sir, what is [the] finest Place you have seen in your Travels.

Atheist. Why really Sir, the Place that most took up my fancy was the King of France's Palace & Gardens at Versailles.

The. I have heard a great deal of the magnificence & beauty of that place; & so did you I suppose, before you saw it; but when you did see it, did it answer your expectation.

Athe. It far exceeded it. For till I saw it I could not imagine the greatness of the whole, the Symmetry of the Parts, the ornaments of architecture, the rich paintings, the magnificent furniture, especially the Pleasant Gardens, with their Statues, Canals & Jett-d'Eaux.

The. I suppose ingenious men of Taste find some defects & superfluities, which they themselves could supply or retrench.

Athe. It may be so. But these who laid & executed this Plan are deservedly admir'd for their ingenuity and Grand Taste.

The. No doubt they did their best: but it is possible it may be exceeded. If I should tell you of a Fabrick that for magnificence & Taste is ownd by Good Judges to be superior, what would you say?

Athe. I suppose you mean some old Roman building or St. Peters at Rome: There may be Heroes in architecture I suppose as well as in arms.

The. You Judge of the mind[,] the contrivance, the ability of the architect—by the greatness & ingenuity of his Work.

Athe. To be sure, to Judge of a man by his actions is the best way.

The. Well then look at this Fabrick of the universe: lift up your Eyes to the cupola of the Sky.[10] Consider.[11]

Athe. Aha, Sir, are you got upon the old Topic? I can make a difference between the works of art, & the necessary effects of Plastic nature.

This like every other argument, [is] easily reducible to regular Syllogisms.

There[12] is no danger from plain and glaring Equivocations: But[,] however[,] the ambiguity of Words is the cause of the greatest controversies and perplexities: different People very often affixing very different Ideas to the same Words, and squabbling not about a disagreement of Sentiments but of Words. Therefore to avoid being impos'd upon or confuted by arguments of this fallacious kind, there is a necessity often to make nice distinctions, that is, to show nicely the ambiguity of Words and their various meanings: that you may discern in what Sense the Proposition is true, & in what it is false.[13]

These Sophisms are not so difficult to be detected either by Natural Sagacity or by the Rules of Logick, as it is hard to determine a Question in Oeconomy, Policy & other cases, where the arguments on both sides are weighty, Solid and far from being Sophistical. As it happen'd in the dispute [between] Cato the Censor, & Scipio Nasica:[14] of whom the former was of opinion that Carthage should be destoy'd for the advantage and security of Rome: the latter insisted that to declare an irreconcileable War again[st] a People who had not given even a plausible pretence, was inconsistent with the Rules of Honour and Justice. In this dispute the arguments of Cato's side were drawn ab Utili, and those of the other ab Honest[um] & it came to this issue, whether the Utile or the Honestum is to be preferr'd when they come in co[nflictio]n with one another. Wherefore if you fall into a controversy of this sort and your adversary has pr[o]ved his advice to be useful: Your business is not so much to confute his Argument, for perhaps that cannot be done, as to show the superiour [adv]antage or the Honour and Justice of your own opinion. And to be sure Honour and Justice should carry it against Utility, or a greater of Utility should carry against a lesser: for when there are Arguments in both Scales, the greater Weight must cast the Balance.

Of this Nature [was] the Question proposed by Rehoboan to his old & his Young Counsellers [whet]her he should answer the tumultuous People mildly or imperiously. The old Men recommended mildness & complyance, till the King having got into the Saddle might establish his full authority: The young men advis'd the contrary: because commonly Inferiours seeing their Govirnours timorous, are ready to encroach mo[re] and more. The Arguments are both good: but the circumstance of the occasion, & especially the event determin'd in favour of the Old Men.[15]

Finis.

---

[1] Extract from Part I, pp. 18–21 of "A Brief System of Logick."

[2] Madison probably should have written "predicates." This word, in one form or another, recurs frequently in Aristotle's "Categoriae" and "De Interpretatione," upon which much in these notes was based. Thus, an English translation of 1b, lines 10–16 of "Categoriae" runs: "When one thing is predicated of another, all that which is predicable of the predicate will be predicable also of the subject. Thus, 'man' is predicated of the individual man; but 'animal' is predicated of 'man'; it will, therefore, be predicable of the individual man also: for the individual man is both 'man' and 'animal' " (E. M. Edghill, ed., "Categoriae and De Interpretatione," *passim*, in Vol. I of William D. Ross, general ed., *The Works of Aristotle Translated into English* [12 vols.; Oxford and London, 1908–52]).

[3] This could have been taken from Watts, *Logick*, p. 25.

[4] This excerpt shows clearly the influence of John Locke's *An Essay Concerning Human Understanding*, first published at London in 1690. See Book II, chaps. x and xi, of this essay.

[5] Extract from Part II, pp. 42–44 of "A Brief System of Logick." Virtually this whole excerpt, except its last two paragraphs, is taken either verbatim or almost verbatim from Watts, *Logick*, pp. 149–53, 165–70.

6 Titus 1:12 ("The Cretans are always liars, evil beasts, slow bellies"). St. Paul, however, merely repeated a common opinion about the Cretans, found in Greek literature as far back, so it has been said, as Epimenides, *ca.* 600 B.C. See also *The Histories of Polybius,* VI, 472.

7 Matthew 4:23.

8 The excerpt here given is from "Sect. 2," entitled "Of Proposition," of "Part 2d," of JM's notes, headed "Of Judgment and Proposition." On p. 37, and continuing on until the notes make junction with this excerpt, they discuss "categorical," "hypothetical," "singular," and "universal" propositions.

9 Extract from Part III, pp. 95–98, of "A Brief System of Logick."

10 Although in its brevity, quality, and conclusion, this dialogue hardly bears comparison with the dialogues led by Socrates, as reported by Plato, there is a faint echo of Socrates in "Phaedo," stating, "I can not help thinking, if there be anything beautiful other than absolute beauty, should there be such, that it can be beautiful only in so far as it partakes of absolute beauty" (Irwin Edman, ed., *Works of Plato* [Modern Library Edition, 1928], p. 166). See also *ibid.,* pp. 217–26, 290–94, 378–79, 434–35, 472–74.

11 Probably the instructor followed up this word by quoting one or both of two biblical passages, or Madison added this word to remind himself of them ("When I consider thy heavens," etc. [Psalms 8:3–4], and "Consider the lilies of the field," etc. [Matthew 6:28–29]).

12 Extract from Part III, pp. 121–22 of "A Brief System of Logick."

13 It is possible rather than probable that the thought in this paragraph was derived from Locke, *An Essay Concerning Human Understanding,* Book III, chap. xi.

14 This dispute in about 150 B.C. between Marcus Cato and Publius Cornelius Scipio Nasica Corculum is mentioned by Plutarch in his "Marcus Cato" (A[rthur] H. Clough, ed., *Dryden's Translation of Plutarch's Lives* [4 vols.; New York, undated], II, 276).

15 I Kings 12:6–21. The "event" was the desertion of King Rehoboam by all the tribes of Israel, except Judah and Benjamin, because he heeded the advice of the "young men" to be a harsher ruler than had been his father, King Solomon.

To Reverend Thomas Martin

RC (LC: Madison Papers).

NASSAU-HALL. August 10th. 69

REVD. SIR,[1]

I am not a little affected at hearing of your misfortune, but cannot but hope the cure may be so far accomplished as to render your journey not inconvenient. Your kind Advice & friendly cautions are a favour that shall be always gratefully remembered, & I must beg leave to assure you that my happiness, which you and your brother so ardently wish for, will be greatly augmented by both your enjoyments of the like blessing.[2]

I have been as particular to my father as I thought necessary for this time, as I send him an account of the Institution &c &c of the College wrote by Mr. Blair[3] the Gentleman formerly elected President of this place, you will likewise find two Pamphlets entitled Britannia's intercession for John Wilks &c,[4] which if you have not seen, perhaps may divert you.

I am perfectly pleased with my present situation; and the prospect before me of three years confinement, however terrible it may sound, has nothing in it, but what will be greatly alleviated by the advantages I hope to derive from it.

The Grammars, which Mr. Houston[5] procured for you amount at 2/10 each to 17/. Your brothers account with Plumb.[6] to 6/7. and Sawneys expences 4/2 the whole 1..7..9, Inclosed you have 15/. the overplus of which you may let Sawney[7] have to satisfy those who may have been at any trouble on his account.

The near approach of examination occasions a surprising application to study on all sides, and I think it very fortunate that I entered College immediately after my arrival, tho' I believe there will not be least danger of my getting an Irish hint as they call it, yet it will make my future studies somewhat easier,[8] and I have by that means read over more than half Horace and made myself pretty well acquainted with Prosody, both which will be almost neglected the two succeeding years.

The very large Packet of Letters for Carolina I am afraid will be incommodious to your brother on so long a journey, to whom I desire my compliments may be presented & conclude with my earnest request for a continuance of both your friendships and sinsere wishes for your recovery, and an agreable journey to your whole Company.

I am, Sir, your obligd friend & Hl. Ser

JAMES MADISON

P. S. Sawne tells me that your Mother and Brothers are determined to accompany you to Virginia; my friendship and regard for you entitle them to my esteem, and assure them that with the greatest sincerity I wish, after a pleasant journey, they may find Virginia capable of giving them great Happiness.[9]

J. M

[1] Reverend Thomas Martin (*ca.* 1742–1770) graduated from the College of New Jersey in 1762. His brief career as a teacher and Episcopal clergyman in Virginia included the two years, 1767–1769, when he lived at Montpelier, tutoring JM and possibly the younger Madison children (*Virginia Gazette* [Williamsburg, Rind], 20 September 1770; Alexander, *Princeton College*, p. 78).

[2] This may suggest that Thomas Martin and his brother Alexander, who stopped

43

in Orange during the summer of 1769 when on his way from North Carolina to New Jersey, helped JM's father to decide that JM should enter the College of New Jersey rather than William and Mary. Alexander Martin (1740–1807) graduated from the College of New Jersey in 1756 and had a notable career in North Carolina politics, serving as governor, delegate to the Constitutional Convention of 1787, and United States senator.

³ Samuel Blair (1741–1818) was elected president of the College of New Jersey in 1767 after John Witherspoon declined the position. When Witherspoon finally accepted the presidency a year later, Blair voluntarily stepped aside. His pamphlet on the college, entitled *An Account of the College of New-Jersey, in which are Described the Methods of Government, Modes of Instruction, Manner and Expences of Living in the Same, etc., with a Prospect of the College Neatly Engraved*, was published at Woodbridge, N.J., by James Parker in 1764.

⁴ *Britannia's Intercession for the Deliverance of John Wilkes, Esq., from Persecution and Banishment. To which is Added a Political and Constitutional Sermon and a Dedication to L . . . B . . .* (6th ed.; London: printed, Boston: reprinted and sold by Daniel Kneeland, at his printing office in Hanover Street, a little below Concert Hall, 1769). The English political reformer John Wilkes (1727–1797) had been expelled from Parliament in 1764 for seditious libel and was outlawed for failing to stand trial.

⁵ William Churchill Houston (*ca.* 1746–1788), tutor and professor at the College of New Jersey, 1769–1783, delegate to the Continental Congress from New Jersey, and member of the Annapolis and Constitutional conventions.

⁶ Probably Benjamin Plum, whose name appeared in the accounts of Princeton merchant Enos Kelsey in 1767–1768 (John Frelinghuysen Hageman, *History of Princeton and Its Institutions* [2 vols.; Philadelphia, 1879], I, 72). Plum took care of further business matters for the Madisons when JM's brother William attended the preparatory school at Princeton in 1774–1775.

⁷ A Madison slave who accompanied JM on the trip to Princeton.

⁸ This remark, together with the general tone of the letter indicating that JM had just arrived at the college, makes it probable that he reached Princeton in the middle of the summer term (perhaps late in July) and immediately began his studies.

⁹ JM evidently sent this letter to Thomas Martin at an undetermined place in New Jersey, where Martin's widowed mother and brothers lived. The intimacy between the Martins and Madisons is further suggested by the following sentences closing a letter from Sam Martin (one of the brothers) to James Madison, Sr., written from North Carolina on 5 September 1780: "My Brother Alexander is now at the Assembly. My mother & Sister Henderson joins me [in] compliments to Mrs. Madison & young Ladies" (original owned by Mr. Charles M. Storey, Boston, Mass.).

For additional comments about this letter, believed to be JM's earliest now extant, see Brant, *Madison*, I, 82–84.

To James Madison, Sr.

RC (LC: Madison Papers).

NASSAU-HALL, September 30th. 69.

HOND. SIR,

I recieved your letter by Mr. Rosekrans,[1] and wrote an Answer; but as it is probable this will arrive sooner which I now write by Doctor Witherspoon,[2] I shall repeat some circumstances to avoid obscurity.

On Wednesday last we had the annual commencement. Eighteen young gentlemen took their Batchelors' degrees, and a considerable number their Masters Degrees; the Degree of Doctor of Law was bestowed on Mr. Dickenson the Farmer and Mr. Galloway, the Speaker of the Pennsylvania Assembly, a distinguishing mark of Honour, as there never was any of that kind done before in America.[3] The Commencement began at 10 O'Clock, when the President walked first into the Church, a board of Trustees following, and behind them those that were to take their Master's degrees, and last of all, those that were to take their first Degrees; After a short Prayer by the President, the Head Oration, which is always given to the greatest *Scholar* by the President & Tutors, was pronounced in Latin by Mr. Samuel Smith[4] son of a Presbyterean Minister in Pennsylvania. Then followed the other Orations, Disputes and Dialogues, distributed to each according to his merit, and last of all was pronounced the Valedictory Oration by Mr. John Henry[5] son of a Gentleman in Maryland. This is given to the greatest *Orator*. We had a very great Assembly of People, a considerable number of whom came from N. York. Those at Philidelphia were most of them detained by Racis which were to follow on the next day.[6]

Since Commencement the Trustees have been sitting about Business relative to the College, and have chose for Tutors the ensuing year, for the junior class Mr. Houston[7] from N. Carolina in the room of Mr. Periam,[8] for the Freshman class Mr. Reeves (a gentleman who has for several years past kept a School at Elizabeth Town)[9] in the room of Mr. Pemberton:[10] the Sophomore Tutor Mr. Thomsom[11] still retains his place, remarkable for his skill in the sophomore Studies having taken care of that class for several years past. Mr. Halsey[12] was chosen Junior Tutor but refused. The Trustees have likewise appointed Mr. Caldwel, a Minister at Elizabeth Town,[13] to take a journey through the Southern Provinces as far as Georgia to make collections by which the College Fund may be inabled to increase the Library, provide an apparatus of mathematical and Philosophical Instruments & likewise to support Professors which would be a great addition to the advantages of this College. Doctr. Witherspoon's business to Virginia is nearly the same as I conjecture and perhaps to form some acquaintance to induce Gentlemen to send their sons to this College.[14]

I am very sorry to hear of the great drought that has prevailed with you, but am in some hopes the latter part of the year may have been more seasonable for you[r] crops. Your caution of frugality on consideration of the dry weather shall be carefully observed; but I am under a necesity of spending much more than I was apprehensive, for the purchasing of every small trifle which I have occasion for consumes a much greater sum than one wou[ld] suppose from a calculation of the necessary expences.

I feel great satisfaction from the assistance my Uncle Beale has recieved from the Springs, and I flatter myself from the continuance of my mother's health that Dr. Shore's skill will effectually banish the cause of her late indisposition.[15]

I recollect nothing more at present worth relating, but as often as opportunity and any thing worthy your attention shall occur, be assured you shall hear from your

Affectionate Son

JAMES MADISON

[1] Probably Alexander Rosecrants (Rosegrant), an infantryman in the Continental Army from Orange County during the Revolutionary War (Orange County Minute Book, No. 2, p. 109, microfilm in Virginia State Library).

[2] John Witherspoon (1723–1794), president of the College of New Jersey, 1768–1794, visited the South in the fall of 1769 to raise money and recruit students for the college (see n. 14).

[3] In addition to honoring John Dickinson and Joseph Galloway, the college also conferred the master's degree on John Hancock. Dickinson and Hancock were popular heroes of the American resistance to the Townshend Acts (Varnum L. Collins, *President Witherspoon*, I, 125). Following Harvard's award of an honorary A.M. to Benjamin Franklin in 1753, that degree was quite often conferred by American colleges, but the College of New Jersey in 1769 was apparently the first of them to grant a doctorate of laws, *honoris causa* (Samuel Eliot Morison, *Harvard College in the Seventeenth Century* [Cambridge, Mass., 1936], p. 491; and Charles F. Thwing, *A History of Higher Education in America* [New York, 1906], pp. 427–28). For a general description of this commencement, see *New Jersey Archives*, 1st ser., XXVI, 520–24.

[4] Samuel Stanhope Smith (1751–1819) was a tutor at the College of New Jersey during most of JM's residence there. Resigning in 1773 to preach in Virginia, he quickly made his mark by his scholarship, piety, and eloquence. By 1775, when he married Dr. Witherspoon's daughter Ann, he and others were ready to found

in Prince Edward County the Academy (the College, 1783 ff.) of Hampden-Sydney, of which he was the first president. In 1779 he returned to the College of New Jersey as professor of natural and moral philosophy. In 1795 he succeeded Witherspoon as president, and held that office seventeen years. The close and long friendship of JM and Smith, probably beginning when JM was in Princeton, may have helped to shape JM's religious views. Smith never wavered in his conviction that his Presbyterian faith squared with right and reason and hence was impregnable against any assault whose force depended upon a new philosophy or new scientific discoveries (Alfred J. Morrison, *The College of Hampden Sidney: Calendar of Board Minutes. 1776–1876* [Richmond, 1912], p. 11; Samuel Holt Monk, "Samuel Stanhope Smith: Friend of Rational Liberty," in Willard Thorp, ed., *The Lives of Eighteen from Princeton* [Princeton, 1946], pp. 86–110).

5 John Henry (1750–1798), later delegate to the Continental Congress, United States senator, and governor of Maryland.

6 The horse races in Philadelphia, scheduled by its famous Jockey Club for 25 and 26 September, had been postponed until Thursday and Friday, the 28th and 29th, in order to avoid conflict with the annual meeting of the Society of Friends (*The Pennsylvania Journal; and the Weekly Advertiser*, 31 August–5 October 1769).

7 William Churchill Houston.

8 In 1769, after five years of service as a tutor at the College of New Jersey, Joseph Periam (*ca.* 1742–1780), who had graduated from there in 1762, was dropped from the faculty and became a schoolteacher in Elizabethtown, N.J. (Alexander, *Princeton College*, p. 79). Brant (*Madison*, I, 74–75) surmises that Periam's adherence to the Berkeleian system of metaphysics may account for his ouster by President Witherspoon.

9 Tapping Reeve (1744–1823), College of New Jersey, '63, was a tutor there for only one year. In 1784, he founded the Litchfield (Conn.) Law School, an institution which attracted students from all over the Union in the early nineteenth century.

10 After less than a year as tutor at the College of New Jersey, from which he had been graduated in 1765, Ebenezer Pemberton (*ca.* 1745–1835) began a long and distinguished career as a teacher, principally in his native New England. Alexander (*Princeton College*, p. 100) states that "on one of the public occasions, while he [Pemberton] was a tutor, he was addressed by Madison, then a student, in a Latin address, valedictory and complimentary, on the part of the class, to the teacher." As late as 28 November 1835, in a letter to Dr. Benjamin Waterhouse, JM referred to this occasion by writing:

"I well recollect Mr. Pemberton in the aspects which his character presented, when I was his pupil; and I readily conceive that your favorable picture is a good likeness of its developements in after life. He must at least have become an adept in the Classics. Being a good scholar at an early day, he could not fail in a long course of teaching others, to be a successful tutor to himself. I have no distinct recollection of the Latin address to him from his pupils including myself, nor of my share in the preparation of it, I suspect that its merit, if it has any, consists rather in the just and grateful feelings of the authors, than in the Latinity which conveys them, if otherwise the greater the merit of our Preceptor" (Harvard University Schools of Medicine and Public Health Library).

11 During his eight years (1762–1770) as a tutor at the College of New Jersey, where he had graduated in 1761, James Thompson occasionally preached in a Presbyterian church at nearby Trenton (Alexander, *Princeton College*, p. 75).

12 Contrary to JM's statement, Jeremiah Halsey (1733–1780), College of New Jersey, '52, declined the College's professorship of mathematics and natural philosophy in 1769. He had been chosen a tutor in 1757, the same year in which he was licensed for the ministry, and when he resigned ten years later to become a mission-

ary in the South, he was the school's eldest tutor. In 1770 he became pastor at Lamington and at Bedminster, in Somerset County, N.J. (John Lafayette Halsey and Edmund Drake Halsey, *Thomas Halsey of Hertfordshire, England . . . with his American Descendants . . .* [Morristown, N.J., 1895], pp. 60–61; Alexander, *Princeton College*, pp. 17–18; John Maclean, *History of the College of New Jersey* [2 vols.; Philadelphia, 1877], I, 273).

[13] For many years, James Caldwell (1734–1781), College of New Jersey, '59, was a distinguished Presbyterian minister at Elizabethtown, N.J. During the Revolution his eloquence helped to stiffen resistance to England and to recruit soldiers for the patriot army (Sprague, *Annals*, III, 222–28).

[14] The southern tours of Witherspoon and Caldwell were highly successful. The latter netted £1,000 for the College of New Jersey and also so much produce that he had to ship it north from Georgia in a vessel chartered for that purpose. Witherspoon's overflow audience in Williamsburg, Va., provided for the college £66, not including the £20 given by Governor Botetourt (*Virginia Gazette* [Purdie and Dixon], 2 November 1769). Although Witherspoon persuaded Henry Lee to send two of his sons to the college, he found that the Anglican influence of Reverend Jonathan Boucher weighed too heavily with George Washington to lure his stepson to the collegiate "nest of Presbyterians" in New Jersey (Varnum L. Collins, *President Witherspoon*, I, 124–29). As a result of his financial drive, Witherspoon, in April 1770, was enabled to purchase David Rittenhouse's ingenious orrery for use in teaching natural philosophy. This scientific apparatus reached the campus of the College of New Jersey one year later (*New Jersey Archives*, 1st ser., XXVII, 144–45, 426; John Maclean, *History of the College of New Jersey*, II, 22–23).

[15] Probably Richard Beale (1723–1771), whose wife Elizabeth was a sister of JM's father. Frances, another of JM's aunts on his father's side, was the widow of Taverner Beale. Dr. John Shore (*ca.* 1731–*ca.* 1802) was a prominent physician of Hanover County (Eugenia G. Glazebrook and Preston Glazebrook, comps., "Virginia Migrations, Hanover County, 1723–1871" [2 vols.; mimeographed; Richmond, 1943–49], II, 48). JM's mother, Nelly Conway Madison (1732–1829), although frequently in ill health, long outlived her husband, James Madison, Sr. (1723–1801). He and Nelly Conway were married on 13 September 1749.

To Richard Paterson

RC (New York Public Library).

March 24th. 1770.

Recievd of Mr. Richard Patterson[1] by order of Mr. Adam Hoops[2] twenty two Shillings and six pence on acct. of Mr. Robert Patterson.[3]

JAMES MADISON

[1] Richard Paterson's mercantile establishment in Princeton, situated on Main Street next to the well-known tavern of Jacob Hyer at the sign of Hudibras, appears to have had an important place in the life of the college. Paterson (d. 1781) was the father of William Paterson, College of New Jersey, '63, later a member of the Constitutional Convention of 1787, governor of New Jersey, United States senator, and associate justice of the Supreme Court (Julian P. Boyd, "William Paterson," in Willard Thorp, ed., *Lives of Eighteen from Princeton*, pp. 2–3; John Rogers Williams, ed., *Philip Vickers Fithian, Journal and Letters, 1767–1774* [Princeton, 1900],

p. 39; *New Jersey Archives*, 1st ser., XXVIII, 423; and John F. Hageman, *History of Princeton and Its Institutions*, I, 64; II, 81).

[2] Adam Hoops (1709–1771) was a prominent Pennsylvania merchant whose business interests ranged widely between the Susquehanna and Delaware rivers. Most probably he and his family had southern connections since a daughter, Sarah, married John Syme, Jr., of Hanover County, Va.; a son, David, was "of Maryland and Virginia"; and another son, Adam, served as an officer of the Maryland line during the Revolution until his capture by the British at the Battle of Camden in August 1780 ("Query on Adam Hoops," *Pennsylvania Magazine of History and Biography*, XXXV [1911], 512; *New Jersey Archives*, 1st ser., XXVIII, 283–84, 452; and F. B. Heitman, *Historical Register of Officers of the Continental Army during the War of the Revolution* [Washington, 1893], p. 227). See JM to his father, 23 July 1770, and JM to Bradford, 3–6 March 1775, for further instances where members of the Hoops family acted as agents for the Madisons.

[3] The identification of "Robert Patterson" and why he should have been in debt to JM (if so) remain in doubt. Probably it was merely coincidental that in 1784 Robert Patterson (1743–1824), professor of mathematics at the University of Pennsylvania, joined with its provost, John Ewing, in testifying that Captain Adam Hoops was sufficiently versed in trigonometry, etc., to qualify for appointment as a surveyor of U.S. public lands (NA: PCC, No. 41, IV, 224–26).

To Richard Paterson

RC (Princeton University Library).

April 3d. 1770[1]

Mr. Richard Patterson Please to let the bearer Mr. Wm. Livingston[2] have fifteen Shillings on acct of your
  Obliged Humble Servant

JAMES MADISON

[1] The date was written over by JM. He may have intended it to be "April 1." On the back of this draft is the endorsement: "Received this 4 of April 1770 of Richd. Paterson the sum of fifeteen shillings on Acct. of James Madison by me. William S. Livingston." Livingston's figure "4" could be a "2."

[2] William Smith Livingston (1755–1794), College of New Jersey, '72, became an attorney in New Jersey and New York and an officer in the Revolutionary army (Alexander, *Princeton College*, p. 155).

To James Madison, Sr.

RC (LC: Madison Papers).

NASSAU HALL. JULY 23d. 1770

HOND. SIR,

I reciev'd yours dated June 4th.[1] & have applied to Mr. Hoops[2] as you directed; he says you must suit yourself in paying him, & if you

49

should let him have a bill of Exchange it must be on your own terms: Forty Pounds £40. New Jersey Currency is the Sum I shall have of him before I get home. my frugality has not been able to keep it below that, consistant with my staying here to the best advantage. I should be glad, if it should be convenient for you, to have my next year's stock[3] prepared for me against I come home, for I shall not be able to stay in Virginia more than 4 weeks at most. Half Jos.[4] pass here to the greatest advantage. I have spoken to several of the present senior class about living with you as Tutor, but they will determine on nothing unless they knew what you would allow them, as it would not be proper for them to remain in suspense 'till I should return here; If you should recieve this [in] time enough to send me an answer by the middle of September & let me know the most you would be willing to give, I think there would be a greater probability of my engaging one for you[.] Inclosed are the measures of my Neck & rists. I believe my Mother need not hurry herself much about my shirts before I come for I shall not want more than three or four at most. I should chuse she would not have them ruffled 'till I am present myself. I have not yet procured a horse for my Journey, but think you had better not send me one as I cant wait long enough to know whether or not you'll have an opportunity without losing my chance, most of the horses being commonly engaged by the Students sometime before vacation begins. If I should set off from this place as soon as I expect you may look for me in October perhaps a little before the middle if the weather should be good. We have no publick news but the base conduct of the Merchants in N. York in breaking through their spirited resolutions not to import, a distinct account of which I suppose will be in the Virginia Gazete before this arrives.[5] their Letter to the Merchants in Philadelphia requesting their concurrence was lately burnt by the Students of this place in the college Yard, all of them appearing in their black Gowns & the bell Tolling.[6] The number of Students has increased very much of late; there are about an hundred & fifteen in College & the Grammar School, twenty two commence this Fall, all of them in American Cloth.

    With my love to all the Family I am Hond. Sir Your Affectionate Son

                                                        JAMES MADISON

[1] Not found.
[2] Adam Hoops.
[3] From its context the ambiguous word "stock," in this instance, probably signi-

fies "allotment of money." For JM's later use of the word in the same sense, see JM to his father, 9 October 1771.

4 The Portuguese johannes, worth about thirty-six shillings, was used in the colonies for hard currency. A half joe was a full johannes, while the double johannes was called a joe.

5 New York merchants, who had maintained the intercolonial non-importation agreement during late 1768 and all of 1769 better than those of any large northern port, finally in the early summer of 1770, to the anger of "patriot" mechanics and other "plain folk," decided to resume buying British merchandise (*Virginia Gazette* [Williamsburg, Purdie and Dixon], 26 July 1770; John C. Miller, *Origins of the American Revolution* [Boston, 1943], pp. 269, 309–10).

6 On 13 July, the students "at the tolling of the College Bell, went in Procession to a place fronting the College, and burnt the Letter by the Hands of a Hangman, hired for the Purpose . . ." (*New Jersey Archives*, 1st ser., XXVII, 203).

Notes on Commentary on the Bible

MS (LC: Madison Papers). With the exception of the extracts from Proverbs, these notes are quoted verbatim, or almost verbatim, from William Burkitt, *Expository Notes, with Practical Observations, on the New Testament of our Lord and Saviour Jesus Christ*, first printed posthumously in London in 1724. The pagination of the editorial footnotes is taken from the sixteenth edition of this work, published in London in 1765. Probably this was the edition which Madison's father received in response to the order of 4 August 1770, which he sent to his Liverpool agents, Clay and Midgeley (MS in Presbyterian Historical Society). Although this is the copy probably used by JM, he may have taken the notes at the College of New Jersey while he was a student there. In view of their structure and the precision with which they mirror Burkitt's own words, these jottings could hardly have been Madison's record of what he heard an instructor say. Although undated, the notes closely resemble in their handwriting other Madison manuscripts penned early in the 1770's.

The four pages of these notes are numbered 4 through 7 consecutively, in an unknown hand, but possibly that of William Cabell Rives. One or more pages, now lost, must have been available to Rives because on pp. 33–34 of the first volume of his *Life and Times of James Madison* are a few notes by Madison on the New Testament, which are not included in the Library of Congress fragment. Rives's paragraph and footnote, devoted to these additional comments, are reproduced below, immediately following what JM wrote on the four extant sheets. Although Rives states that the samples he selected for publication reveal JM's "orthodoxy" and "penetration," he should rather have remarked that they merely manifested the

youthful Madison's interest in the Bible, perhaps at a time when
he felt at least a transient inclination to become a clergyman
(JM to Bradford, 25 September 1773, and n. 2).

[1770–1773]

[Th]e Acts[1]

18. Rulers & great Men are like looking Glasses in the places
where they live, by which many dress themselves. v. 8 &c.

St. Paul went to the Feast at Jerusalem, not to observe the
Ceremony but to Preach to a larger Multitude that he
knew would be there v. 21. &c.

Apollos, though mighty in the Scriptures, yet disdained not
to be instructed farther by Aquila & Priscilla, for he knew
only the Baptism of John. 24 &c

Learned Men, it was a custom among the Jews to allow
them a liberty, tho' no Priests, to teach in their Syna-
gogues. ib[id].

Ch. 19 Holy Ghost. have ye recd. the Holy Ghost since ye Believed. the Apostle does not mean in its Sanctifying operations, but in its miraculous Gifts v. 2d.

Spirit of Prophecy, departed (as the Jews believe) from Israel after the Death of Haggai, Zachariah & Malachi. v. 2d.

Baptizm, Christ's & John's were the same for Substance 2d.

Apostles did greater Miracles than Christ, in the matter, not
manner, of them v. 11

Evil Spirits, none were, that we read of in the old Testament, bodily possessed of, but many in the New, v. 13

Conjuring Books burnt by the believing Jews & Greeks at
Ephesus amounted to 50 000 pcs. of Silver; £800

Saints fall, intimated by Alexander the Copper Smith turning Apostate. v 33

Ch. 20. Sunday, why kept by the Christians, for the Sabbath v. 7

Sleepers under Gods word (at a Sermon), their wretched
contempt of it. v. 9

St. Paul's travelling on foot from Troas to Assos: an happy
example for all the Ministers of Christ. v. 13. &c

Tempt. to neglect the means for our own preservation is to
Tempt God: and to trust to them is to neglect him v. 3
&c. Ch. 27. v. 31

Humility, the better any man is, the lower thoughts he has
of himself v. 19

Ministers to take heed to themselves & their flock. v. 28

Believers who are in a State of Grace, have need of the word of God for their Edification & Building up therefore implies a possibility of falling v. 32.

Grace, it is the free gift of God. Luke. 12. 32–v. 32

Giver more blessed than the Receiver. v 35

Ch. 21.   Affections, Spiritual, are stronger than the natural. v. 1.

Clouds governed by Providence. v. 3d &c.

Sins, or Faults, committed before conversion should not be related to the prejudice of the late Sinner v. 8

Isaiah, going barefoot, the reason of it. v. 11. Isa 20

Ezekiel, packing up his Stuff to remove. v. 11. Ezek. 12

Agedness, how Honourable. v. 16.

Jews, 1000ds & 10 000ds of them believed in St. Pauls days, so, not a few, in the litteral sence, but probably many more saved. v. 20.

Turky & Spaniards alluded to. v. 37 &c.

St. Paul, a Jew by Birth, & a Roman by immunity & privilege v. 39

Ch. 22.   Baptism necessary to be complyed with. v. 16

Carnal Reason, when against the command of God, should be laid by. v. 19

Ch. 23   Conscience[:] it should be inform'd as well as followed. v. 1.

Herod mentioned ib[id].

Magistrates, are not to be treated with ill words, nor flattered v. 4

Sadducees, deny the Resurrection & the existence of Angel or Spirit v. 8

Titles of civil Honour & Respect given to persons in place & power, are agreable to the Mind & will of God. v. 25 Ch. 26. v. 25

Magistrates must do nothing blindfold or blindly. Should know a Cause before they give sentence or Judgment about it. v. 35.

Ch. 24.   Persecution, a persecuting Spirit claps Wings to a Person[.] it makes him swift in his Motions & Zealous in his application & Endeavours. v. 1.

Flattery. Tis Hell and Death to flatter Sinners, or suffer ourselves to be flattered by them v. 2 &c

Judgments & Plagues are staved off for the sakes of God's holy & faithful Servants v. 5 &c.

Sedition may be committed three ways; by the Head, by the Tongue, and by the Hand. v. 10 &c

Church of Rome mentioned. v. 14

Ch. 25. Politicians (Carnal) do not so much consider what is Just & Righteous in it's own nature as what is of use & Advantage to themselves be it Right or wrong v. 9 &c

Dung-hill Cocks of the World know not the Worth of the pearl of Price v. 19 &c.

Ch. 26. Hope is the great excitor of Industry and Endeavour⎱ v. 6 &c.
Expectation puts it upon Action ⎰

Power[:] there is a compelling power and constraining Force in Example v. 11.

Ministers[:] great is the dignity of Gospel Ministers they are God's Messengers v. 16. &c.

Unconverted has little reason to expect to convert others by their Ministry

Ch 27. St. Paul's hazardous voyage to Rome, alluded to the Church in her Militant State here on Earth. v. 12. &c. and the danger of spending our youthful days in folly &c.

Ch. 28. Sinful inferrences are drawn from sorrowful premises. v. 4

Charity[:] no duty more certainly rewarded in another World; so is it frequently rewarded in this, as was Publius, by the miraculous cure perform'd on his Father for his Charity to Paul. v. 8.

Ministers of the Gospel[:] it is the great Duty of them, prudently to prevent, if possible, or presently to remove all Prejudices which may be taken up by their People against their Persons, knowing that, if they have a prejudice against their persons, they will never relish their Doctrine, nor be benefitted by their Ministry. v. 20.[2]

Hope (for the) [sake?] of Israel I am bound: That is; for the Object of Israel's Hope, or the Messiah which they so long expected, & so much hoped for. v. 20.[3]

Sun, the same that softens the Wax hardens the Clay v. 24
See St. Mark. Ch. 14 V. 66 &c.

Gospel stiled the Salvation of God v. 28. & why.

Inquisition & Rome, mentioned, at the end.[4]

Gospels.

Mat.[5] Ch   Jesus is an Hebrew name and signifies a Saviour v. 1.
1st   Christ is a Greek name and signifies Anointed. v. 1

Pollution[:] Christ did by the power of his Godhead purify our nature from all the pollution of our Ancestors v. 5. &c

Until signifies in Scripture as much as never. v 25

Virgin Mary had no other Child (probably) but our Saviour. v. 25

Ch. 2 Bethlehem signifies the House of Bread v. 4 &c.

Rachel is not here the name of a Person but a place v. 18[6]

Ch. 3 Ministers, none to assume the Office before they are sent v. 1.

Papists mentioned v 3. & concerning Auricular confession v. 6

Hermits lives not supported from the instance of John the Baptist preaching in the Wilderness

Sacrament. bad persons upon a profession of Repentance & promise of Amendment may be admitted to the Sacrament. v. 6.[7]

Sins of Omission as Damnable as Sins of Commission v. 10. neglects of Duty as Damnable as Acts of Sin.

Grace, where there is most, there is the greatest sense of the want of it. v. 14.

Ch. 4. Adoption[:] Satans grand design is first to tempt the children of God to doubt of it. v. 3[8]

Ch. 5. Christians who allows themselves in the least Transgression, either of omission, or commission is in a Damnable State. v. 19.

Ch. 6. Prayer, a form o[b]served by our Saviour & which ought to be used by us. v. 9.

Forgiveness, an indispensable Duty. v. 14

Ch. 7. Gifts, distinguished from Grace. v. 21 &c.

Ch. [8.] Marriage not censured nor condemned in Ministers of the Gospel nor the Apostles v. 14

St: Matt. Souls, departed are under the conduct of Angels, good or
Ch. 9. bad to their places of Bliss or Misery. perhaps at their seperation they are not, immediately fi[xed in?] their eternal Mansions v. 24.

Shepherds, or Labourers in Christs Harvest; the idle & lazy, are not so in his Acct. 3[6 &c.]

He who doth not instruct his Flock & feed them with the sincere Milk of the Word, from an Heart full of Love to

God, & compassion to Souls, deserves not the Name of a true Shepherd

Dr. Whitby.[9]

Ch. 10.   Apostles, they were Disciples, before they were Apostles. v. 1

Grace, the want of it doth not disannul a Ministers Office, nor hinder the Lawfulness of his Ministry. Judas, though a Traitor, was yet a Lawful Minister. V. 4.

Lost Sheep, the Israelites so call'd because they were lost in themselves & were in great Danger of being eventually & finally lost, by the Ignorance & Wickedness of their spiritual Guides v. 6.[10]

Preachers, must not be strikers v. 10[11]

Soul, dies not with the Body. 28 V.[12]

Christ's coming. We must distinguish betwixt his intentional Aim, & the accidental Event of it. v. 34[13]

Reward, There is some special & eminent Reward due to the faithful Prophets of God above other Men. v. 41

Ch. 11.   Teaching is in order to the Conversion of Sinners: ⎫
Preaching in order to the Edification of Saints.   ⎬ v. 1.
                                             ⎭

Punishment, there are Degrees of it among the Damned. v. 24

Ch. 12.   Idle words are such as savour nothing of Wisdom nor Piety v. 38 36[14]

Ch. 13.   Unbelief obstructs Christs gracious works in Heaven. v. 58

Ch. 21.   All reformation of manners must begin first at the House of God. v. 13

St. Luke,   Ch. 2d.—the idle are fit for nothing but Temptation to work on. v. 8 &c.

—Such Women whom God has blessed with safety of deliverance should make their first visit to the Temple of God to offer up their Praises & thanksgivings there v. 22d. &c

It is said of some *Turks* that after they have seen *Mahomets* Tomb, the[y] put out their Eyes, that they may never defile them after they have seen so glorious an object. v. 29.

Parts & abilities for the ministerial function are not sufficient to warrant our undertaking of it without a regular Call[15]

Some Proverbs of Solomon.[16]

Chap. 9. V. 7. He that reproveth a scorner getteth to himself Shame &c.

8. Reprove not a Scorner, lest he hate thee.

10. .17 ——;[17] but he that refuseth reproof, erreth

26 As Vinegar to the Teeth, and smoke to the Eyes, so is the Sluggard to them that send him.

XI. 13. A Tale-bearer revealeth Secrets: but he that is of a faithful Spirit concealeth the Matter 12: v. 23[18]

15. He that is surety for a Stranger shall smart for it: & he that hateth suretyship, is Sure. VI. 1. XVII:18[19]

25. The liberal Soul shall be made Fat &c.

XII. 22. Lying Lips are abomination to the Lord: but they that deal truly are his delight.

XIII. 12 Hope deferred maketh the Heart Sick &c.

24 He that Spareth his Rod hateth his Son: But he that loveth him chasteneth him betimes

XIV. 29 He that is Slow to wrath is of great understanding: but he that is hasty of Spirit exalteth folly.

XV. Argumt. Ceremonies to be retained for 3 Reasons from Melancthon[20]

1. A Soft Answer Turneth away wrath: but grievous words stir up anger

3 The Eyes of the Lord are in every Place, beholding the evil and the Good.

5 A Fool despiseth his Father's Instruction: but he &c

XVI 5. Every one that is pround in heart, is an abomination to the Lord. &c

11 A Just weight & balance are the Lord's: all the weights of the bag are his work

16 How much better is it to get Wisdom than Gold: & to get understanding rather to be chosen than Silver

24. Pleasant Words are as an Honey-comb, sweet to the Soul & health to the Bones

25. There is a way that seemeth right unto a Man, but the end thereof are the ways of Death—XIV. 12.[21]

28. ——; a Whisperer seperateth chief Friends[22]

32. He that is Slow to anger, is better than the Mighty; &c

XVIII 8. The Words of a Tale-bearer are as Wounds, & they go down into the innermost parts of the Belly

57

> 13. He that Answereth a Matter before he heareth it, it is folly & shame unto him.
>
> 21. Death & Life are in the Power of the Tongue; & they that love it, shall eat the fruit thereof.
>
> 22 Whoso findeth a Wife findeth a good thing, & obtaineth favour of the Lord.
>
> XX 3 'Tis an honour for a Man to cease from strife: but a fool will be medling;
>
> 9 Who can say I have made my Heart clean; I am pure from my sin
>
> 10 Divers weights and measures are abomination to the Lord. v. 23[23]
>
> 14 It is naught, it is naught, saith the buyer: but when he is gone his way then he boasteth

. . . In[24] one of these notes, referring to a chapter of the Acts of the Apostles, where the Bereans are mentioned as "more noble than those in Thessalonica, in that they received the word with all readiness of mind, and searched the Scriptures daily whether these things were so," he commends their conduct "as a noble example for all succeeding Christians to imitate and follow. . . ."[25]

In a paraphrase on the Gospel of St. John, referring to the passage in which Mary Magdalene is represented as looking into the Holy Sepulchre and seeing two angels in white, one sitting at the head and the other at the feet, where the body of the Saviour had lain, he makes the following reflection:

"Angels to be desired at our feet as well as at our head—not an angelical understanding and a diabolical conversation—not all our religion in our brains and tongue, and nothing in our heart and life."[26]

In the same spirit, commenting on the chapter of Acts, where Jesus says to St. Paul, who had fallen to the earth under the light which shined round about him from heaven, "*Arise*, and *go* into the city, and it shall be told thee what thou shalt *do*," he subjoins this as the proper deduction from the passage: "It is not the *talking*, but the *walking* and *working* person that is the true Christian."[27]

On doctrinal points, the following brief memoranda[28] and references taken from many others of a like character, may serve to show both his orthodoxy and his penetration:

"Omnisciency—God's foreknowledge doth not compel, but permits to be done." Acts, ch. II. v. 23.

"Christ's divinity appears by St. John, ch. XX. v. 28."
"Resurrection testified and witnessed by the Apostles. Acts, ch. IV. v. 33."

1 All of these notes on Acts are exactly copied or paraphrased from pp. 363–93 of Burkitt's volume.

2 By mistake, JM wrote "the" before the first "their" in the paragraph.

3 "Sake" is an editorial guess at the word which JM inadvertently omitted. The antecedent of "they" is "Jews" in verse 19. JM rather than Burkitt supplied the cross-reference to Mark in the next note.

4 By "at the end," JM meant the close of Burkitt's commentary on Acts rather than the close of that book of the Bible.

5 JM's notes on Matthew are all taken from Burkitt's *Expository Notes*, pp. 1–57.

6 "Rachel" signified Bethlehem.

7 Baptism is the sacrament referred to here.

8 The "of it" signifies "whether they are children of God [adoption]."

9 Daniel Whitby, *A Paraphrase and Commentary on the New Testament* (2 vols.; London, 1822), I, 112. These volumes were first published in 1703 and Burkitt, or the editor of his posthumous work, occasionally borrowed comments from them.

10 See Daniel Whitby, *Paraphrase and Commentary*, I, 114.

11 By "strikers," Burkitt meant men equipped with "smiting staves" for their own defense.

12 See Daniel Whitby, *Paraphrase and Commentary*, I, 117.

13 "Event" here means "result," and the antecedent of "it" is His "coming."

14 JM first wrote "38"; then, without deleting it, he corrected his error by entering "36" beside it.

15 This is an extract from Burkitt's comment on verses 46–47.

16 JM, of course, took these extracts from Proverbs rather than from Burkitt's volume.

17 Since JM frequently left out parts of these verses, he inconsistently indicated omission here of "He is in the way of life that keepeth instruction." Perhaps he knew this portion by heart.

18 The cross-reference is to the verse: "A prudent man concealeth knowledge; but the heart of fools proclaimeth foolishness."

19 Each of these verses also deals with suretyship.

20 This line, with its mention of Philipp Melanchthon (1497–1560), a German theologian-reformer who wrote much about church sacraments, is clearly an aside, wholly unrelated to the quotations above or below it.

21 The cross-reference is identical with this verse, except only that "which" is used instead of "that."

22 The portion omitted reads: "A froward man soweth strife." See above, n. 17.

23 This is the only instance among these excerpts from the book of Proverbs when JM summed up the sense of the text rather than quoted it exactly.

24 Here, as mentioned above in the headnote, begins the passage printed in William C. Rives, *History of the Life and Times of James Madison* (3 vols.; Boston, 1859–68), I, 33–34, 34 n.

25 William Burkitt, *Expository Notes*, p. 360, commenting on Acts 17:10–13, but following closely the comment in Daniel Whitby, *Paraphrase and Commentary*, I, 571.

26 Burkitt, *Expository Notes*, p. 300, commenting on John 20:12.

27 Burkitt, *Expository Notes*, p. 335, commenting on Acts 9:6. The "shalt *do*" is "must do" in the King James version.

28 Burkitt, *Expository Notes*, pp. 302, 313, 321, following closely the comments in Whitby, *Paraphrase and Commentary*, I, 489, 512, 519.

To John Boyle

RC (Princeton University Library). Addressed: "To John Boyle, Water Street, Philada. Pr. favr. Mr. Wallace."

PRINCTON May 17th. 1771

SIR,[1]

I wrote to you not long since by Mr. Armstrong[2] but as it is uncertain whether you have seen him, I take this opportunity by Mr. Wallace[3] to acquaint you with a mistake you made in a piece of Cloth I bought of you last winter, occasioned I believe by your giving me the remnant accidentantly instead of the measured piece. When I carried it to the Taylors I found it to be one whole yard short of what I paid you for, that is, 2¼ instead 3¼. If you will please to rectify the mistake by sending the value of the Cloth 34/ by Mr. Wallace who will call on you with this letter, you will much oblige

Yr. Humbl. Sert.

JAMES MADISON

[1] John Boyle, a native of Ireland and linen draper in Philadelphia, signed the nonimportation agreement of 1765 and was a member of that city's "Troop" at the outset of the Revolution. Apparently he died unmarried about 1798 (John H. Campbell, *History of the Friendly Sons of St. Patrick and of the Hibernian Society* [Philadelphia, 1892], p. 100; J. Thomas Scharf and Thompson Westcott, *History of Philadelphia, 1609–1884* [3 vols.; Philadelphia, 1884], I, 272–73).

[2] Earlier letter not found. "Mr. Armstrong" was probably James Francis Armstrong (1750–1816), College of New Jersey, '73, a "fraternity brother" of JM in the American Whig Society, chaplain in the Revolutionary army, and pastor of Presbyterian churches in Elizabethtown and Trenton, N.J. (Jacob N. Beam, *The American Whig Society of Princeton University* [Princeton, 1933], p. 60; Sprague, *Annals*, III, 389–92).

[3] Probably JM's long-time friend, Caleb Wallace (1742–1814), College of New Jersey, '70, and member of the American Whig Society, who at this time was at Princeton preparing for the Presbyterian ministry. After serving as a clergyman for nine years in his native state of Virginia and helping to found Hampden-Sydney College, he was admitted to the bar, moved west of the Appalachians in 1783, and soon became a Virginia Supreme Court judge from the District of Kentucky. From 1792 to 1813 he was a judge of the Court of Appeals of Kentucky (James A. Padgett, ed., "Letters of Caleb Wallace to James Madison," *Register, Kentucky State Historical Society*, XXXV [1937], 205–8; George Selden Wallace, comp., *Wallace: Genealogical Data Pertaining to the Descendants of Peter Wallace & Elizabeth Woods, His Wife* [Charlottesville, 1927], pp. 107–8).

Collegiate Doggerel

Copy by William Bradford in the notebook among his papers in the Historical Society of Pennsylvania. Filling the first half of this eighty-five page notebook is "Father Bombo's Pilgrimage to Mecca in Arabia, Volume II," by Hugh H. Brackenridge and Philip Freneau. This is printed in *Pennsylvania Magazine of History and Biography*, LXVI (1942), 461–78. The doggerel in the remainder of the notebook bears the general title, "Satires against the Tories. Written in the last War between the Whigs & Cliosophian[s] in which the former obtained a compleat Victory." Each of the last three of these nineteen satires is attributed by Bradford to JM. These three are not known to exist in their original form and no reference to them has been found in any letter by or to JM. Ashbel Green, College of New Jersey, '83, and a member of the American Whig Society, stated that "a considerable number of the pieces written by the Whigs [for a pre-Revolution paper war] was preserved and held in great estimation by the Society, while I was a member of the College" (quoted in Jacob N. Beam, *American Whig Society of Princeton University*, p. 61). The records, probably the source of Bradford's copy, apparently were burned in the Nassau Hall fire of 1802.

Interpolated between the title and the text of the first of JM's poems is the statement: "The hand writing is of Mr. Bradford's of whom Mr. Maddison, the name given at the end, was an early friend, J W W." These are most probably the initials of John William Wallace, a kinsman of Bradford, who in 1881 gave Bradford's papers to the Historical Society of Pennsylvania.

Madison's later recollections of his membership in the Whig Society were always happy ones. Writing to it, for example, on 20 January 1827, he expressed the wish that "the Whig Society in amicable competition with its Cliosophic Rival may continue to receive & reflect the lights which will best prepare its members for a useful life, which alone can promise a happy one" (Princeton University Library).

[June 1771–April 1772][1]

The aerial Journey of *the*[2] poet Laureat[3]
of the cliosophic Society

The rising sun his beams had shed
And each affrighted star had fled
When tuneful Spring in rural lays
Began *to* mourn his doleful case

New-englands sons[4] around him came
And many a wanton ruddy dame
Who view'd him nigh a purling stream
Rais'd on a stump to sing his dream.
That very dream in which they say
His soul broke loose from mortal clay
And sought the muses dome on high
Resolv'd with all his art to try
To steal a spark of wit from thence
A scourge for whiggish impudence.
But hear *the* very words he spoke
As from his quivering lips they broke
"Hail gentle shepherds of the grove
Your flocks about this mead may rove
While you attend my mournful tale
And echo sounds it thro' the vale
Soon as the lamp of day was gone
And evening shades oerspread *the* lawn
Tir'd with *the* business of the day
Down on the tender grass I lay.
When sleep had clos'd my slumbering eyes
I spurn'd *the* earth & peirc'd *the* skies
Thro' unknown tracts of air I flew
And pas'd by worlds of various hue
Beseeching every thing to tell
The place on which the Muses dwell.
At length, when coasting thro' *the* spheres
Apollo's song invades my ears
With all the sweet harmonious nine
Whose warbling notes in concert join.
Then by degrees their domes I spy'd
Which blaz'd around on every side
Straight to apollo's hall I went
Half dead with fear, my breath quite spent
Hoping somehow to lurk beneath
And rob him of a laurel wreath
And then a poet laureat rise
The dread of whigs of every size
But while I walk'd about the hall
apollo with the muses all

Came rushing in upon the theif
I cry'd in vain for some relief
The god of day provok'd to find
A villain of so base a mind
Seiz'd on a cudgel rough & great
& mash'd my jaws & crazy pate
Euterpe then a dishclout brought
With grease & boiling water fraught
And well [beswitched?]5 my sides & back
Which lost its hide at every whack
Urania threw a chamber pot
Which from beneath her bed she brought
And struck my eyes & ears & nose
Repeating it with lusty blows.
In such a pickle then I stood
Trickling on every side with blood
When Clio, ever grateful muse
Sprinkled my head with healing dews
Then took me to her private room
And straight an Eunuch out I come
My voice to render more melodious
A recompence for sufferings odious
She brought me to the earth again
And quel'd the Tumults of my brain
Softly wispering in my ear
While she dropt the parting tear
[']Dear friend accept this last behest
Conceal thy folly in thy breast
Forbear to write & only sing
And future sons shall talk of Spring
But mark me well if e'er you try
In poetry with Whigs to vie
Your nature's bounds you then will pass
And be transformed into an ass[']
Then brother shepherds pity Spring
Who dares not write but only sing—["]
—When thus he finished his complaint
He quit the stump & off he went
But soon forgot what Clio said
And wrote an ode & then essay'd

to sing an hymn & lo! he bray'd
And now he stands an ass confess[ed]
Of every scribbling fool, the Jest

MADDISON

Clio's Proclamation

Whereas a certain mongrel race
of tawney hide & grizly face
Have dar'd to prostitute my name
To raise the scribbling fools to fame
I hereby send this Proclamat[io]n
To every land & every nation
Declaring it my full intention
To free the world from this convention
And as a sanction to my word
I'll drive the dogs with fire & sword
Hedlong down to Pluto's coast
There in boiling flames to roast
And then their bodies I'll resign
To gnawing worms & hungry swine
Or to manure the farmers field
For much of dung their trunks will yeild
Very like it in their nature
As sprung from every filthy creature
But first selecting from McOrkle[6]
And every other stinking mortal
Whateer may be of use to those
From whom the wicked wretches rose
The poet Laureat head who scoops
May make a drum for yankey troops[7]
B'ing quite as empty & as sounding
His skull full thick to bear the pounding
While eckley's[8] skin & jakes[9] together
When tan'd will make a side of leather
Just fit to cloath McOrkle bum[10]
Which now becomes a battering ram
And plac'd before a city wall
Will ward of[f][11] many a whizzing ball
And by its monstrous stench may save
Ten thousand yankes from the grave.

Great Allen[12] founder of the crew
If right I guess must keep a stew
The lecherous rascal there will find
A place just suited to his mind
May whore & pimp & drink & swear
Nor more the garb of christians wear
And free Nassau from such a pest
A dunce a fool an ass at best.

J. MADDISON

A poem against the Tories.

Of late our muse keen satire drew
And humourous thoughts in vollies flew
Because we took our foes for men
Who might deserve a decent pen
A gross mistake with brutes we fight
And [goblins?][13] from the realms of night
With lice collected from the beds
Where Spring & Craig[14] lay down their heads
Sometimes a goat steps on the pump
Which animates old Warford's[15] trunk
Sometimes a poisonous toad appears
Which Eckley's yellow carcuss bears
And then to grace us with a bull
Forsooth they show McOrkles skull
And that the Ass may not escape
He takes the poet Laureat's shape
The screetch owl too comes in the train
Which leap'd from Alexander's[16] brain
Just as he scratch'd his grisly head
Which people say is made of lead.
Come noble whigs, disdain these sons
Of screech owls, monkeys, & baboons
Keep up you[r] minds to humourous themes
And verdant meads & flowing streams
Untill this tribe of dunces find
The baseness of their grovelling mind
And skulk within their dens together
Where each ones stench will kill his brother;

J. M.[17]

1 Among his fellow Whigs were JM's close friends, William Bradford, Hugh Henry Brackenridge, and Philip Freneau. The Whigs and their rivals, the Cliosophians, lampooned each other in verse. At least occasionally, after advance notice had been given the entire student body, these outrageous rhymes were read in the Prayer Hall of the College (Jacob N. Beam, *American Whig Society*, pp. 59–65). Although the Whigs customarily reproached the Cliosophians by calling them "Tories," their rivalry had no evident political connotation whatsoever. Judging from the Whigs' frequent references to the humble origins of the Cliosophians, there may have been a social cleavage between the two societies. In this "last war," the Clios' "poetic shots," to which the Whigs were evidently replying, have not been found. See Beam, *American Whig Society*, pp. 43–58, for a general account of the "war."

To determine when JM wrote these verses hinges upon dating "the last war." Another Whig participant, Philip Vickers Fithian, identified an anti-Cliosophian satire of his own as "A Piece written at the Time of a paper-Contention between the Whigg, & Tory Societies, at Nassau-Hall. Read June 22. Anno 1771" (John R. Williams, ed., *Philip Vickers Fithian*, I, 13–15). If this was "the last war" for which JM wrote his doggerel, it too can be dated June 1771. Since the members of the faculty objected to the distraction from study occasioned by the "paper wars," they hardly would have sanctioned an additional outbreak between June and September 1771, when five of the participants were graduated. On the other hand, because three (JM, Brackenridge, and Samuel Spring), and perhaps Freneau also, remained in Princeton until April 1772, the "war" to which JM contributed his doggerel may have occurred between September 1771 and April 1772. Nothing is known of the movements of John Black, the other class of 1771 participant, during the months following his graduation. Fithian's reference to *a* "paper-Contention" rather than *the* "last war," and his mention of opponents different from those ridiculed by JM and his comrades-in-arms, also suggest that different episodes were involved. Furthermore, according to a Cliosophian membership list (cited in Beam, *American Whig Society*, pp. 21–22, 45), one of the Clios lampooned in "the last war" did not join the society until 12 February 1772. If this date is correct, "the last war" took place in the final month or two before JM left Princeton in April 1772. But since the Clio in question, Robert Archibald, is probably the same person whom Fithian refers to as "Richd. Archibald" in his June 1771 satire, the date of Archibald's initiation must be deemed uncertain. Hence it seems impossible to fix the time of "the last war" more definitely than between June 1771 and April 1772.

On the score of their style, the first ten Whig poems in Bradford's copybook have been ascribed to Brackenridge by his and Freneau's biographers. By appending "H. B." to the tenth, Bradford possibly intended to signify that his friend also wrote the uninitialed nine preceding ones. Although Irving Brant (*Madison*, I, 87–88) surmises that a portion of the eighth of these, entitled "Spring's Adventures," may have been by JM, the present editors, lacking proof, are content to leave the "credit" for its particularly scurrilous lines to Brackenridge. Freneau's literary editor severely criticized JM's poems, stating that they are "by all means the worst of the lot. . . . No patriotic citizen will ever venture to resurrect them" (Fred Lewis Pattee, ed., *The Poems of Philip Freneau* [3 vols.; Princeton, 1902–7], I, xviii). The present editors wholly concur with Pattee's literary judgment, even while they render his prophecy inaccurate by publishing these sophomoric outpourings. The verses serve to challenge the accuracy of the widely held opinion that JM was a sedate, humorless, and faultless student, never really young in spirit (L. H. Butterfield, ed., *Letters of Benjamin Rush* [2 vols.; Princeton, 1951], II, 849–50).

2 Words in italics, unless otherwise noted, signify that Bradford used a shorthand

designation of them in his copy. For comment on his shorthand, see Bradford to JM, 1 March 1773, n. 11.

[3] Samuel Spring (1746–1819) of Massachusetts, more than any other Cliosophian, was the favorite target of Whig Society rhymesters. At the College of New Jersey commencement in September 1771 he delivered an oration entitled "The Idea of a Patriot-King." Licensed to preach in 1774, he served as chaplain in the Arnold-Montgomery expedition to Canada in 1775–1776. From 1776 until his death, he was a pastor in Newburyport, Mass. (*New Jersey Archives*, 1st ser., XXVII, 583, 586).

[4] The Whigs frequently put a Yankee tag on the Cliosophians, even though many of their members came from the South.

[5] This word is an editorial surmise to fill in a blank space left by Bradford.

[6] Samuel E. McCorkle (1746–1811), College of New Jersey, '72, for long a prominent Presbyterian minister and academy head at Thyatira near Salisbury, N.C., was a charter trustee of the state university and declined appointment as its first professor of moral and political philosophy and history (William Henry Foote, *Sketches of North Carolina, Historical and Biographical* [New York, 1846], pp. 351, 358, 362, 472, 530–32, 543; Sprague, *Annals*, III, 346–49).

[7] This may refer to the same incident mentioned by Brackenridge in his "A Dialogue," the third of the Whig Society poems copied by Bradford in his notebook. Brackenridge wrote:

> "Thou on thy sounding skin
> Dost clash the din of war; as when of old
> You followed boston's Sons & beat the March
> With Supple fingers on the sheepskin drum."

[8] Joseph Eckley (1750–1811), born in London, graduated from the College of New Jersey in 1772. From 1779 to 1811 he was Congregational pastor of Boston's Old South Church (Justin Winsor, ed., *The Memorial History of Boston* [4 vols.; Boston, 1880–81], III, 406, 415).

[9] This may refer to James Williamson who, with JM and others, received his A.B. at the 1771 commencement (information from Office of the Secretary, Princeton University). His name is given as Jacob Williamson in *New Jersey Archives*, 1st ser., XXVII, 584.

[10] "Bum" in the eighteenth century meant "buttocks."

[11] Bradford wrote "of."

[12] Moses Allen (1748–1779), College of New Jersey, '72, served briefly as pastor of Congregational churches at Wapetaw, S.C., and in St. John's Parish, Ga. After acting for several months as chaplain of the First Georgia Continental Battalion, he died in 1779 while trying to escape from a British prison ship in the Savannah River. He visited JM for several days at Montpelier while on his way to Georgia in 1775 and was urged to spend the winter there (James Stacy, *History of the Midway Congregational Church, Liberty County, Georgia* [Newnan, Ga., 1899], p. 46; Kenneth Coleman, *The American Revolution in Georgia, 1763–1789* [Athens, 1958], pp. 176, 187).

[13] This word is interpolated by the editors to fill a blank space left by Bradford.

[14] Archibald Craig, College of New Jersey, '73, later practiced medicine in Albany, N.Y. (Alexander, *Princeton College*, p. 161).

[15] John Warford (1745–1802), College of New Jersey, '74, served as a Presbyterian minister in Amwell, Hunterdon County, N.J., 1776–1787, and in Salem, Washington County, N.Y., 1789–1802 (William H. Hill, comp., *History of Washington County, N.Y.* [Fort Edward, N.Y., 1932], p. 64).

[16] Isaac Alexander, M.D. (d. 1812), College of New Jersey, '72, was from 1776 to

1778 trustee and headmaster of the Presbyterian Liberty Hall Academy in Mecklenburg County, N.C. (William H. Foote, *Sketches of North Carolina*, pp. 514–15).

[17] Commenting upon poetry in a note to John Quincy Adams on 22 November 1822, JM remarked that he had "never . . . been favored with the Inspiration of the Muses" (LC: Madison Papers).

To James Madison, Sr.

RC (LC: Madison Papers). Addressed to: "Colo. James Madison Orange County Virginia. To be left at Fredericksbg."

PRINCETON October 9th. 1771

HOND. SIR

In obedience to your requests I hereby send you an answer to your's of the 25th. of Sept. which I recieved this morning. My Letter by Dr. Witherspoon who left this place yesterday week contains most of what you desire to be informed of.[1] I am exceedingly rejoiced to hear of the happy deliverance of my Mother[2] & would fain hope your rheumatic pains will not continue much longer. The Bill of exchange was very acceptable, Though I cannot say I have been as yet very much pressed by my creditors. Since I got the Bill I have been making a calculation of my past & future expences & find it nothing more than a bare competency the reason of which I dare say you will not ascribe to extravagance when you read my letter of last week. If I come home in the Spring the purchase of a horse & travelling expences I am apprehensive will amount to more than I can reserve out of my present Stock for those purposes so that it would not be amiss perhaps if you were to send a few Half-Jos: by Dr. Witherspoon or Colo. Lewis's sons[3] if they return, or some safe hand afterwards as best suits you. I should be glad if your health & other circumstances should enable you to visit Dr. Witherspoon during his stay in Virginia.[4] I am persuaded you would be much pleased with him & that he would be very glad to see you. If you should not be able to see him nor send to him[,] Colo. Lewis or any other Gentleman in Fredericksburgh would advance what money I am to have at the least intimation from you. If you should ever send me any Bills hereafter, it will be best for you to make them payable to Dr. Witherspoon, which will give him an opportunity to endorse them, & greatly help me in selling them, if it should so happen that you see him, please to mention it to him[.] I was so particular in my last with regard to my determination about staying in Princton this Winter coming that I need say nothing more in this place, my sentiments being still the same. I am sorry Mr. Chew's Mode of Conveyance will not answer in Virginia. I expect to hear from him in a few days by the return of a man belonging to this Town from New London & shall then acquaint him with it and get it remedied by the methods you propose.[5] Mr James Martin was here at Commencement & had an opportunity of hearing from his Brothers & friends in Carolina by a young man lately come from thence to this College however I shall follow your directions in writing to him immediately & visiting him as soon as I find it convenient. You may tell Mrs. Martin he left his Family at home all well.[6] If you think proper that I should come back to this place, after my journey to Virginia, in the Spring, & spend the Summer here, you may send the Cloth for my coat which I am extremely pleased with & could have wished it had come time enough to have used this Summer past, if you chuse rather I should remain in Virginia next Summer it will be unnecessary.

I am Dr. Sr. Your Affecte. Son

JAMES MADISON

[1] Neither of the letters mentioned in these two sentences has been found.

[2] Reuben Madison (1771–1775) was born on 19 September 1771 (Patricia P. Clark, ed., "Madison Family Bible Records," *Virginia Magazine of History and Biography*, LXVI [1958], 82).

[3] JM probably refers to Colonel Fielding Lewis (1725–1781), brother-in-law of George Washington, a burgess and prominent Fredericksburg merchant. No one of his eleven sons seems to have been graduated from the College of New Jersey, but two of them did attend that institution or its academy early in the 1770's (Merrow Egerton Sorley, *Lewis of Warner Hall: The History of a Family* ... [Columbia, Mo., 1937], pp. 131–265, *passim*; Jane Taylor Duke, *Kenmore and the Lewises* [Garden City, N.Y., 1949], pp. 80–81).

[4] See JM to his father, 30 September 1769, n. 14. Witherspoon preached in Fredericksburg on 13 October 1771 (*Virginia Gazette* [Williamsburg, Purdie and Dixon], 24 October 1771).

[5] Joseph Chew (*ca.* 1725–1798), born in Orange County, the son of Thomas and Martha Taylor Chew, was a first cousin and intimate friend of James Madison, Sr. Leaving Orange about 1745, he thereafter engaged in mercantile enterprises in port towns, including Annapolis, New York, New London, Boston, and Montreal. Because of loyalist sympathies, he probably moved out of the United States in 1776. Letters from him to JM and James Madison, Sr., are in the Madison Papers, LC, and the Presbyterian Historical Society. See also Horace Edwin Hayden, *Virginia Genealogies: A Genealogy of the Glassell Family of Scotland and Virginia* ... (Wilkes-Barre, Pa., 1891), p. 672. Chew's "Mode of Conveyance" and James Madison, Sr.'s substitute for it are not known. It was probably a legal paper.

[6] James Martin was a brother of Thomas and Alexander Martin and "Mrs. Martin" was Thomas' widow (JM to Martin, 10 August 1769, nn. 1, 2, and 9). The "young man" from Carolina has not been identified.

Notes on Salkeld

Ms not found.

[1771–1774]

In an autobiographical sketch sent to James Kirke Paulding in January 1832 (LC: William C. Rives Papers), JM stated that, following his graduation from the College of New Jersey in the autumn of 1771, he devoted much of his time, both at Princeton and later at Montpelier, to a "course of reading" which "mingled miscellaneous subjects with the subjects intended to qualify him for the Bar." JM added, however, that he "never formed any absolute determination" to become a lawyer. Perhaps in this sketch JM predated the beginning of his excursion into the law. On 1 December 1773 (*q.v.*) he wrote, "I intend myself to read Law occasionally and have procured books for that purpose." On 24 January 1774, writing as one who spoke from experience, he characterized legal studies as "coarse and dry."

Hearing that William C. Rives was preparing a biography of Madison, Inman Horner, a lawyer of Warrenton, Virginia, informed Rives by letter on 27 November 1858 (LC: William C. Rives Papers) that he owned the "Manuscript Digest" which JM had made of William Salkeld (1671–1715), *Reports of Cases Adjudged in the Court of King's Bench: With some Special Cases in the Courts of Chancery, Common Pleas, and Exchequer, alphabetically digested under proper heads; From the First Year of King William and Queen Mary, to the Tenth Year of Queen Anne* (2 vols.; London, 1717–18). In his comment upon this "Digest," Horner remarked to Rives: "I have found some in which the Language of the Reporter [Salkeld] has been copied, and some in which it has been abridged and greater precision adopted. But the comparison demonstrates that Mr. Madison is not to be esteemed a mere copyist, that his purpose was to gather the learning of the Judges and their decisions, to separate the wheat from the chaff, or to extract the cream. By my hasty inquiry I am persuaded that his work will be worthy of preservation as a memorial of industry, patience and clear, strong and discriminating mind."

In spite of Horner's judgment of its worth, the "Digest" seems no longer to be extant. In the McGregor Library of the University of Virginia, however, there are four sheets of notes—and a fifth sheet containing only one line of writing—which Horner apparently made in 1858 on the first twenty-nine pages of the "Digest" before informing Rives of its quality, as quoted above. Although Horner indicated that these twenty-nine pages contained summaries of selections from the first 299 pages of Salkeld, and that these twenty-nine were followed by a précis of the next 320 pages of this work, he failed to mention the total length of the "Digest" and the date on it, if any. Moreover, since the original is missing, it cannot be known whether the notes were in JM's youthful hand. Therefore to conclude that he took them when he was reading law in the early 1770's is at best no more than a reasonable assumption.

To reproduce here the notes made by Horner would appear to be unwarranted since, in most instances at least, he merely summarized or commented upon, rather than copied, what Madison had written. The following sample will suffice.

> Hill & Al. v. Lewis. Man[uscript]. Page 16.
> 1. Salk Page 131

This Report occupies two & a half pages in Salkeld, the points are clearly and tersely stated by him, and yet in the Manuscript all the marrow is extricated, and eight separate propositions plainly and fully expressed, are deduced in the Manuscript. It furnishes evidence of an acute, strong and discriminating intellect.

> Griffith v. Harrison. Man. P. 20. 1 Salk. P. 197.
> Mr. M. has in this case copied the Report.

Horner was, above all, impressed by JM's ability to compress the main points of a complicated case, as reported in Salkeld, into a lucid summary filling only a few lines of the notebook. "If he had adopted the Law as a profession," Horner concluded, "his rank at the Bar would have been coequal with his eminence as a Statesman."

From William Bradford

FC (Historical Society of Pennsylvania). The RC is not known to exist. Given below is the text of the first letter copied by William Bradford in his commonplace book. On page 1 of this notebook he wrote, "Letters to and From Mr. James Maddison jr. From October the seventh 1772 to July 28th . . . 1775 inclusive." Unaccountably, Bradford misdated the present letter "October 7th 1773." JM's reply of 9 November 1772 indicates that his friend should have written "October 13th 1772."

Of the thirty-one letters transcribed by Bradford in his copybook, the present editors know of only seven in their original manuscript form. By comparing these seven with the version of them found in this copybook, it becomes evident that Bradford was not always completely accurate, especially when transcribing his own letters. Although he did not alter the general purport of the original, he sometimes shortened or paraphrased a paragraph, or polished a sentence. Evidently he viewed the copying as a literary exercise designed to improve his style as well as to remind him of what he had written to JM. For this reason, the text given below is most probably not word for word what Bradford wrote to JM.

In 1844–1845, Dolley Madison agreed to furnish John William Wallace, a nephew of Bradford, with copies of his uncle's letters to JM if Wallace would make copies for her of JM's letters to Bradford, but the arrangement came to naught because she could not find the Bradford originals at Montpelier (LC: Dolley P. Madison Papers). About thirteen years later, William C. Rives, friend and biographer of JM and an anonymous editor of his writings (the Congressional edition), used at least seven of JM's letters to William Bradford which had been given by Bradford's widow (nee Susan Boudinot) to Elias Boudinot of Philadelphia. (See correspondence of William C. Rives with R. C. and R. H. Weightman of Washington, D.C., now in LC: W. C. Rives Papers, Chronological Series.) These seven originals, together with Bradford's copy of them and of twenty-four others written between 1772 and 1775, comprise, insofar as is known, all the JM–Bradford correspondence now extant. Although R. C. Weightman told Rives that some of JM's letters to Bradford were probably dated at the time of the Constitutional Convention of 1787, neither these letters nor any from Bradford to JM have been found.

October [13th, 1772]. PHILADA

My dear Jemmy

I now perform the promise I made of writing to you when you were last in Philadelphia.[1] I should have given myself that pleasure sooner, had I not heard you were at the —— springs,[2] which made me fearful my letters would miscarry & therefore thought proper to defer it untill I left college.[3] I am now determined to deny myself no longer nor neglect a correspondence which promise me so much pleasure & improvement.

The value of a college-life like most other blessing[s] is seldom known but by its loss. I little thought I should have regretted my leaving Nassau-hall so much as I *feel* I do. But from the congratulations of all around me at my Deliverance (as they please to term it) I would be led to think there was more cause for Joy than sorrow; that I was leaving a state of Bondage and going to enter upon far happier scenes. If a collegiac-life is a state of bondage, like the good old Chinesian I am in Love with my chains. 'Tis the common fault of Youth to entertain extravagant hopes of Bliss in their future life. Tis this that makes us quit College without regret & rush with rapture on the stage of action. Hope is a flatterer we readily beleive; she present[s] the world to our view in a thousand Ideal charms & then tells us, as the prince of the Air did our Saviour, "All these shall be yours."[4] Yet, in my present disposition, I am so far from expecting Happiness hereafter that I look for little but trouble & anxiety. I leave Nassau Hall with the same regret that a fond son would feel who parts with an indulgent mother to tempt the dangers of the sea.

What business I shall follow for life I have not yet determined. It is a Matter which requires deliberation & as I am not pressed by Age[5] I intend to be in no hurry about it. I propose making History & Morality my studies the ensuing winter, as I look upon them to be very necessary in whatever employment I may hereafter engage. "Gnothi se auton"[6] was the celebrated maxim of the antients; & perhaps we shall not find an easier way of doing this than by the study of History. "Human nature is the same in every age if we make allowance for the difference of customs & Education, so that we learn to know ourselves by studying the opinions & passions of others[.]"[7]

Our friend Philip has commenced author. He has published a poem intitled the "America Village" to which he has added three other peices. (1) On a winter Night (2) the miserable life of a pedagogue. (3) an Elegy on an Antient ducth [dutch] house in long Island. Each of these are written in a different kind of verse.[8] I would send you the poem had I an opportunity! It is well worthy your perusal.

We had a numerous tho' not very splendid commencement. Livingston was addmitted to a degree.[9] I had some expectations of seeing you & Ross there. But alas!—You have doubtless heard of Poor Joe's death.[10]

I expect to hear soon from you. When you write be particular; nothing that concerns my dear Jemmy can be indifferent to one who esteems it his happiness to be able to subscribe himself &c.

Wm B——d.

1 JM's "last" visit to Philadelphia was probably in April 1772 on his way home from Princeton. William Bradford (1755-1795), whose father, grandfather, and great-grandfather of the same name were well-known printers in New York City or Philadelphia, received his A.B. and A.M. from the College of New Jersey in 1772 and 1775, respectively. Enlisting as a private in the patriot army in 1776, he rose by merit to a colonel's rank by 1779 when ill health forced him to resign his commission. Following eleven years as attorney general of Pennsylvania, his native state, he served three more on its Supreme Court. From January 1794 until his untimely death nineteen months later, he was Attorney General of the United States.

2 Possibly this was Berkeley Warm Springs, situated in that part of Virginia which is now Morgan County, W.Va. In 1772 JM may have made the first of his many summer visits to this health resort (Brant, *Madison*, I, 108). The dash may signify that Bradford had heard JM mention the place but could not recall its name.

3 Bradford left Princeton following commencement on 30 September 1772, at

which he, as valedictorian of his class, spoke on "The Disadvantage of an unequal Distribution of Property in a State" (*New Jersey Archives*, 1st ser., XXVIII, 277).

[4] "All these things will I give thee" (Matthew 4:9). Bradford's remark about hope being a flatterer was by no means original with him. See, for example, Michael Drayton, *The Barrons' Wars*, Bk. VI, xciv, or Shakespeare, *Richard II*, Act II, scene 2, line 69.

[5] Bradford was seventeen years old.

[6] "Know Thyself." According to Pausanias this was an inscription on the temple of Apollo at Delphi (*Descriptio Graeciae*, Book X, chap. xxiv, paragraph 1). Bradford's "se auton" should have been "sauton."

[7] This sentence is not a quotation from, but a paraphrase of, several paragraphs in David Hume, "An Enquiry Concerning Human Understanding" (Charles W. Hendel, Jr., ed., *Hume Selections* [New York, 1927], pp. 163–65).

[8] Philip Freneau (1752–1832), who was then teaching school in Somerset County, Md. The publication mentioned was *The American Village, A Poem. To which are added, Several other original Pieces in Verse*. By Philip Freneau, A.B. New-York: Printed by S. Inslee and A. Car, on Moor's Wharf, 1772. The titles of the added pieces are: "The Farmer's Winter Evening," "The Miserable Life of a Pedagogue," and "Upon a very ancient Dutch House on Long-Island." See Fred L. Pattee, ed., *Poems of Philip Freneau*, III, 381–400.

[9] William Smith Livingston.

[10] Joseph Ross, College of New Jersey, '71, with whom JM had frequently studied when an undergraduate. If he had not already heard of Ross's death, Bradford's mention of it must have come as a shock (*New Jersey Archives*, 1st ser., XVII, 584).

To William Bradford

RC (Historical Society of Pennsylvania). Addressed to: "Mr. William Bradford Junr. at the Coffee-House Philadelphia[.] By the Post." Bradford's copybook version is also in the Historical Society of Pennsylvania.

ORANGE VIRGINIA Novr. 9th. 1772

MY DEAR BILLEY,

You moralize so prettily that if I were to judge from some parts of your letter of October 13[1] I should take you for an old Philosopher that had experienced the emptiness of Earthly Happiness. And I am very glad that you have so early seen through the romantic paintings with which the World is sometimes set off by the sprightly imaginations of the Ingenious. You have happily supplied by reading and observation the want of experiment and therefore I hope you are sufficiently guarded against the allurements and vanities that beset us on our first entrance on the Theatre of Life. Yet however nice and cautious we may be in detecting the follies of mankind and framing our Oeconomy according to the precepts of Wisdom and Religion I fancy

there will commonly remain with us some latent expectation of obtaining more than ordinary Happiness and prosperity till we feel the
convincing argument of actual disappointment. Tho I will not determine whether we shall be much the worse for it if we do not allow it
to intercept our views towards a future State, because strong desires
and great Hopes instigate us to arduous enterprizes fortitude and
perseverance. Nevertheless a watchful eye must be kept on ourselves
lest while we are building ideal monuments of Renown and Bliss here
we neglect to have our names enrolled in the Annals of Heaven. These
thoughts come into my mind because I am writing to you and thinking
of you. As to myself I am too dull and infirm now to look out for any
extraordinary things in this world for I think my sensations for many
months past have intimated to me not to expect a long or healthy life,
yet it may be better with me after some time tho I hardly dare expect
it and therefore have little spirit and alacrity to set about any thing that
is difficult in acquiring and useless in possessing after one has exchanged
Time for Eternity.[2] But you have Health Youth Fire and Genius to
bear you along through the high tract of public Life and so may be
more interested and delighted in improving on hints that respect the
temporal though momentous concerns of man.

I think you made a judicious choice of History and the Science of
Morals for your winter's study. They seem to be of the most universal
benefit to men of sense and taste in every post and must certainly be of
great use to youth in settling the principles and refining the Judgment
as well as in enlarging Knowledge & correcting the imagination. I doubt
not but you design to season them with a little divinity now and then,
which like the philosopher's stone, in hands of a good man will turn
them and every lawful acquirement into the nature of itself, and make
them more precious than fine gold. As you seem to require that I
should be open and unreserved (which is indeed the only proof of true
friendship) I will venture to give you a word of advice though it be
more to convince you of my affection for you than from any apprehension of your needing it. Pray do not suffer those impertinent fops
that abound in every City to divert you from your business and philosophical amusements. You may please them more by admitting them
to the enjoyment of your company but you will make them respect
and admire you more by shewing your indignation at their follies and
by keeping them at a becoming distance. I am luckily out of the way
of such troubles, but I know you are cirrounded with them for they
breed in Towns and populous places, as naturally as flies do in the

Shambles, because there they get food enough for their Vanity and impertinence.

I have undertaken to instruct my brothers and Sisters in some of the first rudiments of literature,[3] but it does not take up so much of my time but I shall always have leisure to recieve and answer your letters which are very grateful to me I assure you, and for reading any performances you may be kind enough to send me whether of Mr. Freneau or any body else. I think myself happy in your correspondence and desire you will continue to write as often as you can as you see I intend to do by the early and long answer I send you. You are the only valuable friend I have settled in so public a place and must rely on you for an account of all literary transactions in your part of the world.

I am not sorry to hear of Livingston's getting a degree. I heartily wish him well though many would think I had but little reason to do so and if he would be sensible of his opportunities and encouragements I think he might still recover. Lucky[4] and his company after their feeble yet wicked assault upon Mr. Erwin, in my opinion will disgrace the catalogue of names, but they are below contempt and I spend no more words about them.[5]

And now my friend I must take my leave of you, but with such hopes that it will not be long before I receive another epistle from you as make me more cheerfully conclude[6] and Subscribe myself Yr. Sincere and Affecte. friend

JAMES MADISON JUNR.

Your Direction was right however the addition of Junr. to my name would not be improper.

---

[1] Bradford wrote "October 7" in FC.

[2] For a discussion of the nature of JM's illness, possibly epileptoid hysteria, see Brant, *Madison*, I, 105–8.

[3] In 1772, JM's brothers and sisters were Francis (age 19), Ambrose (age 17), Nelly (age 12), William (age 10), Sarah (age 8), Elizabeth (age 4), and Reuben (age 1). Since the first two and the last two of these appear to have been either too old or too young for the "first rudiments," JM's pupils may have been limited to the remaining three.

[4] George Luckey (1750–1823), a Pennsylvanian by birth, was graduated by the College of New Jersey in 1772. Following his ordination as a Presbyterian clergyman in 1775, he preached in Harford County, Md., until 1799 (Alexander, *Princeton College*, p. 155; *Portraits and Biographical Records of Harford and Cecil Counties of Maryland* [New York, 1897], p. 548).

[5] Nathaniel Irwin (1756–1812) was in the class of 1770 at the College of New Jersey. From 1774 until his death he was a clergyman and civic leader at Neshaminy, Bucks County, Pa. Evidently a special friend of JM, Irwin called on him at Montpelier in September 1773 and is said to have visited him in Washington during his

first term as President of the United States (Sprague, *Annals*, III, 333–35). The cause of the "assault" by George Luckey upon Irwin when they were undergraduates is unknown (JM to Bradford, 24 January 1774).

6 This word, torn from the original, is taken from the copy in Bradford's commonplace book.

From Philip Freneau

RC (LC: Madison Papers). Marked by JM "Rcd. Feby. 19. 1773." Freneau specialists have accorded much attention to this letter and have printed it in full at least four times. It is called "Freneau's liveliest known letter" by Philip M. Marsh in his edition of *The Prose of Philip Freneau* (New Brunswick, N.J., 1955), p. 580.

SOMERSET COUNTY IN MARYLAND[1]
November 22d: 1772.

SIR

If I am not wrongly informed by my memory, I have not seen you since last April. you may recollect I was then undertaking a School at Flatbush on Long Island.[2] I did enter upon the business it is certain and continued in it thirteen days—but—"Long Island I have bid adieu, with all its bruitish brainless crew. The youth of that detested place, are void of reason and of grace, From Flushing hills to Flatbush plains, Deep ignorance unrivall'd reigns.["] I am very poetical but excuse it— "Si fama non venit ad aures" if you have not heard the rumor of this story (which by the by is told in various Taverns and eating houses) you must allow me to be a little prolix with it. Those who employed me were some Gentlemen of New York. some of them were bullies, some merchants, and others Scoundrels: They sent me Eight children the eldest of whom was 10 Years. Some could read, others spell and a few stammer over a chapter of the Bible. these were my pupils and over these was I to preside. My Salary moreover was £40,—there is something else relating to that I shall not at present mention. after I forsook them they proscribed me for four days and swore that if I was caught in New York they would either Trounce or maim me: but I luckily escaped with my goods to Princetown—where I remained till commencement—so much for this affair. I have printed a poem in New York called the American Village, containing about 450 Lines, also a few short pieces added; I would send you one if I had a proper opportunity. the additional poems are,—1. a Poem to the Nymph I never saw

—The miserable Life of a Pedagogue—and Stanzas on an ancient Dutch house on Long Island. As to the main poem it is damned by all good and judicious judges—my name is in the title page.[3] this is called Vanity by some—but "who so fond as youthful bards of fame?" I arrived at this Somerset Academy the 18th: of October and intend to remain here till next October. I am assistant to Mr. Bracken[r]idge[.] This is the last time I shall enter into such a business. it worries me to death and by no means suits my "giddy' wandring brain." I would go over for the gown this Time two years[4]—but the old hag Necessity has got such a prodigious gripe of me that I fear I shall never be able to accomplish it. I believe if I cannot make this out I must turn quack—and indeed I am now reading Physic at my leisure hours, that is, when I am neither sleeping, hearing classes, or writing Poetry—for these three take up all my time.

It is now late at night. not an hour ago I finished a little poem of about 400 lines, entituled a Journey to Maryland—being the Sum of my adventures. it begins—"From that fam'd town where Hudsons flood—unites with Streams, perhaps as good; Muse has your bard began to roam." I intend to write a terrible Satire upon certain vicious persons of quality in N. Y—who have also used me ill—and print it next fall. it shall contain 5 or 600 Lines. Sometimes I write pastorals to shew my Wit. "Deep to the woods, I sing a Shepherds care, Deep to the woods, Cyllenius calls me there. The last retreat of Love and Verse I go—Verse made me mad at first and —— will keep me so.["][5] I should have been glad to have heard from you before now; while I was at College I had but a short participation of your agreeable friendship and the few persons I converse with and yet fewer, whose conversation I delight in, make me regret the Loss of it. I have met with a variety of rebuffs this Year, which I forbear to mention. I look like an unmeaning Teague just turned out of the hold of an irish Ship. coming down hither I met with a rare adventure at Annapolis. I was destitute even of a brass farthing. I got clear very handsomely. could one Expect ever to see you again, if I travel through Virginia I shall stop and tallk with you a day or two. I should be very glad to recieve a Letter from you if it can be conveniently forwarded. In short 'Non sum qualis eram" as Partridge says in Tom Jones.[6] My hair is grown like a mop, and I have a huge tuft of Beard directly upon my chin. I Want but five weeks of twenty one Years of age and already feel stiff with age. We have about 30 Students in this academy, who prey upon me like Leaches. ["]When shall I quit this whimp'ring pack, and hide my head in Acomack!" Shall I leave them and go "Where Pokomokes long stream meandring flows.["]⁷ Excuse this prodigious Scrawl—without stile or sense. I send this by Mr. Luther Martin who will forward it to Col. Lee—and he to you I hope.⁸ Mr. Martin lives in Acomack in Virginia, this side the bay. Farewell and be persuaded I remain your

truly humble Servt and friend.

PH. F-r-e-n-e-a-u

[1] Freneau taught briefly, beginning in October 1772, in the academy at Back Creek, near Princess Anne in Somerset County, where Hugh Henry Brackenridge (1748–1816) was principal from 1772 to 1776 (Lewis Leary, *That Rascal Freneau: A Study in Literary Failure* [New Brunswick, N.J., 1941], pp. 45–46; Claude Milton Newlin, *The Life and Writings of Hugh Henry Brackenridge* [Princeton, 1932], p. 25).

[2] This, together with other remarks in this letter, is additional evidence that JM left Princeton in April or early May 1772, before Freneau's return there following his unhappy two weeks in Flatbush (Bradford to JM, 13 October 1772, n. 1).

[3] See Bradford to JM, 13 October 1772, n. 8.

[4] Probably a reference to Freneau's intention to go to England to be ordained as an Anglican minister.

[5] If Freneau composed the satire, he apparently neither published it nor "A Journey to Maryland." They are not known to exist in manuscript.

[6] Henry Fielding, *The History of Tom Jones, a Foundling* (4 vols.; London, 1768), IV (Bk. XV, chap. 12), 129. Idiomatically, "I'm not the man I was." Insofar as is known, Freneau did not realize his hope of visiting JM.

[7] Accomack County, Va., and Somerset County, Md., are separated by the Pocomoke River which flows into Chesapeake Bay.

[8] JM probably knew Luther Martin (*ca.* 1748–1826), who graduated from the College of New Jersey in 1766. Although a Virginia lawyer at this time, Martin is chiefly identified with Maryland. He served as its attorney general, 1778–1805 and 1818–1820, and as one of its delegates in Congress, 1784–1785, and in the Constitutional Convention of 1787. His national prominence, dating from his opposition to the ratification of the Constitution, was enhanced later by his verbal attacks upon President Jefferson and his career as a constitutional lawyer. The "Col. Lee" likely means Henry Lee (1729–1787) of Leesylvania in Prince William County, Va. Lee was a burgess, 1758–1775, a member of the conventions of 1775 and 1776, and county lieutenant during the Revolution. He was the father of "Light-Horse Harry" Lee and the grandfather of Robert E. Lee.

From William Bradford

FC (Historical Society of Pennsylvania).

N. HALL. March 1t. 1773.¹

MY DEAR JEMMY,

You will pardon me for not writing sooner when I inform you that ever since I received your agreeable letter I have [been] roving from place to place without being able to find time to answer it. But I need make no apology, as I know your Goodness will excuse me without one. Punctuality [in][2] answering a letter is what Pope justly call[s] the ceremonial part of friendship which those who have a true taste for[3] the substantial part can sometimes dispense with.

You alarm me, by what you tell me about your[4] health. I beleive you hurt your constitution while here, by too close an application to study; but I hope 'tis not so bad with you as you seem to imagine. Persons of the weakest Constitutions *by taking a proper care of themselves* often out live those of the strongest.[5] Pope, in his letters, is frequently complaining that his health was fast declining & that he looks upon himself as just on the threshhold of another world;[6] yet you see he lived longer than the generallity of mankind do. You, I hope will yet enjoy many days as you seem designed by Providence for extensive usefulness. "Spare useful lives," is a part of the Doctor's petition[7] I always heartily join.

The best thanks I can give you for your advice is[8] to frame my conduct by it. Let me intreat a continuation of it, & be assured I shall always receive it with pleasure & Gratitude. I know not why, but so it is, that that advice of an absent friend makes a deeper impression on me & is more attended to [than][9] the wisest precepts of the wisest Philosopers.

I am afraid you will find me but a dull correspondent however I can be a faithful one. Some have an ingenious way of filling their letters with compliments & professions of regard which for the life of me I cannot obtain. Nor would I if I could. It is true, Compliments have been called the Smoke of Friendship, but I know not whether the metaphor will hold; for where there is smoke there[10] must be some fire, but there may [be] compliments without the least degree of Friendship. Several times I sat down to write to you & as often rose up without being able to tell you any thing that was worth your hearing. When I began this letter I was going upon an old rule I have often heard "to say whatever comes uppermost," But as that always is how heartily I love it is needless to tell you what you already know. I shall therefore give a short account of the several productions of the press in this part of the world.

(*Here an account of *the piece*[?] *against*[?] Dr Witherspoon *precis*[?] *of the* "candid remarks")[11] George Cockings has likewise published a peice which he has christened with the name of Tragedy. I beleive you have read part (I am sure you never read the whole) of his poem, called "War." It may serve to give you some Idea of this Tragedy, when I tell that he seems to have designed it as a compendium of that. The stile is below criticism, & one would think he intended to burlesque blank verse by it. Mather's psalms which you know are prose

divided into six & eight feet, are far preferable.¹² As to Sentiment there
is none in it and the unities *of* time and place (If I rightly understand
what they are) are grosly violated. I think it is Lord Kaims¹³ who ob-
serves "That change of time and place ought never to be indulged in
the same act." But in the middle of the last act the scene shifts from
Quebec to London & the time is considerably advanced. He has, however, happily preserved all the Punctuality of an historian, which may
serve to gratify the curiosity of those who desire to know how Quebec
was taken. But [to] call this peice a tragedy is ridiculous for it has
neither the spirit nor the body of Dramatic poetry.¹⁴

Doctor Smith *has* published an oration *which* he delivered *to the*
Philosophic Society: it is nothing extraordinary but seems to be (as he
himself calls it) "a few loose thoughts thrown together in an evening
or two."¹⁵

You see by my date that I have on[c]e more left the busy town *to*
enjoy *the* quiet of a collegiac Life. If you would allow me to make use
of *the* hackened simile (because it so well describe[s] my case) I *would*
tell *you that* like Noah's Dove I had again sought *the* ark *because* I
found no resting place *for* my foot. I spend my time *very* agreeably &
want nothing to compleat my happiness but your company & conversation. Write soon & beleive me yours

            W—B—D.

---

¹ Bradford wrote from Princeton (Nassau Hall) where he had returned for
graduate study. This letter is evidently a belated reply to JM's of 9 November 1772.
² Bradford wrote "is" instead of "in." Although the editors have not discovered
the exact passage in the writings of Alexander Pope, he frequently expressed almost
the same sentiment. See William Lisle Bowles, ed., *The Works of Alexander Pope,
Esq., in Verse and Prose* (10 vols.; London, 1806), VIII, 286; IX, 354, 375, 378, 387;
X, 237.
³ Bradford repeated "for."
⁴ Here Bradford crossed out "my" and wrote "your" above it.
⁵ Italicized words underlined by Bradford. JM's life span of eighty-five years,
much of it spent in poor or indifferent health, makes this remark of Bradford's
prophetic.
⁶ See, for example, William L. Bowles, ed., *The Works of Pope*, VII, 113–14,
117–19.
⁷ Bradford wrote "pepetition." The first "pe" at the end of one line of his notebook is clearly a copying error. The "Doctor" is undoubtedly Dr. Witherspoon,
whose prayers Bradford was once again hearing. As long as Witherspoon lived he
was referred to as "the Doctor" in JM's correspondence.
⁸ Bradford repeated "is."
⁹ Bradford inadvertently wrote "the" instead of "than."
¹⁰ "Compliments . . . the smoke of friendship" (Alexander Pope to William
Wycherley, 25 March 1705, William L. Bowles, ed., *The Works of Pope*, VII, 13).
The words "smoke there" are unnecessarily repeated in Bradford's notebook copy.

[11] Bradford merely mentions a topic to which he possibly had devoted a paragraph in his letter to JM. The italicized words are in the shorthand used frequently by Bradford in his notebook. On 21 March 1772 President Witherspoon issued his *Address to the Inhabitants of Jamaica, and other West-India Islands, in Behalf of the College of New Jersey (New Jersey Archives*, 1st ser., XXVIII, 289–308; Varnum L. Collins, *President Witherspoon*, I, 143–46). Ostensibly a pamphlet to help raise money and recruit undergraduates from the West Indies, it was widely viewed as an effort to woo support and students from other American colleges, notably the College of Philadelphia (now the University of Pennsylvania) and King's College (now Columbia), through a veiled attack on these institutions. The appearance of Witherspoon's *Address* in the *Pennsylvania Gazette* on 21 and 28 October 1772 and in the *New York Gazette; and Weekly Mercury* on 16 November 1772 called forth at least two sharp rejoinders. One was a letter signed "Causidicus" (obviously a King's College sympathizer) in the *New York Gazette* on 7 December 1772, and the other a pamphlet published in Philadelphia in 1772 entitled *Candid Remarks on Dr. Witherspoon's Address to the Inhabitants of Jamaica, and the other West-India Islands*, attributed to Reverend Thomas B. Chandler of Elizabethtown, N.J. In his letter Bradford evidently included a "précis" of the latter.

The editors have been occasionally baffled by the enigmatic shorthand characters used by Bradford in the file copies of his correspondence. He evidently derived his symbols from James Weston, *Stenography Compleated, or the Art of Short-Hand Brought to Perfection: Being the Most Easy, Exact, Speedy, and Legible Method Extant* . . . (London, 1727), a handbook published in at least eight editions between 1727 and 1748. With the help of this text, Bradford's symbols for short and frequently used words can be deciphered with assurance. On the other hand, the shorthand system of Weston was by no means as simple as the title of his text affirmed it to be. Instead of mastering it, Bradford appears to have combined elements of it with pen strokes of his own invention, especially when using shorthand characters for polysyllabic or unusual words. The question marks inserted by the present editors signify that they may not have correctly transmuted Bradford's symbols into the word or words which he had in mind.

[12] Richard Mather (1596–1669), a clergyman of Massachusetts Bay Colony from 1635 until his death. He was one of the translators of *The Whole Booke of Psalmes* (1640), usually called the "Bay Psalm Book."

[13] Henry Home (Lord Kames), *Elements of Criticism* (3 vols.; Edinburgh, 1762), III, 291. If Bradford had quoted accurately, he would have written: "The unities of place and time ought to be strictly observed during each act. . . ."

[14] The poem to which Bradford alludes as having been read at least in part by JM is George Cockings' (d. 1802) *War: an Heroic Poem, from the Taking of Minorca, By the French, to the Raising the Siege of Quebec* . . . (printed in London, 1760; in Boston by S. Adams, 1762; reprinted and sold in Portsmouth, New Hampshire, by D. and R. Fowle, 1765). Cockings' more recent work was *The Conquest of Canada; or the Siege of Quebec: an Historical Tragedy of Five Acts* . . . (Philadelphia: printed for William Magill, 1772; also printed in Albany by Alexander and James Robertson, 1773). "Punctuality" here, unlike in the first paragraph, means "preciseness."

[15] Shortly before the date of Bradford's letter, Dr. William Smith (1727–1803), provost of the College of Philadelphia and one of the secretaries of the American Philosophical Society, published his speech, *An Oration Delivered, January 23, 1773, Before the Patron, Vice-Presidents and Members of the American Philosophical Society, Held at Philadelphia, For Promoting Useful Knowledge* . . . (Philadelphia: printed by John Dunlap, in Market-Street, 1773).

To William Bradford

RC (Historical Society of Pennsylvania). Addressed: "Mr. William Bradford Jun[r] at the Coffee House Philadelphia." Bradford's copybook version, differing from the recipient's copy by containing a little of Bradford's shorthand, is also in the Historical Society of Pennsylvania and helps to clarify a few indistinct words in the recipient's copy.

VIRGINIA ORANGE COUNTY April 28th. 73

DEAR BILLEY

I received your Letter dated March the 1st. about a Week ago and It is not more to obey your demands, than to fulfill my own desires that I give you this early answer. I am glad you disclaim all punctiliousness in our correspondence. For my own part I confess I have not the face to perform ceremony in person and I equally detest it on paper though as Tully says It cannot blush.[1] Friendship like all Truth delights in plainess and simplicity & It is the Counterfeit alone that needs Ornament and ostentation. I am so thoroughly persuaded of this that when I observe any one over Complaisant to me in his professions and promises I am tempted to interpret his Language thus—As I have no real esteem for you and for certain reasons think it expedient to appear well in your eye, I endeavour to Varnish Falsehood with politeness Which I think I can do in so ingenious a manner that so vain a Blockhead as you cannot see through it. I would have you write to me when you feel as you used to do when we were under the same Roof and you found it a recreation and release from Business and Books to come and chat an hour or two with me. The Case is such with me that I am too remote from the Post to have the same Choice, but It seldom happens that an Opportunity Catches me out of a Humour of Writing to my old Nassovian Friends and you know What place you hold among them.

I have not seen a single piece against the Doctor's Address. I saw a piece advertised for publication in the Phila. Gazette Entitled—Candid Remarks &c. and that is all I know about it. These things seldom reach Virginia and when they do I am out of the way of them.[2] I have a curiosity to read those Authors who write with "all the rage of Impotence" When passion seems to commit a rape on the understanding and engenders a little peevish snarling offspring:[3] not because there is any Excellence or wit in their Writings, but because they implicitly proclaim the Merit of those they are railing against and give them an occasion of shewing by their Silence and Contempt that they are invulnerable. I am heartily obliged to you for your kind offer of sending me some of These Performances. I should also willingly accept Freneau's Works[4] and the Sermons to Doctors in Divinity which I hear are published and whatever else you reckon worth reading.[5] Please to note the Cost of the Articles for I will by no means suffer our acquaintance to be an expence on your part and I have nothing fit to send you to make it reciprocal.

In your next Letter be more particular as to yourself, your Intentions present employments &c. Erwin[6] McPherrin[7] &c &c—The Affairs of College. Is their Lottery like to come to any thing?[8] There has happened no Change in my purposes since you heard from me last. My Health is a little better owing I believe to more activity and less Study recommended by the Phy[si]cians. I shall try if possible to devise some Business that will afford me a sight of you once more in Philada. within a Year or two. I wish you would resolve the same with respect to me in Virginia though Within a shorter time.

I am sorry my situation affords me nothing New Curious or entertaining to pay you for your agreeable information & remarks You being at the Fountain-Head of Political and Literary Intelligence and I in an Obscure Corner—You must expect to be greatly [the] loser on that score by our Correspondence. But as you have entered upon it I am determined to hold you to it, and shall give you some very severe admonitions whenever I perceive a remissness or Brevity in your Letters. I do not intend this as a beginning of reproof but as a caution to you never to make it necessary at all.

If Mr. Horton[9] is in Philadelphia give him my best Thanks for his Kindness in assisting Mr. Wallace[10] to do some Business for [me] not long ago.

I must reecho your pressing Invitations to [write soon which I] do with the more confidence as I have complied [with yours.]

I am Dear [Sir][11] Yours most unfeignedly

JAMES MADISON JUNR.

---

[1] In a letter to Lucius Lucceius, Cicero wrote: ". . . a certain awkward modesty has always restrained me from proposing in person, what I can with less scruple request at this distance; for a letter, you know, spares the confession of a blush" (William Melmoth, trans., *The Letters of Marcus Tullius Cicero to Several of his Friends* [3 vols.; London, 1753], I, 75–76).

[2] See Bradford to JM, 1 March 1773, n. 11. Newspaper delivery must have been erratic in Orange County for JM to have missed all of the printed replies to Witherspoon's *Address*.

3 William Cabell Rives, JM's overly protective biographer, deleted "When" through "offspring," without indicating the omission, from his edition (the Congressional edition) of JM's writings. The Gaillard Hunt edition merely copied from Rives.

4 See Bradford to JM, 13 October 1772, n. 8.

5 These sermons have not been identified, nor is it known whether or not they ever appeared in print. Since Bradford was at this time in Princeton, JM may here refer to a proposed volume by Witherspoon, who had published sermons on clergymen in Scotland which were subsequently reprinted in America. See Varnum L. Collins, *President Witherspoon*, I, 53–55, and II, 241.

6 Nathaniel Irwin.

7 Thomas McPherrin, College of New Jersey, '70, served as a Presbyterian minister in western Pennsylvania from 1773 until his death in 1802 (Alexander, *Princeton College*, p. 136).

8 On 11 March 1772 the trustees of the College of New Jersey authorized President Witherspoon and Jeremiah Halsey to arrange a lottery at New Castle, Del., for the benefit of the institution. They hoped to net a $15,000 profit after distributing prizes in money, ranging in amount from $10 to $6,000, to the purchasers of tickets bearing lucky numbers to be determined by lot. The drawing finally began on 23 May 1774, after nearly eight months of postponement. Although JM had several good friends among the managers of the lottery, he apparently purchased no tickets. The Bradford paper, the *Pennsylvania Journal*, advertised this so-called "Delaware Lottery for the Benefit of the College of New-Jersey" throughout the summer of 1773, and listed the winners in the 13 July 1774 issue. See also *New Jersey Archives*, 1st ser., XXVIII, 542–43, 602–3; XXIX, 289, 352, 387, 417; John Maclean, *History of the College of New Jersey*, I, 315; Wheaton J. Lane, ed., *Pictorial History of Princeton* (Princeton, 1947), p. 11.

9 Probably Azariah Horton, Jr. (d. 1793), College of New Jersey, '70. Apparently he was a deputy commissary general of musters in the Continental Army during the Revolution (*New Jersey Archives*, 1st ser., XXVII, 267; F. B. Heitman, *Historical Register of Officers of the Continental Army*, p. 229; Alexander, *Princeton College*, p. 135).

10 Probably Caleb Wallace. The nature of JM's "Business" is unknown.

11 This word and the bracketed words in the preceding sentence are either torn from the original or are indecipherable because of an ink blot. They have been inserted here from the copy of the letter in Bradford's commonplace book.

From William Bradford

FC (Historical Society of Pennsylvania).

PHILADA. May 27. 1773.

MY DEAR JEMMY

Tis with pleasure I find myself able to give you ample information concerning your Nassovian Friends, many of whom are now in town attending the Synod. Mr. Ervin has been sometime licensed & I hear is very popular in the back parts of Pennsylvania. He has lately commenced a strict Cadoganite; yet [in] spite of Cadogan his health is much impaired and he seems to be in the first stage of a consumption.[1] Our friend McPherrin[2] is likewise fulminating from the pulpit. He is well and in one of his letters desires to be rememb[e]red to you. As to Breckenridge[3] he is still in Maryland. I lately received a letter from him in which he expresses the tenderest concern for You[r] ill state of Health which I acquaint[ed] him with the last time I wrote. He complains of never hearing from you, tho' he has frequently written—and suppose you cannot find an opportuni[ty.]

Keith,[4] Debow[5] & Allen[6] are now in town applying to the presbetry. I could sincerely wish some way was fallen upon for the good of the church; & to prevent persons from "running their heads against the Pulpit (as Dr South says) who might have done their Country excellent service at the Tail of the plow."[7] For I am verily persuaded that these Gentn. are more capable of being benificial to the state by their hands than by their heads.[8] It will perhaps surprize you to hear that the College has chosen Grier[9] Tutor in the place of Mr Devins[10] who has resigned. But it will surprise you still more to hear that Brian is married to Miss Amelia Horner—nay has been so ever since last summer tho' they never acknowledged it till the Fruits of it appeared in a fine Daughter. He is licensed to plead & is now gone to Baltimore. What could be the reason of his marrying her would be hard to determine. It could not be Love—perhaps it was pity.[11] Indeed I know no place so overstocked with Old-Maids as Princeton. So few are the marriages that one a Stranger would be tempted to think the barbarous Custom of burning the Living with the dead prevailed there as well as in the East.

With regard to my Situation I shall be more explicit in my next. Suffice it to say that I have not yet entered on any particular business but continue the study of History and Morality. I have for a long time been roving thro' the regions of Science without steering any direct course. It is now high time "Contrahere Vela"[12] & to confine myself to some limits and follow some settled method of study. As I am now about forming a *Library* of *Books* which I intend shall be my companions thro' Life, I intend to be very carefull in admitting an unworthy member in it. Could you draw up a list of such books as are proper for a private Gentn. Library you would much oblige me by sending it. If I mistake not you have done it already.[13]

News is at a stand—private scandal excepted—that you know can never want Votaries in so populous a city as this. There is now in the

press a petit-peice 'On the Management of Children" by Cadogan.[14]
When you are married I will send you one—or sooner, if you please
   I am your &c &c

                                    W—B—D.

I have sent *you a* bundel of pamphlets by the posts. I hope *they will*
reach *you*.[15]

---

[1] The Synod of New York and Philadelphia met in Philadelphia, 19–27 May
1773. It was the highest court of the Presbyterian Church in America and all ministers were expected to attend (*Records of the Presbyterian Church in the United
States of America. Embracing the Minutes of the General Presbytery and General
Synod, 1706–1788* [Philadelphia, 1904], pp. 436–49). Dr. William Cadogan (1711–
1797) was an eminent English physician, fellow of the Royal Society and of the
College of Physicians. His booklet, *A Dissertation on Gout, and All Chronic Diseases, Jointly Considered, as Proceeding from the Same Causes; What Those Causes
Are; and a Rational and Natural Method of Cure Proposed—Addressed to All In-
valids*, was published in London in 1771 and immediately achieved wide but short-
lived popularity in both England and America. It was reprinted in Philadelphia in
1771 by William and Thomas Bradford. Dr. Cadogan proposed to cure gout and
other diseases, all said to be caused by indolence, vexation, or intemperance, by
exercise and clean living. Cadogan's fellow physicians criticized his shallowness, and
newspaper humorists derided the simplicity of his prescriptions. "Mr. Erwin" (Nathaniel Irwin), perhaps deriving more benefit from Cadogan's prescriptions than
Bradford thought, lived for nearly forty years after this report of ill health.

[2] Thomas McPherrin.

[3] Hugh Henry Brackenridge.

[4] Robert Keith, College of New Jersey, '72, was an itinerant preacher whose
principal service before his death in 1784 was as a chaplain in the Revolutionary
army (Alexander, *Princeton College*, pp. 153–54).

[5] John Debow (1745–1783), College of New Jersey, '72, was licensed to preach in
1773, and occupied a Presbyterian pulpit in Hawfields, N.C., from that time until
his death (*ibid.*, p. 150).

[6] Moses Allen.

[7] The *Dictionary of National Biography* describes the career of the eminent
Anglican divine, Dr. Robert South (1634–1716). Bradford's quotation from South's
writings should be "another [man] run's his Head against the pulpit, who might
have been very serviceable to his Country at the Plough" (anon. ed., *Maxims, Say-
ings, Explications of Scripture, Phrases, Descriptions and Characters, Extracted
from the Writings of the late Reverend and Learned Dr. South* [London, 1717], p.
35). William Livingston of New York, writing in 1768, made nearly an identical
comment (*Proceedings of the American Philosophical Society*, XCI [1947], 307).

[8] Since Moses Allen was a Cliosophian at Princeton, and Keith and Debow were
probably members of the same society, Bradford's disparaging remarks about them
may reveal more about the heat of the rivalry between Whigs and Clios than about
the quality of the pulpit oratory in question. Bradford unintentionally wrote "being"
twice.

[9] James Grier (1750–1791), College of New Jersey, '72, was licensed by the Phila-
delphia Presbytery in 1775, and was pastor of Deep Run Presbyterian Church, Bucks
County, Pa., from then until his death. His appointment as tutor at the College of
New Jersey lasted only one year (Sprague, *Annals*, III, 466–67).

[10] Richard Devens (1749–1835), College of New Jersey, '67, taught school for

three years following his graduation, before returning to the College of New Jersey as a tutor in mathematics from 1770 to April 1773 and from September 1773 to 1774. He is said to have resigned as a tutor because of insanity brought on by too close application to study. So far as is known, he never recovered his reason (Alexander, *Princeton College*, p. 118; John Maclean, *History of the College of New Jersey*, I, 365; Thomas Bellows Wyman, *The Genealogies and Estates of Charlestown, in the County of Middlesex and Commonwealth of Massachusetts, 1629–1818* [2 vols.; Boston, 1879], I, 291).

[11] This scandalous gossip probably concerned Andrew Bryan, College of New Jersey, '72, and Amy Hornor. Her father, Samuel Hornor, died in 1770 leaving a widow and a family of daughters who were often the subject of comment by College of New Jersey students. Little is known of Bryan except that he was admitted to the bar in Baltimore, and was living there in January 1774. His character was dealt with severely by the pious Andrew Hunter, who probably had in mind the same scandal mentioned by Bradford when he wrote Philip V. Fithian on 26 June 1773: "If infamy were law or lies were Gospel he might get license either to plead or preach" (John R. Williams, ed., *Philip Vickers Fithian*, I, 34–36, 90, 138–39; John F. Hageman, *History of Princeton*, I, 31–33; William Paterson, *Glimpses of Colonial Society and the Life at Princeton College*, ed. by W. Jay Mills [Philadelphia, 1903], p. 123). The child alluded to by Bradford was born on 27 March 1773 and died seventeen months later ("Hornor Genealogical Notes," *Pennsylvania Magazine of History and Biography*, XXII [1898], 385).

[12] *Contrahere Vela* (to draw in [my] sails).

[13] See JM to Bradford, 10 June 1773, n. 5.

[14] William Cadogan, *An Essay Upon Nursing, and the Management of Children, from Their Birth to Three Years of Age* . . . (10th Edition; Reprinted in Boston for Cox and Berry, in King Street, 1772). It was also printed by William and Thomas Bradford in Philadelphia in 1773. This work, first published in London in 1748, was generally considered to be Cadogan's best (*Dictionary of National Biography*, III, 639).

[15] The words in italics are in shorthand in Bradford's notebook. The pamphlets have not been identified.

To William Bradford

Copy (Historical Society of Pennsylvania).

June 10th. —73. ORANGE COUNTY.

MY DEAR FRIEND,

I had the pleasure of Mr Wallace's Company & your letter on Tuesday last.[1] He left me to Day but not without requesting me to make mention of his kind remembrance of you when I should write to you. He professes a warm affection for you and you know the sincerity of his professions. I am much obliged to you for your information concerning my friends. I received a Line or two with yours from Mrss Ervin & McPherrin[2] who confirm what you say of them. I hope the fortitude & Zeal with which they enter on the ministerial Duties will procure them esteem and success. As you have a communication with

Mr Brackinridge tell him I write to him by every opportunity and by no means to ascribe his not hearing from me to any want of affection or endeavours in me; for I often lament our unlucky situation.³ Keith Debow &c I wish well but I adopt your opinion of them and had rather see them at the rustic employment you assign them than in the pulpit. Nevertheless it ought to be acknowledged that spiritual events are not limited or proportioned always to human means; yet granting this in its just extent it must be observed that the best human means should be ever employed otherwise it would look like a lazy presumptious dependance on Providence. Grier is a worthy fellow and I am pleased with his preferment; Tho' his want of Majesty and Oeconomy may be unpromising, he has integrity & Industry two very useful requisites. Poor Brian has been long intoxicating his brain with Idleness & disapation. I hope this larger draught of folly he has now taken will sober him again. I seriously pity him.

The *little* bundle *of* pamphlets *is not yet come to hand. Perhaps they may be yet* lying *at* Fredg.⁴ I *shall be* better able to *inform you* in *my* next *whether they have* miscarried or not. You ask my sentiments on the application of your talents; friendship will not allow me to refuse my advice poor as it is; yet in so delicate & important a matter Prudence requires I should hear from you again before I give it; especially as the list of books you desire will fill up the remainder of my paper. I have selected for you the following out of a Catalogue Dr Witherspoon sent me at my request.⁵ The whole is too large to be transcribed here. You shall have it hereafter if you notify your want of it. [Here *was* the Catalogue.]⁶ So for the Doctor[;] what follows I have occasionally noted for my own use: some of them I have not read[.] you have given me a task for which I am wholly unqualified. If they do not answer you must blame yourself—(The Catalg)[.]⁷ Mr Wallace tell[s] me *you are* very sedate and philosophic which makes me love you better than ever I did: I am so myself.⁸

Farewell

J— M— Jr.

---

¹ Caleb Wallace, who apparently reached Montpelier on 8 June, may have brought with him from Philadelphia Bradford's letter of 27 May to JM. At Wallace's request, the Synod of 1773, mentioned at the outset of that letter, had "dismissed" him from the presbytery of New Brunswick, N.J., "to join one of the southern Presbyteries." The Synod of 1772 had commissioned him to go that autumn as "a supply" for six months to churches in Virginia and the Carolinas, but he had been "providentially prevented" from going (*Records of the Presbyterian Church in the United States of America, 1706–1788*, pp. 434, 438, 439).

² The "Line or two" from Nathaniel Irwin and Thomas McPherrin have not been found.

³ Hugh Henry Brackenridge became a schoolteacher in Somerset County, Md., in the autumn of 1772. No early correspondence between him and JM has been found. Bradford entered "I write to him" twice in his copybook.

⁴ Fredericksburg was on the post road between Philadelphia and Williamsburg, but the postmaster at Fredericksburg had no way to get Orange County mail to its destination unless the persons to whom it was addressed called for it, or unless a trustworthy traveler consented to carry it to them.

⁵ This suggests the extent to which JM continued to seek "the Doctors" guidance in his studies after he left the College of New Jersey. JM's letters to Witherspoon have apparently been lost or destroyed. "The Catalogue" may have been a copy of a booklist, preserved in the Princeton University Library, which is entitled, "A Catalogue of Books belonging to His Excellency Jonathan Belcher Esqr: Captain General & Commander in Chief in and over the Province of Nova Caesarea or New Jersey and Territories thereon depending in America[;] Chancellor and vice Admiral in the same." These volumes, numbering about 250 titles, were given to the College of New Jersey by Belcher in 1755.

⁶ Bradford, rather than JM, evidently inserted this bracketed sentence. By "the Catalogue" he probably meant the books JM listed from it. This list, prepared in response to the request of Bradford in his 27 May letter, has not been found.

⁷ Whether this parenthesis was in JM's original letter or was added by Bradford in his copy of it is not clear. The meaning seems to be that, if Bradford does not find the booklists satisfactory, he must blame himself for seeking inexpert advice. "The Catalg" probably means JM's own list rather than Witherspoon's. It, too, is lost.

⁸ The italicized words in this paragraph are in shorthand in Bradford's copy.

Indenture

Summary (MS in Orange County, Va., Court Records; micro-film copy in the Virginia State Library).

16 June 1773. JM, James Madison, Sr., Ambrose Madison, and Francis Madison were witnesses to a deed of sale of a farm in Orange County to Henry Gaines by William and Mary Daingerfield. These witnesses, with the exception of James Madison, Sr., also attested a receipt whereby William Daingerfield acknowledged that he had been paid £28 by Gaines for the property. Strangely, £78 is the price stated in the indenture. The Daingerfields lived in Spotsylvania County.

From William Bradford

FC (Historical Society of Pennsylvania).

DEAR JEMMY,   ABINGTON¹ August 12th 1773.

I have just returned here from Philada where I have been this week past in a constant hurry occasioned by the marriage of a Sister.² I now sit down to answer your agreeable Letter which I could not do sooner altho I greatly desired it; but I hope you will not follow a bad example but reprove my long delay by an early answer; for as I expect soon to determine what profession I shall engage in for Life I am earnest to have the sentiments of so valuable a friend on that subject before I fix my choice. The chief design of my coming to Mr Treat's[3] where I now am was to have Liberty to examine with attention the several callings in Life; every one has its peculiar inconveniences and I am desirous of obtaining a clear Idea of them, that when I enter into public Life I may know what I have to fear and what to expect.

Could I think myself properly qualified for the ministry I should be at no loss what choice to make, As I have always borne in mind that I was born for others as well as for myself I have always been desirous of being in that station in which I could be of most use to my fellow-creature: And in my opinion a divine may be the most useful as well as the most happy member of society. But as there are some insuperable objections to my entering that state My choice is now divided betwixt Law Physic and Merchandize. If I am rightly acquainted with my own genius it points rather to the first than to either of the others. From my childhood my choice has always [been] hovering betwixt Law & divinity, whereas I have constantly had an aversion to physic & trade. But I hope I have diligence enough to overcome this aversion and make all of them equally agreeable & easy. To consult a childs genius in putting him to business is an old rule which however, I beleive, may often be dispenced with; for besides the difficulty and uncertainty in attaining the knowledge of any one's Genius we should remember the advice of an old Philosopher on this very subject, "Optimum eligi facile & suave illud faciet consuetudo."[4] These consideration[s] determined me not to engage rashly in the Study of the Law but to examine the others callings with impartiality and see (supposing my genius the same for all) which would be the most eligible state. The grand objection urged against Law is, that it is prejudicial to morals. It must indeed be owned that the conduct of the generallity of lawyers is very reproachable but that ought not to make their profession so as it is not the necessary consequence of it. Nor do I think there are more temptations in the study of the Law than in Merchandize. As gain is the sole pursuit of the merchant he is much more likely to contract an inordinate desire of wealth than the Lawyers, whose pursuit is as much after fame as Wealth; indeed they are both improper pursuits yet generosity and Benevolence are the product of the one[;] Extortion & Selfishness of the other. Why should a Lawyer be more dishonest than a Merchant? If he is he certainly mistakes his true interest. Honesty is a surer tho' perhaps a slower way of rising than dishonesty. It leads to reputation and reputation to wealth. Besides as I heard Dr Wither-spoon once observe, a man of known probity will have great weight with the Judges and his very appearing in a cause will influence them in its favour. It is then the Lawyers interest to be honest & next to the divine can there be a more useful member of society than an honest Lawyer. Can there be a nobler character than his whose business it is to support the Laws of his country & to defend the oppresed from the violence of the Oppresor: whose whole Life is spent in actions which tend to the public good, in wiping away the tear from the eye of afflic-tion in bringing offenders to Justice or calming the fears of accused innocence? Yet there is one objection against the Study of the Law which has great weight with me. It is overstocked. This indeed holds equally strong against physic tho' it can never do so against Trade. There is so vast a crowd of competitors that I fear it requires greater abilities, & fortune than I possess to rise above or perhaps keep equall with them. "For tho' every crowd has this peculiar quality that over their heads their is room enough yet how to get there is the difficult point; for (continues the humourous dean) it is as difficult to get quit of number as of Hell." "Evadere ad auras &c"[5]

Thus I have fully given you my sentiments on this subject and now desire your unreserved opinion, which you think the wisest choice Law Physic or Merchandize. Beleive me my friend I do not ask your sentiments to pay you the usual compliment on such occasions. It is probable they will have great influence in determining my choice and I request as a test of your friendship that you will be open and un-reserved.

I had a great many things to tell you when I sat down but I have been led into too great a length already. You shall never have occasion "to reprove me for remissness or brevity." I never finish without relunc-tance. While I am writing to you I feel in a manner, in you[r] com-pany & that was always to[o] agreeable to be soon relinquished. I am pleased with an observation I once met with in the Letters *between*[6] Henry & Frances. ["]Writing releives absence—Tis strange that the very action which marks it most should make us feel it least":[7] but seeing I am forced to conclude I comfort myself with the hopes of hearing soon & frequently from you. Beleive me to be

W— B—d.

1 In Montgomery County, Pa., a few miles north of Philadelphia.

2 On 4 August 1773, Tace Bradford (1747–1828) married Joshua Maddox Wallace. See the Wallace genealogy in the *Pennsylvania Magazine of History and Biography*, VIII (1884), xliv.

3 Reverend Richard Treat (1708–1778), Yale, '25, was the Presbyterian minister at Abington from 1731 until his death (Sprague, *Annals*, III, 100).

4 Bradford should have written: *Optimum elige, suave et facile illud faciet consuetudo* (choose what is best; habit will render it agreeable and easy). Pythagoras is credited with this saying by Plutarch (section 8 of "On Exile" in *Morals*).

5 In the "Introduction" to *A Tale of a Tub*, Jonathan Swift wrote: "Now in all assemblies, though you wedge them ever so close, we may observe this peculiar property, that over their heads there is room enough, but how to reach it is the difficult point; it being as hard to get quit of *number*, as of *hell*;

> —— *evadere ad auras*
> *Hoc opus, hic labor est.*"

In a footnote the Latin (Virgil *Aeneid* vi. 126) is translated to read:

> "But to return, and view the cheerful skies;
> In this the task and mighty labour lies."

See John Hawkesworth, ed., *The Works of Dr. Jonathan Swift, Dean of St. Patrick's, Dublin* (12 vols.; London, 1768), I, 43.

6 Italics indicate use of shorthand symbol by Bradford.

7 [Richard Griffith], *A Series of Genuine Letters between Henry and Frances* (2d ed.; 2 vols.; London, 1761), I, 316. The exact quotation, which "Henry" attributed to Montaigne, reads: "Writing relieves Absence: it is an extraordinary Thing, that the very Action which marks it most, should make us feel it least."

To William Bradford

RC (Historical Society of Pennsylvania). Addressed: "To Mr. William Bradford Junr. at the Coffee House Philadelphia Favd. by the Revd Mr. Erwin." A copy of this letter, made by Bradford, is also at the Historical Society of Pennsylvania.

VIRGINIA ORANGE COUNTY [5 September 1773]

DEAR SIR

If I did not love you too well to scold at you I should begin this with upbraiding your long silence contrary to your express promise and my earnest Solicitations.1 The Bundle of Pamplets you sent by the Post has miscarried[.]2 I would not trouble you with sending them again but perhaps if you would enquire of the Post they might still be discovered. I expect this will be handed to you by Mr. Erwin who has been kind enough to extend his Journey this far whose praise is in every mans mouth Here for an excellent Discourse he this Day preached for us.3 He will let you know every thing that Occurs to me worth mentioning at Commencement or Philadelpha if you should not attend the Commencement.[4] Gratitude to him and friendship to yourself and Others with some Business perhaps will induce me to visit Philaa and Princeton in [the] Spring if I should be alive and should have health sufficient. I set too high a Value on Mr. Erwin's Company to write much to you now and besides have the like office of Friendship to several other Friends.[5]

I am Dr. Sr. Yours most Affectionately
Sept 6th. 1773

JAMES MADISON JUNR.

[1] Bradford's letter of 12 August to JM was still on its way to Montpelier.

[2] See Bradford to JM, 27 May 1773, and JM's reply, 10 June 1773.

[3] Nathaniel Irwin. "This Day" probably means Sunday, 5 September. Without dating this letter at its start, JM apparently wrote it on Sunday. Then, the next day, when he entrusted what he had written to Irwin's care, he added Monday's date at the close of the letter.

[4] Although phrased ambiguously, JM evidently means that Irwin will relay Montpelier news to Bradford either in Philadelphia or at the College of New Jersey commencement on 29 September. On that occasion Irwin received an A.M. degree (*New Jersey Archives*, 1st ser., XXIX, 51–57).

[5] In other words, JM was in a hurry because he wished to write other letters, probably also to be carried by Irwin when he left Montpelier on 6 September for Philadelphia. To whom these other letters were addressed and their present whereabouts are unknown to the editors.

From William Bradford

FC (Historical Society of Pennsylvania).

PHILADA. Sept. 24. —73.

MY DEAR JEMMY,

I was on the point of expostulating with you for you[r] long silence when I receiv'd your[s] of Sept 6 by the hands of our worthy friend mr Ervin.[1] I am surprized & chagrined to find you have not received a letter I wrote about six weeks ago. You may remember you promised to give me you[r] sentiments about my employing my talents provided I explained myself more fully upon that head. Eager to have the advice of so valuable a friend upon a point of so much importance to me, I wrote to you as soon as time would permit & desired a speedy answer. I told you &c &c. [here *was a short* abstract of the last letter].[2] But the careless post it seems not content with losing the Pamphlets has also lost my letter. I hope, however, it may be still lying at Fredg.[3] & should you receive it you will answer it soon; if you should not *this*[4] may perhaps be serviceable to you in giving you[r] opinion which of the Different callings you think I had best follow.

About two month[s] ago I wrote to mr Wallace[5] & according to his orders directed the Letter to your Care. I hope you have received and forwarded it. If that has miscarried too: I know not what I shall do. Mr Wallace has, perhaps already begun to entertain the same disadvantageous opinion of me, which I am afraid my supposed Silence made you entertain. Yet methinks it would have been kinder had my friend attributed his not hearing from me to some other cause than my not writing; for you must not Suppose that I would willingly neglect a correspondence with which my interest and happiness are so nearly connected. However I can forgive you as the indulgence with which you treat the remissness you thought me guilty of gives me a pleasure I sensibly feel.

I would willingly have deffered writing till after commencement which will begin in a few days. But I cannot bear to lay under the imputation of remissness and want of friendship so long. I shall therefor conclude this, as the post is upon the point of setting of[f], with assuring you that I am as much as ever your sincere friend.

W— B—D.

[1] Nathaniel Irwin.
[2] Brackets were inserted by Bradford. Words which he wrote in shorthand are italicized. In late September, JM finally received the letter of 12 August from which Bradford evidently included an extract in the present letter.
[3] See JM to Bradford, 10 June 1773, n. 4.
[4] Underlined by Bradford.
[5] Caleb Wallace.

To William Bradford

Copy (Historical Society of Pennsylvania).

Septr. 25th 1773.

MY DEAR FRIEND

I received yours of the 12 August and give you this repeated Testimony of my punctuality. I got your letter to Mr Wallace at the same time much worn and abused. I have given it a new coat & shall forward it as soon as a safe Opportunity serves.

Since you first hinted to me your suspence as to the settled business of your life, I have partook of your anxiety & [though it][1] has been often in my thoughts I feel a backwardness to offer my opinion in so critical a matter and the more so for the weight you are pleased to give it. I have too much esteem and affection for you and am too conscious of my want of capacity and experience to direct in so important an Affair. I must therefore premise that it is my earnest request that you would act the candid open friend as well as in rejecting as in asking advice; for I consult nothing but your real interest, and am sensible of my insufficiency to be a counsellor much more a preceptor. You forbid any recommendation of Divinity by suggesting that you have insuperable objections therefore I can only condole with the Church on the loss of a fine Genius and persuasive Orator. I cannot however suppress thus much of my advice on that head that you would always keep the Ministry obliquely in View whatever your profession be. This will lead you to cultivate an acquaintace occasionally with the most sublime of all Sciences and will qualify you for a change of public character if you should hereafter desire it. I have sometimes thought there could not be a stronger testimony in favor of Religion or against temporal Enjoyments even the most rational and manly than for men who occupy the most honorable and gainful departments and are rising in reputation and wealth, publicly to declare their unsatisfatoriness by becoming fervent Advocates in the cause of Christ, & I wish you may give in your Evidence in this way. Such Instances have seldom occurred, therefore they would be more striking and would be instead of a "Cloud of Witnesses.["]² If I am to speak my Sentiments of Merchandize, Physic and Law I must say they are all honorable and usefull professions and think you ought to *have*³ more regard to their Suitableness to your Genius than to their comparative Excellence. As far as I know your endowments I should pronounce Law the most eligeble. *It*⁴ alone can bring into use many parts of knowledge you have acquired and will still have a taste for, & pay you for cultivating the Arts of Eloquence. It is a sort of General Lover that wooes all the Muses and Graces. This cannot be said so truly of commerce and Physic & therefore less Learning & smaller understanding will do for them. The objection founded on the number of Lawyers should stimulate to Assiduity rather than discourage the Attempt. I greatly commend your determined adherence to probity and Truth in the Character of a Lawyer but fear it would be impracticable. Misrepresentation from a client or intricacy in a cause must often occasion doubt and ignorance till the matter has been considerably debated at the bar; Though it must be allowed there are a thousand cases in which your rule would be safe and highly commendable. I must add after all that if you should enter on a mercantile State (to which peculiar reasons for ought I know may advise)[5] I should be loth to disapprove.

Mr Wallace is not yet settled. He meditate[s] a tour to the South about the last of October which will take up several months I imagine. These few *particulars* I receivd by a letter from him about three weeks ago.[6]

As you have access to New books & have frequent accounts from home, I should be thankfull if you would let me know whenever you light on any worth recommending to a friend. I expect in your next to have a narrative of College affairs and such [other things] as you could not crowd in your last.[7]

We have a very great scarcity of circulating cash in this colony which has reduced the price of provisions & other commodites more than half: I do not meddle with Politicks but this Calamity lies so near the heart of every friend of the Country that I could not but mention it.[8] I do not often write to you in haste but it has happened so now & you must excuse it for it is far from being owing to any Abatement of the Friendship & Affection of Your old &c.

JM JNR.

[1] Probably inadvertently, Bradford wrote "thought is" in his copybook.

[2] Hebrews 12:1. Bradford's copy omits the second quotation mark. By his praise of the Christian ministry JM may imply that it would be his own preferred career if his health improved.

[3] In shorthand in Bradford's copy.

[4] Underlined by Bradford.

[5] Bradford's father and brother had a large printing establishment and bookstore in Philadelphia.

[6] The italicized word is in shorthand in Bradford's copy. Wallace's letter to JM has not been found. Wallace, who was still without a pastorate, planned to comply with an order of the Synod of New York and Philadelphia that he "supply" in the Hawfields and Eno churches in North Carolina and "visit St. Paul's parish in Georgia and preach there some time." Early in 1774, the Hanover Presbytery, Va., licensed Wallace for service there (*Records of the Presbyterian Church in the United States of America, 1706–1788*, pp. 448, 451, 452).

[7] Bradford wrote "others thing." Bradford was at Princeton working for the A.M. degree which the College of New Jersey would confer upon him in September 1775 (*New Jersey Archives*, 1st ser., XXXI, 206). Both his father's business and his own residence on a college campus afforded him unusual opportunity to know about "New books" from "home," that is, England.

[8] Here JM appears to say, almost apologetically, that only the severity of the economic pinch in Virginia could excuse him for mentioning so mundane a subject as "Politicks." This aloofness, manifest in all his surviving correspondence up to this date, and his absorption in matters literary and philosophical were to yield quickly, following the news of the Boston Tea Party (16 December 1773) and its aftermath, to an intense concern about the course of the controversy with the English government.

From William Bradford

FC (Historical Society of Pennsylvania).

PHILADA. Novr. 5th. 1773.

MY DEAR FRIEND,

Your last reached me in a very happy *time*[1] *as I was on the* point of determining what profession *I would* choose & absolutely fixing my choice which had *long been* wavering *between law* & trade! As your *sentiments* coincided with those of *my* [other] *friends*[2] *I have* begun *the study of the law* & intend agreeable to your advice to cultiv[ate in][3] every vacant hour an acquaintance with *divinity* tho at present *I have* no expectations *of a* change of *public character*. Yet in a place *where* deistical *sentiments* almost universally prevail I look upon it as absolutely *necessary* to be *able to defend as well as believe*[4] the *Christian religion. I am studying under* Mr E. Shippen[5] & at present am reading Blackstone Commentaries on the Laws of England *which I am most* pleased *with* & find *but little* of that disagreeable dryness I was taught to expect.

I can give *you but little information with regard to the* affairs of College *which however I believe are in* a flourishing way. I can only say *that the* late commencement did honour to the Graduates & *will* probably *increase the* reputation of Nassau-Hall as *there was* a *very* numerous & polite assembly composed of persons *from all parts of the* Continent.

I *think* I told *you* in a former *letter that* Mr Devins had resigned his Tutorship & retired to New-England. There he spent the summer in galloping pegasus[6] and publishing poems. He has now taken refuge again in the arms of his Alma Mater & was elected Tutor[7] in *the* pla[ce] of Mr Smith[8] who has resigned. Dr Witherspoon & Mr Houston are *by now* [?][9] gone to the southard & so you will probably see one or both of them.

I have the pleasure to inform you that Mr Ervin has a Call from Neshaminy (about 20 miles from *this place*) which I make no doubt but he will accept.[10] I hope Mr Smith may be as well settled. He preached here some time ago & was much liked. His sermon was indeed ingenious & instructive but there was a Luxuriance in it that greatly needed Phocion's pruning knife.[11] This however is a fault that age will correct.

While *you* are complaining of a want of circulating cash we complain of a redundancy. There are now abroad [a] vast number of false dollars so ingeniously counterfieted as scarcely to be distinguished from the genuine. There is also a great quantity of counterfieted Bill[s] made by one ford & uttered by several gentlemen of family & fortune in New Jersey. Can we blame the poor wretches who counterfiet the Coin thro' dread of Poverty when even the "Ministers of Justice," of ample fortunes are detected in doing it.[12]

I have *indeed many* opportunities of consulting the English papers & *know what* books are published but can seldom learn their Character. I would therefore advise you to take the monthly review[13] which will give *you* an account of all the books *which are* published in London & extracts from them: so that if *you do not* chuse to depend upon their Judgment you may judge for yourself. The post will set of[f] very soon & lest I should miss sending this letter, now I must conclude some-what abruptly: If I can oblige you in any manner I beg you will com-mand me freely. To oblige a friend is obliging myself. When you write to Mr Wallace remember me to him

And be assured my Dr Sir that I am yours &c.

W— B—ᴅ

I have sent a few phamplets by Mr Wilkinson[14] which I hope *you will* receive.

[1] This word and the many other italicized words in this letter, unless otherwise noted, were written in shorthand by Bradford in his copybook. For comment about his shorthand, see Bradford to JM, 1 March 1773, n. 11.

[2] Although the shorthand symbols used here by Bradford stand only for "my friends," he either unintentionally omitted the symbol for "other" or felt it was too obvious to include.

[3] The editors have added the bracketed letters, presuming that they are what Bradford intended to write.

[4] The words "defend" and "believe" are italicized because Bradford underlined them for emphasis, but he used shorthand for "as well as."

[5] Edward Shippen (1729–1806), member of a prominent Philadelphia family, was a provincial councilor and a distinguished lawyer and judge, who became chief justice of the Supreme Court of Pennsylvania in 1799. His daughter, Margaret, married Benedict Arnold. Shippen was so highly regarded for his learning and integrity that his mild loyalism during the Revolution did not prejudice the suc-cess of his later career (*Dictionary of American Biography*, XVII, 116–17).

[6] That is, writing poems.

[7] Suffering from temporary attacks of insanity, Richard Devens was obliged to resign from the faculty permanently in 1774.

[8] After three years on the faculty, Samuel Stanhope Smith accepted a pastorate in Virginia.

[9] The meaning of Bradford's shorthand symbol is not clear.

[10] Nathaniel Irwin not only accepted the call but continued to be Presbyterian pastor at Neshaminy until his death in 1812.

11 Phocion, Athenian statesman and general, countered the expansive eloquence of Demosthenes with a blunt recital of "plain facts" about the military weakness of his city.

12 Between 1768 and 1773, Samuel Ford, a New Jersey ironmaster, skilfully forged various paper currency issues of New York, New Jersey, and Pennsylvania. His arrest in Morris County, N.J., in July 1773, his escape, his avoidance of recapture during a far-flung and exciting chase, and the trials and sentencing to death of several of his real or alleged accomplices, were much in the news. Popular excitement was the greater because "ministers of justice" charged Ford and his band with stealing over £6,000 from the New Jersey treasury in 1768. Perhaps with justification, many people believed that the actual culprits in this instance were high-placed colonial officials (*New Jersey Archives*, 1st ser., XXVIII and XXIX, *passim*; Kenneth Scott, *Counterfeiting in Colonial America* [New York, 1957], pp. 239–51; Andrew M. Sherman, *Historic Morristown, New Jersey: The Story of Its First Century* [Morristown, 1905], pp. 117–38).

13 Bradford probably refers to *The Monthly Review* (1749–1845), an influential literary magazine, "printed for R. Griffiths" in London.

14 Probably John Wilkinson (*ca.* 1741–1813), proprietor of the Albemarle Furnace Company, which he founded in 1771. During the Revolutionary War he was commissioned by the state to repair and operate other ironworks in the county. He probably still had business connections in Pennsylvania which required occasional trips northward, for in 1769 he had been in partnership with James Old, an ironmaster in Lancaster County, Pa. (Edgar Woods, *Albemarle County in Virginia* ... [Charlottesville, 1901], pp. 56–57).

To William Bradford

Copy (Historical Society of Pennsylvania).

Dec. 1. 1773.

MY KIND FRIEND

I have had the gratification of receiving both your letters, and the Pamphlets[1] sent by Wilkinson. It is a reflection I am naturally led into whenever I write to you that I always have occasion to be returning my thanks for some kindness received without being able to retaliate. Gratitude is the only fund I can pay you out of which I am sensible your generosity accepts as sufficient: but at the same time Friendship likes it not to be behind hand in favours. My Consolation *however*[2] is that if I am in debt, it is to a liberal Benefactor who thinks as little of his friendly offices as I think much of my Deficiencies.

I am glad you have rescued yourself from your anxiety and suspence and have come to a determination to engage in the study of the Law, which I hope you had better reasons for chusing[3] than I could suggest. I intend myself to read Law occasionally and have procured books for that purpose so that you need not fear offending me by Allusions to that science. Indeed any of your remarks as you go along would afford me entertainment and instruction. The principles & Modes of Government are too important to be disregarded by an Inquisitive mind and I think are well worthy [of] a critical examination by all students that have health & Leisure. I should be well pleased with a scetch of the plan you have fixed upon for your studies, the books & the order you intend to read them in; and when you have obtained sufficient insight into the Constitution of your Country and can make it an amusement to yourself send me a draught of its Origin & fundamental principals of Legislation; particularly the extent of your religious Toleration. Here allow me to propose the following Queries. Is an Ecclesiastical Establishment absolutely necessary to support civil society in a supream Government? & how far it is hurtful to a dependant State? I do not ask for an immediate answer but mention them as worth attending to in the course of your reading and consulting experienced Lawyers & Politicians upon. When you have satisfied yourself in these points I should listen with pleasure to the Result of your reserches.[4]

You recommend sending for the Reviews as the best way to know the present State of Literature and the Choicest Books published. This I have done and shall continue to do: but I find them loose in their principals [and] encourage[r]s of free enquiry even such as destroys the most essential Truths, Enemies to serious religion[5] & extreamly partial in their Citations, seeking them rather to Justify their censures and Commendations than to give the reader a just specimen of the Authors genius. I can rely with greater confidence on you[r] judgment after you have read the Authors or have known their Character from you[r] judicious friends. I am meditating a Journey to Philada which I hope to accomplish early in the spring if no unforeseen hindrances stop me. I shall bring a brother with me to put to school somewhere there, perhaps at Mr Smith's.[6] I need not say how far the desire of seeing you and others is a powerful Inducement and that my imagination daily anticipates the pleasure of this Tour. *who* were *the authors of the* Sermons *you sent* me? *what is the* exchange with *you* now & *what is* it likely *to be in the* spring? Write speedily & forgive my troublesome questions, I am Dr Sir, Your &c.

JM JUNR.

---

[1] Judging from JM's query at the close of this letter, several of these unidentified pamphlets were anonymously published sermons.

[2] Bradford used shorthand for the italicized words in this letter.

[3] In his letter to Bradford, JM may have written "engaging in" because these words appear in the copybook. But Bradford then crossed them out and sub-

stituted "chusing." On the study of law, see above, editorial note on Salkeld, 1771–1774.

4 These are JM's earliest known comments upon a subject which, within a few years, would importantly affect his rise to Virginia-wide, and still later to national, prominence. In 1773 he apparently was beginning to doubt the truth of the axiom that a state church served as an indispensable bulwark of the British Crown, and was already searching for definite evidence that the Anglican establishment in Virginia infringed the rightful liberties of its citizens. Here again, as in his mention of falling prices and politics to Bradford earlier that autumn (25 September 1773), JM apparently could not, or no longer wished to, resist the intrusion of contemporary issues upon his studies. Perhaps, also, this growing interest in the world about him signified that his health had improved.

5 These views, so sharply at odds with JM's later championship of freedom of religion, speech, and the press, may reflect the lingering influence of Dr. Witherspoon's teaching. Students' notes taken between 1772 and 1775 on Witherspoon's "Moral Philosophy, Rhetoric and Eloquence" lectures, now preserved in the Princeton University Library, include warnings against reading ephemeral works dangerous to sound religion and morality.

6 Probably Reverend Robert Smith (1723–1793), a trustee of the College of New Jersey, father of JM's friend and tutor, Reverend Samuel Stanhope Smith, and head of an excellent preparatory school at Pequea, Lancaster County, Pa. (Sprague, *Annals*, III, 172–75). For reasons unknown, JM's father finally decided to enroll his son William (1762–1843) in the preparatory school at Princeton.

From William Bradford

FC (Historical Society of Pennsylvania).

PHILADA. Dec. 25. 1773.

MY DEAR SIR,

The gratefull manner in which you mention *the*[1] few trifles I sent you gives me a most sensible pleasure as it [is][2] a new proof of you[r] friendship. Beleive me my freind I esteem it [a] favor that you put it in my power to oblige; & therefore the best way of showing your gratitude will be to command me freely when I have it in my power to serve you.

I am glad to hear you intend to cultivate an acquaintance with the Law as I promise myself much pleasure and improvement from your remarks upon it. I agree with you that every gentleman who has health & Leisure ought to have a tolerable acquaintance with the Laws & constitution of his Country: yet it is no uncommon thing to find persons of rank & fortune who are utter strangers to both. Blackstone remarks (and every man who is conversant with the world remarks) that there is no nation under heaven that have so valuable a constitution as the English & no nation who [are] so ignorant of the constitution of their

Country.[3] 'Tis in this point I find myself very deficient & I verily beleive I know more of the constitution of Antient Greece & Rome than
of *that* of Great-Britain. This was owing to my ignorance of the English History which I had determined (rashly indeed) not to read till I
had read all that precceeded it. I finding it impossible to be an universal
Historian I propose[4] reading Hume History as soon as time will permit.[5]

I am at present endeavouring to gain an insight into *the* Practice of
our Courts & therefore have not time to investigate the principles of
Government & the English constitution with that accuracy I intend
hereafter to do. Any Question you may propose on that subject will be
highly acceptable: not that I can give you a satisfactory answer, but
because it will make me attend to points, which tho important, I might
pass over without paying the attention they deserve. You will Give me
Liberty in my turn to consult you on any difficulty I may meet with
& thus make your correspondence as instructive as entertaining. Scipio
used daily to thank the Gods that they had introduced him to the Acquaintance of Polybius;[6] nor have I less reason to be thankful that I
once enjoyed your company and now you[r] correspondence.

Mr Breckingridge is well & still in Maryland[7] Mr Freneau passed
thro' here a few days ago but I could not get a sight of him. He intends sailing next spring for England to take Orders.[8] All your friends
this way are well. But I am sorry to inform you that you have lost another of your fellow-Graduates; I mean Neddy Chesman.[9] His exit
was very sudden. He took to his bed on Sunday Evening & the next
Saturday was a Corps. Tis just too weeks since he died.

I have enquired & find the Exchange to be at 79. but it is probable it
will be lower in the spring. I will inform you how it is, should I write
again before I see you. I need not tell you what pleasure Your intention of coming this way gives me. Pray do not let any thing but absolute Necessity frustrate it.

I enclose you an account of the Destruction of the Tea at Boston.[10]
We have taken a more gentle but full as effectual a method of avoiding
the duty. [Th(en) an account of the Arrival of Capt Ayers, treatment
of him & his departure.][11]

I am Dr Sir

W B Junr

---

[1] Italicized words were written in shorthand by Bradford in his copybook.
[2] Bradford had repeated "it."
[3] Bradford might have largely justified this comment by citing William Black-

stone, *Commentaries on the Laws of England* (4 vols.; Oxford, 1765–69), I, 5–6, 51–52.

4 Bradford wrote "have con-" at the bottom of one page and "propose" at the top of a new page of his copybook.

5 David Hume, *The History of England, from the Invasion of Julius Caesar to the Revolution in 1688* (5 vols.; London, 1754–62). Judging from his diaries, preserved by the Historical Society of Pennsylvania, Bradford did not find time to read this work until May and June 1776.

6 Although they are not altogether pertinent, Bradford may have had in mind the remarks attributed to Scipio Africanus the Younger by Cicero in his *De republica* i. 21 and ii. 14; also *The Histories of Polybius*, chap. xxxi, line 24.

7 Hugh Henry Brackenridge continued as headmaster of a school in Somerset County, Md., until 1776.

8 Philip Freneau, having given up his teaching position at Brackenridge's school, was probably on his way north when he passed through Philadelphia. Although he studied theology in 1773–1774, he never went to England to be ordained as an Anglican clergyman (Lewis Leary, *That Rascal Freneau,* pp. 45–52).

9 For Edmund Cheeseman's participation in the graduating exercises of the class of 1771, see *New Jersey Archives*, 1st ser., XXVII, 583–84.

10 Bradford probably inclosed a newspaper clipping telling about the Boston Tea Party of 16 December 1773.

11 The brackets are in Bradford's copybook. The "en" is an editorial insert. In his letter to JM, Bradford likely told him that the arrival on Christmas day in the Delaware River of Captain Ayres and his ship, "Polly," loaded with East India Company tea, gave many Philadelphians a welcome opportunity to express by forceful action their unrestrained enthusiasm over the news of the Boston Tea Party. With Bradford's father as perhaps their chief leader, they warned Captain Ayres that, although he might replenish his ship's stores, he could only avoid a coat of tar and feathers by speedily betaking himself, his vessel, and its tea, back to sea. This the captain did on 27 December. Bradford dated his letter 25 December but evidently waited to post it until the afternoon of the 27th or later (Frederick D. Stone, "How the Landing of Tea Was Opposed in Philadelphia by Colonel William Bradford and Others in 1773," *Pennsylvania Magazine of History and Biography*, XV [1891], 385–93; J. Thomas Scharf and Thompson Westcott, *History of Philadelphia*, I, 285–87).

To William Bradford

RC (Historical Society of Pennsylvania). Addressed: "To Mr. William Bradford Junr. at the Coffee-House Philadelphia." Bradford's copybook version is also at the Historical Society of Pennsylvania.

Jan 24. 1774

MY WORTHY FRIEND,

Yours of the 25 of last month came into my hands a few days past. It gave singular pleasure not only because of the kindness expressed in it but because I had reason to apprehend the letter you recd. last from me had miscarried and I should fail in procuring the intelligence I wanted before the Trip I design in the Spring.[1]

I congratulate you on your heroic proceedings in Philada. with regard to the Tea. I wish Boston may conduct matters with as much discretion as they seem to do with boldness: They seem to have great Tryals and difficulties by reason of the obduracy and *ministerialism* of their Governour.[2] However Political Contests are necessary sometimes as well as military to afford excercise and practise and to instruct in the Art of defending Liberty and property. I verily believe the frequent Assaults that have been made on America[,] Boston especially [,] will in the end prove of real advantage. If the Church of England had been the established and general Religion in all the Northern Colonies as it has been among us here and uninterrupted tranquility had prevailed throughout the Continent, It is clear to me that slavery and Subjection might and would have been gradually insinuated among us. Union of Religious Sentiments begets a surprizing confidence and Ecclesiastical Establishments tend to great ignorance and Corruption all of which facilitate the Execution of mischievous Projects.[3] But away with Politicks! Let me address you as a Student and Philosopher & not as a Patriot now. I am pleased that you are going to converse with the Edwards and Henry's & Charles &c&c who have swayed the British Sceptre though I believe you will find some of them dirty and unprofitable Companions unless you will glean Instruction from their follies and fall more in love with Liberty by beholding such detestable pictures of Tyranny and Cruelty.[4] I was afraid you would not easily have loosened your Affections from the Belles Lettres. A Delicate Taste and warm imagination like yours must find it hard to give up such refined & exquisite enjoyments for the coarse and dry study of the Law: It is like leaving a pleasant flourishing field for a barren desert; perhaps I should not say barren either because the Law does bear fruit but it is sour fruit that must be gathered and pressed and distilled before it can bring pleasure or profit. I perceive I have made a very awkward Comparison but I got the thought by the end and had gone to[o] far to quit it before I perceived that it was too much entangled in my brain to run it through. And so you must forgive it. I myself use to have too great a hankering after those amusing Studies. Poetry wit and Criticism Romances Plays &c captivated me much: but I begin [to] discover that they deserve but a moderate portion of a *mortal's*[5] Time. and that something more substantial more durable more profitable befits a riper Age. It would be exceeding improper for a labouring man to have nothing but flowers in his Garden or to determine to eat nothing but sweet-meats and Confections. Equally absurd would it be for a Scholar and man of Business to make up his whole Library with Books of Fancy and feed his Mind with nothing but such Luscious performances

When you have an Opportunity and write to Mr. Brackinridge pray tell him I often think of him and long to see him and am resolved to do so in the Spring.[6] George Luckey was with me at Christmas and we talked so much about old Affairs & Old Friends that I have a most insatiable desire to see you all. Luckey will accompany me and we are to set off on the 10th. of April if no disa[s]ter befalls either of us.[7] I want again to breathe your free Air. I expect it will mend my Constitution & confirm my principles. I have indeed as good an Atmosphere at home as the Climate will allow: but have nothing to brag of as to the State and Liberty of my Country. Poverty and Luxury prevail among all sorts: Pride ignorance and Knavery among the Priesthood and Vice and Wickedness among the Laity. This is bad enough But It is not the worst I have to tell you. That diabolical Hell conceived principle of persecution rages among some and to their eternal Infamy the Clergy can furnish their Quota of Imps for such business. This vexes me the most of any thing whatever. There are at this [time?] in the adjacent County not less than 5 or 6 well meaning men in close Goal for publishing their religious Sentiments which in the main are very orthodox.[8] I have neither patience to hear talk or think of any thing relative to this matter, for I have squabbled and scolded abused and ridiculed so long about it, [to so lit]tle purpose that I am without common patience.[9] So I [leave you] to pity me and pray for Liberty of Conscience [to revive among us.][10]

I expect to hear from you once more before I see you if time will admit: and want to know when the Synod meets & where:[11] What the Exchange is at and as much about my friends and other Matters as you can and think worth notice. Till I see you Adieu.

JM

NB Our Correspondence is too far advanced to req[uire a]pologies for bad writing & [b]lots.

January 24. 1774

Your Letter to Mr. Wallace is in my hands and shall be forwarded as soon as possible. I hear nothing from him by Letter or fame.[12]

[1] See JM to Bradford, 1 December 1773.

[2] Governor Thomas Hutchinson (1711–1780), who five months later would be superseded by General Thomas Gage. "Ministerialism" connoted subservience to the Lord North ministry rather than true loyalty to the king.

[3] In this paragraph, JM appears to take a middle-of-the-road position toward England's policies. He counterbalances his wish that the Bostonians would temper their boldness with more discretion by implying that his fellow Virginians should mix some boldness with their oversupply of discretion.

[4] What English histories, if any, JM had read is unknown, but he could have come to associate monarchs with tyranny, cruelty, and follies by his study of the *Memoirs of Cardinal de Retz* (above, Commonplace Book, 1759–1772).

[5] JM underlined this word. The period after the next word should have been a comma, and Bradford made the correction in his copybook version.

[6] How or where JM expected to see Brackenridge, who was isolated in his school near the southern boundary of Maryland's eastern shore, is not clear. Brackenridge, however, was still a candidate for an A.M. degree from the College of New Jersey (Claude M. Newlin, *Hugh Henry Brackenridge*, pp. 25–27). For this reason JM may have hoped to meet him in Philadelphia or Princeton.

[7] Luckey, like other candidates for ordination as Presbyterian clergymen in the early 1770's, was probably on an itinerant preaching mission. JM's cordial mention of him contrasts sharply with the opinion expressed in his letter of 9 November 1772 to Bradford (*q.v.*).

[8] Near the beginning of this sentence JM either left out a word or words between "this" and "in" or, as Bradford assumed when transcribing the letter into his copybook, meant the "in" to be "and." Although the unaccustomed fervor displayed by JM in this passage, together with some stronger evidence from other sources (Lewis Peyton Little, *Imprisoned Preachers and Religious Liberty in Virginia* [Lynchburg, 1938], pp. 127–40, 516–21), suggests that he was witnessing "persecution" close by Montpelier, the editors think he more likely had only "the adjacent county" of Culpeper in mind. There, in 1773–1774, flagrant intolerance led to the imprisonment of a half-dozen Baptist preachers (Robert B. Semple, *A History of the Rise and Progress of the Baptists in Virginia* [1810], revised and extended by Reverend G. W. Beale [Richmond, 1894], pp. 382, 481–84).

[9] Judging from this statement, JM was already conspicuous in his own locality as a defender of religious dissenters. In a brief autobiography which he sent to James K. Paulding in 1832, he declared that he was "under very early and strong impressions in favor of liberty both Civil and Religious. His devotion to the latter found a particular occasion for its exercise in the persecution instituted in his County as elsewhere, against the preachers belonging to the sect of Baptists. . . . Notwithstanding the enthusiasm which contributed to render them obnoxious to sober public opinion, as well as the laws then in force, against Preachers dissenting from the Established Religion, he spared no exertion to save them from imprisonment, and to promote their release from it. This interposition, tho' a mere duty prescribed by his conscience, obtained for him a lasting place in the favor of that particular sect." Fortunately, he concluded, American independence brought with it religious freedom (LC: William C. Rives Papers). Apparently it was religious issues, more than tax and trade regulation disputes with England, which were rapidly luring JM away from his beloved studies and arousing his interest in contemporary politics.

[10] The bracketed words in this and the preceding sentence, illegible in the original letter, were taken from Bradford's copybook version. William C. Rives, one of the anonymous editors of the Congressional edition of JM's papers, made the

sentence say: "So I must beg you to pity me, and pray for liberty of conscience to all" (Madison, *Letters* [Cong. ed.], I, 12). Rives sometimes made improper alterations in JM's phraseology, but it is possible that here the handwriting may have been less faded when he read it than it is now. In any event, JM clearly wrote "Liberty of Conscience" instead of the expression "religious Toleration" used by him in his letter to Bradford on 1 December 1773. If JM in each instance took special care to state exactly what he meant, he had moved to a significantly more liberal position during the month intervening between these two letters.

[11] The Synod of New York and Philadelphia of the Presbyterian Church convened in Philadelphia on 18 May 1774.

[12] "Fame" in the eighteenth century frequently signified "public report or rumor" rather than "eminence." If Bradford's letter to Caleb Wallace is the same one mentioned by JM in his letter of 25 September 1773, Wallace's whereabouts in North Carolina or Georgia must have been unknown to JM (JM to Bradford, 25 September 1773, n. 6).

From William Bradford

FC (Historical Society of Pennsylvania).

March 4. 1774. PHILADA.

DEAR SIR,

I purposely delayed answering yours of January 24th to this time that I might be better able to give you the Intelligence you wanted. I hope however it will reach you before you set out and perhaps time enough to be answered.

I agree with you that a Student of Law should not to[o] much indulge his taste for polite-Learning as it has a tendency to make the mind averse to severer Studies. Yet the Lawyer as well as the Divine has this advantage that every kind of Learning will be *benificial*[1] to him in his profession: where as to most others it can at best be but ornamental. Some parts of the Law are indeed dry & disagreeable enough; but you should not call it a barren Study—Far from it: It bears *Golden* fruit, my friend. Rather say the Belles letters are unprofitable—

"For what's the worth of any thing
"But as much money as 'twill bring."   Butler.[2]

Or allow it to be a barren study; even then it will but the more resemble those cou[n]tries that abound [in] Gold:[3] It is this that attracts so many to engage in the profession & that makes them pore over the dry Pages of Littleton and Coke[4] with more pleasure than those of Homer or Cicero. They had rather with Eneas seek the *Golden* branch, even in a *desert*, then loll on the sides of Parnassus tho' surrounded with flowers.[5] Helicon may be pure and refreshing indeed but 'tis Patoclus with his golden sands that has charms for them.[6] But for my own Part I must confess that with all this *rich* encouragement I cannot apply myself so closely as I would wish to do: but I hope that as I advance the journey will be plesanter.

I received a Letter a few days ago from Finley[7] in which he tells me that Breckenridge is sick and the disorder he labours under a dangerous one: But the ludicrous manner in which he mentions it inclines me to think it is not so bad as he would have me imagine.[8] Of Ervin Mr McPherrin &c I have hear[d] nothing new.[9] Doctor Witherspoon was down a few days past & informed me that Dod was married to a Girl in Brunswick: but he put the Cart before the horse: he was a father before he was an husband. I beleive it was the Girls friends that forced the Old fellow's head in the noose.[10] Linn is married to one of the Daughters of that Mr Blair who resided some time at Princeton.[11] 'Tis said Reese intends to follow the example but (to use the news-paper stile) this wants confirmation.[12]

I am sorry to hear that Persecution has got so much footing among you. The discription you give of your Country makes me more in love with mine. Indeed I have ever looked on America as the land of freedom when compared with the rest of the world, but compared with the rest of america Tis Pennsylvania that is so. Persecution is a weed that grows not in our happy soil: and I do no[t] remember that any Person was ever imprisoned here for his religious sentiments however heritical or unepiscopal they might be. Liberty (As Caspipina says in his Letters) [is] the Genius of Pennsylvania; and it[s] inhabitants think speak and act with a freedom unknow[13]——I do indeed pity you; & long to see you according to your own expression, "breathing our purer air." The Synod will meet here about the middle of may.[14] You will then have an opportunity of seeing most of your Nassovian friends, and higthing[15] the felicity that friends long seperated enjoy when they meet.

We have several publications here the cheif of which is, "Caspipina Letters." It is conjectured they are written by Mr Duche: for the Author in one place says, "My name contains the Initials of my Profession" & signs his Letters Tamoccaspipina, which is thus decyphered. ["]The Assistant Minister Of Christ Church And St. Peters In Philadelphia In North America—That is, Mr Duche."[16] I have not yet read them with attention but as far as I can judge they a[re] very *pretty*.[17] You shall have one when you visit us.

I am impatient to see you & will write no more as it reminds me you are yet afar of[f]. But must conclude *with*[18] assuri[n]g you That I am &c

                                                        WBJUNR.

[1] Bradford underlined this word in his copybook.

[2] Samuel Butler, *Hudibras*, Part II, Canto I, lines 465–66. If Bradford had quoted accurately he would have written.

> "For what is *Worth* in any Thing,
> But so much *money* as 'twill bring?"

[3] Bradford wrote "it Gold" instead of "in Gold." At this point in his copybook, Bradford bracketed and crossed out a passage following the colon, as well as a succeeding sentence. The former reads: "for naturalists tell us that the more any place abounds in that precious metal the more wild & barren it is." The sentence, however, is too heavily inked out to be legible.

[4] Sir Edward Coke, *The First Part Of The Institutes of the Lawes of England, Or, A Commentarie upon Littleton* [Sir Thomas Littleton] *not the name of a Lawyer onely, but of the Law it selfe* (2d ed.; London, 1629).

[5] Virgil *Aeneid* vi. 141–48, 203–11.

[6] Bradford's mention of Patroclus, the close friend of Achilles whom Hector slew outside the walls of Troy, is far-fetched. Bradford seems to mean that the Greeks mainly sought rich spoil when they besieged Troy. He probably had read Alexander Pope's translation of Homer's *Iliad* xx. 100. Here, although not referring directly to Patroclus, Homer mentioned the "golden sands" of the Scamander River near Troy. The mercenary emphasis of this paragraph may have shocked JM by its sharp contrast with the disdain of money-chasing expressed by Bradford in his letter of 12 August 1773 (*q.v.*). His altered attitude, however, was perhaps merely a pose congenial to his penchant for satire and literary allusions rather than reliable evidence that he had come to accept a financial standard as the principal gauge of a successful career.

[7] Ebenezer Finley (1754–*ca.* 1790), College of New Jersey, '72, was the eldest son of Samuel Finley, president of the college from 1761 to 1766. Ebenezer Finley is incorrectly reported to have become a doctor in Charleston, S.C. (Alexander, *Princeton College*, p. 151). Actually, he moved to the Ohio country (information from Office of the Secretary, Princeton University).

[8] Brackenridge had been ill earlier in the year but by March was well on the road toward recovery (Claude M. Newlin, *Hugh Henry Brackenridge*, pp. 26–27).

[9] Nathaniel Irwin and Thomas McPherrin.

[10] "Dod" was probably Thaddeus Dod (1740–1793) who was "old" when he began his theological studies shortly after his graduation in 1773 from the College of New Jersey. Sprague's statement (*Annals*, III, 356) that Dod married Phoebe Baldwin in Newark may not contradict Bradford's word if it is interpreted to mean that her home was in New Brunswick.

[11] William Linn (1752–1808), a graduate of the College of New Jersey in Bradford's own class of 1772, married Rebecca (or Rebecka) Blair early in 1774. She was a daughter of Reverend John Blair (1720–1771), who had been professor of divinity at the college and served as its acting president for some months preceding Witherspoon's arrival from Scotland. In his notebook, Bradford made copies of his sprightly correspondence of 1774–1775 with his close friend Linn. These letters often refer to the same persons mentioned in the JM-Bradford correspondence, and hence serve to illuminate it. Linn, a Pennsylvanian, served as a Presbyterian

chaplain in the patriot army, transferred to the Dutch Reformed Church in 1787, acted as president of Queen's College (Rutgers) from 1791 to 1794, and occupied the pulpit of the Collegiate Church in New York City until 1805 (*Pennsylvania Magazine of History and Biography*, XLI [1917], 350; Sidney Irving Pomerantz, *New York, an American City, 1783–1803* [New York, 1938], p. 377).

12 Probably Oliver Reese, a Pennsylvanian, who graduated in 1772 from the College of New Jersey. He died on 7 October 1775 in Wilton, S.C., where he had accepted the pastorate of a Presbyterian church (Alexander, *Princeton College*, p. 158; *South Carolina Historical and Genealogical Magazine*, X [1909], 222). Bradford's copybook contains a fragment of an undated poem entitled, "A pastoral Elegy on the Death of Oliver Reese."

13 Bradford wrote "in the Genius" instead of "is the Genius." Unaccountably, he failed to complete this sentence in his copybook. What he likely omitted was "n elsewhere in America."

14 See JM to Bradford, 24 January 1774, n. 11.

15 Bradford wrote this word above a deleted "contributing" and probably meant "heightening."

16 The twenty letters of Caspipina (Reverend Jacob Duché [1737–1798], who became chaplain of the Continental Congress and still later a Tory) were originally printed anonymously in the *Pennsylvania Packet*, beginning in March 1772, and were first reprinted in book form, again anonymously, as *Observations on a Variety of Subjects, Literary, Moral and Religious; in a Series of Original Letters, Written by a Gentleman of Foreign Extraction ... Revised by a Friend* (Philadelphia, 1774).

17 Bradford underlined this word.

18 Bradford used a shorthand symbol for this word.

To William Bradford

RC (Historical Society of Pennsylvania). Addressed: "To Mr. William Bradford Junior At the Coffee-House Philadelphia." A copy of this letter, made by Bradford, is also at the Historical Society of Pennsylvania.

April 1st. 1774. VIRGINIA ORANGE CY.

MY WORTHY FRIEND

I have another favour to acknowledge in the receipt of your kind Letter of March the 4th. I did not intend to have written again to you before I obtained a nearer communication with you but you have too much interest in my inclinations ever to be denied a request.

Mr. Brackenridge's illness gives me great uneasiness: I think he would be a loss to *America:* His merit is rated so high by me that I confess if he were gone, I could almost say with the Poet That His Country could furnish such a Pomp for Death no more.[1] But I solace myself from Finley's ludicrous description as you do.

I agree with you that the World needs to be peopled but I should be sorry it should be peopled with bastards as my old friend Dod and

—— —— seem to incline.² Who could have thought the old monk had been so letcherous. I hope his Religion, like that of some enthusiasts, was not of such a nature as to fan the amorous fire.

Our Assembly is to meet the first of May When It is expected something will be done in behalf of the Dissenters: Petitions I hear are already forming among the Persecuted Baptists and I fancy it is in the thoughts of the Presbyterians also to intercede for greater liberty in matters of Religion. For my part I can not help being very doubtful of their succeeding in the Attempt. The Affair was on the Carpet during the last Session; but such incredible and extravagant stories were told in the House of the monstrous effects of the Enthusiasm prevalent among the Sectaries and so greedily swallowed by their Enemies that I believe they lost footing by it and the bad name they still have with those who pretend too much contempt to examine into their principles and Conduct and are too much devoted to the ecclesiastical establishment to hear of the Toleration of Dissentients, I am apprehensive, will be again made a pretext for rejecting their requests. The Sentiments of our people of Fortune & fashion on this subject are vastly different from what you have been used to. That liberal catholic and equitable way of thinking as to the rights of Conscience, which is one of the Characteristics of a free people and so strongly marks the People of your province is but little known among the Zealous adherents to our Hierarchy. We have it is true some persons in the Legislature of generous Principles both in Religion & Politicks but number not merit you know is necessary to carry points there. Besides[,] the Clergy are a numerous and powerful body[,] have great influence at home by reason of their connection with & dependence on the Bishops and Crown and will naturally employ all their art & Interest to depress their rising Adversaries; for such they must consider dissenters who rob them of the good will of the people and may in time endanger their livings & security.

You are happy in dwelling in a Land where those inestimable privileges are fully enjoyed and public has long felt the good effects of their religious as well as Civil Liberty. Foreigners have been encouraged to settle amg. you. Industry and Virtue have been promoted by mutual emulation and mutual Inspection, Commerce and the Arts have flourished and I can not help attributing those continual exertions of Gen-[i]us which appear among you to the inspiration of Liberty and that love of Fame and Knowledge which always accompany it. Religious bondage shackles and debilitates the mind and unfits it for every noble enterprize every expanded prospect. How far this is the Case with Virginia will more clearly appear when the ensuing Trial is made.³

I am making all haste in preparing for my Journey: it appears as if it would be the first of May before I can start which I can the more patiently bear, because I may possibly get Some company by that time and it will answer so exactly with the meeting of the Synod.⁴ George Luckey talks of Joining me if I can wait till then. I am resolutely determined to come if it is in my power: If any thing hinders me it will be most likely the indisposition of my Mother who is in a very low state of health and if she should grow worse I am afraid she will be more unwilling to part with my brother as she will be less able to bear a Separation. If it should [so un]fortunately happen that I should be forced [to put]⁵ off or give out coming, Luckey on his Return to Virginia will bring me whatever publications you think worth sending and among others Calpipnis⁶ Letters. But whether I come or not⁷ be assured I retain the most ardent affection and esteem for you and the most cordial gratitude for your many generous Kindnesses. It gives me real pleasure when I write to you that I can talk in this Language without the least Affectation and without the suspicion of it, and that if I should omit expressing my love to you your friendship can supply the Omission or if I make use of the most extravagant expressions of it your Correspondent Affection can believe them to be sincere. This is a satisfaction & delight unknown to all who correspond for business or conveniency; but richly enjoyed by all who make pleasure and Improvement the business of their Communications.

Farewell

JM

P.S. You need no longer direct to the Care of Mr. Maury.⁸

¹ "America" is italicized because JM underlined it. "The Poet" could have been Seneca, Francis Bacon, or John Milton. Bacon attributed the phrase "Pompa mortis magis terret quam mors ipsa" (The pomp of death alarms us more than death itself) to Seneca. Though Seneca did use the words "pompa mortis" in *Oedipus* i. 126, it was in quite a different sense from that which Bacon implied. Bacon was probably thinking of "Stultitia est timore mortis mort" (It is folly to die of the fear of death) from Seneca's Epistle 70 (W. Gurney Benham, ed., *Putnam's Dictionary of Thoughts* [New York, 1930], p. 622). Lines 15–16 of Milton's "On Shakespeare" are:

> And so sepulchered in such pomp does lie,
> That kings for such a tomb would wish to die.

² JM probably intended Bradford to interpolate the name of Dod's wife in the blank (Bradford to JM, 4 March 1774, n. 10).

³ Although the Presbyterians and Baptists, beginning in 1769, brought more and more pressure on the colonial legislature to grant them religious toleration or

liberty, they were unsuccessful until 1776. In the session of 1774, however, when the dissenters again petitioned for redress, the House of Burgesses appeared to be more sympathetic but eventually adjourned without extending relief (*Journals of the House of Burgesses of Virginia, 1766–1769*, pp. 205, 252; *1770–1772*, pp. 186, 249; *1773–1776*, pp. 92, 102, 103, 189, 225).

⁴ The Synod of New York and Philadelphia of the Presbyterian Church met in the latter city from 18 to 26 May 1774. Although JM was an Anglican, many, if not most, of his college friends were Presbyterians.

⁵ The bracketed syllable and words are editorial inserts to replace those which the breaking of the letter's seal probably effaced.

⁶ "Caspipina."

⁷ At the bottom of Bradford's copybook version of this letter, he wrote: "NB. The beginning of May Mr Maddison arrived at Philada. & spent a few days: he the[n] proceeded on his way to Albany & returned in a fortnigh[t] staid a little while with us & then set of[f] for Virginia." This note is the only known record telling of JM's northern trip. Why he should have gone to Albany is especially puzzling.

⁸ Probably James Maury (1746–1840), friend and business agent of JM, well-known Fredericksburg merchant in the 1770's, and U.S. consul at Liverpool, 1790–1830 (*Virginia Magazine of History and Biography*, XXVII [1919], 375–76; *Journal of the Executive Proceedings of the Senate of the United States of America* [Washington, 1828——], I, 48; IV, 52).

To William Bradford

RC (Historical Society of Pennsylvania). Addressed: "To Mr. William Bradford Junr. at the Coffee-House Philadelphia." Bradford's copybook version is also at the Historical Society of Pennsylvania.

July 1. 1774.

DEAR SIR

I am once more got into my native land and into the possession of my customary enjoyments Solitude and Contemplation, though I must confess not a little disturbed by the sound of War blood and plunder on the one Hand and the Threats of Slavery and Oppression on the Other.¹ From the best accounts I can obtain from our Frontiers The Savages are determined in the extirpation of the Inhabitants, and no longer leave them the alternative of Death or Captivity. The Consternation and timidity of the White people who abandon their possessions without making the least resistance are as difficult to be accounted for as they are encouraging to the Enemy. Whether it be owing to the unusual Cruelty of the Indians the want of necessary implements or ammunition for War or to the ignorance & inexperience of many who,

since the establishment of peace, have ventured into those new Settlements, I can neither learn nor with any certainty conjecture. However
It is confidently asserted that there is not an Inhabitant for some Hundreds of miles back which have been settled for many years, except
those who are forted in or embodied by their Military Commanders.[2]
This state of things has induced Lord Dunmore, contrary to his Intentions at the Dissolution of the Assembly to issue Writs for a new Election of Members whom he is to call together on the 11th. of August.[3]

As to the Sentiments of the people of this Colony with respect to
the Bostonians I can assure [you] I find them generally very warm in
their favour. The Natives are very unanimous and resolute, are making
resolves in almost every County and I believe are willing to fall in
with the Other Colonies in any expedient measure, even if that should
be the universal prohibition of Trade.[4] It must not be denied though
that the Europeans especially the Scotch and some interested Merchants
among the natives discountenance such proceedings as far as they dare
alledging the Injustice and perfidy of refusing to pay our debts to our
Generous Creditors at Home. This Consideration induces some honest
moderate folks to prefer a partial prohibition extending only to the
Importation[5] of Goods.

We have a report here that Governor Gage has sent Lord Dunmore
some Letters relating to public matters in which He says he has strong
hopes that he shall be able to bring things at Boston to an amicable
settlement. I suppose you know whether there be any Truth in the
Report or any just foundation for such an Opinion in Gage.[6]

I[t] has been said here by some that the appointed Fast was disregarded by every Scotch Clergyman though it was observed by most
of the others who had timely notice of it. I cannot avouch it for an
absolute certainty but it appears no ways incredible.

I was so luckey as to find Dean Tuckers Tracts on my return Home
sent by mistake with some other books Imported this Spring. I have
read them with peculiar satisfaction and illumination with respect to
the Interests of America & Britain. At the same time his ingenious and
plausible defence of Parliamentary Authority, carries in it such defects
and misrepresentations as Confirm me in political Orthodoxy[,] After
the same manner as the specious Arguments of Infidels have established
the faith of Enquiring Christians.[7]

I am impatient to hear from you and do now cordially renew the
stipulation for that friendly correspondence which alone can comfort
me in the privation of your Company. I shall be punctual in trans-

mitting you an account of every thing that can be acceptable, but must freely absolve you from so strict an obligation which your application to more important Business will not allow, and which my regard for your ease & Interests will not suffer me to enjoin.

I am Dear Sir your faithful friend

JAMES MADISON JUNR.

[1] Although the date of JM's return to Montpelier is unknown, the opening words of this sentence imply that he had been home only a short time. If religious intolerance was the spur which initially aroused his concern about contemporary events (see his letter of 24 January 1774), the military and political affairs stressed in the present letter probably served as an additional prod to end his absorption in study and reading. Besides indicating an improvement in his health, his journey through the middle colonies may well have widened his horizons and quickened his interest in public affairs. On the other hand, the complete omission in this letter of his customary inquiries about old friends and his unusually meager mention of books may merely signify that his meetings and conversations while on his trip had temporarily made these favorite subjects irrelevant.

[2] JM here refers to the attacks by Shawnee and other Indians on white trappers, traders, surveyors, and settlers in western Pennsylvania and Virginia, including what is now the Little Kanawha Valley of West Virginia, and eastern Kentucky. This struggle, known as Lord Dunmore's War, began in the spring of 1774, climaxed in the repulse of the Indians at the hard-fought Battle of Point Pleasant on 10 October, and ended shortly thereafter with the Treaty of Camp Charlotte. By this preliminary pact, and its confirmation about a year later at Pittsburgh, insofar as the Shawnees and several other tribes living in what is now southern Ohio were concerned, Kentucky was opened to undisturbed settlement by the whites. The background of the conflict is a tangled story of a boundary dispute between Virginia and Pennsylvania in the Monongahela Valley, of bitter intercolonial rivalries between land speculators, including John Murray, Earl of Dunmore (1732–1809), of his determination and that of some Virginians to have the middle Kentucky area settled, and of the brutal murder of members of the family of a Mingo chieftain (Logan) by a party of whites (Reuben Gold Thwaites and Louise Phelps Kellogg, eds., *Documentary History of Dunmore's War, 1774* [Madison, Wis., 1905]; Thomas Perkins Abernethy, *Western Lands and the American Revolution* [New York, 1937], pp. 106–15).

[3] The unenthusiastic response of the tidewater-dominated House of Burgesses in mid-May 1774 to Governor Dunmore's request that he be financially enabled to recruit a special military force, sufficiently large and well equipped to crush the Indians speedily, contrasts sharply with JM's anxiety because of the frontier crisis. Besides the fact that Montpelier was nearer to the panic-stricken border than it was to Williamsburg, close relatives of his father had fought Indians and suffered from their depredations during the French and Indian War. Although some of JM's kinsfolk living on the frontier may have supplied him with those "best accounts" mentioned earlier in this letter, he more likely read them in the *Virginia Gazette* (Williamsburg, Rind) of 2 and 21 June 1774. Governor Dunmore had dissolved the House of Burgesses in late May because it called for prayer and fasting on 1 June, the day when the Boston Port Bill was to go into effect. Following the dissolution, a "rump session" of the House met in Raleigh Tavern, resolved to boycott most East India Company wares, and instructed the legislature's Committee of Correspondence to invite all the other colonies to a general congress

(First Continental Congress). Although on 17 June the governor issued the writs mentioned in this letter, he further prorogued the Assembly on 8 July—this time until early November. The Indian war kept him on the frontier from 10 July until 4 December. For this reason, as well as because he knew that a majority of the burgesses would oppose his demands, he by successive prorogations prevented them from meeting until 1 June 1775. By then his effective power as governor had ended (*Virginia Gazette* [Williamsburg, Rind], 14 July and 8 December 1774; *Journals of the House of Burgesses of Virginia, 1773–1776*, pp. 132, 163–73; Force, *American Archives*, 4th ser., I, 350–51, 419, 523, 1014).

4 Charles Ramsdell Lingley in his *The Transition in Virginia from Colony to Commonwealth* (New York, 1910), pp. 87–90, states that mass meetings in at least fifty-four of the sixty-one Virginia counties passed resolutions between the summer of 1774 and spring of 1775. Many of these resolves appear in Force, *American Archives*, 4th ser., I, *passim*.

5 Underlined by JM.

6 On 30 May and 26 June 1774 General Thomas Gage (1721–1787) wrote to the Earl of Dartmouth expressing a restrained optimism about being able to effect "an amicable settlement" (Clarence Edwin Carter, ed., *The Correspondence of General Thomas Gage, 1763–1775* [2 vols.; New Haven, 1931–33], I, 355–57).

7 JM probably refers to Josiah Tucker (*ca.* 1712–1799), *Four Tracts Together with Two Sermons* (2d ed.; Glocester, 1774). Tract IV by this anti-mercantilist Dean of Gloucester must have been of especial interest to JM. In this tract the Dean argued, on grounds of economic benefit to England, that the American colonies should be encouraged to separate entirely from England (Robert Livingston Schuyler, ed., *Josiah Tucker: A Selection from His Economic and Political Writings* [New York, 1931], pp. 281–369). JM apparently deemed a denial of any rightful authority of Parliament over the colonies to be an "orthodox" constitutional position.

From William Bradford

FC (Historical Society of Pennsylvania).

August. 1st. 1774

DEAR SIR,

I am sorry to find your letter confirms the accounts we have received of the depredations of the Indians; which I hope was a slight & private quarrell with Cressop & others; for such accounts as these generally increase in horror as the distance increases. I am apprehensive the death of Sir William Johnston (of which you must undoubtedly have heard[) will] be attended with disagreeable consequences, & serve to encourage the enemy even more than the timidity you condemn in the white-people. 'Tis said he concluded a treaty with them a few hours before he died;[1] but that will not prevent them joining with those in Virginia if they think it their interest to do so; they [are] a people who pay but little regard to the Faith of Treaties, & whose general character is well drawn by our friend Breckenridge when he calls them

"Wild as the winds, unstable as the sea,
Cruel as death & Treacherous as Hell"[2]

I have hopes that the congress which it is expected will meet at this City next month will do something towards effectually warding of[f] the attacks of Slavery and fixing the boundaries of our Liberties. Till that is done I am apprehensive all our endeavours will [be] of but little use, as they will not reach the root of the disorder: they may procure a repeal of the present acts, but that like the repeal of the stampt-act will be but a temporary relief & leave us exposed to the attacks of some future ministerial scoundrel who like North may be ambitious of "laying us at his feet."[3] It is recommended to our delegates to insist on the repeal of certain acts we deem oppressive & the confirmation (or if they please the *grant*[4]) of certain rights, that are necessary to our Liberty. If this measure should be adopted by the Congress & this "bill of rights" be confirmed by his majesty, or the parliament, the Liberties of America will be as firmly fixed, & defined as those of England were at the revolution.[5] We expect much from the delegates of Virginia & Boston; for several of those appointed for this province are known to be inimical to the Liberties of America. I mean Galloway the author of the detestable peice signed Americanus in the time of the Stampt Act; & one Humphries an obscure assemblyman who but the moment before he was appointed voted against the having a congress at all. I am informed the State of affairs is still worse in New York where nothing but Dissention prevails. I hope they will not communicate any of that spirit to the Congress.[6]

Indeed my friend the world wears a strange aspect at the present day; to use Shakespear's expression "the times seem to be out of joint."[7] Our being attacked on the one hand by the Indians, & on the others, our Liberties invaded by a corrupt, ambitious & determined ministry is bring[ing] things to a crisis in America & seems to fortell some great event. In Europe the states entertain a general suspicion of each other; they seem to be looking forward to some great revolution & stand, as it were with their hands on their swords ready to unsheath them at the earliest warning. The obstinate & bloody contention of the Turk & Russian, the overthrow of Liberty in Sweden & Corsica, the Death of Lewis and the Accession of a young ambitious monarch to the throne of France lead us to imagine there is something at hand that shall greatly augment the history of the world:[8] Many of our good people &

among the rest Mr Halsey[9] have calculated the commencement of the Millenium in the present Century, & others with equal probability, the consumation of all things: and indeed when the plot thickens we are to expect the conclusion of the drama.

I thankfully accept your indulgence in not expecting punctuality in my answering your Letters. The hurry of Business and the bustle of the town renders it impossible to write in haste & not forget much of what I intended to tell you; & I seldom send away a letter without recollecting that I have done so. If you hear of Mr Wallace[10] you will not forget to inform me. I have his interest too much at heart to be indifferent about his Wellfare.

I am yours &c

WB.

[1] Michael Cresap (1742–1775), border leader and pioneer, was widely, but probably unjustly, accused of the murder of members of Mingo Chief Logan's family at Yellow Creek on 30 April 1774, thus precipitating Lord Dunmore's War (JM to Bradford, 1 July 1774, n. 2). Sir William Johnson (1715–1774), serving under royal commission as "Agent and Superintendent" of the Six Nations and their affairs, died suddenly on 11 July in New York while endeavoring to restrain the Iroquois from joining the Indians of western Pennsylvania and Virginia in their uprising against the whites. Thanks mainly to Johnson's influence, most of the Iroquois remained neutral during the war.

[2] The first line of this quotation should read: "Unstable as the sea, wild as the winds." The couplet is from "The Rising Glory of America," written in 1771 by Freneau and Brackenridge and read by the latter on the occasion of their graduation from the College of New Jersey. In 1772 it was published in Philadelphia by Joseph Crukshank for R. Aitken, bookseller (Fred L. Pattee, ed., *Poems of Philip Freneau*, I, 49, 64).

[3] William Cobbett, ed., *The Parliamentary History of England from the Earliest Period to the year 1803* (36 vols.; London 1806–20; continued as *Hansard's Parliamentary Debates*), XVII, 1159–1356 (7 March to 27 May 1774), *passim;* Lord North's speeches in support of the measures known later by the colonists as the "Intolerable Acts."

[4] Underlined by Bradford.

[5] "An Act Declaring the Rights and Liberties of the Subject, and Settling the Succession of the Crown," usually known as the Bill of Rights, was enacted by Parliament in December 1689 as one of the reforms accompanying the "Glorious Revolution."

[6] During the controversy over the Stamp Act, Joseph Galloway (1731–1803), wealthy Philadelphia lawyer and speaker of the provincial legislature of Pennsylvania, published in the *Pennsylvania Journal* (Philadelphia) of 9 January 1766 "the detestable peice" signed "Americanus," upholding the hated tax law. In September 1774, at the First Continental Congress, his conciliatory "Plan of Accommodation on Constitutional Principles" failed to gain the support of the "radical" delegates, mainly from New England and Virginia. Among Galloway's supporters in the Congress was Charles Humphreys (1714–1786), a Haverford Quaker who, after long service in the legislature of his colony, closed his political career by voting against

the adoption of the Declaration of Independence by the Second Continental Congress. Of like opinion, Galloway fled to England in 1778 and remained there until his death (Worthington Chauncey Ford *et al.*, eds., *Journals of the Continental Congress, 1774–1789* [34 vols.; Washington, 1904–37], I, 43–51).

7 "The time is out of joint" (*Hamlet*, Act I, scene 5, line 188).

8 After six years of war, Russia forced Turkey to sign a humiliating peace treaty on 21 July 1774. In May of that year, Louis XVI, then twenty years of age, succeeded to the throne of France upon the death of his grandfather, Louis XV. During the preceding five years France had been consolidating its hold upon Corsica, after ending its independence and ousting its hero, Pasquale Paoli, in 1769. In Sweden, Gustavus III was crushing all attempts to lessen his prerogative.

9 Reverend Jeremiah Halsey, pastor of the Presbyterian church at Bedminster, N.J., served as trustee of the College of New Jersey in the 1770's. At the meeting of the Synod of New York and Philadelphia, 17–23 May 1775, he was the only clergyman who dissented from the paragraph of the pastoral letter affirming allegiance to King George III (*Records of the Presbyterian Church in the United States of America, 1706–1788*, pp. 378, 468–69).

10 Caleb Wallace.

To William Bradford

Copy (Historical Society of Pennsylvania).

VIRGINIA August 23. 1774.

DEAR SIR,

The receipt of your's of the first inst. was peculiarly acceptable to me; the enjoyment of your Company at Philada. has so revived & increased my pristine Affection for you, that I found great pleasure in that token of you[r] Affectionate Kindness. And tho' it is with the utmost chearfulness I emancipate you from the bondage of a punctual correspondence yet I find I cannot do without an occasional Line from you. As to myself I shall continue to write something or other as long as I perceive you have patience or time to read it.

I informed you in my last of the unhappy condition of our Frontiers from the irruption & cruelty of the savages; tho' I still beleive it to be true in great measure yet it is suggested by some that the mischiefs have been grossly magnified & misrepresented; and that it is possible some may find their Interest in doing it.[1] Lord Dunmore is now at Pittsburg intending to march shortly with 2 or 3000 men to the indian Towns and to extirpate those perfidious people intirely: But his Lordships intentions & expectations meet with the greatest derision from those versed in Indian affairs who affirm that he will find no body at the Towns but a few old squaws & superannuated warriors, & that the destruction of their Huts & properties will by no means recompense us for the charges of the expedition. Besides the absence of those troops will certainly embolden the enemy to range with less controul & greater havoc among the Frontier settlers. If these Apprehensions should be well-grounded it is probable his Lordship's conduct will breed some altercations between him and this assembly who will certainly examine into the expediency & success of so expensive a project before they pay the men he has employed for it.[2]

I have seen the instructions of your committee to your representatives & greatly admire the wisdom of the advice & the elegance and cogency of the diction. In the latter especially they are vastly superior to what has been done by our convention.[3] But do you not presume too much on the generosity & Justice of the crown, when you propose deffering all endeavours on our part till such important concessions & novel regulations are obtained; Would it not be advisable as soon as possible to begin our defence & to let its continuance or cessation depend on the success of a petition presented to his majesty. Delay on our part emboldens our adversaries and improves their schemes; whilst it abates the ardor of the Americans inspired with recent Injuries and affords opportunity to our secret enemies to disseminate discord & disunion. But I am mounting into the sphere of the general Congress to whose wisdom and Judgment all private opinions must give place. This Colony has appointed seven delegates to represent it on this grand occasion, most of them glowing patriots & men of Learning & penetration. It is however the opinion of some good Judges that one or two might be exchanged for the better.[4] The Conduct of your Assembly in chusing galloway & Humphries seems to forbode difficulties and divisions which may be strengthened by the deputees from N.Y. It also seems to indicate a prevalency of selfish Quakers in your House which frustrate the generous designs & manly efforts of the real friends to American Fredom. I assure you I heartily repent of undertaking my Journey to the North when I did. If I had it to perform now, the opportunity of attending the Congress would be an infinite addition to the pleasures of it. I cannot help congratulating you on your happy situation in that respect. I comfort myself however under the privation of such an happiness with the hope that you will befriend me in sending a brief account of whatever is singular and important in their proceedings that can not be gathered from the public papers. Indeed I could wish their Debates were to be published which might greatly illuminate the minds of the thinking people among us and I would hope there would be sufficient abilities displayed in them to render us more respectable at Home.

With this I send a letter to Mr Ervin which I beg you will forward.[5]
I am Dr Sir Your &c.

JM JR.

[1] See JM to Bradford, 1 July 1774, n. 2. There is no doubt that the Indians killed, maimed, or captured many whites and destroyed much of their property, but an accurate accounting cannot be made, if for no better reasons than the indistinctness of the geographic area to include, the impossibility of identifying the particular Indian tribe responsible for each of the long series of forays, and the lack of agreement upon when to begin, whether in 1764 at the close of the preceding war or at some later date in the next decade. In his comment, however, JM reflected a charge, often made in the summer of 1774, that Dunmore and his fellow land speculators had exaggerated the extent of the depredations as an excuse for expending the colony's "blood and treasure" to crush the Indians and thereby profit financially from opening the frontier, especially Kentucky, to survey and settlement. The need to provision twelve hundred or two thousand troops would also reduce the amount of surplus food which individual Virginians might otherwise send to the beleaguered Bostonians (Force, *American Archives*, 4th ser., I, 593, 787).

[2] The victory of Colonel Andrew Lewis and Virginia militia over the Indians in the Battle of Point Pleasant at the mouth of the Kanawha River extricated Governor Dunmore, then at Pittsburgh, from a difficult situation. The victory, together with the satisfactory peace of Camp Charlotte, brought him congratulatory addresses as a gratifying sequel to the earlier accusations that he had welcomed, if not fomented, the conflict with the Shawnees. In 1775, the House of Burgesses voted £350,000, Virginia currency, to pay the cost of the war (Hening, *Statutes*, IX, 61, 68).

[3] The instructions of 23 July 1774 of the Pennsylvania provincial assembly to its delegates to the First Continental Congress and the corresponding instructions of 6 August 1774 of the Virginia Convention are in Force, *American Archives*, 4th ser., I, 608–9 and 689–90, respectively. Although those of Virginia, unlike those of Pennsylvania, commanded the representatives to "express, in the first place, our faith and true allegiance" to King George III, they declared in favor of an intercolonial non-importation and non-exportation agreement, denied any authority to Parliament over a colony's internal polity, and favored "resistance and reprisal" against Governor Gage if he did not desist from his "despotick" course in Boston. On the other hand, the much briefer instructions of Pennsylvania merely directed its delegates to concert upon a plan best calculated for "obtaining a redress of *American* grievances, ascertaining the *American* rights, and establishing that union and harmony which is most essential to the welfare and happiness of both countries; and, in doing this . . . to avoid every thing indecent or disrespectful to the mother state." Although JM politely complimented "the diction" of the Pennsylvania directive, his comments later in this paragraph make clear that he favored the much bolder course enjoined upon the Virginia delegation.

[4] Peyton Randolph, Richard Henry Lee, George Washington, Patrick Henry, Richard Bland, Benjamin Harrison, and Edmund Pendleton comprised the delegation (Force, *American Archives*, 4th ser., I, 689). Which "one or two" of these JM had in mind is not certain; perhaps he deemed Henry too fiery, or Randolph or Bland too moderate.

[5] Nathaniel Irwin. JM's letter to him has not been found. JM evidently misdirected his letter for Bradford to Irwin, and vice versa. At the bottom of his file copy Bradford wrote: "This letter by mistake was directed to Mr Ervin."

Indenture

MS (Orange County, Va., Court Records).

[22 September 1774]

This Indenture made the twenty Second day of September in the year of our [Lord] one thousand Seven hundred and Seventy four Between James Madison of the County of Orange and Nelly his wife of the one part and James Madison Junior of the said County of the other part Witnesseth that the said James Madison and Nelly his wife for and in Consideration of the Sum of Thirty pounds Current money of Virginia by the said James Madison Junior to the said James Madison in hand paid before the Sealing and Delivering of these presents the Receipt whereof is hereby Acknowledged have granted bargained and Sold and by these presents do grant bargain and Sell and enfeoff Unto the said James Madison Jr. his heirs and Assigns forever a part of that Tract or parcel of Land known by the name of Black Level Containing two hundred Acres more or less and bounded as followeth Viz Beginning at three small Pines and a Red Oak at the head of a Valley in the patent Line Corner to Burr Harison[1] the North thirty four degrees West one hundred and eighty poles[2] thence North fifty degrees East 180 poles thence South thirty four degrees East to the patent Line thence along the said Line to the beginning To Have and to hold the said two hundred Acres of Land together with all houses woods waters profits hereditaments and Appurtenances whatsoever to the same belonging and the Reversion and Reversions Remainder and Remainders[3] Rents and profits there of and all and Singular other the premises to the said James Madison Junr. his heirs and Assigns forever to the only proper use and behoof of the said James Madison Junr. his heirs and Assigns forever and to no other use or purpose whatsoever and the said James Madison and Nelly his wife for themselves their heirs Executors and Administrators do Covenant grant and agree to and with the said James Madison Junr. his heirs and Assigns forever that he the said James Madison at the time of Sealing and Delivering these presents is seized[4] and possessed of an indefesable Estate of inheritance in Feesimple[5] in the said two hundred Acres of Land and premises and that full power and Lawful authority to Convey the same in as full and ample manner as the same is hereby Conveyed and the said James Madison Junr. his heirs and Assigns shall and may at all times hereafter peacibly hold and enjoy all and Singular the said parcel of Land and premises with the Apurtenances without lett or Molestation from the said James Madison and Nelly his wife their heirs or Assigns or any other persons whatsoever and the said two hundred Acres of Land with the Appurtenances shall forever hereafter remain unto the said James Madison Junr his heirs and Assigns discharged of and[6] from all former and other gifts grants bargains Sales Mortgages rights titles Judgments and Executions Whatsoever and also that the said James Madison and Nelly his wife and their heirs the said Land and premises with the appurtenances unto the said James Madison Junr. his heirs and Assigns against the Claim of all persons whatsoever shall and will warrant and forever defend by these presents In Witness whereof the said James Madison and Nelly his wife have hereunto set their hands and Seals the day and year first above written

Signed Sealed and Delivered ⎫   JAMES MADISON   (L S)
In the presence of   ⎭   NELLY MADISON   (L S)
FRANCES TAYLOR[7] SAMUEL FRENCH[8] AMBROSE MADISON[9]

Memorandom that quiet and peacible possession and seisen of the within mentioned Lands and premises was had and taken by the within named James Madison Junr. of and from the within named James Madison on the day and year within written according to the form and effect of the within written Deed

JAMES MADISON

At a Court held for Orange County on Thursday the 23d of Novr. 1775 This Indenture with Memorandum of Livery[10] and Seisen Endorsed thereon from James Madison Gent. to James Madison Junr. was Acknowledged by the said James Madison Senior and Ordered to be Recorded
    Test
                                        JAMES TAYLOR Clk Cur[11]

---

[1] There were three or four Burr Harrisons living in Virginia at this time (Horace E. Hayden, *Virginia Genealogies*, p. 513). The editors have been unable to identify the one who owned land adjoining Montpelier, but the one whose residence was closest to JM's was Burr Harrison (1738–1822) of Fauquier County, a member of a family of extensive landowners. He was a militia colonel in 1776–1777 and a paymaster in the Continental Army in 1780–1781. After the war he moved to Chester County, S.C. (John H. Gwathmey, *Historical Register of Virginians in the Revolution* [Richmond, 1938], p. 354; *Virginia Magazine of History and Biography*, XXIV [1916], 211).

[2] A pole is a rod or perch; hence it measures 16½ feet.

[3] An estate in expectancy, which becomes an estate in possession upon the deter-

mination of a particular prior estate, created at the same time and by the same instrument; distinguished from a reversion, in which the residual interest is reserved by the grantor.

4 That is, "made the owner of."

5 That is, in contrast to "fee tail," an estate which the owner is free to sell, give, or bequeath to anyone.

6 Probably a word such as "free" or "immune" was omitted here.

7 Francis Taylor (1747–1799), JM's second cousin, was clerk of the Orange County Committee of Safety in 1775. Between 1776 and 1781 he served successively as an officer (captain to colonel) in the 2d and 15th Virginia Regiments, and in the regiment guarding British prisoners at Charlottesville. Following the Revolution, he accumulated a large landed estate in Kentucky and the Indiana country, as well as in Orange County ("Francis Taylor's Diary," typescript, p. 4, owned by E. H. Taylor Hay of Chicago).

8 Unidentified, unless he was Ensign Samuel French of Orange County, named in a "Memorandum concerning Military Service of Baptists" (Boyd, *Papers of Jefferson*, I, 662). He appears to have been a laborer and a militia corporal in the French and Indian War (*Virginia Magazine of History and Biography*, II [1894–95], 147; III [1895–96], 201).

9 JM's brother Ambrose (1755–1793), who was only nineteen years of age in September 1774.

10 The act of delivering legal possession of property.

11 Clerk of the Court. James Taylor (1738–1808), JM's second cousin, was at first the deputy clerk and later the clerk of Orange County between 1762 and 1798, the year before he emigrated to Jefferson County, Kentucky (Orange County Order Book, No. 6, p. 630, microfilm; and J. Estelle Stewart King, ed., "Abstracts of Early Kentucky Wills and Inventories," typescript, 1931, p. 132, both in Virginia State Library).

From William Bradford

FC (Historical Society of Pennsylvania).

PHILADA. October 17th 1774.

DEAR SIR,

My silence has been long & perhaps you will tell me unkind; but I plead your release from strict pu[n]ctuality in bar to any reproofs of that sort: And do not think that I plead this because I [have] no better plea: but because It would take up more time than I can spare to tell you all the causes of my silence: yet they may be comprehended in two word[s] Sickness & Business.[1] But tho they prevented me from writing to you they could not prevent me thinking frequently and tenderly on You; for beleive me, whether sick or well, busy or at liesure, I am most sincerely yours.

The Congress have sate much longer than was expected & have not yet adjourned, but it is expected they will do so in a few days. Their proceedings are a profound secret & the doors open to no one; so that were you here as you wish[ed] your curiosity would be but poorly gratified in that respect; yet there is so great a concourse of gentlemen from all parts of the Continent that you would have an opportunity of forming some very valuable & agreeable connections & amply recompensing yourself for your disappointment with regard to the hearing the debates of Congress. Philadelphia has become another Cairo; with this difference that the one is a city swarming with Merchants the other with politicians & Statesmen. The Congress sits in the Carpenter's Hall in one room of which the City Library is kept & of which the Librarian tells me the Gentlemen make great & constant use.[2] By which we may conjecture that their measures will be wisely plan'd since they debate on them like philosophers; for by what I was told Vattel, Barlemaqui Locke & Montesquie[u] seem to be the standar[d]s to which they refer either when settling the rights of the Colonies or when a dispute arises on the Justice or propriety of a measure.[3] Whether these dispute[s] shall be published at large; or the resolves with the reasons of them; or only the resolves by themselves I cannot pretend to say: Be that as it will, when they are published you shall have them by the earliest opportunity.[4] A Gentleman of my acquaintances goes next week to Fredericksburg & I will send you by him some of the political phamphlets with which our city is filled; but which you may not have seen. I have been able to read but few of them & that with no great attention: I believe however some of them are worthy your perusal. I send you, now, a poem on divine revelation which Mr. Breckenridge spoke at Commencement & has published.[5] He desired me to do so & requested you to recommend it to your friends if you think it has any merit in order to assist the sale that the printer may not be a loser by him. I am afraid he has published it at an improper time; the political storm is too high for the soft still voice of the muse to be list[e]ned to; & indeed this does not seem the proper time for poetry unless it be such as Tyrtaeus wrote.[6] I am glad however that our friend seems determined that these blossoms of Genius shall not "waste their sweetness in the desert air."[7] It will encour[a]ge him to make still greater attempts & tutor him to heights he would once have trembled at. If I may be allowed to judge he appears to have rather a strong and masculine Genius than a just & delicate taste: Imagination is his province. The consequence of this will be that his writings tho' enriched with many original beauties will be obscured with Faults which even a moderate Genius would have avoided. Perhaps the pun on the word Tartarean in this poem will justify the latter part of this remark.[8] But where is the man that ever bestrode pegasus and did not sometimes get a fall.

I went yesterday to hear our classmate McCorkle predicate: & I assure you his sermon was very orthodox: The point he chiefly Laboured to prove was "that the Laws of God were superior in wisdom to the Laws of men"; & I think his arguments on this part were in a gr[e]at measure unanswerable; the rest had a great deal of chronology but very little instruction in it. However he is better than many that I have heard.[9] Duffield & Lewis Wilson are chosen tutors at College: I am somewhat surprised at the Latter's accepting so troublesom[e] & so ungrateful a task.[10]

How came you to direct my letter to Mr Ervin & his to me when you wrote last: you must have been as absent as the Menalcas of Bruyere.[11] 'Tis the first time I have been honoured with the title of "reverend." Should you & I ever write treason you must be more careful to whom you direct what you write. I hope you are so of your billet-doux.

There is no news at present: when the Congress breaks up you shall hear from me again.

I am &c

W BRADFORD JUN

P S. If you *have* any *friends* in Baltimore to *whom* I could direct the Pamphlets *etc.*[?] I wish to send you, I could *oblige* you often in that way.[12]

W.B.

---

[1] In a letter of 24 September 1774 to William Linn, Bradford wrote: "I have been sick ... very sick: I was within an ace of supping with my progenitors" (Historical Society of Pennsylvania).

[2] Francis Daymon was the librarian of the Library Company of Philadelphia. The availability of its books was one reason why the delegates to the First Continental Congress, in spite of the objections of Joseph Galloway and a few others, selected Carpenter's Hall as a meeting place (*Journals of the Continental Congress*, I, 27; Edmund Cody Burnett, *The Continental Congress* [New York, 1941], pp. 33–34; Austin K. Gray, *Benjamin Franklin's Library: A Short Account of the Library Company of Philadelphia, 1731–1931* [New York, 1936], pp. 27–28).

[3] Although the delegates may have frequently consulted the works on political philosophy and international law of John Locke, Charles Louis de Secondat, Baron de La Brède et de Montesquieu, Jean Jacques Burlamaqui, and Emeric de Vattel, they

merely quoted Montesquieu and Cesare B. Beccaria in their series of "Addresses"; and Beccaria only in the one entitled, "To the Inhabitants of the Province of Quebec" (*Journals of the Continental Congress*, I, 106). General Charles Lee, who was not a member of the Congress, apparently had a large share in drafting this address (John Richard Alden, *General Charles Lee: Traitor or Patriot?* [Baton Rouge, 1951], p. 60).

4 Bradford was in an advantageous position to know what went on behind the closed doors of the First Continental Congress. His father, William, and his older brother, Thomas, besides publishing *The Pennsylvania Journal; and the Weekly Advertiser*, were the official printers of the Congress. Following its adjournment on 26 October, the Bradfords at their "London Coffee House" address brought out the first edition of the *Journal of the Proceedings of the Congress held at Philadelphia, September 5, 1774*.

5 [Hugh Henry Brackenridge], *A Poem on Divine Revelation; Being an Exercise Delivered at the Public Commencement at Nassau-Hall, September 24, 1774* . . . (Philadelphia: Printed and Sold by R. Aitken, Bookseller, opposite the London-Coffee-House, Front Street, 1774).

6 An elegiac poet of about 650 B.C., whose poetry praised the laws, patriotism, and heroism of his fellow Spartans during the second Messenian War.

7 From line 56 of Thomas Gray's *Elegy Written in a Country Churchyard*. Bradford's "their" should be "its," and his "in" should be "on," to conform with the original.

8 The reference is to the lines:

> . . . Night on the east comes down
> With gloom Tartarean, and in part it rose
> From Tartary beneath the dusky pole.

Bradford's strictures upon the quality of the poem appear to have been shared by other critics during his own and later generations. Brackenridge used the same heroic style of verse in his poems on the Battle of Bunker Hill and on the death of Montgomery at Quebec, but most of his later literary output was satirical (Brackenridge, *Poem on Divine Revelation*, p. 13; Claude M. Newlin, *Hugh Henry Brackenridge*, pp. 30–33).

9 In a letter on [1?] November to William Linn, Bradford commented further: ". . . for three sundays past have been entertained with hearing [Samuel] McCorkle, [Oliver] Rees, and [Israel] Evans . . . : I have a great inclination to laugh at the first; but you would chide me if I did" (Historical Society of Pennsylvania).

10 John Duffield, a Pennsylvanian, delivered the Latin oration at the College of New Jersey Commencement in 1773, and served as tutor for two years. He was a surgeon in the 3d Continental Artillery in 1782–1783 (F. B. Heitman, *Historical Register of Officers of the Continental Army*, p. 160). Bradford's surprise because Lewis Feuilleteau Wilson (1753–1803), College of New Jersey, '73, accepted a humble tutorship may have reflected the fact that he was a wealthy West Indies planter's son and had received his early education in England. Undecided between a career as a physician or as a Presbyterian minister, he became the former in 1775 and practiced medicine successfully for eleven years. From 1793 until his death, he was a pastor at Concord, N.C. (*New Jersey Archives*, 1st ser., XXIX, 52–57; John Maclean, *History of the College of New Jersey*, I, 365; Sprague, *Annals*, III, 570–75).

11 See JM to Bradford, 23 August 1774, n. 5. For the absent-minded and blundering "Menalcas," see Jean de La Bruyère's essay "Of Man" in *The Works of Monsieur De La Bruyère* (2 vols.; London, 1713), II, 211–18.

12 Bradford used shorthand symbols for the italicized words.

To William Bradford

Copy (Historical Society of Pennsylvania).

VIRGINIA Nov: 26. 1774.

DEAR SIR,

The pamphlets & letters[1] you sent me were safely delivered about ten days after the date of them. I esteem it a singular favor that you should be so thoughtfull of obliging me at a time when your attention must necessarally have been employed on many more important considerations. Your readiness also to serve me on any future occasion demands my acknowledgments. I have no acquaintance in Baltimore I could confide in for that purpose. If I should hereafter make any I shall take the Liberty in consequence of your offer to give you notice of it (To go to Dunlaps to stop paper. *Got several back etc.*)[2] A part of the men that went out with Lord dunmore against the Shawnese towns we hear were attacked on the 10 of last month by 7 or 800 Indians. The fight continued the whole day and was extremely obstinate on both sides; Our men kept the field: The loss of the Indians was considerable. This it seems was the last effort of the Savages for they immediately sued for peace as the only method to save themselves & their *Towns*[3] from destruction. The peace was granted in order to save the lives of many prisoners the Indians had got among them, but on what terms I cannot say.[4]

The proceedings of the Congress are universally approved of in this Province & I am persuaded will be faithfully adheared to.[5] A spirit of Liberty & Patriotism animates all degrees and denominations of men. Many publickly declare themselves ready to join the Bostonians as soon as violence is offered them or resistance thought expedient. In many counties independent companies are forming and voluntaraly subjecting themselves to military discipline that they may be expert & prepared against a time of Need. I hope it will be a general thing *thro'ought*[6] this province. Such firm and provident steps will either intimidate our enemies or enable us to defy them. By an epistle from the yearly meeting of the Quakers in your City to their bretheren & friends in our Colonies I observe they are determined to be passive on this Critical occasion from a regard to their religious principles mixed I presume with the Leaven of civil policy.[7]

If america & Britain should come to an hostile rupture I am afraid an Insurrection among the slaves may & will be promoted. In one of our Counties lately a few of those unhappy wretches met together & chose a leader who was to conduct them when the English Troops should arrive—which they foolishly thought would be very soon & that by revolting to them they should be rewarded with their freedom. Their Intentions were soon discovered & proper precautions taken to prevent the Infection. It is prudent such attempts should be concealed as well as suppressed.[8]

I heard a few days since that our friend mr Wallace is in a declining state of health: His friends suspect the beginnings of a Consumption: But Death has no sting for him.[9] Mr Brackenridge I understand is nobly engaged in a paper war with the Teachers of a rival & a neighbouring School.[10]

I was told by a Quaker Gentleman from Philada that a complaint of being persecuted in New-England was laid before the Congress by the People called baptists. Did Truth or prejudice dictate to the Quaker in his report.[11] Are the Transactions of the Congress so well known that you could inform me what Character our delegates have left behind them for Oratory Zeal & Literature.

Vale

J MADDISON JR.

(the first[?] part of this letter compressible[?] abridged.)[12]

[1] What these were is not known although "the pamphlets," at least, may have included, besides Brackenridge's poem, several relating to the dispute between the colonies and Great Britain.

[2] The italicized words are in shorthand in Bradford's copybook. Apparently JM had asked Bradford to stop his subscription to the weekly [John] *Dunlap's Pennsylvania Packet, or, the General Advertiser*, published in Philadelphia. "Got several back" is probably Bradford's vague summing up of JM's stated reason for cancellation. During the rest of his life JM was occasionally annoyed by the slowness with which newspapers reached the Orange, Va., post office.

[3] Word underlined by Bradford.

[4] For the Battle of Point Pleasant and Treaty of Camp Charlotte, see JM to Bradford, 1 July 1774, n. 2, and 23 August 1774, nn. 1 and 2.

[5] Here JM especially has in mind the non-importation, non-exportation, and non-consumption resolutions of the First Continental Congress, known as the "Association."

[6] Word underlined by Bradford.

[7] James Bowden, *The History of the Society of Friends in America* (2 vols.; London, 1850–54), II, 298–99.

[8] To what particular incident JM referred has not been determined. Planters took care that slave unrest in one locality was not noised about lest it cause disaffection in other areas. When, in the late spring and summer of 1775, the long-continued disagreements between Governor Dunmore and the House of Burgesses came to the pitch of armed conflict, he was accused of instigating a revolt of the

slaves. The Governor's course in the autumn of 1775 amply justified this charge (*Journals of the House of Burgesses of Virginia, 1773–1776*, p. 245; David John Mays, *Edmund Pendleton, 1721–1803* [2 vols.; Cambridge, Mass., 1952], II, 56–57).

9 In his letter of 17 March 1775, JM assured Bradford that the rumor about Caleb Wallace's ill health had been false.

10 For a possible sample of the ammunition used in this "paper war," see Bradford to JM, 4 January 1775, n. 6. The war may have broken out when Eden School, which was near Brackenridge's school at Back Bay, was named the one free school in the area, and a road to it was ordered built (Elizabeth Merritt, ed., *Proceedings and Acts of the General Assembly of Maryland, October 1773 to April 1774, Archives of Maryland*, LXIV [Baltimore, 1947], 341, 345, 360, 376).

11 Although no "complaint" of this kind seems to have been made to Congress, Reverend Isaac Backus (1724–1806), other prominent New England Baptists, and leading Pennsylvania Quakers met on the evening of 14 October in Carpenter's Hall with Continental Congress delegates from several of the New England and middle colonies. There, Backus presented "An Appeal to the Public" and President James Manning of Rhode Island College (Brown University) a "Memorial," asking that the legal disabilities of Baptists in Massachusetts be removed. John Adams and his fellow delegates from that colony agreed to do what they could to have these grievances redressed upon their return home. The memorial appears in full in Alvah Hovey, *A Memoir of the Life and Times of the Rev. Isaac Backus, A.M.* (Boston, 1859), pp. 204–10. See also L. H. Butterfield *et al.*, eds., *Diary and Autobiography of John Adams* (4 vols.; Cambridge, Mass., 1961), II, 152–54; III, 311–13).

12 Bradford used shorthand for the italicized words.

From William Bradford

FC (Historical Society of Pennsylvania).

PHILADELPHIA Jany. 4. 1775.

MY DEAR FRIEND

Agreeable to your request I waited on Mr Dunlap & stopd *your paper*[?] *ours now follows*[?] [*Got Ferguson at Bell's and will send it as soon as* possible etc]¹

With regard to the Complaints of New-England Baptist I can learn nothing. I believe there was none. I suppose you have by this time read the *Journal*² of the Congress by which you will see the Secresy was one of their first resolves; they have observed it so faithfully that we know but little of the Delegates Characters as Scholars & Orators, but those of Virginia are highly celebrated for their zeal. *Your* province seems to take the lead at present; that silent spirit of Courage which is said to reign there has gained you more credit than you can imagine. One fleeson an Upholster[er] has made two Colours for the Fairfax Company; the Motto's "Pro aris & focis" & "Aut Liber aut nullus.["] He has orders also to procure a number of Drums & 200 Muskets as speedily as possible.[3] This is doing something to purpose; but Pennsylvania seems as if it had expended all its vigor in the time of the Stampt-act; or surely it would catch some of that martial spirit that is kindled all around it. But the great Number of Quakers among us will always prevent our doing much that way: "*Their* dear delight is peace," for which I beli[e]ve (with you) they have more reasons than one.[4] As to New-York I think it has the least public Virtue of any City on the Continent. I have heard several express their apprehensions of its Constancy. Rivington is encouraging the Cause of Administration there with all his might: he is daily publishing pamphlets against the proceedings of the Congress & the Cause they are engaged in. Some of them are grossly scurrilous, particularly "A Dialogue between a Southern delegate & his Spouse on his return from the Congress." One of them entitled "a Friendly address to all reasonable americans" (said to be written by Dr Cooper or Dr Chandler) is very artfully done, & I am afraid has had some bad effects on the lower Class of people. Genl. Lee & several others have answered it. If you have not seen it you shall have [it] as soon as possible.[5]

I am sorry to hear of Mr Wallace's declining health. If you write to him advise him to a Journey this way & ask him for me why I never hear from him. Mr Breckenridge when he was here spoke to Aikin about publishing a Satire he had written against some drunken, swearing ministerial parsons who infested his neighbourhood & one Ennis master of [the] School. It was written in Hudibrastic verse in which you know he excells: he repeated part of it & [I] think it had more of the Spirit of Butler than the one I sent you had of Milton. I know not why he delays sending it unless the Skirmish with yon Schoolmaster you speak of engages his attention too much to think of any [thing] else.[6]

Your fear with regard to an insurrection being excited among the slaves seems too well founded. A letter from a Gentleman in England was read yesterday in the Coffee-house, which mentioned the design of administration to pass an act (in case of a rupture) declaring ["]all Slaves & Servants free that would take arms against the Americans." By this you see such a scheme is thought on & talked of; but I cannot beleive the Spirit of the English would ever allow them publickly to adopt so slavish a way of Conquering.

Adieu

W B——D.

PS. Your quondam Chum Livingston, boy as he is, has become a husband.—A run a way match with one Miss Lot.[7]

Memorandum sent Sepr. 1816, to Mr. Delaplaine at his request

(5813)

James Madison was born on the 16. of March 1751. His parents James Madison. and Nelly Madison (before her marriage Nelly Conway) resided in the County of Orange in Virginia. at the time of his birth they were on a visit to her mother who resided on the Rappahannock in the County of King & Queen. At the age of about 12 years. he was placed under the tuition of

Donald Robertson, from Scotland; a man of great learning, and an eminent teacher in the County of King & Queen. With him he studied the latin and greek languages; was taught to read the French but not to speak; and beside arithmetic and Geography, made some progress in algebra and Geometry. Miscellaneous literature also was embraced by the plan of the School.

Having remained 3 or 4 years with Mr. Robertson, he prosecuted his studies for a year or two under the Revd Thomas Martin, the Parish Minister of the established Church, the Church of England as it was then called, and who lived with his father as a private tutor.

In the year 1769. by the advice of Mr. Martin (and of his brother Alexander Martin) both of whom had been educated at Nassau Hall in N. Jersey, he was sent to that Seminary, of which Dr. Witherspoon was then President, (the climate of William & Mary, being regarded as unfavorable to the health of persons from the mountainous region) for the sequel of his Education. He there went thro' the ordinary course of studies and in the year 1771½ received a diploma of Bat: of Arts. His health being at the time too infirm for a journey home. he passed the ensuing winter

AUTOBIOGRAPHICAL SKETCH

MADISON'S DIPLOMA

¹ The italicized words represent a somewhat doubtful decoding of Bradford's shorthand symbols. The final pair of brackets are Bradford's. He apparently had canceled JM's subscription to Dunlap's newspaper, replaced it with a subscription to the Bradfords' *The Pennsylvania Journal; and the Weekly Advertiser*, and would forward to Montpelier, at the first opportunity, Adam Ferguson's (1723–1816) *An Essay on the History of Civil Society* (Edinburgh, 1767), which Robert Bell (*ca.* 1732–1784), Philadelphia printer and bookseller, republished in 1773.

² Bradford underlined this word and the two other words italicized later in this letter.

³ In October 1774 the Fairfax County (Virginia) Committee of Safety asked its chairman, George Washington, who was then in Philadelphia attending the First Continental Congress, to procure the colors and other equipment needed by the Committee's "independent militia company." "For our altars and firesides" and "either freedom or nothing" signified its revolutionary spirit and its purpose. Washington placed the order with Plunket Fleeson, whose upholstery, drapery, and wallpaper shop was patronized by the socially elite of Philadelphia (Kate Mason Rowland, *The Life of George Mason, 1725–1792* [2 vols.; New York, 1892], I, 181–82; Douglas Southall Freeman, *George Washington, a Biography* [7 vols.; New York, 1948–57; Vol. VII by J. A. Carroll and M. W. Ashworth], III, 393; and William Henry Egle, ed., *Proprietary, Supply, and State Tax Lists of the City and County of Philadelphia, for the Years 1769, 1774 and 1779* [Harrisburg, 1897], p. 251).

⁴ On the day following Bradford's letter, a Quaker "Meeting for Sufferings . . . for Pennsylvania and New-Jersey," held in Philadelphia, addressed "An Epistle . . . To our Friends and Brethren in these and the adjacent Provinces," embodying counsel of identical tenor with that of the quotation (Force, *American Archives*, 4th ser., I, 1093–94). The pacifism of Quakers was often attributed by their opponents to an unwillingness to have political unrest lessen their business profits.

⁵ Bradford's comment about James Rivington (1724–1802) is somewhat unfair because he had not altogether barred Whiggish articles from his widely read *New-York Gazetteer*. To ardent patriots, however, Rivington was "*that* JUDAS," "a most wretched, jacobitish, hireling *incendiary*." In 1774, he published the anonymous *A Dialogue, Between a Southern Delegate, and his Spouse, on His Return from the Grand Continental Congress, a Fragment, ascribed to the Married Ladies of America, By Their Most Sincere, and Affectionate Friend, and Servant Mary V. V.*, and the anonymous (but probably by Myles Cooper [1737–1785], Anglican clergyman and president of King's College) *A Friendly Address to all Reasonable Americans, on the Subject of Our Political Confusions: in which the Necessary Consequences of Violently Opposing the King's Troops, and of a General Non-Importation are Fairly Stated*. Most likely it was Thomas Bradbury Chandler (1726–1790), Anglican rector of St. John's Church, Elizabethtown, N.J., who replied in the anonymous *The Strictures on the Friendly Address Examined, and a Refutation of Its Principles Attempted* (New York, 1775) to General Charles Lee's *Strictures on a Pamphlet, Entitled, a "Friendly Address to All Reasonable Americans . . ."* (Philadelphia, 1774). See Arthur M. Schlesinger, *Prelude to Independence: The Newspaper War on Britain, 1764–1776* (New York, 1958), pp. 222–27. Lee (1731–1782), a professional soldier whose later conduct in the American army would arouse much controversy, may have been the more outspokenly Whiggish in 1774–1775 in the hope of gaining a high, if not the highest, command in the patriot forces in the event of war.

⁶ The poem which Brackenridge discussed with Robert Aitken (1734–1802), a Philadelphia printer, was apparently never published, unless possibly in pamphlet or newspaper form. Brackenridge's "Hudibrastic verse" recalls his undergraduate days at the College of New Jersey (Collegiate Doggerel, June 1771–April 1772), while his Miltonic imitation was *A Poem on Divine Revelation* (Bradford to JM,

17 October 1774, n. 5). "Ennis" probably should have been "Innis," a teacher at Eden School in Princess Anne, Md., and a zealous Loyalist. Eden School was established in 1770 and destroyed by fire in 1804. Although Brackenridge's poem seems not to be extant, an apparent answer to it in verse was "The Devil's Triumvirate," about three hundred lines in length, and written by "Aristophanes" (MS owned by Mrs. E. H. Cohn, Princess Anne, Md.). It attacks Brackenridge, Samuel Wilson, and Luther Martin for leaguing with Satan in their strictures upon Innis and Loyalist ministers. After chiding Brackenridge for his "fertile Genius at a Knack of turning fair white into Black," the anonymous poet ordered him

> In Dust and Ashes now repent
> The horrid Lies thou dos't invent
> 'Gainst Men of Probity and Candour
> Tho' nought can come from thee but Slander
> Thou'rt so far gone in Defamation
> That I dispair of Reformation.

7 William Smith Livingston married Catherine Lott, daughter of Abraham Lott of Beaverwyck, near Morristown, N.J. (*Pennsylvania Magazine of History and Biography*, LXX [1946], 294 n., 297 n.).

To William Bradford

RC (Historical Society of Pennsylvania). Addressed: "To Mr. William Bradford Junr. at the Coffee-House Philadelphia." Bradford's copybook version is also at the Historical Society of Pennsylvania.

VIRGINIA ORANGE COUNTY
Jany 20. 1775

MY WORTHY FRIEND

Your very acceptable favours by Mr. Rutherford arrived safe but I perceived by the date, had a very tedious passage which perhaps may be attributed to the *craziness* of the Vessel in which you embarked them. I ought to mention in particular that I did not receive them till after I wrote my last as an apology for my not then acknowledging it[1]

I entirely acquiesce in your Opinion of our friend Brackenridge's Talents and think his poem an indubitable proof of what you say on that Head.[2] It certainly has many real beauties in it and several Strokes of a strong original Genius but at the same time as you observe some very obvious defects which I am afraid too are more discernible to common readers than its excellencies[.] If this be the case, I am apprehensive it will not answer the end proposed which as I collect from his Letter to me,[3] was to raise the Character of his Academy by the fame of its Teacher. It is on this account, he says, he desires it might have a pretty general Reading in this Government:[4] for my own part

I could heartily wish for the Honour of the Author and the success of the performance that It might fall into the Hands only of the Impartial and Judicious. I have shewn it to some of our middling sort of folks and am persuaded it will not be much relished by that Class of my Countrymen. The Subject is itself frightful. Blank Verse in some measure unintelligible at least requires stricter attention [than]⁵ most people will bestow, and the Antiquated Phraseology however eligible in itself disgusts such as affect modern fashions. In short the Theme is not interresting enough nor the dress sufficiently alamode to attract the notice of the generality. The same Merit in a Political or humorous Composition would have rung the Author's fame through every province in the Continent. Something of this kind I am encouraged to expect soon from a passage of his Letter in which he mentions a design of finishing a Poem then in hand, on the present Times and from the description he gives of it (if it be not too local) I doubt not will meet with the publick's Applause. He informed me it would be ready for the Press in three months from the time he wrote: If so you must have seen [it] by this time.⁶

We are very busy at present in raising men and procuring the necessaries for defending ourselves and our fr[i]ends in case of a sudden Invasion. The extensiveness of the Demands of the Congress and the pride of the British Nation together with the Wickedness of the present Ministry, seem, in the Judgment of our Politicians to require a preparation for extreme events[.] There will by the Spring, I expect, be some thousands of well trained High Spirited men ready to meet danger whenever it appears, who are influenced by no mercenary Principles, bearing their own expences and having the prospect of no recompence but the honour and safety of their Country.⁷ I suppose the Inhabitants of your Province are more reserved in their behaviour if not more easy in their Apprehensions, from the prevalence of Quaker principles and politics. The Quakers are the only people with us who refuse to accede to the Continental Association[.] I can not forbear suspecting them to be under the controul and direction of the Leaders of the Party in your Quarters for I take those of them that we have to be too honest and simple to have any sinister or secret Views and I do not observe any thing in the Association inconsistent with their Religious princ[i]ples. When I say they refuse to accede to the Association my meaning is that they refuse to Sign it, that being the method used among us to distinguish friends from foes and to oblige the Common people to a more strict observance of it: I have never heard whether the like method has been adopted in the other governments.⁸

I have not seen the following in print and it seems to be so just a specimen of Indian Eloquence and mistaken Valour that I think you will be pleased with it. You must make allowances for the unskillfulness of the Interpreter.

The Speech of Logan a Shawanese Cheif, to Lord Dunmore

I appeal to any White man to [say]⁹ if ever he entered Logan's Cabin hungry and I gave him not meat, if ever he came cold or naked and I gave him not Cloathing. During the Course of the last long and bloody War, Logan remained Idle in his Tent an Advocate for Peace; Nay such was my love for the Whites, that those of my own Country pointed at me as they passed by and said Logan is the friend of White men: I had even thought to live with you but for the Injuries of one man: Col. Cresop, the last Spring in cold blood and unprovoked cut off all the Relations of Logan not sparing even my Women and Children. There runs not a drop of my blood in the Veins of any human Creature. This called on me for Revenge: I have sought it. I have killed many. I have fully glutted my Vengeance. For my Country I rejoice at the Beams of Peace: But do not harbour a thought that mine is the Joy of fear: Logan never felt fear: He will not turn his Heal to save his life. Who is there to mourn for Logan? Not one.¹⁰

If you should see any of our Friends from Princeton a little before the time of your intending to writ[e] to me and could transmit any little Intelligence concerning the Health &c of my little brother there, it would [be] very acceptable to me & very gratifying to a fond Mother; but I desire it may only be done when it will cost you less than 5 Words.¹¹

We had with us a little before Christmas the Reverend Moses Allen on his return from Boston to Charles Town. He told me he came through Phila. but did not see you: though he expresses a singular regard for you and left his request with me that you would let him hear from you whenever it is convenient: promising to return the Kindness with punctuality. He travelled with considerable equipage for a Dissenting Ecclesiastic and seems to be willing to superadd the Airs of the fine Gentleman to the graces of the Spirit. I had his Company for several days during which time He preached two Sermons with general Approbation. His discourses were above the common run some degree and his appearance in the Pulpit on [the] whole was no discredit to [him.] He retains too much of his primitive Levity but promises amendm[ent.] I wish he may, for the Sake of himself his friends and his flock. I [shall] only add that he seems to be one of those Genius's that are forme[d] for shifting in the world rather than shining in a College and that I really believe [him][12] to possess a friendly and generous Disposition. You shall ere long hear from me again[.] Till then

    Vive Vale et Cetare[13]

JAMES MADISON JUNR.

[1] "Mr. Rutherford" was probably Robert Rutherford (1728–1803) of Frederick County, who was connected with the Madisons through the marriage of a daughter to one of JM's cousins. He was a burgess during most of the sessions from 1766 to 1773, a state senator from 1776 to 1790, and a United States congressman from 1793 to 1797 (T. K. Cartmell, *Shenandoah Valley Pioneers and Their Descendants: A History of Frederick County, Virginia* ... [Winchester, Va., 1909], pp. 254–55). The "favours" which he brought may have been books or pamphlets with no covering note from Bradford. Although the comments about Brackenridge are clearly in response to what Bradford had written on 17 October, JM had evidently received that letter before he wrote "my last" to Bradford on 26 November.

[2] *A Poem on Divine Revelation.*

[3] Letter not found. Henry Marie Brackenridge, Hugh Henry's son, lost many of his father's papers in "an accident" while journeying down the Mississippi River (William F. Keller, author of *The Nation's Advocate: Henry Marie Brackenridge and Young America* [Pittsburgh, 1956], to the editors, 23 November 1957).

[4] JM's use of the word "Government" instead of "province" may reflect the fact that at that time the extralegal county committees of safety and the Association exercised more effective control in Virginia than did Governor Dunmore and other officials of the Crown. On the other hand, Dunmore himself used the word "Government" as an equivalent of "province." Perhaps JM also merely meant this.

[5] "That" in the original.

[6] See Bradford to JM, 4 January 1775, n. 6. JM repeated the phrase "it would."

[7] Governor Dunmore wrote on 24 December 1774 to the Earl of Dartmouth: "Every County . . . is now arming a Company . . . for the avowed purpose of protecting their Committees, and to be employed against Government, if occasion require" (Force, *American Archives*, 4th ser., I, 1062).

[8] The Association (JM to Bradford, 26 November 1774, n. 5) was enforced by local committees in each colony. JM's aristocratic outlook is mirrored in his reference to "the Common people" here and to "our middling sort of folks" earlier in this letter. As a matter of fact, some of the Virginia planters themselves needed to be "persuaded" to abide by the terms of the Association. The Quakers of northern Virginia belonged to the Philadelphia Yearly Meeting.

[9] JM's word was "day," but he probably meant to write "say" as in the 4 February 1775 *Virginia Gazette* (Williamsburg, Dixon and Hunter) version.

[10] Colonel Michael Cresap was often charged with the brutal murder of the family of Logan (*ca.* 1725–1780), the Mingo chieftain who became a staunch ally of the British during the Revolutionary War. His Indian name was Tah-gah-jute. The crime was probably committed by Daniel Greathouse and his group of Indian traders (Reuben G. Thwaites and Louise P. Kellogg, eds., *Documentary History of Dunmore's War, 1774*, pp. 10, 12, 15–17, 19, 378). However this may be, the chieftain's moving speech during the peace negotiations between the Shawnees and Dunmore at Camp Charlotte late in 1774 was translated for the governor by Logan's brother-in-law John Gibson. See JM to Bradford, 1 July 1774, n. 2, and 23 August 1774, n. 2. By what means JM secured a copy is unknown, but his is the earliest

written version now extant. Bradford had it printed in his family's *Pennsylvania Journal* on 1 February 1775; a somewhat different version appeared in the *Virginia Gazette* three days later. Thereafter it was frequently reprinted, usually in the form sent by JM to Bradford. Jefferson included it in his *Notes on the State of Virginia*, together with a condemnation of Cresap. As late as 1797, Luther Martin, Cresap's son-in-law and by then a prominent Maryland Federalist, attacked Jefferson for defaming Cresap (Brant, *Madison*, I, 281–91).

[11] In May 1774, William Madison enrolled in the preparatory school at Princeton.

[12] The bracketed letters or words in this paragraph signify either inadvertent omissions by JM or bits of the writing which disappeared when the right-hand edge of the original page became tattered. In several instances Bradford's file copy supplied the editorial inserts.

[13] This expression means, "Be happy, farewell, etc." The "Vive, vale" is from Horace *Epistolae* i. 6. 67.

From William Bradford

FC (Historical Society of Pennsylvania).

MY DEAR FRIEND,
                                                          [3–6? March 1775][1]

I would have answered your most acceptable epistle of the 20 Jany had not the conclusion given me hopes of "eer long hearing from you again." You must have received a letter I wrote in the beginning of Jany. soon after you dispatched your last unless it be as long on its Voyage as the one I sent by Rutherford was.

I thank you for Logan's speech. I admire the nervous & untutor'd eloquence of it. Like Timanthes "Plus pingitur quam intelligitur."[2] The last sentence is particularly pathetic & expressive; it raises a crowd of Ideas & at one stroke sets in a strong light the Barbarity of Cressop, the sufferings of Logan and his contempt of death. I thought it a pity that so fine a specimen of "Indian Eloquence & mistaken Valour" (as you justly call it) should languish in obscurity and therefore gave a copy of it to my brother who inserted it in his paper; from which it has been transcribed into the others & has given the highest satisfaction to all that can admire & relish the simple Beauties of nature. I need make no apology for publishing what I suppose must be public your way, tho you say you have not seen it in print.

I am glad to hear you are so industrious in Virginia in preparing for the worst. There is no hopes of this province learning the military Exercise unless it be when we ought to be making use of it. Our provincial Convention was called (it is thought) principally for the purpose of setting on foot independant companies appointing officers &c; But so great an opposition was expected that it was not even proposed. They however passed a few harmless resolves lest [it] should be said, "they march'd up the hill & so march'd down again."[3] It is happy for us that we have Boston in the front & Virginia in the rear to defend us: we are placed where Cowards ought to be placed in the middle; & perhaps the bravery that surrounds us may prevent our want of it being detrimental to the cause of freedom. But we are not totally destitute of public virtue. Our Assembly is strinuous in supporting & recommending the resolutions of the late Congress & have appointed Delegates for the ensuing one. Among these was Galloway; but he declined it with declaring that the proceedings of the Colonies were against his Judgment & against his Conscience. Methinks this fellow's Conscience has become very tender since he laid aside the attorney; but I am afraid he can contract or dilate it at pleasure & make it strain at a Gnat or swallow a camel as best suits his purpose.[4] As to the N York Assembly, they have resolved to petition the king & remonstrate to the parliament, but will have nothing to do with the Congress. They have absolutely refused to nominate delegates, but I hope their Constituents will do it for them; I observe the Committee of that City have called a meeting to consult upon the matter.[5] Was it not too late a petition from the several assembli[es] might perhaps be advantageous to our cause. Most of the Governors[6] have assured their respective assemblies (from private instructions I suppose) that such petition will be duly attended to; I imagine there is nothing prevents the parliament repealing the oppressive acts but their Pride & therefore a little submission on our side by affording them an opportunity of receeding with credit might not be amiss. But if, as is probable our fate is already determined in parliament[,] Union among ourselves, & a strict adhearence to the measures of the Congress is the only means of safety.

I had a letter the other day from Mr Breckenridge in which he gave me the disagreeable task of telling him what the public said of his peice. I have enquired but can meet with nobody that has read it, & shall therefore plainly tell him so & lay the fault on the subject the times & the publisher. He says nothing about his Canto's, which I am impatient to see. They would serve to counterbalance several satire[s] that have been published this way against the Congress & patriotic party.[7]

I wrote to Mr Duffield about your brother and have the happiness to inform you that he is well—the formost scholar in his class & what is still better yt he is a good boy.[8] I hope I shall hear from you soon, but I am afraid the business of the supreme Court will prevent me writing to you again for some time.[9] But whereever I am, or whatever

I am doing I cannot forget you. You frequently obtrude on my thoughts & are frequently the subject of my conversations with those who know & love you. I find that your friendship & correspondence makes a great part of my happiness and that time but serves to increase my fond attatchment to you. Forgive my friend these overflowings of an heart devoted to you. I know you will esteem it the Language of the heart & believe me sincere when I subscribe myself

    your affectionate friend

W.B.

[1] Because Bradford refers to an action of the New York City "Committee of Sixty" on 1 March (below, n. 5) but omits mention of the results of that action on 6 March, he probably wrote this undated letter between the 3d and 6th of that month.

[2] In his *Natural History*, book 35, chapter 10, Pliny commented that Timanthes, a celebrated Greek painter of about 400 B.C., "atque in hujus operibus intelligitur plus semper, quam pingitur." One English version of this runs, "for albeit a man shall see in his [Timanthes'] pictures as much art as may be, yet his wit went alwaies beyond his art" (Philemon Holland, trans., *The Historie of the World, Commonly called, the Naturall Historie of C. Plinius Secundus* [London, 1601], p. 536).

[3] This is a somewhat inaccurate quotation from the anonymous nursery jingle about "the noble Duke of York" and his "ten thousand men." During its meetings of 23 to 28 January, the Convention of the Province of Pennsylvania unanimously approved what the First Continental Congress had done, pledged to enforce its recommendations, and adopted twenty-seven resolutions, mostly designed to encourage and regulate domestic manufactures (Force, *American Archives*, 4th ser., I, 1169–71).

[4] In December 1774 the Pennsylvania Assembly led all other colonial legislatures in ratifying the work of the Continental Congress and in naming delegates to the second meeting of that body, scheduled for the following May. Among those chosen to attend was Joseph Galloway. Although he at once and repeatedly declared that he would not serve, he was not released by the Assembly from his commission until 12 May 1775. This revocation closed his political career in Pennsylvania (Oliver C. Kuntzleman, *Joseph Galloway, Loyalist* [Philadelphia, 1941], pp. 127, 132–33).

[5] After resolving to petition George III and memorialize Parliament, the New York Assembly on 23 February, by a 17 to 9 vote, declined to appoint delegates to the Second Continental Congress (Force, *American Archives*, 4th ser., I, 1287–90). On 1 March the "Committee of Sixty" of New York City set 6 March as the date for a meeting of the city's voters to decide how those delegates should be chosen (*ibid.*, 4th ser., II, 4, 48–49).

[6] Between "Governors" and "have," Bradford inadvertently wrote "this was."

[7] Thus ended Brackenridge's high hopes that his *A Poem on Divine Revelation* would be a success. The "Canto's" were probably his never published, anti-Tory satires (Bradford to JM, 4 January 1775, n. 6).

[8] John Duffield, a tutor at the College of New Jersey, was Bradford's close friend.

[9] Service in the patriot army delayed Bradford's admission to the bar until 1779. Early in 1775 he was probably the student assistant of a Philadelphia attorney who was preparing the briefs of cases to be heard by the provincial Supreme Court, scheduled to convene on 10 April.

To William Bradford

Copy (Historical Society of Pennsylvania).

[Early March 1775][1]

DEAR SIR,

I intend to throw this in the way of Mr David Hoopes[2] who I hear is setting out for Philada. As it is uncertain whether he may get it I shall only return a short answer to yours of Jany 4th. [Mr Dunlap's mistake about price of his paper—the 2 Vol. of Papers too dear & vide lit.][3]

We had a report here a few days [ago] that the New Yorkers had again given way & that the assembly had voted the proceedings of the Congress illegal. It raised a surprizing spirit of indignation & resentment which however Subsided on the report's being contradicted. The intimation you gave me of the state of affairs there prepared me to hear it without Surprize.

I lately saw in one of our Gazettes a pamphlet in answer to the friendly address &c: by what you informed me I conjecture it to have been written by Genl. Lee. It has much Spirit and Vivacity & contains some very sensible remarks. Some of our old bigots did not altogether approve the Strictures on the Clergy & King Charles; but it was generally, nay with this exception, universally, applauded.[4] I wish most heartily we had Rivington & his ministerial Gazetteers for 24. hours in this place. Execrable as their designs are, they would meet with adequate punishment. How different is the Spirit of Virginia from that of N York? A fellow was lately tarred & feathered for treating one [of] our county committees with disre[s]pect; in NY. they insult the whole Colony and Continent with impunity![5]

Some persons have expressed to me a curiosity to See the Friendly Address &c and as you mention it as the best performance on that Side of the dispute & promise to Send it with Ferguson &c I should be obliged to you for it.[6] If you should See Mr Hoops and are acquainted with him if he is not to much encumbered on his return perhaps he would be kind enough to bring them. I shall add no more at present for the reason above mentioned, but that I am Yours most Sincerely & affectionately:

JM JUN.

[1] JM probably wrote this undated letter early in March because on the 17th he mentions it as having been sent "very lately" by David Hoops.

[2] David Hoops (*ca.* 1757–post-1791), a son of Adam Hoops, was probably in Virginia to plan his move there as a Louisa County farmer. By 1777 he was farming in Frederickville Parish, about thirty-five miles from Montpelier, but shortly thereafter he moved back to Pennsylvania. He was related by marriage to Patrick Henry's half-brother, Colonel John Syme, Jr. (Malcolm H. Harris, *History of Louisa County, Virginia* [Richmond, 1936], p. 162; *Pennsylvania Magazine of History and Biography*, XXV [1911], 512).

[3] Bradford's brackets evidently inclose a mention of two subjects about which JM wrote at some length in his original letter, as signified by *vide lit.* To what "2 Vol." he referred is unknown, but apparently he had been overcharged for Dunlap's newspaper (JM to Bradford, 26 November 1774, n. 2; and Bradford to JM, 4 January 1775, n. 1).

[4] See Bradford to JM, 4 January 1775, n. 5. Confident that Reverend Myles Cooper had written the anonymous *Friendly Address*, Charles Lee opened his reply (*Strictures on a Pamphlet*) to it by accusing every high "Ecclesiastick" of the Church of England of "want of candour and truth, the apparent spirit of persecution . . . and the zeal for arbitrary power." He then continued: "I believe there are at least ninety-nine Americans in a hundred, who think that Charles the First was an execrable tyrant; that he met with no harder fate than he deserved; and that his two Sons ought, in justice, to have made the same exit." JM probably read Lee's essay in the *Virginia Gazette* (Williamsburg, Purdie) of 3 February 1775.

[5] This episode has not been identified. On 10 March 1782, however, Thomas Parker, in a letter to Governor Benjamin Harrison of Virginia, mentioned the tar and feathering of Tories in Isle of Wight County seven years before (William P. Palmer *et al.*, eds., *Calendar of Virginia State Papers and Other Manuscripts* [11 vols.; Richmond, 1875–93], III, 92). In the *Magazine of History and Notes and Queries*, III (New York, 1906), 156, a letter from Williamsburg of 27 November 1774 is summarized, telling of a pole erected opposite the Raleigh Tavern, "upon which was hung a large mop and a bag of feathers and under it a bucket of tar."

[6] For Ferguson's essay, see Bradford to JM, 4 January 1775, nn. 1 and 5.

To William Bradford

Copy (Historical Society of Pennsylvania).

VIRGINIA 17th March 1775.

DEAR SIR,

This I expect will be delivered to you by the Revd. Mr Samuel Smith[1] who will inform you of every thing respecting our affairs that I could let you know by Letter. I wrote to you very lately by Mr David Hoops in answer to yours contain[in]g a few lines from Mr Irvin.[2] If it should fail of coming to you it will be proper I should know of it because I there mentioned what I desired as to Dunlap & the Collection of papers I wanted & would not now unnecessarally trouble you with a repetition. Inclosed you have a small pitance for reimbursing you for your layings out on my account for the time past and any other trifles you may be kind enough to send me. Mr Smith will return he says about the middle of June and will bring ferguson[3] for me, if you will put it in his hands and any thing else that he can conveniently carry[.] I have the pleasure to hear by him that our friend Mr Wallace is not in that perilous state, I was induced by a false rumour to make you beleive he was.[4]

1 Samuel Stanhope Smith.
2 The "few lines" from Nathaniel Irwin have not been found.
3 For Ferguson's essay, see Bradford to JM, 4 January 1775, n. 1; and JM to Bradford, [early March 1775].
4 Caleb Wallace (JM to Bradford, 26 November 1774). Here Bradford ended his file copy of this letter, the only version of it known to be extant.

From William Bradford

FC (Historical Society of Pennsylvania).

April 4th. [1775][1]

My dear Sir

Though the business that at present surrounds me on every side, makes writing inconvenient, yet I cannot let Mr. Hoops[2] return without a few Lines to one I value so much.

[Mr Dunlap's paper &c][3] I send with this Furguson which I could not get for less *than* 12/ tho' you will perceive it is somewhat soil'd. I also send the friendly address &c. & The other side of the Question.[4] I dare not add more for fear of encumbering Mr. Hoops.

The Supream & Oyer & Terminer Courts[5] which are just a[t] hand will keep me closely employed for some time. They begin the tenth day of this month when Young McAllister, (who you may remember was expelled from college) is to be tried in conjuntion with one Stewart a printer for counterfeiting the 50/. bills of Credit of this province. Clymer, with whom McAllister was studying Law, & several others are to be council for them but the fact is so plain, that the Eloquence of Gabriel could not prevent their conviction: whether their Youth, join'd to the intercession of their friends may induce the Governor to pardon them I cannot say.[6]

Adieu

W B Jun

[1] Bradford left out the year in his notebook copy.

[2] David Hoops.

[3] Bradford's brackets probably signify that he had expanded upon this subject in the original copy of this letter.

[4] See Bradford to JM, 4 January 1775, n. 5. In his file copy, Bradford denoted the italicized word by a shorthand symbol.

[5] An "oyer & terminer" (to hear and decide) court in Pennsylvania was a tribunal with criminal jurisdiction.

[6] John M'Allister and Andrew Stewart (or Stuart). See Bradford to JM, 2 June 1775. M'Allister's name does not appear on any undergraduate roster of the College of New Jersey known to the editors. Clymer was probably Daniel Cunyngham Clymer (1748–1819), College of New Jersey, '66, a prominent Philadelphia lawyer who entered state politics after moving to Reading, Pa., in 1782 (*Pennsylvania Magazine of History and Biography*, III [1879], 287, n. 3).

To William Bradford

Copy (Historical Society of Pennsylvania). This letter, the original of which is lost, was delivered by Patrick Henry, who arrived in Philadelphia on 17 or 18 May.

VIRGINIA May 9th. 1775.

MY DEAR FRIEND

I this day received your favor by Mr Hoopes but have not yet got the articles I find came along with it. Mr Hoopes lives at no very great distance so that I shall not be long without them.[1]

We have lately had a great alarm here about the Governor's removing a large quantity of powder from our magazine and conveying it on board a ship of war:[2] Not less [than][3] 600 men well armed and mounted assembled at Fredg. on this occasion, with a view to proceed to Wmsburg. [to] recover the powder & revenge the insult: The propriety of such a step was warmly agitated and weighty arguments adduced both for & against it: At length the advice of Peyton Randolph, Edm. Pendleton, Richd. H. Lee, and George Washington Esqrs. delegates for the Congress, to return home was complied with.[4] The reasons however that induced these Gentlement to give this advice did not appear satisfactory to Patrick Henry Esqr. another of our delegates whose sentiments were not known at Fredg. This Gentleman after the dispersion of the troops at the above named place under the authority of the committee of his County and at the head of an Independant Company undertook to procure redress, which he resolutely accomplished by taking of the King's Quit-rents as much money as would replace the powder which had been removed so far that it could not be come at.[5] This affair has prevented his appearing at the Congress as early as his Colleagues, and has afforded me this opportunity of sending you a few lines. I expect his conduct as contrary to the opinion of the other delegats will be disapproved of by them, but it [has][6] gained him great honor in the most spirited parts of the Country and addresses of thanks are already presenting to him from different Quarters: The Gentlemen below whose property will be exposed in case of a civil war in this Colony were extremely alarmed lest Government should be provoked to make reprisals. Indeed some of them discovered a pusilanimity little comporting with their professions or the name of Virginian.[7]

I sent last fall to England for a few books, among which was priestly's treatise on Government. The present state of our affairs seems to threaten that it may be a long time before our commercial intercourse will be renewed:[8] If this sd. appear to you to be the Case (& the session of the Congress will enable you to form a good guess), and it should be convenient in other respects, I should be glad you would send me the above treatise by the return of Mr S. Smith.[9] The short time I had to scribble these few lines is already expired, & I must for the present bid adieu to my beloved friend.

J M JUN.

[1] David Hoops. In his copybook Bradford repeated "shall not."

[2] This occurred in Williamsburg on 20 April 1775. In this paragraph, JM, of course, reported what he read or was told, not what he saw. The "large quantity" was fifteen half-barrels (Force, *American Archives*, 4th ser., III, 389–90).

[3] Bradford wrote "that" instead of "than."

[4] 29 April 1775. For this advice to be given by the conservative Randolph and Pendleton occasions no surprise, but Richard Henry Lee, and perhaps even Washington, might have been expected to advocate a less cautious policy.

[5] Patrick Henry and his company appear to have easily persuaded Richard Corbin, the receiver general, to give them £330 from the king's funds in his custody. If this sum proved to be more than adequate to purchase as much powder as had been "unlawfully" taken by Governor Dunmore, the balance would be returned to Corbin (Force, *American Archives*, 4th ser., II, 540).

[6] Bradford inadvertently wrote "his" instead of "has."

[7] JM, living in the "spirited" up-country, obviously approved of what the men of Hanover had done. By the "Gentlemen below" he meant the planters along the lower York and James rivers.

[8] JM probably refers to Joseph Priestley (1733–1804), *An Essay on the First Principles of Government; and on the Nature of Political, Civil, and Religious Liberty* (London, 1768). Under the Association the non-importation agreement had gone into effect on 1 December 1774.

[9] Samuel Stanhope Smith.

Address to Captain Patrick Henry and the Gentlemen Independents of Hanover

MS not located. Text from the *Virginia Gazette* (Williamsburg, Purdie), 19 May 1775, supplement. Patrick Henry apparently sent the original manuscript, possibly in JM's hand, to Alexander Purdie, who most likely destroyed it after setting the type. Peter Force in his *American Archives*, 4th ser., II, 539–40, followed the *Gazette*'s version although, probably inadvertently, he substituted "county magazine" for "country magazine." On the other hand, William Cabell Rives in his *History of the Life and Times of James Madison*, I, 95, stated that he reproduced the address from a copy of it in JM's hand. The Rives version alters that of the *Gazette* by using the word "opportunity" instead of "occasion," and "in which" instead of "where." No copy of the address in JM's hand is known to the present editors. Among his papers in the Library of Congress is a copy of the four resolutions which accompanied the address, but the penmanship is not JM's. The evidence that he drafted the address and the resolutions is inconclusive at best.

[9 May 1775]

The committee for ORANGE county, met on Tuesday the 9th of May, taking into their consideration the removal of the powder from the publick magazine, and the compensation obtained by the independent company of Hanover; and observing also, that the receipt given by Capt. PATRICK HENRY, to his Majesty's Receiver General, refers the final disposal of the money to the next Colony Convention, came into the following resolutions:

1. That the Governour's removal of the powder lodged in the magazine, and set apart for the defence of the country, was fraudulent, unnecessary, and extremely provoking to the people of this colony.

2. That the resentment shewn by the Hanover volunteers, and the reprisal they have made on the King's property, highly merit the approbation of the publick, and the thanks of this committee.

3. That if any attempt should be made at the ensuing Convention to have the money returned to his Majesty's Receiver General, our delegates be, and they are hereby instructed, to exert all their influence in opposing such attempt, and in having the money laid out in gunpowder for the use of the colony.

4. That the following address be presented to Capt. PATRICK HENRY, and the Gentlemen independents of Hanover.

GENTLEMEN,

We, the committee for the county of Orange,[1] having been fully informed of your seasonable and spirited proceedings in procuring a compensation for the powder fraudulently taken from the country magazine, by command of Lord Dunmore, and which it evidently appears his Lordship, notwithstanding his assurances, had no intention to restore, entreat you to accept their cordial thanks for this testimony of your zeal for the honour and interest of your country. We take this occasion also to give it as our opinion, that the blow struck in the Massachusetts government is a hostile attack on this and every other colony, and a sufficient warrant to use violence and reprisal, in all cases where it may be expedient for our security and welfare.

James Madison, chairman, *James Taylor, Thomas Barbour, Zachariah Burnley, Rowland Thomas, James Madison, jun. William Moore, James Walker, Lawrence Taliaferro, Henry Scott, Thomas Bill.*[2]

[1] The Orange County Committee of Safety, organized on 22 December 1774, had JM's father as its chairman, Francis Taylor as its clerk, and JM as one of its members. Prior to 9 May 1775 the committee's only known activities were to oblige Francis Moore, Jr., to make a public apology for violating the Association by gambling, and to burn some "execrable" Tory pamphlets found in the possession of Reverend John Wingate (*Virginia Gazette* [Williamsburg, Dixon and Hunter], 28 January, 11 March, and 15 April 1775).

JM apparently was one of the men of Orange County who carried the committee's address and resolutions to Patrick Henry. At any rate the latter, who was then at Port Royal, Va., on his way to the meeting of the Second Continental Congress in Philadelphia, consented to take with him JM's letter of 9 May to Bradford. Henry took his seat in Congress on 18 May.

In the Lloyd W. Smith Collection of the Morristown National Historical Park, Morristown, N.J., is the following acknowledgment by Patrick Henry of the Orange County Committee's address and resolutions:

PORT ROYAL may 11th. 1775

SIR.

I think myself & the Volunteers of Hanover peculiarly happy to find, that the Reprizal we have made for the purpose of compensating the Colony for the Loss of the Powder from the Magazine, has met with the Approbation of your Committee. Give me leave to assure you Sir, that nothing called us forth upon that Occasion, but Zeal for the public Good.

I can discover nothing improper for the public Eye in the several Votes & Resolutions sent me. The Gentm. who are now so kind as to escort me, wish it (together with similar Votes of three other Cotys recd. today,) to be printed.

Be pleased to present my best Compliments to the Committee & believe me to be Sir yr. mo. obedt. sert.

P. HENRY JR.

JAMES MADISON ESQR.

² Thomas Barbour (1735–1825) was justice of the peace for some forty-five years, a burgess from 1769 to 1775, a member of the General Conventions of 1774 and 1775, sheriff in 1776 and 1777, and county lieutenant, 1784–1786 and 1789–1791. Replacing William Moore as major of militia in 1778, he served for three years with this rank, and the next three as lieutenant colonel. When JM declined to be county lieutenant in 1784, Barbour assumed that office. His plantation, Bloomingdale, neighbored Montpelier on the west. He and his sons, James and Philip Pendleton Barbour, were close friends of the Madisons (W[illiam] W. Scott, *A History of Orange County, Virginia* [Richmond, 1907], pp. 70–71, 183, 214). Zachariah Burnley (*ca.* 1730–1800) succeeded James Madison, Sr., as county lieutenant. He also served the county as justice of the peace, burgess, sheriff, and delegate in the General Assembly, 1780–1781. Thereafter he appears to have withdrawn from public life (Emma Dicken, comp., *Our Burnley Ancestors and Allied Families* [New York, 1946], pp. 44–46; William G. and Mary Newton Stanard, comps., *The Colonial Virginia Register* [Albany, 1902], pp. 173–75, 177, 191, 194, 196). Rowland Thomas (*ca.* 1725–*ca.* 1800) was a justice of the peace for eighteen years and sheriff for six years before moving to Spotsylvania County around 1787. Later he moved to Kentucky (Orange County Order Book, No. 6; Minute Books, Nos. 1 and 2, microfilm in Virginia State Library). William Moore (1740–1802) was a state assemblyman during the Revolution, and sheriff of Orange County from 1784 to 1789. He was usually known as "Major Moore" because of his rank in the militia when he resigned his commission in 1778. A lifelong friend of the Madisons, he was apparently a half brother of JM's mother (D. N. Davidson, comp., "Several Famous Families of Orange County, Virginia" [mimeographed; Orange, Va., 1934]). James Walker (*ca.* 1729–*ca.* 1785) was a justice of the peace for thirteen years, a burgess in 1761–1767, 1769–1771, and 1775, sheriff in 1771–1772, a delegate to the Virginia Convention of March 1775, and a state senator in 1777–1778 (Orange County Order Book, No. 6; Minute Book, No. 1, *passim*). Lawrence Taliaferro (1734–1798) of Rose Hill was commissioned a justice of the peace and a militia captain in 1768. He remained in militia service and commanded the "Culpeper Minute-Men" at the Battle of Great Bridge on 9 December 1775. In 1778 he was appointed lieutenant colonel of the Orange County militia (Orange County Order Book, No. 7, p. 514; *Lineage Book of the National Society of the Daughters of the American Revolution*, LXVI [1923], 155). "Henry Scott" was apparently a printer's error for Johnny Scott (*ca.* 1738–1805), justice of the peace for twenty-four years, a militia captain and commissary from 1775 to 1778, and a delegate to the General Assembly from 1781 to 1783 (Orange County Minute Books, Nos. 1–3, *passim*). "Thomas Bill" was a printer's error for Thomas Bell (*ca.* 1739–1796), justice of the peace from 1769 to 1792 (*ibid.*).

From William Bradford

FC (Historical Society of Pennsylvania).

PHILADA. June ye 2d. 1775.

MY DEAR FRIEND,

I have two of your epistolary favours to acknowledge[,] the one handed to me by the Revd Mr Smith, some time ago & the other since by Patrick Henry Esqr. I also received 22/6. & as it exceeds what Ferguson &c Cost I shall consider you as the Cestui que Use of the surplus.[1]

I have but little to tell you of the Congress; they keep their proceeding so secret that scarce any thing transpires but what they think proper to publish in the papers. They meet every day & continue long in debate but it is said are very unanimous. I can however (inter nos) inform you that they begin to entertain a great Suspicion that Dr. Franklin came rather as a spy than as a friend, & that he means to discover our weak side & make his peace with the minister by discovering it to him. It was expected he would have given the Congress some very useful information with regard to affairs at home, but hitherto he has been silent on that head & in every respect behaved more like a spectator than a member. These particulars were communicated to a Gentleman I am acquainted with by Coll: Lee who was highly offended with the Doctor & declared he should not leave the Congress till he had removed or confirmed that suspicion.[2]

The back Counties of this province are very busy in learning the military Exercise. Mr. Armstrong informs me that in Lancaster County alone there are above 3000 men training to arms who associate not only to defend themselves at home if attacked; but have solemnly engaged to leave all & march wheresoever & whensoever their assistance is needed.[3] We are equally industrious in Philada. and propose having a General review next monday: & I hope in a month or two we shall be able to meet without dread the most disciplined troops. I wish the infatuation of the ministry may not oblige us to employ our arms against our fellow subjects; but should matters come to that expected issue I am persuaded this city will not be wanting in the day of Battle. A surprizing unanimity prevails here & all our tories have recanted or fled for it: We have two Companies composed intirely of Quakers, who dress in a neat uniform & many others of that society are in the other Companies: So much, have the sufferings of boston excited the resentment & courage of that peace-loving People.[4] We have authentic accounts that the people of Boston suffer all the distress of famine[,] that Milk is sold in small quantities at the rate of a crown Pr Quart, that the Country people bring no fresh provisions in the town & that the little salt meat they have is excessively high. Tho' the[y] have liberty to leave the town on particular days, yet as they are obliged to wait on several officers to procure a pass, (which only serves for the day on which it is procured & for which a dollar is extorted from the poorest inhabitant*) and as they are all stoped at the Gate &c to be searched,

* This appears to be a mistake.

they get out but slowly. The army it is said are likewise in want of fresh provisions; which set them upon stealing some sheep from the Islands: but the attempt miscarried, it seems.[5]

In my last I informed you of McAllister & Stuart being apprehended for conterfeiting the bills of Credit of this province: they have since been convicted, & condemned but both at different times escaped out of gaol: The Gaoler is confined on suspicion of being privy to their Escape.[6] We have just receivd an account of some of the Magistrates of this province being imprisoned near fort-pitt by Ld. Dunmores officers. I hope We shall have no disturbance about boundaries at a time when unanimity is so necessary.[7]

As our ports are to be shut up the 20th. July it is probable you will not receive the books you sent for very soon. I will therefore send Priestly's treatise on Government by Mr Smith and if the resolves of the Congress or any thing new is published before he goes, you shall have it by him.[8] All friends this way are well. I hope you are so too; si valeas valeo[9]

Adieu

W B JUN

[1] See JM to Bradford, 17 March 1775. The Anglo-French legal expression "Cestui que" means a person who retains a beneficial interest in property which has been vested legally in a trustee.

[2] Although Bradford's suspicion of Benjamin Franklin was, of course, entirely unwarranted, it was shared by many others, including Bradford's brother Thomas, during the first weeks of the Second Continental Congress. Returning from nearly eight years as a colonial agent in England only one day before being chosen a delegate to the Congress, Franklin remained silent during its early sessions. Richard Henry Lee (1732–1794) had probably been led to distrust Franklin by his brother, Arthur Lee, who while in London came to believe that the Pennsylvanian's ambition for a higher office kept him from vigorously asserting colonial rights (Carl Van Doren, *Benjamin Franklin* [New York, 1938], pp. 480–81, 527–29).

[3] Bradford may have heard this news from John Armstrong, Jr. (1758–1843), whose father, a prominent lawyer and judge, was then helping to raise troops in western Pennsylvania (Charles Page Smith, *James Wilson, Founding Father, 1742–1798* [Chapel Hill, 1956], pp. 44, 66–67).

[4] On 26 August 1775, a member of Congress at Philadelphia wrote to a gentleman in London: "The very *Quakers* in this and other Provinces are in arms, and appear in the field every day in their regimentals, and make as good a figure as the best" (Force, *American Archives*, 4th ser., III, 435–36).

[5] The asterisk and footnote are Bradford's. Bradford did not exaggerate the scarcity and high prices of food in Boston or the difficulties besetting its citizens who wished to leave that city (Force, *American Archives*, 4th ser., II, 375–76, 423, 425, 441, 666, 798, 1735–36). On 23 May 1775 the Massachusetts Provincial Congress took steps to stop the "plunder or purchase" by the British of "Hay, Cattle, Sheep, and many other things" owned by residents of the Boston harbor area (*ibid.*, II, 818). In this connection, on 27 May hot skirmishes between detachments of the

opposing armies occurred on Hog and Noddle's islands, although Bradford probably had not heard of them (*ibid.*, II, 719–20).

6 On 27 May 1775 Governor John Penn offered a reward for M'Allister's capture (*Pennsylvania Archives*, 4th ser., III, 515–16). On 7 June 1775 a reward was posted in Philadelphia for the apprehension of Stewart (Kenneth Scott, *Counterfeiting in Colonial Pennsylvania* [New York, 1955], p. 141).

7 Although the successful outcome of Lord Dunmore's War had temporarily ended the Indian menace in the Pittsburgh neighborhood, the peace merely invited a resumption there of the old and bitter jurisdictional dispute between Virginia and Pennsylvania (*Pennsylvania Archives*, 1st ser., IV, 618–20; Boyd, *Papers of Jefferson*, I, 235–36, 245; Solon J. Buck and Elizabeth Hawthorn Buck, *The Planting of Civilization in Western Pennsylvania* [Pittsburgh, 1939], chap. viii).

8 Reverend Samuel Stanhope Smith did not set out for Virginia until 17 July 1775.

9 This expression appears to be a shortened form of the often used "si vales, bene est; ego quidem valeo," meaning "if you are well, 'tis good; as for me, I am well."

To William Bradford

Copy (Historical Society of Pennsylvania).

June 19th. 1775.

MY DEAR FRIEND

I received another acceptable pledge of your friendship two days ago in a letter dated June 2d. and, as usual, must begin this by discharging a debt of Gratitude to which the further accounts I have of your friendly services and intentions intitle you. I hope I have an inexhaustible fund of that however destitute I may be of other virtues. But I assure you I am often grieved at reflecting that I have it not in my power to give you a better evidence of it than verbal declarations Yet I have that opinion of your goodness that I am persuaded you would be satisfied even without them.

Little did I ever expect to hear that Jeremiah's Doctrine that "the heart of man is deceitful above all things & desperately wicked"[1] was exemplified in the celebrated Dr Franklin, & if the suspicions against him be well founded it certainly is remarkably exemplified. Indeed it appears to me that the bare suspicion of his guilt amounts very nearly to a proof of its reality. If he were the man he formerly was, & has even of late pretended to be[,] his conduct in Philada. on this critical occasion could have left no room for surmise or distrust. He certainly would have been both a faithful informer & an active member of the Congress. His behaivour would have been explicit & his Zeal warm and conspicuous. We have a report he[re] that Bland one of our delegates has turned traitor & fled from Philada. I hope it is not true tho' some unfavorabl[e] Hints have been thrown out of late to his prejudice.[2] Virgil certainly gave a great proof of his knowlege of human nature when he exclaimed "Quid non mortalia pectora cogis auri sacra fama?["][3] Tho' appointed a member[4] of Congress Bland is in needy circumstances & we all know age is no stranger to avarice. The conduct of these two delegates with many concurring circumstances I think suggest the apprehensions that some Golden prospects will be opened to the Congress by the ministry before they make their ultimate appeal to the Sword. A prospect that could captivate the heart of a franklin could almost make me shudder for the tempted. But when I consider the united virtue of that illustrious Body every apprehension of Danger vanishes. The signal proofs they have given of their Integrity & attachment to Liberty both in their private & Confederate capacities must triumph over Jealously itself. However should it come to the worst I am persuaded that the Union Virtue & Love of Liberty at present prevailing thro'out the Colonies is such that it would be as little in the power of our treacherous friends as of our avowed enemies, to put the yoke upon us. An attempt to sell us would infallibly purchase to the authors present Vengeance & eternal infamy.

A rumour is on the wing that the provincials have stormed Boston & with the Loss of 7,000 have cutt off or taken Gage & all his men. It is but little credited. Indeed the fact is extremely improbable: but the times are so remarkable for strange events; that improbability is almost become an argument for their truth.[5]

Our friend Mr Wallace I hear is well & has entered into the Connubial state with one Miss McDowell, daughter of one of the representatives of Bottatourt County.[6] Since I wrote last a Dysentry hath made an Irruption in my father's family. It has carried off a little sister about seven & a brother about four years of age.[7] It is still among us but principally among the blacks. I have escaped hitherto, & as it is now out of the house I live in, I hope the danger is over. It is a disorder pretty incident to this Country & from some symptoms I am afraid will rage more generally this year than common. Our Burgesses from the County are not yet returned from Willmsbg. where they hold their Assembly. So I cannot give you any particulars of their proceedings. The news papers will do that I expect: I understand Lord Dunmore by deserting his Palace & taking Sanctuary on board the Ship of War, under pretence of the fear of an Attack on his person, has surprized & incensed them much, As they thought it incredible he should be actuated on that occasion by the Motive he alledges. It is judged more likly to have proceeded from some intelligence or Instructions he has received from his friends or superiors to the North. It is said the Governor of N Caroliana has treated his Assembly nearly in the same manner. Some will have it that Lord Dunmore removed from Wmsbg. & pretended danger that he might with more force & consistency misrepresent us to the ministry. His unparralled malice to the people of this Colony since the detection of his false & wicked letters, sent home at the time he was professing an ardent friendship for us must lead us to suppose he will do us all the Injury in his power. But we defy his power as much as we detest his Villany.[8] We have as great unanimity & as much of the Military Ardor as you can possibly have in your government; & the progress we make in discipline & hostile preparations is as great as the Zeal with which these things were undertaken. The strength of this Colony will lie chiefly in the rifle-men of the Upland Counties, of whom we shall have great numbers. You would be astonished at the perfection this art is brought to. The most inexpert hands rec[k]on it an indifferent shot to miss the bigness of a man's face at the distance of 100 Yards. I am far from being among the best & should not often miss it on a fair trial at that distance. If we come into an engagement, I make no doubt but the officers of the enemy will fall at the distance before they get withing 150 or 200 Yards. Indeed I believe we have men that would very often hit such a mark 250 Yds. Our greatest apprehensions proceed from the scarcity of powder but a little will go a great way with such as use rifles. It is imagined our Governor has been tampering with the Slaves & that he has it in contemplation to make great Use of them in case of a civil war in this province. To say the truth, that is the only part in which this Colony is vulnerable; & if we should be subdued, we shall fall like Achilles by the hand of one that knows that secret.[9] But we have a good cause & great Courage which are a great support. I shall just add that among other incouragement we have a prospect of immense crops of Grain.

Adieu

J M Jun

[1] JM inserted "of man"; otherwise he accurately quoted Jeremiah 17:9.

[2] Largely because of ill health, Richard Bland (1710–1776) withdrew from Congress in early June. Tories, and especially several Anglican clergymen, spread the report that his American patriotism had not withstood a British offer of a lucrative position as tax collector. On 28 July, the Virginia Convention completely exonerated him, and two weeks later re-elected him to Congress. On 12 August, pleading that he was "an Old man, almost deprived of sight," he declined the appointment (*Journals of the Continental Congress*, II, 243–44; Force, *American Archives*, 4th ser., III, 369, 371, 379–80).

3 *Aeneid* iii. 56–57, "cursed greed for gold, to what crimes dost thou not impel the human breast." JM's "fama" should have been "fames."

4 In copying, Bradford inadvertently preceded "a member" with "a mem."

5 Except for a few minor skirmishes, no engagements between American and British troops around Boston occurred after Lexington and Concord until the Battle of Bunker Hill on 17 June. Perhaps JM had heard a garbled version of a mistaken report, sent on 13 June by an unidentified Virginia delegate in the Continental Congress to "his friend in Williamsburgh." This told how, with "merely trifling" losses, fifteen hundred Americans had fought an equal number of British troops on Noddle's Island in Boston Harbor and killed or wounded two hundred of them (Force, *American Archives*, 4th ser., II, 974).

6 Caleb Wallace married Sarah (1755–*ca.* 1775), daughter of Samuel McDowell (1733–1817), a burgess from Augusta County from 1772 to 1776, and a member of the Virginia Council of State in 1781 (William H. Whitsitt, *Life and Times of Judge Caleb Wallace* [Louisville, 1888], pp. 31–32; Jos. A. Waddell, *Annals of Augusta County, Virginia, from 1726 to 1781* [Staunton, Va., 1902], pp. 121–22).

7 Elizabeth (b. 1768) died on 17 May 1775 and Reuben (b. 1771) on 5 June 1775.

8 Dunmore shifted his residence from the governor's palace at Williamsburg to the British man-of-war "Fowey" at Yorktown on 8 June. At about the same time, his letters of 29 May and 24 December 1774 to the Earl of Dartmouth, telling about the recalcitrant American Whigs, were published in colonial newspapers. On 10 June 1775 the Virginia House of Burgesses adopted Jefferson's "Address," rejecting Lord North's so-called "Conciliatory Proposals" of 20 February. On 24 June the Burgesses, after bidding defiance to Dunmore, adjourned their final session under British rule (*Journals of the House of Burgesses of Virginia, 1773–1776*, pp. 280–83; Force, *American Archives*, 4th ser., I, 387–88, 1061–63; II, 1023, 1130, 1198, 1200–1202, 1223–24; Boyd, *Papers of Jefferson*, I, 170–74). Governor Josiah Martin (1737–1786), who had prorogued the North Carolina Assembly in early April, fled from the provincial capital to Fort Johnston on the Cape Fear River, between 24 May and 2 June 1775.

9 See JM to Bradford, 26 November 1774, n. 8.

From William Bradford

FC (Historical Society of Pennsylvania).

July 10th 1775

MY DEAR FRIEND

I did intend to have delayed writing to you till Mr Smith's return to Virginia; but I believe that will not be early & I am not fond of delaying the discharge of an Epistolary debt. He was married last week to Miss Anna Witherspoon & proposes to spend some time at Princeton & at his fathers.[1] He desired me to mention this to you lest you should suppose he had returned without calling upon you.

The Congress talk of removing in a week or two to Hartford in Connecticut that they may be nearer the seat of War & receive earlier and more authentic intelligence than at this distance it is possible to obtain.[2] They have published a "Declaration of the Causes & necessity of taking up arms", and another "Address to the inhabitants of G. Britain [."][3] I have been seeking an opportunity of sending you these but cannot find one: however they will be immediately published in all the papers & probably will reach you nearly as soon as this. They are written (particularly the last) with a Spirit that will charm you. As I read them Pleasure vibrated thro' every nerve & I thank my God that I was born in an age & country capable of producing such Gallant spirit. By the address I find they have prefered another petition to the King & to remove every imputation of obstinacy (say they) we have requested his majesty to direct some mode by which the united applications of his faithful colonists may be improved into a happy & permanent reconciliation. The declaration & address have gone to England in a vessel which saild yesterday: & I suppose the petition accompanies them.[4]

Mr Kirkland (an Indian missionary at Onida) came to town a few days ago to engage the Congress to propose a treaty to the five nations which he thinks they would readily come into. He informed that those tribes are very favorable to our Cause notwithstanding the constant endeavors that have been used to excite them against us. Guy Johnston sometime ago sent them the War Belt but they returned him a belt of peace. The Congress is to take the matter under Consideration to day; & I hope will be able so to conduct matters that we shall either receive assistance from these nations or have nothing to fear from them[.][5] Mr Kirkland proposes on his return to send some of their Chiefs this way & hopes by seeing our military preparations they will banish that contemptable opinion of strength they have been industriously taught to entertain, & consequently [be] more willing to join us. He also informed me that the five nations lately resolved in a Conference meeting that they would not admit any White People to settle among them. They had observed that those tribes that did so, soon became extinct & they have wisely gaurded against the same fate. ["]The great God (said they to some white people) does not chuse we should live together: he hath Givin you a white skin & said live you on that side of the river: to us he hath given a Red skin & said live you on tother side the river—let us not disobey him." They are however fond of treating with the white people & of being considered important by them.

I heartily wish your Riflemen & ours were at the Camp. There are about 200 collected in this province and are to set off soon.[6] When the[y] arrive I am mistaken if the young officers complain of want of Promotion: there will be vacancies enough for them to rise in.

I am grieved to hear the dysentery prevails so much with you, & for the loss you have sustained. If the disorder should not abate I would recommend a Journey this way to you: & if you can find nothing to amuse you here you may prosecute your Journey to Cambrige. An Enthusiasm (almost equal to that which prevailed in Europe for the Crusades) has seized many in this city & carried them to the Camp; & yet they are not wanted. It is said the american lines a[re] 20 miles in length & that soldiers arrive so fast from all Quarters that it is difficult to find provision for them all.[7] I received a letter from Mr Rees a few days ago in which he informs me of a Negro conspiracy having been discovered at Charlestown.[8] I hope Virginia will have no disturbances of that Kind.

I am &c.

W B Jun

[1] See JM to his father, 30 September 1769, n. 4. Samuel S. Smith's father, Robert, was a clergyman at Pequea, Pa.

[2] Benjamin Harrison to George Washington, 21–23 July 1775: "The debate about our remove was taken up yesterday [22 July], and determined in the negative" (Force, *American Archives*, 4th ser., II, 1697–98).

[3] Thomas Jefferson and John Dickinson were the principal authors of "A declaration by the Representatives of the United Colonies of North America, now met in General Congress at Philadelphia, setting forth the causes and necessity of their taking up arms," adopted by Congress on 6 July 1775 (*Journals of the Continental Congress*, II, 140–57; Boyd, *Papers of Jefferson*, I, 187–219). Richard Henry Lee was probably the main draftsman of "The Twelve United Colonies, by their Delegates in Congress, to the Inhabitants of Great Britain," adopted 8 July 1775 (*Journals of the Continental Congress*, II, 163–70).

[4] Often called the "Olive Branch Petition," this document written by John Dickinson bore the title, "To the king's most excellent Majesty." Congress adopted it on 8 July (*ibid.*, II, 158–62). On the same day Congress asked Richard Penn to carry the three addresses, and a letter to the Lord Mayor of London. He sailed on 12 July (*ibid.*, II, 162 n., 172).

[5] For forty years following his graduation in 1765 from the College of New Jersey, Reverend Samuel Kirkland (1741–1808) was a missionary among the Oneida Indians. Believing that he and other "dissenting missionaries" were influencing the six Iroquois tribes to favor the patriot cause, Colonel Guy Johnson (1740–1788), the Crown's Indian superintendent, ordered these clergymen out of central New York. Although the patriots charged Johnson with endeavoring to incite the Iroquois against the settlers, he protested that he was merely trying to keep them neutral. Kirkland appeared before Congress on 10 July 1775. On 30 June it had named a committee to draft "proper talks to" the Indians (Force, *American Archives*, 4th ser., II, 661–62, 841–43, 911–12, 1116–17, 1309–10; *Journals of the Continental Congress*, II, 123, 172–73).

[6] On 22 June the Continental Congress asked Pennsylvania to increase from six to eight the number of its riflemen companies (*ibid.*, II, 104). On 8 July, William and Thomas Bradford wrote with exaggeration in an open letter "to the Printer of a Publick Paper in London" that Pennsylvania had raised one thousand riflemen, "the worst of whom will put a ball into a man's head at . . . one hundred and fifty or two hundred yards . . ." (Force, *American Archives*, 4th ser., II, 1609).

[7] On 27 July 1775, George Washington wrote to John A. Washington that his

troops, including the sick and absent, numbering about sixteen thousand, guarded a semicircle around Boston stretching for eight or nine miles (Force, *American Archives,* 4th ser., II, 1736). These soldiers were in greater need of tents, gunpowder, and other munitions than of food (*ibid.,* II, 1119–20).

8 Probably Oliver Reese. Early in May a letter was received from Arthur Lee in London "intimating that a plan was laid before Administration, for instigating the slaves to insurrection." This was doubly alarming since it was already assumed that the Negroes "entertained ideas, that the present contest was for obliging us to give them their liberty." Prompted by fears of the Negroes as well as of British invasion, the people of Charleston patrolled day and night and the city was declared in mid-June to resemble a "garrison town" (John Drayton, *Memoirs of the American Revolution . . .* [Charleston, 1821], I, 231; Force, *American Archives,* 4th ser., II, 1129). A committee was appointed on 4 June 1775 to investigate reports of slave insurrections, and "trials of several Negroes suspected and charged of plotting an insurrection" were conducted during the week of 18 June. Of Jerry, a slave convicted at that time and hanged on 18 August, Henry Laurens wrote: "I am fully satisfied that Jerry was guilty of a design & attempt to encourage our Negroes to Rebellion & joining the King's Troops if any had been sent here." Although the superintendent of Indian affairs in South Carolina was impeached in June for "endeavoring to incite the Creek & Cherokee Indians to act against this Colony," Laurens was convinced by 2 July that "we have nothing to fear from within; not even from the Indians." But even though the "Rumours & Whispers of Insurrections are no more heard—nevertheless we are constantly upon our guard & the Militia are by parties trained every day" (*Extracts from the Journals of the Provincial Congresses of South Carolina, 1775–1776* [Columbia, S.C., 1960], p. 37; Henry Laurens to John Laurens, 18 June, 23 June, and 21 August 1775, and to James Laurens, 2 July 1775, all in South Carolina Historical Society; David D. Wallace, *South Carolina: A Short History, 1520–1948* [Chapel Hill, 1951], pp. 260–62).

From William Bradford

FC (Historical Society of Pennsylvania).

PHILADA. July [18, 1775][1]

MY DEAR SIR,

I wrote to you last week by the post. Mr Smith gives me an opportunity of sending you a few more lines which friendship will not allow me to neglect.[2]

I have seen the address to the six confederate indian Nations. It sets forth that our fathers left britain on the faith of Contracts which have been faithfully observed on our part, that the king's ministers grew jealous of us, that they sent armies to rob & kill us, therefore requesting if any application be made to them by those wicked ministers to refuse them, that we only desire that peace may continue between us. "We do not ask you (says the address) to take up the hatchet against the soldiers of the great King. We ask that it may be buried deep & peace

& harmony subsist between us[.]" They are desired to acquaint the tribes on the river St. Lawrence with this talk: & on the return of their messengers to pay a visit to the general congress: & in the conclusion "We have lighted up a small council fire at Albany that we may hear each other & more fully disclose our minds to one another.["] This is to be translated into Indian by Mr Kirkland and Genl. Schuyler is to deliver the belts, which are to be larger than any ever sent to the five nations: & as the Indians judge of the importance of the business by the Largeness of the belt there is no doubt but this matter will excite universal attention among them.[3]

It is said the Declaration is to be translated in several Languages and sent abroad. I am also privately informed that they are preparing an address to foreing states inviting them to trade with us.[4] If this be true it may serve to explain what I heard Coll Hancock say the other day: "that he made no doubt but Boston would soon be in the peaceable possession of the original proprietors: nay continued he, I should not be surprized if Britain should court a reconciliation by offering to indemnify us for all our Losses." As I knew not his Grounds for such a speech I must confess it appeared to me a very extradinary one. I believe the Congress have lay aside the design of removing from Philada. But they talk of adjourning next saturday for a few weeks.[5]

I had the pleasure this morning of seeing Aaron Burr who is going to the Camp with one Mr Ogden.[6] I hope I shall hear from you soon, but I had rather see you. If the Congress should not remove it may be an inducement to you, to pay us a visit after their adjournment.

With this you will recieve Priestly, a few pamphlets, & a small map of Boston harbour.[7]

I am Dr Sir &c

W B Jun

P.S. The suspicions against Dr Franklin have died away: whatever was his design at coming over here, I believe he has now chosen his side, and favors our cause.[8]

---

[1] In his notebook copy, Bradford neglected to complete the date of this letter. He mentioned, however, in his diary, which is now in the Historical Society of Pennsylvania, that he wrote to JM on 10 and 18 July.

[2] Reverend Samuel Stanhope Smith was about to return to Virginia with his bride, Ann Witherspoon.

[3] "A Speech to the Six Confederate Nations...from the Twelve United Colonies," adopted by the Continental Congress on 13 July, was to be accompanied by "Three Strings, or a small Belt," "The large belt of intelligence and declaration," and "A small belt." After Reverend Samuel Kirkland and General Philip Schuyler

(1733–1804) took these to the "central council house" at Onondaga, the Six Nations were asked to make them known to their seven allied tribes along the St. Lawrence River, and then meet again (as they did) with agents of Congress in August at Albany. Bradford's two quotations should have read as follows: "We don't wish you to take up the hatchet against the king's troops. We desire you to remain at home, and not join on either side, but keep the hatchet buried deep.... We depend upon you to send and acquaint your allies to the northward ... that you have this talk of ours.... And when they return, we invite your great men to come and converse farther with us at Albany, where we intend to re-kindle the council fire which your and our ancestors sat round in great friendship" (*Journals of the Continental Congress*, II, 177–83; III, 351).

4 Although on 15 July Congress declared that for the next nine months any ship-master could export American produce to the value of whatever gunpowder, salt-peter, sulphur, or other military stores he brought in from abroad, it delayed until 6 April 1776 before completely opening American ports to world trade (*ibid.*, II, 184–85, 200–201; IV, 257–59).

5 Congress adjourned 1 August and reconvened 5 September 1775. John Hancock of Boston was at this time the president of the Continental Congress.

6 Bradford and Aaron Burr had been graduated in the same class at the College of New Jersey. Following the death of his parents, Burr lived with his uncle, Timothy Edwards, in Elizabethtown. Armed with a letter of introduction from John Hancock to George Washington (Force, *American Archives*, 4th ser., II, 1689), Burr and Matthias Ogden (1755–1791), who had also lived with the Edwards family, joined the patriot forces besieging Boston. They later served with distinction in the ill-fated Montgomery-Arnold campaign against Canada.

7 For Joseph Priestley see JM to Bradford, 9 May 1775, n. 8. The map was probably "A New Plan of Boston Harbour from an Actual Survey, Engrav'd for the Penn-sylva. Magazine," which was printed in June 1775 (*Pennsylvania Magazine or American Monthly Museum*, I [1775], between p. 240 and p. 241).

8 See Bradford to JM, 2 June 1775.

To William Bradford

Copy (Historical Society of Pennsylvania).

VIRGINIA ORANGE: July 28—1775.

MY OBLIGING FRIEND

I received your favor of the 10th. inst. and have since had a sight of the declaration and Address from the Congress. I must concur with you in every[1] encomium that can be bestowed on them, particularly the last mentioned which for true Eloquence may vie with the most applauded Oration of Tully himself. These performances must be chiefly owing to a few illustrious writers of that body. Is it discoverable who are the original Authors of them? I think the traces of Livingstons pen are visible in the one we are now speaking of. You are a better Judge & better acquainted with his Genius & writings[2]

Our convention is now sitting, and I believe intends to strike a considerable sum of money & to raise 3 or 4,000 men as an Army to be in immediate pay. The independants, who I suppose will be three times that number will also have their pay commence as soon as they are called to action.[3] The Preparations for War are every where going on in a most vigorous manner. But the Scarcity of Ammunition is truly alarming. Can you tell how they are supplied in N England and what steps are taking to procure a sufficiency for the time to come. I was a little induced from the confident assertion of the Congress that foreign Assistance if necessary was ["]*undoubtedly* attainable," to think & hope that some secret Overtures had been made to them. If so I imagine they are wrapped up in impenetrable secresy as yet.[4] Hath any thing further been whispered relative to the conduct of Dr Franklin?[5] I yesterday heard a report that the Indians on the back of us who are to be treated with the last of next month by Commissioners appointed by the Convention indicate a great indisposition to enter into friendly engagement with us at this Juncture. The report adds that there were some frenchmen with them and this determination was formed at their instigation. If there is any truth in this, it will probably be known at Philada. before this reaches you; As indeed every thing of importance is drawn there by the Congress before private intelligence can be conveyed.[6]

I was much surprized to hear of the marriage of our friend Mr Smith. I had never heard of such a manuvre's being in agitation, And if I forget not Allen (who ought to know) told me there were some engagement with Thompson from that Quarter which he could not in honor break & from which she was unwilling to release him. And if I did not mistake him (I speak with caution you observe) Thompson intended a trip to Princeton to settle affairs. However I intermeddle little with such matters; & something that might set the affair in a different Light may have escaped my attention or memory.[7] A Letter to Mr Smith is in company with this. It is directed to him at Princeton to the care of Plum.[8] If he should be in Philada. at the time you get this I should be glad you would give him notice of it. Or if by going to Princeton you think it will miss of him in that case you would oblige me by taking it out of the office and conveying it to him. I have requested him to bring me two pamphlets "An apology for the Church of England as by Law Established" &c by Josiah Tucker—and An Essay on Toleration with a particular view to the late Application of the Dissenting Ministers to Parliament &c. by Phil. Turneaux. If he should not be in Town after he recieves this & you could procure them and send them to him with Priestly before he sets off for Virginia you would lay me under another Obligation.[9]

A Scotch Parson in an adjoining County refused to observe the fast or preach on that day. When called on he pleaded Conscience, alledging that it was his duty to pay no regard to any such appointments made by unconstitutional authority. The Committee it seems have their Consciences too: they have ordered his Church doors to be shut and his salary to be stopped, and have sent to the convention for their advice. If the Convention should connive at their proceedings I question, should his insolence not abate if he does not get ducked in a coat of Tar & surplice of feathers and then he may go in his new Canonicals and act under the lawful Authority of Gen. Gage if he pleases. We have one of the same Kidney in the parish I live in. He was sometime ago published in the Gazette for his insolence and had like to have met with sore treatment; but finding his protection to be not so much in the law as the favor of the people he is grown very supple & obsequious.[10]

The Dysentery has been again in our family & is now among the slaves. I have hitherto Escaped and hope it has no commission to attack me. It is less severe [than] it was at first.[11] I am obliged to finish in great haste to have an opportunity that Just offers for sending this Letter to the Post.

Adieu.

J M Jun

[1] Bradford's file copy repeats "every."

[2] Although JM probably had in mind William Livingston (1723–1790), whose spirited pamphlets attacking established churches found a receptive audience, it was Robert R. Livingston (1746–1813) who had been on the committee of the Second Continental Congress which drafted the "Address to the Inhabitants of Great Britain" (*Journals of the Continental Congress*, II, 80). Even so, Richard Henry Lee was probably the principal author of that address.

[3] In August 1775 the Virginia Convention provided for the levying of a variety of taxes, the issuance of £350,000 of paper money, the recruiting of 1,445 soldiers for the defense of the colony, and the raising of over eight thousand minutemen for the protection of their respective districts. These new forces were to take the place of the former militia, volunteers, and independent companies (Force, *American Archives*, 4th ser., III, 377–411, 424–27, 456; George Mason to Martin Cockburn, 24 July and 22 August 1775, in *Calendar of Virginia State Papers*, I, 267–68).

[4] The expression "undoubtedly attainable" is from Congress' "Declaration ... of ... the causes and necessity of ... taking up arms." The first formal step toward initiating "secret Overtures" for foreign aid occurred on 29 November 1775, when Congress created a Committee of [Secret] Correspondence.

[5] See Bradford to JM, 2 June 1775, n. 2, and 18 July 1775.

[6] Both the Virginia House of Burgesses and the Continental Congress appointed commissioners to treat with the western Indians at Fort Pitt (*Journals of the House*

of Burgesses, 1773–1776, p. 282; *Journals of the Continental Congress,* II, 183; III, 433; Force, *American Archives,* 4th ser., III, 76). Delay by the Indians in coming to the fort, as well as friction between the commissioners from Virginia and Pennsylvania over whether the one or the other province owned the forks of the Ohio River, protracted the negotiations. Eventually, in October 1775, the Indians signed a treaty agreeing not to take the warpath (Reuben Gold Thwaites and Louise Phelps Kellogg, eds., *The Revolution on the Upper Ohio, 1775–1777* [Madison, Wis., 1908], p. 125).

7 Reverend Samuel S. Smith married Ann Witherspoon at Princeton on 28 June 1775 (Willard Thorp, ed., *Lives of Eighteen from Princeton,* p. 92). The "Thompson," whom JM evidently believed had been engaged to Miss Witherspoon, was probably Reverend James Thompson. At that time he and Reverend Moses Allen lived in Charleston, S.C.

8 Probably Benjamin Plum. JM's letter to Smith has not been found.

9 Josiah Tucker, *An Apology for the Present Church of England as by Law Established, occasioned by a Petition said to be preparing by certain Clergymen, and Others, to be laid before Parliament, for abolishing Subscriptions, in a letter to one of the Petitioners* (Glocester, 1772); Philip Furneaux (1726–1783), *An Essay on Toleration: with a particular view to the late application of the Protestant Dissenting Ministers to Parliament, for amending and rendering effectual the Act of the first of William and Mary, commonly called the Act of Toleration* (London, 1773). JM's letter could not have reached Bradford before Smith left Princeton or Philadelphia for Virginia.

10 On 12 June 1775 the Continental Congress designated 20 July as a day of "public humiliation, fasting and prayer" (*Journals of the Continental Congress,* II, 87–88). The "Scotch Parson" was Reverend James Herdman, who was licensed in 1770 as a minister of the established church in Virginia and assigned in 1774 to Bromfield Parish, which included parts of what was then Culpeper County. Although the Convention appears to have offered no "advice," the Culpeper Committee of Safety ordered Herdman's expulsion from the county "from and after the 19th day" of October 1775. He departed so hastily that he left behind a portion of his library. He is last heard of in 1777 as a "foreigner" in Henrico County, where he once more refused to take the oath of allegiance (*Virginia Magazine of History and Biography,* XLI [1933], 143; *Virginia Gazette* [Williamsburg, Dixon and Hunter], 20 January 1776; *Virginia Gazette* [Williamsburg, Purdie], 31 January 1777; Raleigh Travers Green, comp., *Genealogical and Historical Notes on Culpeper County, Virginia* [Culpeper, 1900], p. 35). The recalcitrant Orange County minister was Reverend John Wingate (*ca.* 1746–1789), who, after being licensed to preach in 1771, was assigned in 1774 to St. Thomas Parish, Orange County, where he christened JM's youngest sister, Frances Taylor Madison, in October of that year. He surprised the Committee of Safety on 25 March 1775 by refusing to give up "seditious" pamphlets in his possession on the ground that they were not his personal property. Two days later the pamphlets were seized and burned in the presence of the Orange Independent Company. Some time later he left the parish. At the time of his death he resided on the island of Grenada in the British West Indies (*Virginia Magazine of History and Biography,* XLI [1933], 305; LXVI [1958], 82; Force, *American Archives,* 4th ser., II, 234–35; *Gentleman's Magazine and Historical Chronicle* [303 vols.; London, 1731–1907], LIX, Part II [1789], 955).

11 Bradford probably miscopied JM's "than" as "that." In the Boston Public Library is a letter of 5 July 1775 from James Madison, Sr., in which he writes: "My Wife was taken two days ago with the same disorder my children died with. I hope She will have it favourable. It is above a fortnight since any of my family at home had it." The letter was addressed to Oliver Fowler.

Commission as Colonel of
Orange County Militia

MS (Henry E. Huntington Library). The words and numbers in script type signify that the clerk inserted them in ink. Otherwise, the original of this commission is in print. Each of the seven signatures appears to have been written by the man whose name is subscribed. The commission forms were probably printed by Alexander Purdie, editor of the *Virginia Gazette* of Williamsburg.

[2 October 1775]

The COMMITTEE of SAFETY for the Colony of VIRGINIA
To *James Madison Junr. Esqr.*

BY Virtue of the Power and Authority invested in us, by the Delegates and Representatives of the several Counties and Corporations in General Convention assembled, we, reposing especial Trust and Confidence in your Patriotism, Fidelity, Courage, and good Conduct, do, by these Presents, constitute and appoint you to be *Colonel* of the Militia of the County of *Orange*; and you are therefore carefully and diligently to discharge the Trust reposed in you, by disciplining all Officers and Soldiers under your Command. And we do hereby require them to obey you as their *Colonel*. And you are to observe and follow all such Orders and Directions as you shall from Time to Time receive from the Convention, the Committee of Safety for the Time being, or any superiour Officers, according to the Rules and Regulations established by the Convention.[1]

Edmd. Pendleton

Thos. Lud. Lee

GIVEN *under our Hands, at Williamsburg this 2d. Day of October* Anno Domini 1775.

P. Carrington

Dudley Digges

Carter Braxton

Js. Mercer

John Tabb.[2]

1 The Virginia Committee of Safety, created by the General Convention which convened at Richmond on 17 July 1775, was empowered to conduct the defense of the colony during the recesses of the Convention and in accordance with its regulations. The military aspect of this defense was to be provided by armed men of three types—the "regulars" (state line), the minutemen, and the militia. The last of these was in the nature of a reserve force, to be used against the enemy in emergencies. The highest officer of the militia of each county was the county lieutenant (Hening, *Statutes*, IX, 9–35). In Orange County in 1775, JM's father held this office. JM, by virtue of this commission, became his father's second in command. Although there is no doubt that the son had undergone military training (JM to Bradford, 19 June 1775) and would occasionally be called "Colonel" in later years, he rarely, if ever, served in the field with the militia of Orange County. Referring to himself in the third person in his "Autobiographical Notes" (Princeton University Library), written at some time between 1816 and 1831, he spoke of "causes preventing him from entering the army, viz his feeble health, and a constitutional liability to sudden attacks, somewhat resembling Epilepsy, and suspending the intellectual functions." In short, in spite of his colonelcy, JM was not a veteran of the Revolution and never claimed to be. In 1775, Orange County was divided by the county lieutenant into muster districts, with the militia in each district commanded by a captain. In the Mills College Library, Oakland, Calif., is a letter dated "October 1775" from JM's father to "Capt. James Hunter," geographically defining his muster district and ordering him to prepare a roster of the men therein who were liable for militia service.

2 Besides the signers of this commission, George Mason, John Page, Richard Bland, and William Cabell were also members of the Virginia Committee of Safety in 1775 (Hening, *Statutes*, IX, 49). As chairman of this committee, Edmund Pendleton (1721–1803) of Caroline County, who had just completed twenty-three years as a burgess, was *de facto* governor of the colony, or at least of the patriots among its citizens. Thomas Ludwell Lee (1730–1778) of Stafford County, had occasionally been in the House of Burgesses between 1758 and 1775. His training in the law helped to qualify him as a judge of the General Court of Virginia for several years before his death. He was one of a notable group of brothers including Richard Henry, Francis Lightfoot, Arthur, and William Lee (Cazenove Gardner Lee, Jr., *Lee Chronicle: Studies of the Early Generations of the Lees of Virginia*, ed. by Dorothy Mills Parker [New York, 1957], pp. 72–73). Paul Carrington (1733–1818) of Charlotte County, a lawyer and officer of militia, served as a king's attorney before the Revolution, as a judge of the higher courts of his state from 1778 to 1807, and held numerous less important public offices. Dudley Digges (1718–1790) of York County had had long experience as a burgess and colonel of militia before the Revolution. Besides serving as a delegate to the General Conventions of 1774–1776, he was a member of the Council of State and a state examiner of claims during the war (Lyon Gardner Tyler, ed., *Encyclopedia of Virginia Biography* [5 vols.; New York, 1915], II, 9). Prior to the Revolution, Carter Braxton (1736–1797) was of local prominence as a burgess and sheriff of King William County. From 1776 until his death he was usually a member of either the Virginia House of Delegates or of the Council of State. When serving in the Continental Congress, 1776–1777, he signed the Declaration of Independence. Before the Revolution, James Mercer (1736–1793) of Hampshire County had served as a captain in the French and Indian War and as a burgess. During his later career he was chiefly distinguished as a judge of the General Court and the Court of Appeals, 1779–1789, and of the reorganized Court of Appeals, 1789–1793. John Tabb (*ca.* 1737–1798), son of a rich Amelia County merchant, served successively between 1771 and 1776 in the House of Burgesses, the general conventions, and on the state Committee of Safety. In 1777 he was colonel of the militia of his county. Shortly before his death his daughter Martha married Congressman William B. Giles (*ibid.*, II, 33–34).

18. That religion, or the duty which we owe to our CRE-
ATOR, and the manner of difcharging it, can be directed only
by reafon and conviction, not by force or violence; and therefore,
that all men *are equally entitled to* ~~fhould~~ enjoy ~~the fulleft toleration~~ in the exercife of
religion. according to the dictates of confcience, unpunifhed and
unreftrained by the magiftrate, ~~(unlefs, under colour of religion,~~
~~any man difturb the peace, the happinefs, or fafety of fociety)~~
And that it is the mutual duty of all to practife Chriftian forbearance, love, and charity, towards each other.

(Unlefs the prefervation of equal liberty and free ex
ercife of the State are manifeftly in dangered)

That Religion or the duty we owe to our Creator. and the
manner of difcharging it, being under the direction of
reason and conviction may not of violence or compulsion, all
men are equally entitled to the full and free exercise of it according
to the dictates of Conscience; and therefore that no man or class of men
ought, on account of Religion to be invested with peculiar emoluments or
privileges; nor subjected to any penalties or disabilities unless under &c

x suggested by J. M. [illegible]
the same finally agreed to.

RELIGIOUS AMENDMENT TO THE VIRGINIA DECLARATION OF RIGHTS

CAPITOL OF VIRGINIA

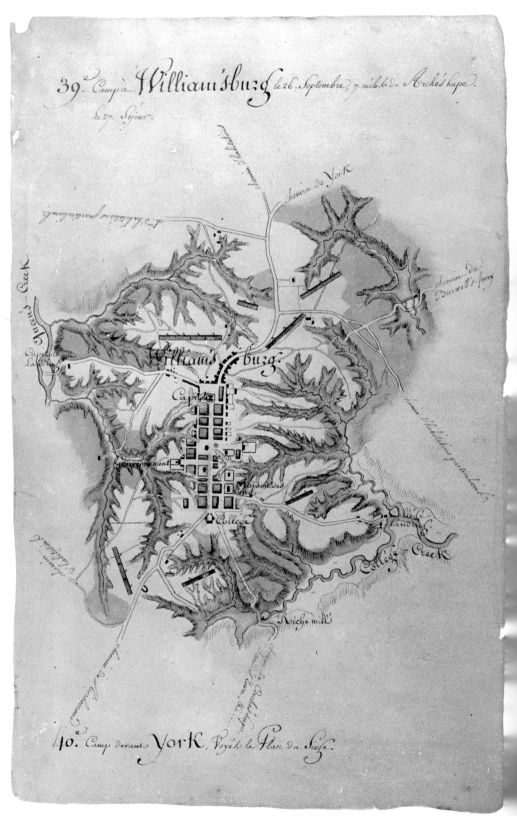

WILLIAMSBURG AND SURROUNDING COUNTRY

Certificate of Election of James Madison, Jr., and William Moore

MS (Virginia State Library). On the reverse is merely the word "Orange."

[25 April 1776]

ORANGE S S.[1]

I hereby Certify, that Jas. Madison Jr, And William Moore Esqrs., Are duly Elected Delegates, for the Sd. County, to Serve in General Convention, for one year then Next following,[2] Given Under my hand, and Seal, this 25th Day of April, 1776,

THO: BARBOUR

S: O: C[3]

[1] *Salutem Sciatis*—that is, "Greeting. Let it be known."

[2] The Convention of July 1775 at Richmond provided that on the regular "court day" in April of each year the properly qualified freeholders of every county should choose "two of the most fit and able men" from among their own numbers to attend "General Conventions." These normally were to assemble at Williamsburg on the first Monday in May (*The Proceedings of the Convention of Delegates for the Counties and Corporations in the Colony of Virginia, Held at Richmond Town, in the County of Henrico, on Monday the 17th of July 1775* [Richmond, 1816], p. 47; Hening, *Statutes*, IX, 54–55). "Court day" in Orange County was "the fourth Thursday," hence 25 April 1776.

[3] Thomas Barbour, sheriff of Orange County.

Case of William Aylett

MSS (Virginia State Library). Papers of Committee of Privileges and Elections of the Convention of Delegates, convened 6 May 1776 at Williamsburg.

[8–22 May 1776]

EDITORIAL NOTE

When JM, a delegate from Orange County, took his seat in this Convention on 8 May 1776, he was at once appointed to the Committee of Privileges and Elections. This large group, ultimately numbering nearly half of the 130 delegates, concerned itself primarily with the validity of their election and with alleged instances of individual Virginians manifesting disloyalty to the patriot cause. As a young and inexperienced legislator, JM probably contributed little to the work of this committee. For this reason, a reproduction of its extensive minutes, which in no instance mention his name, will be limited to the first item of business after JM became a member. The Convention of 6 May to 5 July 1776, however, was an important chapter in his political education, and the disputed-election case of William Aylett of King William County will illustrate one type of problem necessarily engaging his attention. Other matters in which, as a member of other committees, he directly participated, were the settlement of claims against Virginia arising from "the late expedition against the Indians," the counting of ballots cast in the elections of governor and members of the Privy Council, and, above all, the preparation of a declaration of rights and plan of government for the province (see Declaration of Rights, 16 May–29 June 1776). For the committees, see *The Proceedings of the Convention of Delegates Held at the Capitol, in the City of Williamsburg, in the Colony of Virginia, on Monday, the 6th of May, 1776* (Richmond, 1816), pp. 16, 17, 25, 78, 79, 81.

[18 May 1776]

The Committee of Privileges and Elections, have according to Order,[1] inquired into the Information, touching the Election of Delegates for the County of King William, to them referred, And it appears to your Committee from the Poll taken at the said Election by Owen Gwathmey Gentn. Sherif of that said County,[2] that at the close of the Poll the Number of Votes stood as follows

> For William Aylett[3] 78
> Richard Squire Taylor[4] 73
> Carter Braxton[5] 39

It also appears to your Committee from the Testimony of the said Owen Gwathmey, that some time before the Poll was closed,[6] Mr. Aylett, declined standing a Candidate, and made a Public declaration of it and at the same time desired that Mr. Braxton might be elected.

That after Mr. Aylett's resignation, he[7] made proclamation several times for the Freeholders to come in and Vote, before he closed the Poll.

It also appears to your Committee from the Testimony of Benjamin Temple,[8] that he with many others who had voted at the Election, applied to Mr. Aylett during the Poll, and desired he would decline in favour of Mr. Braxton, which he accordingly did, and the people generally seemed well pleased, that Mr. Braxton should be returned a Delegate; but that there was not a sufficient Number, who had not voted to have elected Mr. Braxton and in case the Poll had been continued, most of them would have voted for Mr. Taylor. That Mr. Dandridge Claiborne had been proposed as a Sub-Delegate,[9] but on hearing Mr. Taylor was a Candidate, he declined. That the Poll was kept open so long as any person would come in to Vote, and that the Sheriff, before he closed it, made Publication several times for the Freeholders to come and vote, And that in any event Mr. Taylor would have been elected.

It further appears to your Committee from the Testimony of Drury Ragsdale[10] that after Mr. Aylett declined, there was a sufficient Number, in his Opinion, who had not voted to set Mr. Braxton before Mr. Aylett. That many, who did not vote after Mr. Aylett's resignation, looked on it to be unnecessary, considering Mr. Braxton as elected of course: that the Poll was kept open a considerable time, after the People declined going in to Vote. That the Deponent informed many, while the Poll was taking, of the consequences of leaving Mr. Braxton out. That for some time after the Poll was begun, Mr. Braxton's friends were backward in giving their Votes, but afterwards they exerted themselves to promote his Interest. That the Deponent with Mr. Fox,[11] the day after the Election was making a Calculation how many persons were at the Election who did not Vote, and they made the Number about 42, which would have mostly voted for Mr. Braxton and Mr. Aylett; but that in any event Mr. Taylor would have been elected.

It also further appears to your Committee from the Testimony of James Quarles[12] that he did not vote at the Election, on account of Mr. Ayletts resignation; that he thought, until the day of Election, that Mr. Taylor offered only as a Sub-Delegate, and many people in the lower Parish thought as he did.

And it further appears to your Committee from the Testimony of Archibald Govan,[13] that he did not vote at the Election, thinking Mr. Braxton could not get a sufficient Number of Votes to elect him; but in case he had voted it would have been for Mr. Braxton; that on Mr. Aylett's resignation in favour of Mr. Braxton, the People in General seem'd to be well pleased; that before Mr. Aylett resigned, Mr. Braxton had not friends enough to set him before Mr. Aylett or Mr. Taylor, but some were of a different Opinion; but that in any event Mr. Taylor would have been elected.

Upon the whole matter your Committee came to the following Resolution vizt.

Resolved as the Opinion of this Committee that the said William Aylett and Richard Squire Taylor are duly elected Delegates for the said County of King William.[14]

[22 May 1776]

The Committee of Privileges and Elections have had under their Consideration, an Information (to them referred) that William Aylett

Esqr., a Delegate for the County of King William had accepted a Military Post of Proffit in the Continental Army, by which his Seat in this Convention is become vacated: And it appears to your Committee that the said William Aylett, since his Election, hath accepted a Commission, appointing him Deputy Commissary General to the Continental Forces in Virginia.[15] Whereupon your Committee came to the following Resolution, Vizt.

Resolved, as the Opinion of this Committee, that the said William Aylett hath vacated his Seat in this Convention.[16]

[1] On 9 May, the Convention was assured by the committee that in its opinion the certificates of election from King William County, along with those from thirty-six other counties or corporations (e.g., the College of William and Mary), were evidences of valid elections. Later that day, however, upon hearing that the sheriff of King William County "hath returned a delegate as duly chosen . . . who had a lesser number of votes than two other candidates," the Convention referred the matter to the Committee of Privileges and Elections for investigation and report (*Proceedings of the Convention*, May 1776, p. 9).

[2] Owen Gwathmey III (1752–1830) was a brother-in-law of George Rogers Clark and sheriff of King William County for several years after 1776. Later he moved to Kentucky and died at Louisville (*Lineage Book of the National Society of the Daughters of the American Revolution*, XIV [1902], 250; XCV [1927], 172).

[3] William Aylett (1743–1780) had been a burgess from 1771 to 1775 and a delegate to the three general conventions of 1775. He would be Virginia's commissary of stores and agent for trade in 1776–1777. He also served as deputy commissary general of purchases for the southern department, with a colonel's rank in the continental line, from 1776 until his death (*Journals of the Continental Congress*, IV, 315; VIII, 477; Louis A. Burgess, ed., *Virginia Soldiers of 1776* [2 vols.; Richmond, 1927], II, 944–47; Elizabeth Hawes Ryland, ed., *King William County, Virginia, from Old Newspapers & Files* [Richmond, 1955], pp. 55, 62; *Journals of the Council of State*, I, 62, 248, 296, 398, 403).

[4] Richard Squire Taylor (d. 1810) was sheriff of King William County in 1764 and a justice of the peace between 1764 and 1771. He was also a delegate to the General Assembly of October 1776 and a trustee for the improvement of Pamunkey River navigation in 1789 (*Bulletin of the Virginia State Library*, XIV [1921], 56–110, *passim*; Earl G. Swem and John W. Williams, eds., *A Register of the General Assembly of Virginia 1776–1918 and of the Constitutional Conventions* [Richmond, 1918], p. 1; Hening, *Statutes*, XIII, 73).

[5] See JM's commission as colonel, 2 October 1775, n. 2.

[6] Voting for delegates to the General Convention was viva voce, and the polls were kept open by the sheriff in "April annually, on the several days appointed by law for the holding of the county or co[r]poration courts respectively, and at the places where such courts are accustomed to be held" (Hening, *Statutes*, IX, 54).

[7] The sheriff.

[8] Benjamin Temple (*ca.* 1735–1802) rose from lieutenant's rank in the French and Indian War to a colonelcy by 1783, after serving through the Revolution in the dragoons. From 1784 until 1800 he was continuously a member of one or the other house of the Assembly of Virginia, and was a delegate in 1788 to its convention to ratify the Federal Constitution (F. B. Heitman, *Historical Register of Officers of the Continental Army*, p. 394).

⁹ Equivalent to an alternate. William Dandridge Claiborne (1756–1811) left the College of William and Mary in 1776 to join the patriot army. In 1777–1779 he was a major of militia. His one term as a member of the state legislature during the Revolution was followed between 1785 and 1798 by considerably more service in that body. He was sheriff of King William County in 1790 and from 1802 to 1804. Since he was only twenty years of age in 1776 and the vote for delegates was confined to those twenty-one or older, Claiborne would hardly have been eligible to stand for an office for which he could not even vote (Elizabeth H. Ryland, ed., *King William County*, pp. 62, 73, 81; Hening, *Statutes*, VIII, 305–7; IX, 54).

¹⁰ Drury Ragsdale, Jr. (1750–1804), was a captain during the Revolution—at first of his county's militia and, from 1777 to 1783, of the 1st Continental Artillery. He was a member of the Virginia General Assembly in 1783 (F. B. Heitman, *Historical Register of Officers of the Continental Army*, p. 339).

¹¹ Possibly Thomas Fox (*ca.* 1750–1802), who, while serving in the Virginia continental line as a second lieutenant and later as a first lieutenant, was taken prisoner by the British when Charleston surrendered in May 1780 (*ibid.*, p. 181; Elizabeth H. Ryland, ed., *King William County*, pp. 70–71).

¹² Although the identification is not certain, he likely was the James Quarles who moved to Albemarle County in 1776, served as captain and major in the 2d Regiment of the state line during the Revolution and as sheriff of his county in 1782–1783 (Boyd, *Papers of Jefferson*, III, 344–45, 439; VI, 175; Edgar Woods, *Albemarle County in Virginia*, pp. 299–300; H. R. McIlwaine, ed., *Official Letters of the Governors of the State of Virginia* [3 vols.; Richmond, 1926–29], I, 175, 266; II, 115–16). On the other hand, he may have been the James Quarles of King William County who was known as "General" after the Revolution because of his service as paymaster general for a time during that war (Louis A. Burgess, ed., *Virginia Soldiers of 1776*, I, 332–34).

¹³ Probably he was a relative of the Tory Archibald Govan, who left for England early in 1776, and whose land in King William County escheated to the state four years later (*Virginia Gazette* [Williamsburg, Dixon and Hunter], 20 January 1776; *Calendar of Virginia State Papers*, I, 396; VII, 86; VIII, 96, 155).

¹⁴ Following the submission of this report, the Convention "*Ordered*, That the sheriff do amend the certificate of the election of delegates for the said county of King William, agreeably to the foregoing resolution" (*Proceedings of the Convention*, May 1776, p. 18).

¹⁵ On 20 May,
"The Convention being informed, that William Aylett, Esq., a delegate for the county of King William, had accepted a military post of profit in the continental army, by which his seat in this Convention is become vacated.
"*Ordered*, That the said information be referred to the Committee of Privileges and Elections; and that they inquire into the truth thereof, and report the same, together with their opinion thereupon, to the Convention" (*ibid.*, p. 20).

¹⁶ On 22 May, having heard this report, the Convention "*Ordered*. That the President [Edmund Pendleton] be desired to issue his warrant for the election of a delegate for the county of King William, in the room of the said William Aylett" (*ibid.*, p. 23). Aylett never attended the Convention. In fact, it received from him on 7 June a "memorial" bearing upon a matter connected with his new position as deputy commissary general (*ibid.*, pp. 37, 82). Although unnoted in the *Proceedings of the Convention*, a certificate dated 13 June 1776 in the Virginia State Library makes clear that Braxton was elected, vice Aylett, as a delegate from King William County. Braxton, however, could not have attended the Convention even during its closing days because he was in the Continental Congress at Philadelphia from 23 February until at least 9 July 1776 (*Journals of the Continental Congress*, IV, 167; V, 530).

Declaration of Rights and Form
of Government of Virginia

[16 May–29 June 1776]

EDITORIAL NOTE

When JM returned to Virginia in 1772, after three years at the College of New Jersey, the colony was in the throes of a religious revival. Baptist preachers, usually zealous but unlettered, itinerated through the province paying little heed to the statutes regulating the holding of religious services. This disregard of law was compounded by derogatory attacks on the Established Church. As might be expected, many of these clergymen were arrested and committed to jail, where they languished until they gave bond not to preach. JM sympathized with them. Though the Baptists were active in his own county of Orange, they had not been arrested there since 1768.

As early as 1 December 1773, in a letter to William Bradford, JM questioned the need for ecclesiastical establishments and sought information about religious toleration in Pennsylvania. (Also see JM to Bradford, 24 January 1774, and n. 9.) Both observation and extensive reading convinced him that religious liberty was a sacred right. Virginians generally held a less liberal view. Those who wished to relieve the dissenters of their disabilities usually took as a model the English Toleration Act of 1689. This led to proposals which would exempt the dissenters from legal penalties without extending them complete religious freedom.

The necessity for some revision of the statutes relating to the Established Church had been recognized by the House of Burgesses as early as 8 May 1769, when a Committee for Religion was first appointed and directed to prepare a bill exempting dissenters from the penalties of the law. For various reasons, action on such a measure was put off from session to session until the House of Burgesses expired on the eve of the Revolution. Meanwhile, the need for reform had become acute.

JM was elected a delegate from Orange County to the Revolutionary Convention which met on 6 May 1776. Except for his appointment two days later to its Committee on Privileges and Elections (above, Case of William Aylett, 8–22 May 1776), he is not mentioned in the proceedings until 16 May, when he was added to the committee named the day before "to prepare a declaration of rights, and such a plan of government as will be most likely to maintain peace and order in this colony, and secure substantial and equal liberty to the people" (*Proceedings of the Convention*, May 1776, pp. 16–17).

This committee was appointed after the Convention had faced up to the fact that a satisfactory accommodation with Great Britain was impossible and hence that independence was essential. JM, a junior member of the committee, was not expected to take an active part in writing the constitution. George Mason, whose great talents were acknowledged by all, was the chief architect of both the Declaration of Rights and the Form of Government. The only extant copy of his first draft of the Declaration, the one which he gave to Thomas Ludwell Lee about 25 May 1776, is now in the George Mason Papers in the Library of Congress.

The committee amended Mason's draft before reporting the Declaration to the Convention on 27 May. The report was referred to the committee of the whole and the Declaration was ordered "printed for the perusal of the members" (ibid., p. 25). Copies of this printed broadside were hurried north by the postrider. In Philadelphia, where the Second Continental Congress was sitting, the Pennsylvania Evening Post printed the committee's draft of the Virginia Declaration of Rights in full on 6 June 1776, as did the Pennsylvania Gazette six days later. R. Carter Pittman has called attention to the fact that this draft became one of the most influential constitutional documents in American history. It was republished all over America, in England, and in Europe. Its provisions were copied by Franklin into the Pennsylvania, and by John Adams into the Massachusetts, declarations of rights of 1776 and 1780, respectively (Virginia Magazine of History and Biography, LXVIII [1960], 110).

Although JM most probably was interested in all parts of the Virginia Declaration of Rights, only its last paragraph, that providing for religious toleration, stirred him to action. On his copy of the printed broadside of the Declaration, he prepared an amendment designed to establish absolute religious freedom in Virginia rather than the limited toleration which Mason envisioned. Since JM was a junior member of the Convention and always shrank from speaking in public, he sought an influential sponsor for his proposal. Patrick Henry, who had pleaded eloquently the cause of imprisoned Baptists on many occasions, was an obvious choice. But when Henry introduced the amendment in the Convention, he was at once asked whether he intended to disestablish the Church, for such was the apparent intent of the amendment. Henry "disclaimed such an object," as Edmund Randolph tells us (ibid., XLIV [1936], 47). With the sponsor in retreat, the amendment was doomed. JM then drafted a second amendment providing for a degree of religious freedom without disestablishing the Church. The key words of this proposal were written into the last article of the Virginia Declaration of Rights, adopted in its entirety by the Convention on 12 June 1776.

This final version of the Declaration was not published outside of Virginia for about a half-century. During this time, the committee's draft, which contained none of JM's handiwork, passed in the world at large as the official text. JM meanwhile continued to press for religious freedom in Virginia and achieved success with the passage of Thomas Jefferson's Statute for Religious Freedom on 16 January 1786. Jefferson was then in France, and it was JM who pushed the bill through the General Assembly (Boyd, Papers of Jefferson, II, 545–53).

The combination of circumstances set forth above contrived to deny JM the acclaim to which he was justly entitled. By his first important public act, he sought to assure complete religious freedom to all Virginians. Unable to gain the support of a majority in the Convention for so advanced a measure, he at least won a significant victory by replacing George Mason's words, "fullest Toleration in the Exercise of Religion," with his own, more liberal, "free exercise of Religion." Continuing to strive for the goal he failed to reach in 1776, he attained it a decade later when the legislature of Virginia enacted the statute mentioned above. This memorable reform, however, became identified with Jefferson's name, even though JM mainly deserved to be credited with its achievement.

Printed below, in chronological sequence, are copies of (*a*) George Mason's original draft of the article on religion in his proposed Declaration of Rights; (*b*) that article as revised by the committee; (*c*) JM's rejected amendment and his accepted amendment of that article; and (*d*) the article on religion in the Declaration of Rights adopted by the Virginia Convention. Finally, there is an editorial note on "Independence and Constitution of Virginia," written by JM in his old age. Most of this long manuscript comprises a careful copy of public documents or extracts from them. Since these were not a product of JM's thought, they will not be reproduced in this volume. While he was transcribing them, however, he occasionally interpolated comments of his own or appended a footnote. These are all quoted at appropriate places in the editorial note.

George Mason's Proposed Declaration of Rights

MS (LC: Papers of George Mason). The first and longer portion of this manuscript, including its provision about religion, is in the hand of George Mason. The last five lines on its third page and all of the concluding fourth page are in the hand of another member of the committee, Thomas Ludwell Lee, who signed this last page at its close.

EDITORIAL NOTE

This document is probably the paper mentioned by Thomas L. Lee in his letter of 1 June 1776 to his brother, Richard Henry Lee, then in Philadelphia attending the Second Continental Congress: "I enclosed you by last post a copy of our declaration of rights nearly as it come through the committee" (Kate M. Rowland, *Life of George Mason*, I, 240). The articles in this copy are unnumbered. They total twelve only, and the one on religion is the ninth. Thomas L. Lee comments, near the end of the manuscript:

> Another [Article] is agreed to in committee condemning the use of general warrants; & one other to prevent the suspension of laws, or the execution of them.
>
> The above clauses, with some small alterations, & the addition of one, or two more, have already been agreed to in the Committee....

In other words, the following proposal by Mason was as he first wrote it, and before it was amended by the committee.

[*ca.* 20–25 May 1776]

[9] That as Religion, or the Duty which we owe to our divine and omnipotent Creator, and the Manner of discharging it, can be governed only by Reason and Conviction, not by Force or Violence; and

therefore that all Men shou'd enjoy the fullest Toleration in the Exercise of Religion, according to the Dictates of Conscience, unpunished and unrestrained by the Magistrate, unless, under Colour of Religion, any Man disturb the Peace, the Happiness, or Safety of Society, or of Individuals. And that it is the mutual Duty of all, to practice Christian Forbearance, Love and Charity towards Each other.[1]

Committee's Proposed Article on Religion

Broadside (LC: Madison Papers). At the top of the first of its two sheets, JM wrote, "the original was draughted by Col[?] George Mason, & amended by the Committee."

EDITORIAL NOTE

When the committee laid its amended draft of George Mason's proposed Declaration of Rights before the Convention on 27 May, that body ordered it "to be committed to a committee of the whole Convention" and "*Resolved, that this Convention will on Wednesday next* [29 May], *resolve itself into a committee on the said declaration; and that, in the mean time, the same be printed, for the perusal of the members*" (*Proceedings of the Convention, May 1776*, p. 25). Judging from the size of the type used and certain characteristics of the type face, the printer of this broadside was Alexander Purdie of Williamsburg, publisher of a *Virginia Gazette*, but he did not reproduce this proposed Declaration of Rights in his paper. On the other hand, Dixon and Hunter printed it in their *Virginia Gazette* on 1 June 1776. The preamble of the Declaration, as it was furnished to the members of the Convention, reads, "*A* DECLARATION *of* RIGHTS *made by the representatives of the good people of* VIRGINIA, *assembled in full and free Convention; which rights do pertain to us, and our posterity, as the basis and foundation of government.*" Omitting this preamble, Dixon and Hunter merely prefaced their copy of the Declaration in the *Virginia Gazette* of 1 June with these words, "A DECLARATION *of* RIGHTS *reported from the committee who were appointed to draw them up, now under consideration of the Convention.*" On the other hand, the *Pennsylvania Gazette* of 12 June 1776 reproduced the preamble as it was reported by the committee to the Convention.

[27–28 May 1776]

18.[2] That religion, or the duty which we owe to our CREATOR, and the manner of discharging it, can be directed only by reason and conviction, not by force or violence; and therefore, that all men should enjoy the fullest toleration in the exercise of religion,[3] according to the dictates of conscience, unpunished and unrestrained by the magistrate unless, under colour of religion, any man disturb the peace, the happiness, or safety of society. And that it is the mutual duty of all to practice Christian forbearance, love and charity, towards each other.

Madison's Amendments to the Declaration of Rights

Broadside (LC: Madison Papers). JM wrote the earlier of his two amended readings ("A" below) in the space beneath the article about religion in his printed copy of the Declaration of Rights submitted to the Convention by the committee. The Convention rejected this amendment after it had been introduced and defended by Patrick Henry. JM then framed a second proposal ("B" below) by interlining the printed article about religion and writing two more lines immediately under it. A facsimile of these amendments appears in this volume.

EDITORIAL NOTE

There is no certain evidence known to the editors which fixes the time when either JM's first or second amendment was laid before the Convention or its committee of the whole. The official journal of the Convention merely reveals that the drafting committee's report, having been printed, was debated on 29 and 30 May and 3, 4, 5, and 11 June 1776. The session of 11 June seems to be the most likely occasion since the journal for that day records that "The Convention then proceeded to the consideration of the amendments reported to the declaration of rights, and having gone through the same, and agreed thereto, *Ordered,* That the said declaration of rights, with the amendments, be fairly transcribed, and read a third time."

Furthermore, it perhaps may be assumed that the Convention debated the articles in succession, from the first to the last. If so, the one on religion would have been the final one discussed. On 12 June the Convention unanimously adopted "A DECLARATION of RIGHTS" (*Proceedings of the Convention,* May 1776, pp. 25–43, *passim*).

[29 May–12 June 1776]

A

That[4] Religion or the duty we owe to our Creator, and the manner of discharging it, being under the direction of reason and conviction only, not of violence or compulsion, all men are equally entitled to the full and free exercise of it accordg to the dictates of Conscience; and therefore that no man or class of men ought, on account of religion to be invested with peculiar emoluments or privileges;[5] nor subjected to any penalties or disabilities unless under &c[6]

B

18. That religion, or the duty which we owe to our CREATOR, and the manner of discharging it, can be directed only by reason and conviction, not by force or violence; and therefore, that all men are equally entitled to enjoy the free exercise of religion,[7] according to the dic-

tates of conscience, unpunished and unrestrained by the magistrate, Unless the preservation of equal liberty and the existence of the State are manifestly endangered;[8] And that it is the mutual duty of all to practice Christian forbearance, love, and charity towards each other.[9]

Article on Religion Adopted by Convention

Printed text (*Proceedings of the Convention*, May 1776, p. 43).

[12 June 1776]

16. That religion, or the duty which we owe to our CREATOR, and the manner of discharging it, can be directed only by reason and conviction, not by force or violence; and therefore, all men are equally entitled to the free exercise of religion, according to the dictates of conscience; and that it is the mutual duty of all to practise Christian forbearance, love, and charity, towards each other.[10]

Independence and Constitution of Virginia

MS (LC: Madison Papers). This undated document of twenty pages bearing the above title is entirely in JM's hand.

[1827?]

EDITORIAL NOTE

Although the date when JM prepared this manuscript must remain uncertain, it could well have been written in the autumn of 1827, during his exchange of letters with George Mason's grandson about the Virginia Declaration of Rights and first Form of Government, and at a time when a revision of the state constitution was much in the public mind.

The manuscript has considerable unity of content but its eight final sheets, dealing wholly with the first constitution of Virginia, are separately paged. This fact may warrant some doubt whether they were written immediately following the completion of the first twelve pages. If they were not, however, JM's general title with its mention of "Constitution" would be misleading. Furthermore, the first twelve pages justify the use of the word "Independence" in the title only to the extent that the latter half of page one and most of page two are filled with an accurate copy by JM from the journal of the Convention of its resolves of 15 May 1776, instructing Virginia's delegates in the Second Continental Congress "to propose to that respectable body, to declare the United Colonies free and independent States" (*Proceedings of the Convention*, May 1776, pp. 15–16).

The first half of page one of this manuscript contains JM's transcription of the journal entry of 10 May (*ibid.*, p. 11) recording that a "Committee of the County of Augusta" had sent to the Convention a statement "representing the necessity of making the confederacy of the United Colonies the most perfect, independent, and lasting, and of framing an equal, free, and liberal Government that may bear the test of all future ages." Clearly pertinent to JM's subject, these recommendations must have attracted his special interest because he not only copied the full entry but wrote "Quere—its date" in the left-hand margin, and "[quere, as to the *date* of this representation, and whether the document be on the public files]" at the close of the paragraph. Whether he received an answer to these questions is unknown but, if he did, he succeeded where the present editors have failed. Apparently the "representation" from the Augusta County Committee is lost (Jos. A. Waddell, *Annals of Augusta County*, p. 241).

Beginning at the bottom of page two of the manuscript and continuing to the middle of page four are JM's extracts of salient entries in the Convention journal between 15 May and 29 June 1776, dealing with the appointment of the committee to prepare a Declaration of Rights and plan of government and with the timetable of action by the Convention upon the committee's proposals about each of these subjects, and especially the Declaration of Rights.

This portion has three brief interpolations by JM, not taken from the journal. After "Mr. Treasurer," listed among the twenty-eight Convention members comprising the first appointees to the committee to propose a Declaration of Rights and a Form of Government, JM inserted "[Robert Carter Nicholas]" so as to make clear who was then the provincial treasurer. After noting, "May 18. Ordered that George Mason be added to that Committee," JM wrote, "[It is inferred that he was not before present: especially as his name is not on any one of the numerous Committees of antecedent appointment. His distinguished talents, if present, could not have been overlooked.]" JM's inference was correct. His very similar comment in a letter to George Mason's grandson on 29 December 1827 (Madison, *Letters* [Cong. ed.], III, 607) may signify that he prepared this manuscript at about that time. His final interpolation in this section of the manuscript is an addition of "[see a printed copy in the hands of J. M.]" after copying the journal entry of 27 May 1776, providing for the printing of the committee's proposed Declaration of Rights.

After dividing vertically the last seven and one-half pages of this first part of the manuscript into two columns of approximately equal width, JM transcribed in the left-hand column the Declaration of Rights, "as printed by order of the Convention" (*q.v.*) immediately after 27 May 1776, when it received its committee's draft of the document. In the right-hand column, opposite the relevant item in the left-hand column, JM copied the amended wording, if any, of the Declaration of Rights "As agreed to by the Convention" (*q.v.*).

Except that at the outset of his accurate transcription of the proposed Declaration, JM footnoted, "It was drafted by George Mason," he refrained from interspersing either column of these pages with any comments of his own until he had reached the end of his copying with the article on religion in the committee's draft of the Declaration. Above its closing word he placed an asterisk, drew an ink line across the left-hand column, and penned under this line the following remarkable footnote:

"On the printed paper here literally copied is a manuscript variation of this last article making it read 'That Religion or the duty we owe to our Creator, and the manner of discharging it, being under the direction of reason and conviction only, not of violence or compulsion, all men are equally entitled to the full and free exercise of it, according to the dictates of Conscience; and therefore that no man or class of men, ought, on account of religion to be invested with peculiar emoluments or privileges, nor subjected to any penalties or disabilities, unless under colour of religion, the preservation of equal liberty and the existence of the State be manifestly endangered.' "

"This variation is in the handwriting of J. M. and is recollected to have been brought forward by him with a view, more particularly to substitute for the idea, expressed by the term *'toleration,'* an absolute and equal right in all, to the exercise of religion according to the dictates of conscience. The proposal was moulded into the last article in the Declaration, as finally established, from which the term 'toleration' is excluded."

Forgetting what he had done in the Convention, probably over fifty years before, JM in this note blended his first and second amendments of the committee's article on religion (*q.v.*) into a largely meaningless whole.

From this analysis of the content of the first twelve pages, it is evident that the Declaration of Rights is their main subject rather than the "Independence" or "Constitution" specified in the general title of the manuscript.

On the other hand, the last eight pages deal altogether with the constitution. They, as JM indicated by his bracketed note at the top of the first page, are in the main devoted to a "copy of a printed paper, in the hands of J.M." This "paper," now among his manuscripts in the Library of Congress, is a two-page leaflet, or broadside, probably printed about 10 June 1776, and entitled "A PLAN OF GOVERNMENT." Immediately beneath this caption are the words, *"Laid before the Committee of the House, which they have ordered to be printed for the perusal of the members."*

Perhaps it was soon after JM received his copy as a member of this committee that he used his quill pen to make this statement read, "Laid before the Committee appointed for that purpose, which they have ordered to be printed for the perusal of the members of the House." JM followed this amended form when he copied the document in his old age, but added a footnote reading:

"An alteration in the handwriting of J.M. erases 'of the House' and inserts after 'Committee,' *appointed for that purpose;* and adds, at the end, after 'members' *of the House,* making the whole read—Laid before the Committee appointed for that purpose, which they have ordered to be printed for the perusal of the members of the House.

"From this correction, it appears that what was laid before the Committee was printed by its order not by that of the Convention, as was done in the case of the 'Declaration of Rights' reported by Mr [Archibald] Cary, from the appointed Committee; nor is there in the Journal any order for printing any plan of Government reported to the Convention, from a Committee."

Except for this alteration, JM accurately copied this "plan of government" in full. The plan was the one submitted by George Mason to the committee of the Convention. Julian Boyd prints an annotated copy of it in his *Papers of Thomas Jefferson*, I, 366–69. Barring the footnote mentioned above, JM's transcription is devoid of any further comment by him until he reached its close. He then added the following footnote:

"It is not known with certainty from whom this first draught of a Plan of Government proceeded. There is a faint tradition that Meriwether Smith spoke of it as originating with him. What is remembered by J.M. is that George Mason was the most prominent member in discussing and developing the Constitution in its passage through the Convention. The Preamble is known to have been furnished by Thomas Jefferson."

In a letter to a grandson and namesake of George Mason on 29 December 1827 (Madison, *Letters* [Cong. ed.], III, 605–8), JM, after calling Mason "the master builder of the Constitution, and its main expositor and supporter throughout the discussions which ended in its establishment," somewhat inconsistently expressed strong doubt whether Mason could have been the author of "the primitive draft" represented by the printed "plan of government" which had been submitted to and printed by the committee in June 1776. The passage of over fifty years led JM to forget that this plan was by Mason, even though he correctly recalled the dominant role of Mason in shaping the recommendations of the committee and in steering them, with amendments, through the Convention (cf. with *ibid.*, III, 451–52; also see Brant, *Madison*, I, 236). JM, however, correctly stated to Mason's grandson that the preamble of the constitution had been borrowed from drafts prepared by Jefferson (Boyd, *Papers of Jefferson*, I, 331, 337–40, 377–79).

In copying Mason's printed plan, JM filled the left-hand column of the closing eight pages of his manuscript. Judging from his heading of the right-hand column, "Copy of the Constitution as finally agreed to, by the Convention of 1776," he intended to present, except for its preamble, the same sort of parallel arrangement which he had completed for the proposed and the official Declaration of Rights. In the case of the constitution, however, he laid the work aside after transcribing its first article and the opening ten words of the second article, which comprised the only alteration of that article as proposed by Mason. In other words, except for JM's heading, given above, and these two entries, the right-hand column of this manuscript's last eight pages is entirely blank.

---

[1] For many years everyone interested in the Declaration of Rights, including JM, believed that Mason's first draft of it was a paper in his hand, bearing the caption, "Copy of the first Daught [*sic*] by GM." This paper has been reproduced in facsimile at least twice—once between p. 240 and p. 241 of Vol. I of Kate M. Rowland, *Life of George Mason*, and again in *Virginia Cavalcade*, I [1951], 15–18. The copy in the biography, however, omits a few marginal notes by Mason. A transcript of this "first Daught," made by someone unknown and also lacking those marginal notes, came into the possession of JM and is now among his papers in

the Library of Congress. He accepted its caption as bona fide, and in his old age he had his brother-in-law, John C. Payne, who often served as his amanuensis, go through it and mark the variations between its text and that of the draft recommended by the committee to the Convention. This exercise appeared to reveal that the Convention, during its debates on the committee's draft, struck out many of its alterations of Mason's "original" and returned in the final version to what he had first proposed. It is now known, however, that the "Copy of the first Daught by GM" was compiled by him in 1778 from his true first draft–of which the article on religion is quoted above–, from the committee's proposal, and from the draft finally adopted by the Convention (Brant, *Madison*, I, 235–40). In Mason's fictitious first draft, the article on religion corresponds in its wording exactly with what the committee proposed to the Convention (*q.v.*) except that Mason had a "the" before "safety of society," near the close of the article. On the docket of JM's copy of Mason's misleading document, William C. Rives, JM's first biographer, wrote a fairly lengthy commentary, interesting today as evidence of his unquestioned acceptance of that document as being what it purported to be.

² Unlike Mason's proposed Declaration of Rights, the article on religion had now been assigned the final place in the document. Furthermore, because the committee added articles to those proposed by Mason, the article on religion had become No. 18, rather than No. 9.

³ From this emphasis upon "toleration" only, it is evident that, if JM attempted to have the committee accept his amendment (*q.v.*), he was unsuccessful.

⁴ JM put a cross above this word, and another cross in the left-hand margin, followed by "suggested by JM & [includes?] clause finally agreed to." This "clause," of course, is "all men are equally entitled to the full and free exercise of it [religion]."

⁵ If this had been adopted by the Convention, it would in effect have disestablished the Anglican Church. The proposal serves to make clear that this amendment must have been the earlier of the two amendments, even though both are written on the same sheet with no designation by JM as to which preceded the other.

⁶ By "&c," JM evidently meant that after "under" should follow the words of the committee's version–"colour of religion, any man disturb the peace, the happiness, or safety of society. And that it is the mutual duty of all to practice Christian forbearance, love, and charity, toward each other."

⁷ Between the words "therefore" and "religion," the committee's version reads, "that all men should enjoy the fullest toleration in the exercise of."

⁸ Between the words "Unless" and this semicolon, the committee's version reads, "under colour of religion, any man disturb the peace, the happiness, or safety of society."

⁹ This second amendment appears to have been introduced in the Convention by Edmund Pendleton (Brant, *Madison*, I, 247). Julian Boyd in *Papers of Jefferson*, I, 345 n., states that, probably before 27 May and possibly even before 14 May when Jefferson reached Philadelphia for the meeting of the Second Continental Congress, he had sketched a constitution for his state and sent it to a member of the Virginia Convention. This draft included the guarantee that "All persons shall have full & free liberty of religious opinion, nor shall any be compelled to frequent or maintain any religious service or institution [but seditious behavior to be punble . . . by civil magistrate accdg to the laws already made or hereafter to be made]" (*ibid.*, p. 344, brackets are Jefferson's; see also, pp. 330–31, 364–65 n.). Although Madison may have seen this proposal before he prepared his amendments, he did not need it to convert him to the side of religious freedom. He had been its passionate advocate as early as January 1774 (JM to Bradford, 24 January 1774).

¹⁰ This final form of "A Declaration of Rights" appeared in the *Virginia Gazette* (Purdie), "Postscript," on 14 June 1776, and in the *Virginia Gazette* (Dixon and Hunter) on 15 June 1776.

From William Bradford

Letter not found.

20 May 1776. In "A Memorandum Book and Register, for the months of May & June 1776," now in the Historical Society of Pennsylvania, William Bradford wrote on 20 May:

". . . went to the town meeting[1] where notwithstanding the badness of the day ther was a great number of inhabitants & it was resolved 1. That the present Government was inefficient 2. That the Assembly could not legally form a new one: 3. That a Convention be chosen for that purpose; & several others of the like nature: this gives the Coup de Grace to the King's authority in this province. In the afternoon I gave Mr. Maddison an account of this meeting, of our defeat at Quebec[2] & several other articles of intelligence."

[1] "A very large number" of Philadelphians assembled in the State House at the call of the Committee of Inspection and Observation of the City and Liberties. The gathering declared that since the provincial legislature still desired a reconciliation with England it was not fitted to carry out the 15 May resolution of the Second Continental Congress, asking each colony to establish a government adequate "to the exigencies of their affairs." Therefore the "town meeting" resolved to bypass the legislature and call upon the people of the province to elect a Convention for the purpose of deciding how the recommendation of Congress could be made a reality in Pennsylvania (Force, *American Archives*, 4th ser., VI, 517–19).

[2] The arrival of British reinforcements in the St. Lawrence River early in May was the final blow which led the patriot army to abandon its siege of Quebec and withdraw from Montreal. This bad news reached Congress on 18 May (*Journals of the Continental Congress*, IV, 362).

To William Bradford

Letter not found.

Ca. 21 May 1776. In "A Memorandum Book," Bradford noted on 28 May 1776: "This morning I recieved a Letter from Mr Maddison who is a member of the Virginia Convention, informing me of the declaration of Independency made by that body."[1]

[1] Since the resolution calling upon the delegates of Virginia in the Second Continental Congress to propose that "the United Colonies" be declared "free and independent States" was adopted by the Convention on 15 May (Force, *American Archives*, 4th ser., VI, 1524), this missing letter must have been written by JM on that date or a short time thereafter. More of its content is probably indicated in Bradford's memorandum of 3 June (*q.v.*).

To James Madison, Sr.

RC (LC: Madison Papers; and Massachusetts Historical Society: French Collection). Originally this letter must have consisted of two sheets, with each sheet folded twice, horizontally. Splitting along the folds as the manuscript aged, it divided into six separate strips. The first of these, upon which JM probably wrote the date, the salutation, and the opening few lines of his message, has disappeared. Although the portion immediately following this missing one and the section containing the closing lines of the letter are now in the Massachusetts Historical Society, two of the three middle fragments are in the Library of Congress. The other lost strip, probably comprising nine or ten lines, would directly precede the portion on which the letter closes. The fraying at each fold where the pages split caused a line or some part of a line to disappear. Therefore, the missing words have had to be supplied by conjecture. In like manner, the left-hand margins of the fragments in the Library of Congress have been so clipped as to cut off words or parts of words. Here, too, the editors have indicated, within brackets, what JM may have written. On the reverse of one of the fragments in the Library of Congress there appears in JM's hand, "To [C]ol. James Madison, Orange County [carrie?]d by [Capt. Thomas W?]alker." Noted below is internal evidence permitting the letter to be dated with considerable assurance at Williamsburg early in June 1776. JM had been there since 8 May as one of the two representatives of Orange County at the colonial "Convention of Delegates."

[1–15 June 1776]

would be adviseable to make the best terms you can with him. I intend to apply myself to him on my return home. I have not had an opportunity since I red. your last[1] of taking the opinion of Col Pendleton[2] on Ignatius's Queries,[3] but I shall speak to him on the subject as soon as I can find him at leasure, which his close engagement in business occasions to be not very often the case. Col. Henry[4] says that half blood entitles to personal Estates and that the money arising from the Sale of the Land must be considered as Chattels if the person who sold it was duly authorised by the Intestate. that is, if the bargain was so made as to bind the Intestate of

will of course bind the Heirs. so do not [forget?]   [he?] also said that [Ne?]gros was to be considered as Chattels, as the   Intestate died with. I suppose the Law is plain enough in that instance.[5] [Nothing rem]arkable has happened at Quin's Island since the Enemy took [it. The]y are very active in fortifying it and those who are acquainted [with] the place are of opinion it will be impossible to dislodge them. Our [arm]y in field amount to abt. 500 Regulars I believe and are very [short of?] conveniences.[6] Mr. Crig went from this place yesterday with a [pack]et[?] homewards, and will give you a more particular acct.[7] [Many] of the Maryland Convention betray a disposition exceed[ingly?]

[adverse to?] the American Cause. Independ[ent] of the Recommendation[8] [to detain the?] person and papers of Govr. Eden and to form a New Gove[rn]mt. [representative?] of the people, they have resolved that their present Governt. [is exerc?]ised under the Authority of the Crown and they confess the obliga[tion of its? rep]resentative[s] to obey the Mandates of the Ministry,   & they have not only given Eden permission to leave the Colony   [b]ut have insulted this Colony with a request that our Cruisars [should? fore]bear molesting him as he passes our Coasts. and have sent [us their?] proceedings respecting him among which is an address containing[9]   [de?]clared it during the

apply
that the Persons who take them should be sworn. I expect it will avail noth[ing] and that the whole work will be to do over again.[10] It is uncertain when the Convention will rise. Most of the members seem determind to go home to their Har[vests] and I expect the House will adjourn at that season though it is obvious th[e] Business will be by no means finished by that time. We shall expect the [Horses?] down about the 20th. of the Month if you do not hear from me again. Major Moore is well as usual. He grunts as much and eats as hearty a[s] an[y] man in Williamsburg.[11]

I am Dr Sir your affectionate son

Js MADISON JUNR

[1] Not found. It probably would have furnished an identification of the "him" in each of the two preceding lines. If JM's word "last" was used precisely, it signifies that his father had written to him more than once since he arrived in Williamsburg.

[2] Edmund Pendleton, president of the Convention, and also chairman of Virginia's Committee of Safety.

[3] In the Orange County Order Book, No. 8, p. 356, a microfilm of which is in the Virginia State Library, appears the following, under date of 23 May 1776: "Administration granted Ignatius Tureman on the Estate of George Tureman Decd Where-

upon he with James Madison Gent his Security Entered into And Acknowledged Their Bond for the Same in the Sum of £500. Cont. Money." Ignatius Tureman (d. 1784) moved to Spotsylvania County by 1782 (Spotsylvania County Court Records, Will Book E, pp. 572, 584, on microfilm in Virginia State Library).

4 Patrick Henry, then a delegate to the Convention from Hanover County.

5 It would appear that George Tureman, probably of King and Queen County (*Virginia Magazine of History and Biography*, IV [1896–97], 296; XXXII [1924], 156), died intestate before effecting a sale of his property in Orange County. Its court permitted Ignatius Tureman, with JM's father as his security, to be the administrator of this portion of the deceased's estate. George Tureman's potential heirs evidently included some half-brothers or other relatives not wholly of his "blood." Being in doubt about their legal share, if any, in the estate, and doubtful whether the administrator could go ahead and sell Orange County property which the deceased had taken steps to sell, Ignatius Tureman asked the elder Madison to have JM seek the advice of Edmund Pendleton, one of the ablest lawyers in Virginia. Unable to catch him at a leisure moment, JM posed the questions to Patrick Henry. How the Tureman estate issue was finally settled is unknown.

6 Gwynn's Island, in Chesapeake Bay near the mouth of the Piankatank River, was occupied by Lord Dunmore, the royal governor of Virginia, and some four hundred of his Negro and white henchmen from about 1 June to 10 July 1776. JM may have greatly underestimated the number of Virginia troops facing Dunmore, since Pendleton in a letter of 1 June to Jefferson put the figure at two thousand (Boyd, *Papers of Jefferson*, I, 297, 454–55, 468–69; H. R. McIlwaine, ed., *Official Letters of Virginia Governors*, I, 6–7, 10).

7 Probably Reverend Elijah Craig (*ca.* 1743–1808), pastor of the Blue Run Baptist Church in Orange County. He was twice jailed as a dissenting preacher in Culpeper County and is asserted to have been jailed also in Orange County. Craig represented the interests of his denomination at the state Revolutionary conventions and the general assemblies. In 1786 he migrated to Kentucky (J. H. Spencer, *A History of Kentucky Baptists* [2 vols.; Cincinnati, 1885], I, 87–88; Lewis P. Little, *Imprisoned Preachers and Religious Liberty in Virginia*, pp. 133, 516, 524). At Williamsburg Craig sold a rifle to one Charles Smith, a soldier in Captain Thomas Walker's company of the 9th Virginia Regiment (*Calendar of Virginia State Papers*, VIII, 186). While returning to his place of residence in Albemarle County, Walker seems to have stopped at Montpelier to deliver JM's letter to his father (see headnote).

8 This apparently refers to two resolutions of the Continental Congress. On 10 May 1776 it "recommended to the respective assemblies and conventions of the United Colonies, where no government sufficient to the exigencies of their affairs have been hitherto established, to adopt such government as shall, in the opinion of the representatives of the people, best conduce to the happiness and safety of their constituents in particular, and America in general" (*Journals of the Continental Congress*, IV, 342). The royal government of Maryland was evidently deemed not to be "sufficient" for the above-mentioned "exigencies" because on 16 April the Congress "earnestly requested" the Council of Safety of Maryland "immediately to cause the person and papers of Governor Eden to be seized and secured" (*ibid.*, IV, 285–86).

9 Conservative in temper and well disposed toward the amiable Governor Robert Eden (1741–1784), the Council of Safety and the General Convention in Maryland not only spurned the requests of Congress but even, as JM indicates, asked the authorities at Williamsburg to assure Eden an unmolested passage out of Chesapeake Bay. This request, being laid before the Virginia Convention on 31 May, makes certain that the letter of JM to his father could not have been written before that date (*Proceedings of the Convention*, May 1776, p. 30). The Virginians probably

felt the more "insulted" by the Maryland Convention's presumption because two weeks before, on 15 May, the Virginia Convention had "unanimously" instructed their delegates in the Continental Congress to propose that "the United Colonies" declare their independence (above, Declaration of Rights, 16 May–29 June 1776).

10 Without having the missing strip preceding this final fragment of the letter, the antecedent of "it" is wholly speculative. Possibly JM had mentioned the work going on in the Convention to make the governmental transition from colony to commonwealth. The famous Declaration of Rights was adopted unanimously on 12 June; discussions were in train about what the rest of the state's written constitution should be, and an ordinance was under consideration "to enable the present magistrates and officers to continue the administration of justice, and for settling the general mode of proceedings in criminal and other cases till the same can be more amply provided for." This bill, by prescribing an oath to be taken by the "several persons named in the commission of the peace in each country" and by suggesting its provisional nature in its title, seems to coincide with what JM writes in the partial sentence and the first sentence of this fragment (Hening, *Statutes*, IX, 126).

11 Major William Moore, JM's fellow delegate from Orange County. The mention of the 20th as being in the future fixes, of course, the date after which this letter could not have been written and also suggests that JM had probably sent at least one other letter from Williamsburg to his father. As already mentioned, the Convention remained in session until 6 July.

From William Bradford

Letter not found.

3 June 1776. In his "Memorandum Book" (see 20 May 1776) Bradford wrote:

"As my friend Maddison had desired me in his last to give him a sketch of the Constitution of this province and of that of Connecticut which might be useful to him as a member of Convention, I determined to return an early answer & wrote a rough draught of a Letter for that purpose. The constitution of Connecticut I learnt from douglas¹ who is no very good historian & a little viva voce information I picked up as I travelled thro' the province in my [journey] to the Camp at Cambrige last fall.² . . . In the Evening I copied the Letter to Mr. Maddison. . . ."³

1 William Douglass, M.D. (*ca.* 1691–1752), *A Summary, Historical and Political, of the First Planting, Progressive Improvements, and Present State of the British Settlements in North-America* (2 vols.; Boston, 1749–53). Douglass gives an account of Connecticut in Part III of his second volume.

2 Perhaps this journey, together with his increasingly active role in the Revolution, explains why Bradford found no time after July 1775 to copy in his commonplace book his continuing correspondence with JM.

3 Neither this letter nor its "rough draught" is known to be extant.

To James Madison, Sr.

RC (LC: Madison Papers). On the cover sheet, William C. Rives wrote, many years later, "after this insert Declaration of Rights & Constitution." This was done in Madison, *Letters* (Cong. ed.), I, 21–28, which Rives edited.

WILLIAMSBURG June 27—1776

HON'D SIR,

I this day disposed of the Bill of Exchange I brought down to Col. Zane[1] at 42%. and filled up the Blank for the sum with £.180. I take this earliest opportunity of acquainting you with it that no inconvenience may arise from your making any engagements inconsistent with the sale I have made. I was unwilling to take so low a price for the Bill but thought it the best that could be done at this time. If the Exchange sd. rise hereafter it will be very uncertain whether our remoteness from the market wd. not have disabled us from taking advantage of it.[2]

It is impossible for me to say when the Convention will adjourn, but am pretty certain it will not be so soon as was expected when I wrote by Troilus.[3] It is said that 7 Ships, some very large, have within a few days past come to the aid of Dunmore Whether they be transports or Ships of War is not yet determined.[4] This is all the News we have at present.

I am dear sir, Yrs. affectely,

JAMES MADISON JR.

[1] Isaac Zane, Jr. (d. 1795), a Pennsylvania-born merchant, distiller, and miller of Frederick and Shenandoah counties, Va. His public service included membership in the House of Burgesses from 1773 to 1775, in the general conventions of March, July, and December 1775 and of May 1776, and in the House of Delegates from 1776 to 1795. He was also a colonel of militia. In his will he bequeathed ten guineas to Jefferson and another ten to either JM or his father (*Tyler's Quarterly Historical and Genealogical Magazine*, VI [1924–25], 272).

[2] A bill of exchange was ordinarily drawn against a merchant with whom the drawer had a financial balance in his favor. Being negotiable, the bill might pass from hand to hand for months before ultimately reaching the drawee. Although in a colony like Virginia, where specie was rare, these bills were legal currency (Hening, *Statutes*, VI, 85), they had no fixed value and were usually accepted by a creditor at a heavy discount. This fluctuation might reflect, for example, a drop in tobacco prices and hence a decline in the credit of the signer of the bill of exchange or of the merchant against whom it was drawn.

[3] No doubt a slave, and probably the one who had brought horses to Williamsburg from Montpelier about a week earlier (JM to James Madison, Sr., [1–15 June 1776]). JM's letter, conveyed to his father by Troilus, has not been found.

4 See JM to James Madison, Sr., [1–15 June 1776], n. 6. The figure "7" agrees with the number of anchor cables cut by the British fleet in its hurry, on 10 July, to get beyond the range of the patriot guns. Four of these ships were the "Fowey," "Dunmore," "Otter," and "Roebuck" (Boyd, *Papers of Jefferson*, I, 461–62).

Case of Unsettled Claims from Dunmore's War

MS (Virginia State Library). Mostly in the hand of John Tazewell, clerk of the Virginia House of Delegates.

EDITORIAL NOTE

On 29 June 1776, immediately after adopting the "form of government," or state constitution, which it had framed, the Virginia Convention heeded the eleventh and twenty-second articles by electing a governor (Patrick Henry) and eight members of the Council of State. JM acted as one of the four tellers for each of these elections (*Proceedings of the Convention*, May 1776, pp. 78–79; Hening, *Statutes*, IX, 112–19). This council selected John Page to be its president, thereby also making him the lieutenant governor of the commonwealth. In accordance with Article XXII of the constitution, the adjournment of the Convention on 5 July transformed its members into the personnel of the House of Delegates of the legislature. Before it convened at Williamsburg on 7 October, the qualified voters, balloting on varying dates in August and September in the districts defined by an ordinance of the Convention, elected a Senate of twenty-four members (*ibid.*, IX, 128–30). Thus the bicameral legislature of the sovereign Commonwealth of Virginia came into being, with JM a charter member of the House of Delegates. His term in that body expired with its adjournment on 21 December 1776.

Much of its business was channeled through three large committees—the Committee of Privileges and Elections, the Committee of Propositions and Grievances, and the Committee of "Publick" Claims. JM was named to the first of these, a group comprising over fifty delegates (*Journal of the House of Delegates of Virginia, Anno Domini, 1776* [Richmond, 1828], p. 4). He served on the long-standing Committee for Religion, and on the special committees for unsettled claims against the state arising from Lord Dunmore's War, for preparing a letter to the delegates of Virginia in the Continental Congress about the disputed boundary between that state and Pennsylvania, for drafting a bill to abolish some special privileges of the Anglican Church and some disabilities of dissenters, and for examining the enrolled bills (*ibid.*, pp. 13, 14, 41, 68, 77).

If the journal of the House of Delegates and the remnant of other legislative papers in the Virginia State Library can be trusted, JM was not the chairman of any committee, nor the draftsman of any committee report, nor the introducer of any motion during this session. Although its journal omits mention of the participants in the debates, he probably spoke seldom, if ever, from the floor. Thomas Jefferson, one of the most prominent members of the House of Delegates, recalled many years later how youthful JM appeared to be and how silent his shyness kept him when in a large group. On the other hand, although possibly not referring to this particular session, Jefferson added that young Madison demonstrated unusual skill in the wording of committee reports and resolutions (Edward Coles to Hugh Blair Grigsby, 23 December 1854, reporting what Coles had been told by Jefferson, RC in Virginia Historical Society). No extant document of this session, however, is in his hand, nor is any so distinctive in expression or thought as to be confidently attributed to him. Moreover, he seems never to have mentioned this meeting of the House of Delegates as one to which he contributed significantly.

For these reasons, one sample only is furnished of the work of this session. This is a report of the "unsettled claims" committee of which JM was a member. It was chosen, not because it suggests JM more than any other manuscript, but merely because, in its length and the interest of its subject matter, it fairly well typifies the extant reports of the special committees.

[9 December 1776]

The Committee[1] appointed have According to Order Examined the Reports of John Harvie & Joseph Neville[2] to whom it was referred to Settle such of the Claims against the Public On Account of the late Expedition Against the Indians as remained Unsettled, and to revise those that had been Settled in West Augusta, have Agreed upon a report and Come to a resolution thereupon, as Follows.

It appears to your Committee by the Testimony of Sundry Witnesses, that while the Forces under the Command of the Earl of Dunmore, on the late Expedition Against the Indians, were encamped near the Shawanese Towns, Colo. William Crawford was Ordered to take the Command of a Detachment of two hundred and fifty men, and to march against a Town of the Seneca Nation of Indians, Distant from the Camp about thirty miles, his Lordship at the same time Assuring him, that if any Plunder was taken, it shou'd be Equally Divided among the Captors. It further Appears that the Party took at the said Town Several Prisoners, with Plunder in Indian Goods, Horses[?], Silver Trinkets, and Other Articles, which were sold by Consent of the said Captors, the sale Amounting to three hundred & five Pounds fifteen Shillings & a half Penny, when the Captains of Each Company, became Responsible for the Purchases made by their men.[3] It Likewise appears that another Party Commanded by Colo. McDonald, on an Expedition against the upper Shawanese Towns, after distroying the same, took Plunder which was sold in like Manner, to the Amount of thirty five Pounds Eleven Shillings & three Pence.[4] It further Appears to your

Committee that the Commissioners on Settling the Expences of the late Indian War, Stopped Out of the pay of the Different Officers, the said two sums, Amounting in the whole to three Hundred and forty One Pounds six Shillings and three Pence half Penny.

Resolved as the Opinion of this Committee, that the Captors had an Undoubted right to the said Plunder, and in Order that Strict Justice shou'd be Done them, a Commissioner Ought to be Appointed, to Recieve from the Treasury, the said sum of three hundred & forty One Pounds Six Shillings and three Pence half Penny, and to Call upon each of the Officers who Commanded Parties in the said Detachments, (on Oath) for lists of the Names of the Men who Served, and the said Commissioner Pay each of them, their Proportionate Parts of the said Sum of Money.

1776 Decr. 9
Agreed to by the House of Delegates

JOHN TAZEWELL[5] C. H. D.

Ordered that Mr. James Wood[6] be appointed a Commissioner for the purposes mentioned in the within Resolution.

JOHN TAZEWELL C. H. D.

Dec Xth[7] 1776
Agreed to by the Senate

J. PENDLETON[8] C. S.

---

[1] Unsettled monetary claims arising from military service in, or goods furnished for, Lord Dunmore's expedition of 1774 against the western Indian tribes were presented to the Virginia Convention of July 1775. Even that early, John Harvie (1742–1807), from the West Augusta district, was named to one or another of the special committees appointed to determine the validity of these claims (*Proceedings of the Convention*, July 1775, pp. 14–15, 21, 23–24). On 16 January 1776, the Convention, which had assembled on 1 December 1775, named Harvie to settle the rightful claims of this nature of petitioners living in five western counties, and named Joseph Neaville (Neavill, Neville, 1730–1819) of Hampshire County to act in the same capacity for four other counties. They were ordered to render an accounting at the next convention (*The Proceedings of the Convention of Delegates held at the Town of Richmond, in the Colony of Virginia, on Friday, the 1st of December, 1775. and afterwards by adjournment in the City of Williamsburg* [Richmond, 1816], p. 99). At the sessions of 25 and 27 May of this "next convention," the reports of Harvie and Neaville were referred for examination to a committee of sixteen delegates, with Archibald Cary of Chesterfield County as its chairman and JM as one of its members. This committee reported on 14 June 1776 (*Proceedings of the Convention*, May 1776, pp. 25, 47, 54). It was the Cary committee, "revived" by the House of Delegates on 15 October 1776, but with Thomas Lewis of Augusta County as its new chairman because of Cary's election to the Senate, which rendered the present report. It was accepted by the House of Delegates on 9 December and by the Senate two days later rather than on 10 December as is indicated at the close of the manu-

script report. Included in the report printed in the journal was a separate recommendation by the committee to pay Private John Hardin, Jr., £20 "in Consideration of the wound he received in the service of this Country" when under the command of Captain Daniel Morgan on his "Expedition against the upper Shawanowo Towns" (*Journal of the House of Delegates, 1776*, pp. 14, 88, 91). Hardin had been wounded while on the expedition mentioned in n. 4, below (Reuben G. Thwaites and Louise P. Kellogg, eds., *Documentary History of Dunmore's War*, p. 155 n.).

2 After serving as a delegate of Virginia in the Continental Congress from May 1777 until December 1778, Harvie became in May 1779 the register of the Virginia Land Office, a position which he continued to hold for twelve years. For a time during the Revolution he had the rank of colonel in the Virginia militia by virtue of his role as a purchasing agent. Briefly in 1788 he was secretary of the commonwealth. Besides serving as a captain in Dunmore's War, a burgess from 1773 to 1776, a member of the conventions of 1775 and 1776, and of the House of Delegates in 1777, 1780, and 1781, Neaville was a militia brigadier general during the Revolution and helped determine the boundary between Pennsylvania and Maryland. He represented Virginia in the United States Congress, 1793–1795.

3 Late in October 1774, with his force of about 250 men, Major William Crawford (1732–1782) destroyed a settlement of Mingo Indians on the west bank of the Scioto River, near the present site of Columbus, Ohio. The Mingos were said to be an offshoot of the Senecas and were often called the "Iroquois of the Ohio" (*ibid.*, pp. 28 n., 303–4; Virgil A. Lewis, *History of the Battle of Point Pleasant* ... [Charleston, W.Va., 1909], p. 12). Born in Berkeley County, Va., Crawford moved to Pennsylvania in 1768 after serving as an officer in the French and Indian War and in the campaign against Pontiac. Crawford's activities as a surveyor of western lands brought him into close association with Washington. His military career on the frontier during the Revolution ended tragically in 1782 when the Wyandottes captured him in the Ohio country and tortured him to death at Sandusky.

4 Early in August 1774, a detachment led by Major Angus McDonald (1733–1779) burned five Shawnee villages, near the present town of Dresden on the Muskingum River in Ohio (Reuben G. Thwaites and Louise P. Kellogg, eds., *Documentary History of Dunmore's War*, pp. 151–56). McDonald, whose home was near Winchester in Frederick County, had fought in the French and Indian War. By his surveying activities in 1774 on behalf of Washington and other veterans of that conflict, he had helped to precipitate Dunmore's War. Loyalist in his sympathies, McDonald declined Washington's offer of a lieutenant colonel's commission in April 1777 (Fitzpatrick, *Writings of Washington*, III, 211 n.; VII, 297 n.; XXXVII, 505–6).

5 John Tazewell (*ca.* 1741–1781), a Williamsburg lawyer, served as clerk of the Virginia conventions of 1775 and 1776, and of the House of Delegates from 1776 to 30 October 1777. In May 1778 he became an associate justice of the General Court of Virginia.

6 James Wood (1750–1813) of Frederick County had commanded a company in Dunmore's War, and served as a colonel of the Virginia continental troops from 12 November 1776 to 1 January 1783. His long political career included service in the House of Burgesses, the Convention of 1776, the legislature for twelve years, and the Privy Council for twenty years, as lieutenant governor, and as governor of Virginia from 1796 to 1799. He was president of the Society of the Cincinnati in Virginia from 1784 until his death (*Proceedings of the Convention*, December 1775, pp. 75, 77, 86; *Journal of the House of Delegates, 1776*, p. 52; Lyon G. Tyler, ed., *Encyclopedia of Virginia Biography*, II, 46).

7 From this date to the end, the paper is in Pendleton's hand rather than Tazewell's.

8 John Pendleton, Jr. (*ca.* 1749–*ca.* 1807), of Richmond and Henrico County, was a nephew of Edmund Pendleton. He was clerk of the Virginia Committee of Safety in 1775–1776 and clerk of the state Senate in the session of May–June 1777. Following a term on the Richmond Common Council, 1783–1784, he retired to his Henrico County farm (*Proceedings of the Convention,* December 1775, p. 102; *Journal of the House of Delegates,* May 1777, p. 109).

To James Madison, Sr.

RC (LC: Madison Papers). Unless JM failed to add his customary close and his signature to this letter, at least its final page is lost. So, too, is the address sheet. The salutation and contents of the letter make it certain that he was writing to his father, who was in Fredericksburg.

ORANGE [29] March, Saturday 1777[1]

HOND SIR,

The family have been pretty well since you left us except Anthony.[2] He was taken on Wednesday morning with a strong Ague succeeded by a high fever and accompanied with a pain in his Stomach and side. The Swelling in his Arm also increased very considerably and became hard and painful. I was a good deal at a loss in what manner to proceed with him being unable to form any Judgmt. of the nature of the Tumor or the effect a proper treatment of his other complaints might have on it. I ventured however to have a pretty large quantity of blood taken from him and had his arm kept moist by the usual Poultices, which has answered every purpose I cd. have hoped. His fever and pain have gradually abated and I have no doubt but he will be perfectly recovered from them in a few days, and the Swelling on his arm seems to be subsiding fast.

The following odd affair has furnished the Ct. of this County with some very unexpected business.

Two persons travelling from Phila. to the Southward one of them a French man and an officer in the Continental Army and the other a man of decent figure came to the Ct. House on the evening of the Ct. day[3] and immediately enquired for a member of the Committee;[4] and being withdrawn with several members into a private room they gave information, that they fell in with a man on the road a few miles from the Ct. house who in the cours[e] of Conversation on public affairs gave abundant proof of his being an adherent to the King of G. B. and a dangerous Enemy to the State, that he run into the most outrageous abuse of our proceedings and on their threatening to inform agt. him in the most daring manner bid defiance to Committees or Whoever shoul[d] pretend to judge or punish him. They said the man they alluded to had come with them to the Ct House and they made no doubt but they could point him out in the Crowd. On their so doing the Culprit appeared to be Benjamin Haley.[5] As the Committee had no jurisdiction in the case it was referred to a justice of the Peace. Every one seemed to be agreed that his conduct was a direct violation of Law and called aloud for public notice; but, the Witnesses being travellers and therefore unable to attend on at a Trial, it was thought best not to undertake a Prosecution which promised nothing but impunity and matter of triumph to the offender. Here the affair dropped and every one supposed was entirely at an end. But as the French man was accidently passing through the room where Haley was, he took occasion to admonish the people of his being a disaffected person and upbraided him for his Tory principles. This introduced a debate which was continued for some time with great heat on the part of the Frenchman and great insolence on the part of Haley. At the request of the latter they at length both appeared before a Justice of the peace. Haley at first evaded the charges of his antagonist, but after some time, said he scorned to be a *counterfeit* and in answer to some questions that were put to him, signified that we were in the State of rebellion and had revolted from our lawful Soverign and that if the King had justice done him his Authority would still be in exercise among us. This passed in the presence of 20 or 30 persons and rendered the Testimony of the Travellers needless. A warrant for arresting him was immediately issued and executed. The criminal went through his examination in which his very Pleas seemed to aggravate his guilt. Witnesses were summoned sworn and their evidences taken. And on his Ob[s]tinate refusal to give security for his appearance he was committed to close goal [gaol]. This happened about 8 OClock. I have since heard he begged abt. one OClock in the morning to be admitted to bail & went hom[e] but not without threats of revenge and making public declaration yt. he was King George's man. I have stated the case thus particularly not only for your own satisfaction, but that you may, if an opportunity occurs, take the advice of some Gentleman skilled in the Law, on the most proper & legal mode of proceeding against him.[6]

Ambrose requests you will enquire whether any pretty neat Shoe Boots are to be had in Fredg. and the price of them.[7]

[1] The monthly "Court Day," to which reference is made in the letter, was Thursday, 27 March 1777. For this reason the "Saturdy" must have been the 29th.
[2] A slave. JM frequently refers to slaves as members of "the family."

3 Above, n. 1. The American officer and his companion have not been identified.

4 That is, the Orange County Committee of Safety, of which JM's father was a member.

5 Benjamin Haley or Healey (*ca.* 1730–1800) was frequently involved in litigation, usually as the defendant, in the Orange County Court from 1755 until his death (Orange County Order Book, No. 6, pp. 126, 526; Orange County Minute Book, No. 2, p. 372; Orange County General Index to Orders and Minutes, No. 3—these are on microfilm in Virginia State Library).

6 "Benjamin Haley appeared in Discharge of his recognizance for attributing the right of Kingly Power. . . . Several Witnesses being Examined, The Jury returned With their Verdt. Guilty, 12/ [shillings]. fine & one Hours Imprisonment and ordered that the Sher. take him into Custody &c." (Orange County Minute Book, No. 2, pp. 61–62). This record, by further noting that Haley "denied the charge," apparently contradicts what JM reported to his father. Much more surprising, however, in view of the severity of the law against Tories passed by the October 1776 session of the legislature of which JM had been a member, was the extreme leniency of the sentence imposed on Haley. This law (Hening, *Statutes*, IX, 170–71) provided that anyone convicted of "advisedly and willingly maintain[ing] and defend[ing] the authority, jurisdiction, or power, of the king or parliament of Great Britain" could, upon conviction after a jury trial, be sentenced to pay a fine of up to £ 20,000 and to languish in prison for up to five years. Why Haley's neighbors treated him so generously can only be surmised. Probably they knew him as a contentious, hotheaded fellow who meant, or could do, no harm. Perhaps, too, in the light of the doubts expressed by JM, they were not certain that they had acted legally. The preamble of the above-mentioned law stated that its purpose was to punish "all persons who are so wicked as to devise the destruction of good government, or to obstruct the operation of the laws." Had Haley attempted to do either of these? Furthermore, the law, by requiring every sheriff to read it "at the door of the courthouse of his county, on some court day on or before the first day of April next [1777]," might be interpreted as not in effect until that day. Whether the sheriff of Orange County had complied with this provision is not known.

7 At this time JM's brother Ambrose was at the outset of his nineteen months of service as lieutenant and paymaster of the 3d Virginia Regiment. In 1779 he was captain of a Virginia company guarding British prisoners at Charlottesville (F. B. Heitman, *Historical Register of Officers of the Continental Army*, p. 282).

Defeated for Election to Virginia House of Delegates

MS (LC: William C. Rives Papers). The statement below, in the hand of JM's brother-in-law, John C. Payne, is an extract from page 5 of an autobiographical sketch written in the third person and inclosed by JM in his letter to James K. Paulding of January 1832. JM first drafted this brief memoir in 1816 and revised it from time to time during the next sixteen years. No mention of this election in any paper written by or to JM in 1777 is known to exist.

[24 April 1777]

In the election of Delegates to the Legislature for the ensuing year (1777), he was an unsuccessful candidate. Previous to the Revolution the election of the County representatives was as in England, septennial, and it was as there, the usage, for the Candidates to recommend themselves to the voters, not only by personal solicitation, but by the corrupting influence of spirituous liquors, and other treats, having a like tendency. Regarding these as equally inconsistent with the purity of moral and of republican principles; and anxious to promote, by his example, the proper reform, he trusted to the new views of the subject which he hoped would prevail with the people; whilst his competitors adhered to the old practice. The consequence was that the election went against him: his abstinence being represented as the effect of pride or parsimony.[1]

[1] On 16 May 1777 the *Journal of the House of Delegates* records that "A petition of sundry freeholders of the county of Orange, whose names are thereunto subscribed, was presented to the House, and read; setting forth, that Mr. Charles Porter, one of the candidates at the election of delegates for the said county, on the 24th of April last, did, contrary to an ordinance of Convention [Hening, *Statutes*, IX, 57], make use of bribery and corruption during the said election, and praying that the said election may be set aside." The next day, Bolling Stark, chairman of the Committee of Privileges and Elections to which this petition had been referred, pointed out that the proper course would be for the memorialists and Porter to examine witnesses before at least two justices of Orange County and return the depositions to the committee. Neither the petition nor evidence that a hearing took place has been found. On 9 June, however, the House of Delegates rejected the plea of the petition for lack of proof to sustain the allegations of bribery and corruption (*Journal of the House of Delegates*, May 1777, pp. 14, 18, 67). About two weeks before the House of Delegates took this adverse action, the Orange County Court on 29 May 1777 nominated JM and his father and fourteen other men "Justices of the Peace and also of Oyer & Terminer" (Orange County Minute Book, No. 2, p. 62). JM declined the office. In the mid-1780's, when JM was a member of the House of Delegates, Porter was the other representative of Orange County. Charles Porter (*ca.* 1741–1791), a tavern keeper from 1766 to 1772, was the owner of the Tudor Hall plantation in Orange County by the time of the Revolution. At its outset he was a lieutenant of militia but shared in the siege of Yorktown in 1781 as a colonel of militia. He served as a member of the House of Delegates, 1777–1779 and 1784–1789 (Orange County Order Book, No. 7, p. 396; Order Book, No. 8, p. 230, and *passim*, microfilm in Virginia State Library; Earl G. Swem and John W. Williams, eds., *Register of the General Assembly*, pp. 4, 6, 9, 20, 22, 24; W. W. Scott, *History of Orange County*, pp. 75, 136). When writing the second sentence of this statement, JM evidently forgot that the British Septennial Act of 1716 did not extend to the province of Virginia. The royal governor, at his pleasure, could dissolve the House of Burgesses and call for a new election.

From Samuel Stanhope Smith

RC (LC: Madison Papers). Since the address sheet is lost, it cannot be known whether Smith sent the letter to JM at Montpelier or at Williamsburg.

[November 1777–August 1778][1]

DEAR SIR

This is the first time I have had an opportunity to write to you since your election to your new & honourable office. I rejoice that your country has been able, in spite of all your modesty, to discern your merits; & that she has had virtue enough to place you in a station where your talents will not be useless to her. Altho I could wish you had the same opinion of yourself that others have, & then I confess I should be glad to see you a degree or two lower but where your services would be more important. For I am really afraid that the Assembly doth not sufficiently consult her own dignity while so many of her most deserving members are distributed among the honorary & profitable offices of the State; & so few are left who can give a lustre to her councils, or authority to her decisions; or even perhaps guide her deliberations with regularity & prudence. You are better acquainted however, what reason there is to fear any loss of dignity in our own legislature and in our representation in the Congress of the States. But when I began my letter, I had it not in view to lead you into political scruples. Perhaps it may prove a relaxation to you in the midst of other business, to attend to a few metaphisical ones. I would not have troubled you on such subjects, if I had not known your taste for them, & your quick discernment of every error or mistake; & even of every hint that may lead to the discovery of any truth.[2] I promise myself this benefit at least, that I shall see some mistakes or superficial reasonings that I am not aware of at present; & that I may receive some clue that may serve to exercise my thought anew, & lead to a more perfect investigation of this   .[3]

You have frequently attacked me on that knotty question of *liberty* & *necessity* that has so much embarrassed philosophers, & has raised such furious war among divines. I have lately had occasion to write on several philosophical subjects, & among others, on this question.[4] I shall send you the result of my thoughts upon it; not at length, but with the utmost conciseness I am able, knowing that you are so well acquainted with the subject; that it is sufficient barely to state my opinion, without any long detail of the reasonings that support it,

which are apt to grow tedious, where they are not necessary. I write
with the prospect of my own improvement, & not of your information,
& therefore beg in return your candid animadversions on my scheme
with your own thoughts on the same subject.

I am Sir   Yr M obt servt

SAML S. SMITH[5]

Being reasonable & moral agents, it is a question of no small importance whether Virtue & Vice are any more than names to distinguish actions without merit or blame & whether we are free in the
exercise of volition as well as of action, & wherein that liberty consists;
or whether reason, sense, & volition be only a more refined & delicate
species of machinery? In this inquiry there are several terms to be
explained & defined, such as *power, motive, volition*. And the whole
question of liberty & necessity relates to the connexion betwixt motive
& volition. Mr. Hume resolves the idea of *power* into that of *succession;*
with this addition that the succession hath been observed to be constant, so that on the appearance of the object which is called the cause,
the mind by *custom* & *experience* is led to infer the appearance of the
other called the effect. For what is power? saith he. If it be any thing
different from observed uniform succession, must it not mean to express the whole *energy* that is in any *cause* to produce the *effect*? And
then [he] appeals to all men whe[th]er they have any idea of that peculiar *constitution* of things, of that *nature* that is the source of the necessary
connexion of the effect with the cause or of that *influence* that creates
the change? He concludes they ha[ve] not, & therefore returns to his
first hypothesis that *power* & & *constant succession* are the same. I believe indeed, that if we have any idea [of] power different from Mr.
Hume's, we derive it from the exertions & the feeli[ngs] of our own
minds. When I press against an obstacle that resists my action[?] when
I attempt to raise a weight that requires a sensible effort, I am conscious
of a certain *nisus*,[6] an energy which gives an idea, or is itself the idea,
of the *force* or *power* of the *cause* that acts upon the object & produces
an *effect*. Like every other simple idea it is to be explained on[ly] by
the feeling. And happily for this argument it is one of the most common [sen]sations of the human mind. When we exert any external effort when we ch[oose?] when we call up one set of ideas & dismiss
another, when we arrange[,] compare & reason from them, in innumera-
ble instances we have the idea of an or[der?] that operates its effects,
of a *power* to controul & govern our own actions & thoughts. An obscure idea of the same nature we apply to material & inanimate causes.
And altho it is true that that idea does not explain the *invisi[ble]* con-

stitution of things, nor the intrinsic *nature* of the *causal influence,* so that a priori we could infer the existence of the effect from the operation of the cause; yet, I cannot conceive that this circumstance annihilate[s] the idea of power as Hume supposes it does. May we not make the same observation on the notices of every sense? Is heat in our sensation the same as it exists in the fire or in the sun? Can we explain the secret magic of nature in giving a[ll] the perceptions of beauty from certain compositions of colour, figure, extensio[n] &c? Yet who ever doubts but the ideas of beauty & of heat are real, & represen[t]ations of their objects sufficient for all the purposes of life? The represe[nt]ation of the energy, & efficiency of causes which we have in the idea of pow[er] is no less proper than those of the objects of any of our senses whatever. If it were not a real idea & as different from mere succession, as it is from heat or colour, the terms power, energy, force, &c every where used by philosophers, & [in] which Mr. Hume is as liberal as any writer, would be only so much waste of ink & paper, being absolutely void of meaning. I cannot conceive that they could have had existence in any language. Nay, the idea of power is a more perfect representation of its object, when its object is the operations and exertion of the human mind, than are the ideas of many other senses. For us ideas of *thought, affection,* & any of these mental mov[e]ments, are in this respect more perfect than all others. Our ideas are the things themselves, or at least a consciousness of their *nature* & *presence* that always attends them. Of this class is *power*—especially that exercise of it that is exerted in volition arresting the process of thought, directing it on a new train of objects, & all the modes of chusing, refusing, & acting. How different is that exertion that is employed in fixing the attention on one object; in calling up this set of ideas, & dismissing another, in changing, turning, suspending, & producing action from the simple idea of succession that arises from contemplating external objects, or our own ideas as they follow in a train? The idea of *power* seems to be so plain, & well-defined, that none but a philosopher too enamoured of the product of his own brain, is capable of denying it. And when this idea is acknowledged, as by plain & unsophisticated reason & experience I think it must[,] the *liberty* of *moral action* necessarily follows. For if we have any clear idea of power at all, we have a clear distinction betwixt the power of another operating upon us; & our own power exerted upon others, or on ourselves. In the one case we have the feeling of liberty, & of being masters of [o]ur own actions; in the other we are sensible of constraint, & of being subject to a foreign controul. To every plain man the perceptions of power & liberty are as distinct, certain & precise as any perceptions whatever & are always conjoined. If a philosopher therefore is inclined to represent them as false or delusive, what medium will he use for that purpose? He can make use of none plainer than the ones in question. And if they are to be esteemed delusive, by what criterion shall we annex certainty to any principle of human nature? We enter at once into the regions of absolute doubt & scepticism Experience the great test of moral as well as phisical science, proves the power we have over our ideas, & our actions. And the exercise of power proves that we are free. Human liberty is as evident & undelusive as the principles of our nature. The question therefore no longer can be whether we enjoy liberty? but wherein that liberty consists which it must be confessed we do enjoy? There are philosophers, & among these is the distinguished name of Locke, who assert that *liberty of will* is an absurd expression.[7] The will is not, nor cannot be free. The mind necessarily chuses what pleases it, & refuses what displeases it. And the objects arround us necessarily produce pleasure or pain by their correspondence with the principles of human nature, or their opposition to them. So that we cannot avoid being pleased with the one, & displeased with the other. Our liberty therefore only consists in being able to do what we please, to perform what we chuse & regards not volition, but the action consequent upon our choice. But [v]olition, or choice itself, is involved in desire, or aversion; these necessarily [r]esult from the emotions of pleasure & pain; & these last are necessarily [c]onnected with the presence of certain objects to the senses, or imagination.

If this theory were true, liberty were not worth inquiring after; it were not worth enjoying. Lord Kame[s] would have offered up a very reas[on]able act of devotion, when he praised the penetration of his Maker who could discern that to be *good* which weak & short-sighted mortals thought to be *evil*. Virtue & vice are not much concerned in the external action[s] of men, abstracted from their will & intention. Moral good & evil have their seat here, so that if we have any moral liberty, or are the capable subjects of virtue or vice, of praise or blame, we must be free in the exercise of volition, as well as of action. We always act upon motive and in reference to some end. If the influence of motive upon the mind i[s] necessary and irresistible, the virtue or the vice in that case, if any there can be, is not imputable to us, but to the constitution of nature, & to the design of its Author who hath established such a necessary connexion.

The nature of motive is explained in the term; that it is something

that rou[ses,] excites, & moves the mind to action. The human constitution hath not been left without a variety of springs to set it in
motion. We have instincts, sens[es,] appetites, capacities of pleasure &
pain, with correspondent objects adapted to them by the *design* of
Nature, whose presence is ordained to excite similar emotions & feelings. Every object of nature that can come within our knowlege is so
adapted to some principle of the constitution, as to be either agreable
or offensive & capable of inspiring either aversion or desire. So that
each of these objec[ts] when it is present with a certain concurrence
of circumstances; or, if not the object, at least the principl[e] it affects
& the feeling it raises, may rouse & excite the mind & be a motive of
volition. The mind is always moved by some of these principles, appetites, affectio[ns,] passions, or by a sense of interest, of duty, which
seem to have been implanted by natu[re] for that purpose. But before
they move volition they assume the form of desires. A present good
produces joy but no volition unless it may probably be lost; when the
desire of its continuance prompt the will, & engage us to pursue the
means to retain it. The will is only excited by something not in possession which we would acquire; or by some immediate uneasiness
from which we desire to be free. Desire seems to be the immediate
urgent motive of the will; the principles above mentioned & their
correspondent objects are the primary & more remote motives, being
the source of desire. Desire by almost all fat[al]ists has been considered
as a modification of volition. So far is this from bei[ng] the truth that
it is properly ranked among the class of affections. Beauty p[ro]duces
an emotion of pleasure, a pleasing emotion is the cause of the affectio[n]
of love, & while its object is yet absent or unpossessed affection assumes
th[e] form of desire. Desire is the immediate motive of choice & volition & as this gradually changes & approaches to the other, like
prismatic colours & indeed like all other neighbouring & conjoined
principles of nature, their extre[me?] limits are scarcely, if at all, discernible. Which circumstance, perhaps, has deceived so many philosophers to confound them together. But every species of affection, desire
not excepted[,] terminates upon the objects themselves towards which
our actio[ns] are directed & regards *them* as *good* or *evil:* And volition
solely regards our own actions considered as proper to attain the objects of our happiness; or to remove the immediate uneasiness that
presses us. These actions are either corporeal or mental. The former
are easily understood; by the latter I mean the *indulgence* we may
chuse to give to any of our internal affections or inclinations. Before
I exert any outward action, I may chuse to contemplate the object of

any affection so long as to raise desire to the highest degree. It is seldom that an affection is suddenly raised to a great height, or acquires irresistible force at the first view of its object: this is the effect of *indulgence*. It depends upon the will; & comes under this denomination of *mental action*.

Having ascertained the power we exercise over our own minds, & shown motive to be the desire of possessing some good, or of removing some present uneasiness with which we are pressed; for the both of these may by a little subtlity be ultimately resolved into the same thing; yet, in practice we find ourselves sometimes more immediately & forcibly urged by the one, & sometimes by the other. And having also stated a distinction betwixt desire & volition it is time to consider the connexion betwixt the will & the motives by which it is excited. How far it is free, or how far it is necessary & the one involved in the other. Such is the fate of philosophy from the narrowness of the human mind that an accurate & scrutinous inquiry into almost any subject only serves to multiply perplexity & doubt, to discover how little we know & how many difficulties occur at every step that seem to baffle research. Certainty & well defined knowlege is the lot of but few subjects. Men have subtlety enough to raise objections, but not penetration sufficient to give them a satisfactory solution. This hath been peculiarly the fortune of the present question. The reality of virtue & vice at least as the proper objects of reward & punishment from a supreme & righteous Judge hath been brought into doubt & agitated with great heat by different parties almost from the earliest dawn of philosophy. On one hand it is maintained that all our actions are governed by the laws of necessity & fate. Reason indeed contains a finer species of machinery; but still, it is no more than the machinery of reason.[8] So that virtue & vice can have neither merit nor demerit considered as our actions; but are imputable solely to that primary & original influence from which they are derived, whether that be blind fatality, or a supreme intelligent cause. On the other hand are the patrons of liberty who maintain that we are accountable for our actions, & that in order to [be] this we must be under no constraint or compulsion. There must be no necessary & irresistible connexion established betwixt moral causes & their effects; betwixt motive & volition. And even among the latter there are some who verge nearer to the doctrine of necessity, while others pride themselves in flying from it to the remotest distance. I embrace the side of liberty, & shall endeavour to explain it consistently with our experience. Experiment in morals as well as in phisics is the only proper source of truth, & guide of reasoning. Nothing can be more fallacious than to begin with any abstracted theory of divine prescience, a subject so far superior to human intellect, & from thence to reason down to the actions of creatures. It will be sufficient if we can understand a subject nearer home. And in investigating this it is by no means necessary that we should warp our own experience in order to reduce the prescience of the Deity to the state & mode of human knowlege. If we shall be able to deduce our moral liberty from its proper source, let us not be afraid to avow it, tho' it should be atten[d]ed with this consequence that God's ways are not as our ways, nor his thoughts as our thoughts.[9]

It is confessed that when any object is presented to the mind or the sen[ses] which is exactly fitted by nature to some correspondent principle[,] its proper emotion &c necessarily arises; we are to inquire therefore whet[her] the necessary existence of a motive before the fancy, doth consequently involve a necessity of action & choice? Even tho' we should admit, according to the opinion of the fatalists that each motive singly might necessarily controul the mind; yet one scarcely ever appears single & alone. As[10] many as we have particular senses often offer themselves at once. And frequently their number is greatly multiplied, many addressing themselves to each sense & to each affection: which circumstance affords the mind a great advantage in exerting its power over its own volitions. For even if one affection, or object of desire, being present to the mind at on[ce] should be able to attract this[?] with an irrestib[l]e force, because it is the only happiness at that time in view: Yet when so many necessary forces meet together & mutually oppose each other's influence: reduced almost to a ballance they become more manageable, & subject to her power & controul. Perhaps the reason why many writers have been so much embarrassed by the antagonists of human Liberty, is, that being persuaded to consider *Desire* as a modification of the *will*, & finding a degre[e] of Desire necessarily to arise from the preference of its object by an unguarded concession, they have been led to involve necessity in the *nature* of *volition*. But we have found that *will* regards only ou[r] own *actions*, & is their immediate mover. Indeed, when two objects are offered to me that I may take but one of them: th[ere] is a choice or preference in which the will at the first view seems to regard the *object immediately*. However if we wi[ll] examine accurately it will perhaps be found even here to terminate in our own action, the *receiving* of one, & the *neglecting* of the other. This solution of the matter becomes more prob[a]ble [w]hen the choice is made between objects acknowleged to be [e]qual in value, which therefore raise an equal degree of desire. Because if *desire* necessarily arose from the presence of the objects [a]nd *volition* were involved in that *desire*, we should with equal [n]ecessity chuse both: nor could [we] seperate the one from the other. A conclusion that contra[d]icts the most plain & well defined experience, & therefore must [be] false. So that tho' *desire* regards the *object itself*, *volition* only regards the actions or endeavours we use to obtain it, and prompts us to [ex]ert them. Yet still the same question will be returned upon us [by] the advocates of fatalism, so hard is it to relinquish a favourite scheme: since it is confessed that external objects by their correspondence with the principles of the human constitution necessarily affect us with a degree of pleasure or pain, & produce propor[t]ionate desires. Is not that an acknowledgement, that the movements of the will are governed by the same necessity? By no means. Because then we should chuse many & even contrary objects [a]t once; & use equal efforts to acquire them: we might pursue our own interest, & a pleasure that is destructive of it at the same time & at [the?] same time be generous & uncharitab[l]e to the same person for it is a matter of experience that so many, different objects of desire may solicit the mind at once. That conclusion is absurd & proves the premises to be false. But the inquirer seems to be led [i]nto it by the error that I have taken notice of before, confounding desire with volition. Let me repeat a little & Suppose that the influence of one motive, if it were single & alone, & the mind at the same time affected by no [o]ther, should necessarily controul the will. Yet that is a circumstance in which we seldom or never find ourselves. The [m]ind is usually solicited by many motives at the same time, many perhaps that are not coincident & some that even directly [o]ppose their influence to others. Will it follow because a motive in its full power, & uncontrouled by any other, might [h]ave had a necessary effect: that it will be attended with the same necessity when diminished by the force of its antagonist? In that case it will be so much weakened that the mind will not be irresistably attracted[?]; but have an evident conscious liberty & freedom of movement. This is an effect that flows from the combination of a variety of senses, propensions, instincts &c & their ballance in one constitution. They mutually correct each other's impulse and however each alone might draw with irresistable force: yet all together produce a state of mind loose & free to move as several bodies within their common sphere of attraction, but not near enough to be drawn into contact. Take any mot[ion?] arround or among each other with great ease. They are calculated to *rouse* and *animate* the mind and *set it in motion,* but d[o] not *necessarily deter-*

mine its mov[e]ments towards any *precise point*. How! is the mind then left to run at random without any certain & definite influence or direction in its motions? If she is not led by motive: if motive hath not a certain & necessary influence, is she driven by accident amid a sea of motives: or doth she move in blind & unmeaning exertions without any determinate aim? That question implies a consequence that is plainly not well deduced. Must all be accident that is not necessity? May we not be excited to action: may not these actions be guided to a determinate end without being compelled. Are not *Reason* & *Conscience* sufficient preservatives against the fickleness of chance? Be it so you say, but how doth reason, how doth conscience, or any other principle, direct our choice If[11] not by exhibiting the *proper*, the *beautiful*, the *prudent*, the *obliga[tory]* by presenting some *motive* to the mind? If that motive is stronger than its antagonist it produces choice & action; if weaker, it is only witness to the other's triumph. We never act but for some end: under the influence of some *motive*. That motive is something that *pleases* us: that *pleases us most* for the present. If then we are so formed as *necessarily* to act from *motive of some kind*,—for to act without motive were to act irrationally,—must not that *motive* which is *most pleasing* for the present govern us with a *necessary* sway? No, we can produce experience to the contrary. And first we are not conscious of such necessity; we perceive as great ease & freedom of movment as if we were actually fre[e] which would not be probable on the supposition of a necessary force. In the next place, when I reflect upon the subject; & make trial of m[y] own power, I find I can suspend or vary my actions as I plea[se]. But when I say my *action* & my *will* may be varied as *I please*, doth not that imply *another motive*, either a *desire of finding the truth in this controversy*, or a fantastic *pride of shewing* my power whose presence hath now the same necessary effect the former motive had till overpowe[red] by the appearance of this? But I can dismiss this, & resume the other, or one different from both. I acknowlege I have some *end* in view, some *motive*. But as often as I make trial, I can *do* or *forbear*: I can *act in this way* or *another*; So that I find no moti[ve] necessary in its influence, but I can change it for a different one. And when finally I submit to this influence of the last or proceed in my usual [c]hannel, I am contented with the consciousness that I *could* do otherwise; & tho' I am *guided* by the *influence of motives*, I am satisfied from many trials, & an induction from many particular experiments, that I am not *subject* to any *necessary & irresistible attraction*. The last motive, tho' I make no experiment upon *it*, I conclude by a reasonable *induction* to be nothing different in this respect from others which I have so often found to have their influence barely from *persuasion*, not from *necessity*. *Still* [t]his is confessing that the mind must be *roused* to action, & *guided* in acting [by] some *motive*. It cannot *otherwise* exert a single *volition*. Somewhere necessity must lie, even contrary to all experiments in favour of liberty [i]n other cases. This is a matter that merits our attention & seems to promise a crisis to this question. Experiment appears to favour the conclusion already drawn, that, in the common course of life no particular motive hath a necessary & irresistible power over the Will. Experiment makes it equally plain that we never act without a motive.

Before we proceed farther, let us inquire into the reason of this. It is now known & received by all philosophers almost, that the sole inlets of our knowledge are the *senses*. We have no ideas but what have obtained admission this way. Every simple idea therefore is derived from some [o]bject actually existing in nature, making its proper impression upon its correspondent sense. And every compound idea is made up of simple ideas thus admitted by thier proper senses. So that it is impossible [to] *think* without having some real existences before the mind. It is nothing strange then that it is impossible for us to *chuse* or *will* without having *some object* in view: because *volition* implies *thought*, & *thought* implies *idea*, & *idea* implies its *object*. If one *volition supplants* another it must therefore plainly regard a *different object*. And that *object* must be within the *view* of the mind before we can *will* any thing concerning it. But is that any more than saying we are *human creatures* who are so limited as [t]o be capable of no ideas except of those few *actual existences* that have impressed our senses: & therefore when we exert volition, if we think at all in the case, it must be of some *object*, & every *object* we have confessed has some *tendency* to *affect* the mind with *desire*. But is that proving that these objects of thought & volition have a necessary power to controul the mind? may not the mind be so formed as to contemplate and judge among them, to will & act as they seem calculated to promote its *happiness?* That I presume almost any reasonable man will acknowlege to be the truth. And if so, it proves that no particular object in itself is possessed of influence, that is irresistible & controuling. It only gains *any* influence by its connexion with our *happiness*. And however every *motive*, that is every *object* of nature, *necessarily* excites a *degree* either of *pleasure* or *pain;* yet doth not any one on that account necessarily controul the will. This subject hath been explained before. And *any one may* be the *immediate* motive of volition, when we consider it as ou[r] *present happiness or good. Here* then it will be said is the *point* wher[e] necessity exists. Let us examine it. What is hapiness? It is gratifying our different senses, & capacities of pleasure, & indulging, in contemplation or possession the objects that do gratify them. Happiness may be derived fro[m] enjoying as many objects as afford pleasure, & from avoiding as many as afford pain; so that positively or negatively it may be derived from *every motive* of the will; that is, from *every object of nature* that comes withj[n] the reach of our capacities. Our happiness consists of a variety of degrees, & of kinds extreamly different. Our present enjoyment or happiness depends on a variety of circumstances, & many of them in our own power. If there is proposed to me a social meeting, for festivity or friendship: there are many principles of human nature that such an interview will gratify: I know that I can be happy there, & I may chuse to attend. In the height of my social enjoyment I can call to mind my closet, my books, & my papers, & I know that I may derive happiness from thence. I may either choose to continue with my friends or to remove to my study. I am concious that I can find happiness in both. There are *many situations* in which I can [be] happy by gratifying some *propensions of nature.* These *situation[s]* therefore only become more *complex motives* to the mind: & She may chuse among them with the same *freedom* as hath been *shewn* to be possible among other motives. To be happy in such *situations* it is only necessary to hav[e] the *single* motives & *agreeable circumstances* that attend them *presented* to us by some *foreign guide,* or *called up* by the native *power* of the mind; & by the same *power* to *exclude* the ideas that *oppose* & *thwart* the[m.] Of such a *power* we are conscious; & have occasion frequently to exert it[.] When I am solicited to action I *recollect* that by this *power* I may render myself happy in *many* situations, which prevents my rushing with *necessary* violence on *any one* before me, and if they are proposed to my *choice,* I find that I am not *necessarily* confined to *any one* because it is my *present greatest good.* I may be in a *humour;* or disposition for one; rather than another, whic[h] may incline me to chuse it; tho with the utmost ease & freedom. Bu[t] I find, at the same time, that I can alter that choice, when I recollect that this *humour* is *transient* it *depends* on circumstances and that it is even in my *power* to *change* it or give it *another tone,* by calling up a different *scene* of images to the fancy. In general indeed we comply with this transient disposition; but such *experiments* when occasion invites, prove that it lays us under no *necessary* controul. So that we have only found upon this inquiry that *necessity* is annexed to *happiness* in *general;* not to any *particular kind* of it. We cannot deliberately & designedly chuse to be *miserable* & renounce all *happiness;* but we by no means fee[l] ourselves under the necessity of choosing any *particular species* and *degree* of happiness alone. This power of calling forth, arranging, of giving presence & liveliness to new ideas, & new scenes merits particular attention both as a principle of nature, & for its great importance [in] the exercise of the moral freedom of the mind. What that *power* is, it is difficult [to] explain or learn except from experience. It would seem necessary, at first view that an idea should be already in the mind before she could exert any [o]peration concerning it. For when she attemps to recall any image without having some previous determinate aim: that is without antecedently having some part of the image she would recall: it seems to be letting her [r]un at a blind hazard to hit upon the first that accident may throw in her way. But to have an idea before it is recalled is absurd, & quite useless to [m]y purpose. Some explanation of this matter must be attempted. We usually think in a train & every idea almost is suggested by the one immediately before. This train is assisted & conducted by the relations which we conceive the objects that compose it to have one to another. Contiguity may dispose the mind to pass readily along neighbouring objects: & by contrast, she may suddenly pass to the greatest distance, & transport the thought to remote regions of the Earth or of the universe. So resemblance & dissimilitude, cause & effect, proportion or disproportion, the natural & moral connexions of men; & innu[me]rable relations aid & conduct the train of thought: And when once a subject hath been introduced to the mind she is naturaly disposed to trace its [r]elations, to consider its parts, & their mutual dependencies & connexions among each other. This she may do & repeat her work till she has acquired [th]e clearest, strongest and most impressive conception of it that is possible. Wherein then consists the *power* that hath been so often mentioned? & what [i]s its *utility?* This train of ideas *is not* so impetuous, but it may be resisted[,] its flow is not *necessarily so continual* that it cannot be *suspended.* We are [of]ten conscious of its suspension: which is performed by that *power* of mind in question. Like every other primary principle of human nature; it seems to be [i]nexplicable: except by its operations. However it is [a] matter of experiment and [on]ly needs the trial, to convince any inquirer, that the mind can suspend her [tr]ain of thought, & put herself in an attitude of attention, circumspection, and [in]quiry. In exerting this power, she hath always some *general purpose* in [vi]ew. So that while in this situation she contemplates the ideas that rise up before her according to the forementioned relations: if any, even a slight [vo]lition[?], seems to lead to her *general purpose*, she can leave those that are [less?] intimate, & pursue *that:* till she finds a subject that suits her *aim:* when [she?] can again suspend a farther progress in that kind of inquiry, & survey h[er] chosen subject in all its extent, & its relations by a similar operation. [Then?] having found the *power*, about which this question has been raised, to [c]onsist in suspending the train of our ideas, & throwing the mind into a state of [at]tention; & taken notice of that particular quality of our train of ideas; that they are sug[ge]sted & linked together by the relations which objects bear to each other: by which this *power of suspension* &c can be productive of any farther consequence; Let us now examine its utility. If our ideas were [co]nstantly to flow in an unbroken train without this power of suspension, [o]ur volitions would also partake of the same uniformity. For every motive must be some *idea:* nor doth the mind ever exert her *will* but in consequence [o]f some motive. If then her train of ideas & the *motives* of volition involved [in] them were conversant with objects that would lead, for instance, to vice [&] self-injury: tho none of these objects separately can be a necessary cause of volition, as *hath been proved* before; yet, if we chuse at all, & that would be almost unavoidable, we must chuse under the influence of some idea of the pres[ent] train: no other being at that time in the mind & it being impossible by the supposition, to call up any new image, or to vary the train in any degree. All our liberty in that case would be to make a choice among the variety of objects immediately within the view of the mind: & these all leading to vice & self-injury, we should only have the liberty of chusing among many vices. But by the exertion of this *power* so often mentioned, suspending the train, & so suspending volition: we may call forth a different train of images; run thro' al[l] their different relations, contemplate them in various lights, repeat the view till it becomes so vivid as to carry the will in opposition to its rival. Herein consists its utility that it enables us to ballance on[e] motive against another, & to overcome vice by virtue altho' it is also attended with this consequence[,] that it makes it possible for virtue to [be] overcome by vice. Which indeed is necessary to constitute as moral agen[ts] & capable of merit or of blame. Here a very natural inquiry arises whether that act of suspension be not exerted in consequence of some motive? And if so, the question returns whence com[es?] it that this motive is present with the mind just at the moment she needs its assistance? Is it from new suspension? which would run us back into an endless chain of

206

absurdities or is it by some peculiar appointment of nature, always ready to support our faltering virtue? This inquiry leads us to a subject that hath long lain in obscurity, & I know not whether there is any philosopher that hath given a satisfactory solution of it. We are to suppose our constit[u]tion to have been origonally created with an equal ballance, proportion and subordination among all its *principles*. Man must have be[en] placed in the midst of objects suited to these different *principles*. For a while at least the system would move with regularity; Every principle, I have said before, makes a necessary part of the constitution: & upon the presence of their corresponding objects they are necessarily affected with some emotion, sentiment, or passion. These emotions, sentiments, & passions are the *motives* of the *will*. Among other principles inherent in the human heart that are motives of action we percieve a calm *self love*, instinctive *benevolence* & *a sence of duty*. Which seem to have been appointed the guardians of our Virtue against the extravagances to which inferior passions might be carried. In a state of Innocence we can conceive that they might have been effectual guardians. Whether suc[h] a state has ever existed or not is immaterial to the argument: Let us at least suppose it: to some it would help to illustrate the reasoning. I will here divide motives into two classes, the one may be called *occasional*, the other *habitual*. The former are those emotions & [de]sires that arise only on the presence of their objects to the sense or fancy. Among the latter are to be distinguished [c]alm *self love*, & a *sense of duty;* making duty here to comprehend the principle of *benevolence*, as most of our duties regard the welfare of others. I [c]all them habitual, because they constantly attend us. The *one* is intimately linked with the *consciousness* of our *existence*, the *other* instantaneously & necessarily arises with *every passion* to guard it from excess: & especially when that *passion* approaches the limits of *right* & *wrong*. They [n]eed no effort of the suspending power to bring them into view. They are already & always present, & are the *motives* we are inquiring after, in consequence of which that *power* is exerted, when our *Liberty* is concerned in the preservation of our *virtue*. So apply this to practice. In the supposed state of innocence, man could be [in]fluenced by a multitude of objects & desires as he is at present. They would be [p]ersonal motives of volition as they occurred in train. To a certain limit they might be indulged with safety. But as they approached near to the limit & began to acquire a strength that might possibly carry them beyond it, those habitual principles, the constant authoritative guardians of virtue, might perhaps with ease give the train of ideas & motives a new direction. Or if there [e]ver should occur a difficulty, as those evidently might in a free mind, then might one or both of these habitual motives produce a suspention of volition, & of the present train of thought: The mind would have in [v]iew some *general purpose* as was mentioned above, its *best interest*, or its *duty;* which are indeed coincident. Then the first relation whether strong or slight that seemed to tend towards *this purpose* it might seize, & pursue till it perceived some object of *duty*, or *interest* that appeared proper to counterballance the motive that was likely to be too powerful. And then [i]ndulge[12] the train of thought thro its obvious relations till it formed a sufficient poise[13] for its antagonist, & delivered the mind from the danger of undue influence, & restored her to her former ease of movement. These principles could never interpose their authority, or have any influence [i]f the connexion betwixt motive and volition were necessary. The volition would have already had effect before the act of suspension could be [e]xerted. It is true they [are] thus far necessary, that the mind never chuses or exerts volition without a motive: & when it alters its choice from one, it is by turning its attention to another, & having the latter in the room of the former. This is done either by the natural course of succession in a train: or by the accidental exibition of some new object by a foreign cause: or by the *power* of the mind excited by some of her *habitual principles* calling forth different ideas & engaging her in a new train. By the repeated [e]xercise of this power man might have forever confirmed his innocence; fixed boundaries in practice to all his passions & as they were created in just proportion &c have established that proportion by habit which would be habitual virtue. And when innocence is lost the only way in which he can recover it or reasonably attempt its recovery is by the repeated, & more painfull exertion of *this power*, recalling the lost images of virtue: contemplating them, & using them as motives of action, till they overcome those of vice again & again untill after repeated struggles, & many foils[14] they at length acquire the habitual superiority. Whatever might have happened in innocence, we still retain the resemblance of it even in this imperfect state. Where *vice is predominat*, we may have moral freedom, as well as under the *predominancy of virtue*. As in innocence, virtue may acquire such a stable habit that the ideas of vice may be attended with so much abhorrence as for ever to seem a necessary barrier against its practice: so many vicious inclinations proceed by indulgence to such a degree as to possess at least all the *appearances of necessity:* & every

repitition of vice from the first infraction of the boundaries of innocence to that fatal period, is one step more towards necessity & increases the difficulty of a return to virtue. But if vice ever becomes too
powerful for the feeble exertions of duty; if it should even increase to
a necessary & irresistible force, that doth not take off the guilt, as if
we had been created subject to the laws of fatalism, because it is a necessity induced by voluntary wickedness. This by the by demonstrates
the great importance of an early virtuous education. The result of the
whole is that *liberty consists* in such a *proportion* of external objects to
the *principles of human nature*, as [a]llways to raise so[me] *emotion*
or *desire* sufficient to be a *motive* of *volition*, but not to determine the
will with *absolute necessity*. The mind is always determined in it[s]
volition by motive[.] That motive is neither uneasiness alone as Mr.
Locke[?] supposes, nor pleasure as others have it supposed, each thinking it necessary to reduce it to some single thing: but some times the
one affects the mind most, & sometimes the other. Among motives she
chuses *freely*, commonly following the present *tone of humour or inclination & concurrence* of objects—here pleasure is her motive. When
she avoi[ds] pain uneasiness is her immediate motive. She has a power
of varying her train of thought & therefore her motives: so that if each
motive apart governed with necessity which is not the case it may be
controuled by this *power*, that would be able to creat[e] a species of
liberty even in these difficult circumstances. *This power* is exercised
in consequence of certain *habitual motives* inseperably inherent in the
mind, which however we sufficiently experience have no necessary
force. Among these *self-interest* and *duty* are investe[d] by nature
with peculiar *dignity* & *authority*. When *duty* operates the very *command* & *feeling* that we *ought*, carries great force; & seems to b[e] a
peculiar kind of motive. It is uncertain to me whether it belongs to the
[c]lass of *pleasure* or *uneasiness:* or whether it be not entirely *different*
from *both:* & of that *nature* that its *slightest command*, even apart from
the hope of reward [&] fear of punishment, is fitted to ballance* the
liveliest feelings of the others, [p]urly because it is duty; a *generous &
inexplicable perception* whose influence [is] only known by being *felt*.
But when it adds its sanctions of *approbation* & *remorse*, here are motives both of *pleasure* & *uneasiness*. The wisdom & goodness of our

---

* I say it is fitted to ballance the motives of pleasure and uneasiness: not that it
always *actualy* controuls them, but that it is attended with a *feeling* that I cannot
express, that it is in our *power*, & that we *ought* [to] act according to its dictates
in opposition to every other motive.

Maker is evident in making these motives *habitual*, that they may not wait to be called for: which probably would be but seldom done if they were not intrinsic & inherent in the constitution; & that they may always be ready to bring in aid to cope with vice, & to assist virtue. For they are not themselves the only support of virtue. Her objects have a correspondence with the mind as well as others, & are attended with the most serene & refined, tho' not the most impetuous pleasures. And these habitual motives of *duty* & *interest*, by means of the power we have over our own [i]deas, presenting to the view the *images* that are favourable to virtue, [c]all in *their* pleasures in aid of their own *influence* and *authority*. Here is an excellent foundation for liberty[,] no motive in itself controuling the will with absolute necessity. And when one motive is like to be too hard for human infirmity, the *power* of calling up another that may ballance it: And the *exertion* of that power, not left to the present partial & dangerous *inclination* but excited[15] by habitual ever present motives that are always acting, & always the guardians of virtue. Yielding to them which we feel we *ought*, & we have *power* to do, I always *except* the case of too confirmed vice, tends directly to virtue; *vice* triumphs whenever they are *resisted*.[16]

Thus for my own amusement I have given some reflexions on the subject of liberty & necessity. I wrote them, perhaps you will think, in too much has[te] & gave them to be transcribed by another for want of sufficient time to do it myself. Looking over it I perceive several superfluous observations, & would probably perceive many more both superfluous & defective, if I were no[t] in such haste to expose my own folly. But if I write to a discerning critic I hope I do also to a candid friend, whose severest animadversions will be made to me. And to me I care not how severely every sentence be sifted, for I am really more anxious to find the truth in this question than to invent or maintain any new modes of expression.

You will easily perceive that there is a difference betwixt the power of suspension which I have supposed, & that so vigorously maintained by the Arminians.[17] They call it a power in the will of suspending & determining its[elf?] in which they say that *liberty* consists. And their antagonists can press them back thro an endless & absurd chain of suspensions & determination[s.] I have made liberty to consist in a different point; this suspending pow[er] to regard the train of thought, & the *motives* of action; not the *will* solely, or even principally; & to prevent the same endless absurdity from pressing this doctrine that has been so successfully urged against the Arminian, the habitual motives of *duty* & calm *self-interest* are introduced, that by their *authority* & *dignity ought* to govern the mind. They are always virtuous motives; we know sufficiently that they are not necessary in their operation; but if we will attend to them they are sufficient to create a poise[18] to vice by calling up the images & motives of virt[ue.] I am here talking only as a philosopher. As a Divine I might say that the strength of vicious habit might require some heavenly assis[t]ance or afflatus to make them always effectual. I have suppose[d] the state of innocence on this very account; lest some should den[y] the influence of these habitual motives, in a state so depraved as the present. When you write to[19] do pray, if you have time or paper after answering this long epistle, inform me whether you can assig[n] any cause for the existence of a Deity, that may not also be assigned for the existence of the universe alone. I do not doubt his being. But I doubt whether it can be proved by *speculative* reasoning, & is not rather a kind of indelible sentiment of the heart.[20]

I am   yr very hble servt

SAML S SMITH

[1] The first five sentences of this letter suggest that Smith wrote it after he heard of JM's election by the House of Delegates to the Council of State of Virginia. JM was elected to this office on 15 November 1777 and attended his first meeting of the council on 14 January 1778. Although Smith would more likely congratulate JM upon this honor shortly after its conferral, rather than later, there is no known primary evidence to support this supposition. All that can be said with assurance is that JM had sent his friend a written commentary upon some of the matters mentioned in this letter before Smith wrote again to him on 15 September 1778. Smith was a founder and the first president of Hampden-Sydney Academy (JM to James Madison, Sr., 30 September 1769, n. 4). This school, heavily dependent for its first faculty upon men who had been with JM at the College of New Jersey, opened its doors in 1776 and became a college in 1783. On 8 November 1775, the trustees of the academy nominated JM to membership on their board. He helped to manage a lottery on the academy's behalf in 1777 (*Virginia Gazette* [Williamsburg, Purdie], 4 July 1777, supplement). Although he continued on the board until 1820, he apparently attended none of its meetings (Hening, *Statutes*, IX, 321–22; JM to Reverend Moses Hoge, 20 April 1820, LC: Madison Papers; William Henry Foote, *Sketches of Virginia, Historical and Biographical* [Philadelphia, 1850], pp. 397–98).

[2] Smith visited Montpelier occasionally between 1773 and 1775, and had been a tutor at the College of New Jersey during JM's student days there.

[3] In the original the word "truth" is crossed out at this point but no word was substituted. Smith possibly intended to insert "problem."

[4] Smith probably published nothing on any philosophical subject at this time. His paragraph suggests that, before he polished his essay for the press or for use as a lecture, he wanted the benefit of JM's frank and thorough criticism.

⁵ Writing in a smaller hand than usual, Smith seems to have interlineated this formal close *after* he had appended his long essay. He terminated the letter with an even more respectful adieu. He intended above all in the essay to explore the meaning and scope of the antithetic concepts, "liberty & necessity," and to effect a reconciliation between them. In pursuit of this goal he dilated at somewhat tedious length upon thought—its origin, meaning, nature, mode of expression, and limitations. Smith's empiricism reflected the influence upon him of John Locke, *An Essay Concerning Human Understanding* (London, 1690), David Hume, *A Treatise of Human Nature* (3 vols.; London, 1739–40), and Henry Home (Lord Kames), *Essays on the Principles of Morality and Natural Religion* (Edinburgh, 1751). As Smith well knew, he could refer casually to these authors because JM had become familiar with their works as a result of his own study and President John Witherspoon's courses at the College of New Jersey. Smith included a chapter "On Volition" in his *The Lectures Corrected and Improved, Which Have Been Delivered for a Series of Years in the College of New Jersey; on the Subjects of Moral and Political Philosophy* (2 vols.; Trenton, N.J., 1812), I, 275–99. Although differing in expression from, and lacking the detailed argument found in, the essay mailed to JM, this chapter maintains the same general position as the essay.

⁶ The striving of man to attain a higher level of existence and, if possible, to become as a god.

⁷ "It is as insignificant to ask whether man's will be free as to ask whether his sleep be swift or his virtue square" ("An Essay Concerning Human Understanding" in *The Works of John Locke* [10 vols.; London, 1812], I, 227).

⁸ This sentence is especially obscure in its meaning. Smith's point may be that man, by means of the mechanical process of reasoning alone, cannot distinguish between virtuous and wicked acts.

⁹ Isaiah 55:8.

¹⁰ Beginning at this point, Smith let a clerk take over for the balance of the essay portion of the letter. Smith then amended what the clerk had copied, revising words frequently, adding bits between the lines, and deleting two portions of considerable length near the close of the essay. To record all these emendations in detail would require much more space than their importance warrants.

¹¹ Following "If" the copyist inserted "it" by mistake.

¹² Instead of "[i]ndulge," the copyist erroneously wrote "[i]ndulgence."

¹³ Used in the sense of "counterpoise."

¹⁴ Used in the sense of "failures."

¹⁵ Clarity seems to require the retention of this word, even though it appears to be deleted in the manuscript.

¹⁶ At this point, because Smith struck out twenty-three more lines on virtue and vice, the essay part of this letter comes to an end. From here to the close, the manuscript is in his own hand.

¹⁷ Followers of Jacobus Arminius (1560–1609), a Dutch theologian who argued against the doctrine of predestination and irresistible grace and on behalf of freedom of the will.

¹⁸ Above, n. 13.

¹⁹ The "to" should probably have been replaced by a comma or followed by "me."

²⁰ Smith's comments of 15 September 1778 (*q.v.*) upon JM's now missing reply suggest that JM did not treat the matter broached in these concluding sentences. On the other hand, in a letter of 20 November 1825, JM appears to agree that the existence of God cannot be demonstrated by "speculative reasoning" (Madison, *Writings* [Hunt ed.], IX, 229–31).

Virginia
Piedmont and Mountain Areas

PENNSYLVANIA

MARYLAND

KENTUCKY AREA

TENNESSEE AREA

NORTH CAROLINA

Pittsburgh

Wheeling
Fort Statler
Redstone

Morgantown

Marietta

Point Pleasant (Fort Randolph)

Ashland

Cumberland
Berkeley Springs
Harpers Ferry
Winchester
Front Royal
Culpeper C. H.
Orange C.H.
Castle Hill
Richmond

Montpelier
Barboursville
Charlottesville
Monticello
Staunton

Lynchburg
Hampden-Sydney College
Roanoke

Danville
Roanoke Rapids
Halifax

Yadkin River
Guilford C.H.
Greensboro
Hillsboro
Raleigh

Salisbury

Charlotte

Rivers labeled: Muskingum River, Hocking River, Ohio River, Little Kanawha River, Monongahela River, Tygart River, Cheat River, S. Branch Potomac River, Cacapon River, Shenandoah River, Potomac River, Rappahannock River, Rapidan River, Youghiogheny River, Elk River, Gauley River, Greenbrier River, Great Kanawha River, Gwyandot River, New River, James River, Appomattox River, Tug Fork, Clinch River, W. Fork Holston River, S. Fork Holston River, Little River, Staunton River, Banister River, Dan River, Roanoke River, Catawba River, Haw River, Cape Fear River, Tar River, Neuse River, Big Sandy River

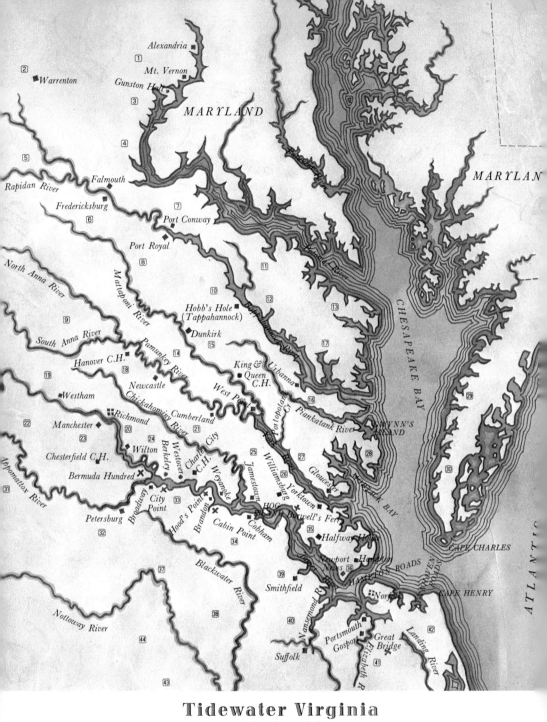

Tidewater Virginia

at the close of the
Revolution

WILLIAM BRADFORD

WILLIAM MADISON

JOHN WITHERSPOON

PATRICK HENRY

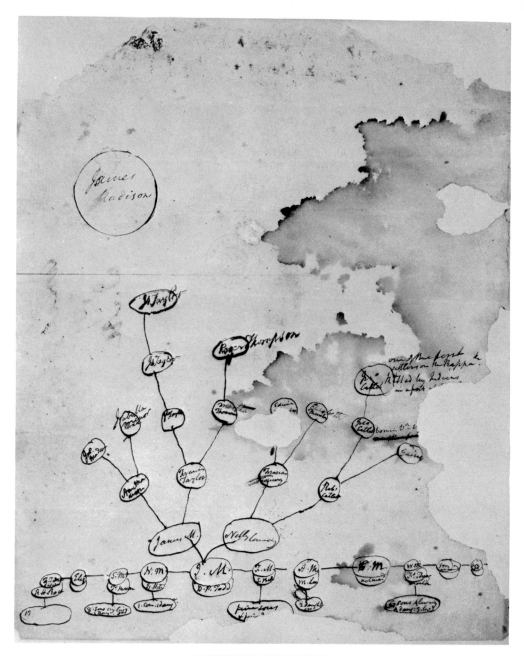

MADISON FAMILY TREE

THE MADISON FAMILY TREE

This family tree, framed under glass, is in LC: Madison Miscellany. For reasons given below, JM could hardly have prepared the chart earlier than the close of 1813 or later than September 1819. He apparently left among his papers at the time of his death a brief statement about his forebears. This document, now lost, came into the possession of his niece, Mrs. Lucie Hartwell Conway. She permitted Bishop William Meade of Virginia to print a copy of it in his *Old Churches, Ministers and Families of Virginia* (2 vols.; Philadelphia, 1857), II, 96–97. This statement does little more than present in prose form the material on JM's chart about his ancestors. Several of the chart's cramped entries, however, are inaccurate and several others are the more difficult to read today because a water stain has partially obliterated them. The remainder of this note seeks to clarify what JM jotted down on the chart about his paternal and maternal ancestors in Virginia, and about his brothers and sisters and the number of their children.

John Madison, the second of that name in Virginia, and his wife, Isabella Minor Todd, had a son, Ambrose (d. 1732), who married Frances Taylor (1700–1761) in 1721. Frances Taylor was a daughter of James Taylor (*ca.* 1674–1729), probably the second rather than the third of that name in Virginia, and of his wife, Martha Thompson (1679–1762). The son of Ambrose and Frances Taylor Madison was James Madison, Sr. (1723–1801), the father of JM.

A son of Edwin Conway (*ca.* 1642–1698) and his wife, Elizabeth Thornton, was Francis Conway (1697–1733). Rebecca Catlett (d. 1760), whom Francis married about 1718, was the granddaughter of Elizabeth Underwood and John Catlett, killed by Indians in a fort at Port Royal on the Rappahannock River in 1670, and a daughter of John's son of the same name (1658–1724) and his wife, Elizabeth Gaines. Nelly Conway (1732–1829), one of the children of Francis and Rebecca Catlett Conway, married James Madison, Sr., on 15 September 1749.

Omitting JM, but otherwise reading along the horizontal line of his chart from left to right, the children of James and Nelly Conway Madison were:

1. Frances Taylor (1774–1823) married Dr. Robert H. Rose (d. 1833) in 1800. Their eldest child was born either late in that year or in 1801. Although JM's failure to mention any of their children might suggest the date when he made the chart, his omission in this regard is misleading for reasons given in items 3 and 8, below. Those reasons most probably warrant the conclusion that the Roses' seven sons and four daughters went unmentioned because of JM's inadvertence or uncertainty about their number.

2. Elizabeth (1768–1775).

3. Sarah Catlett (1764–1843) married Thomas Macon (1765–1838) in 1790. JM's note apparently reads "8 sons six livg[;] 1 daugr. do [living?]." He could not have known that Sarah and Thomas had seven (not eight) sons until 1808, when the seventh was born. Furthermore, they had two daughters, one born

in 1794 and the other in 1803. The latter died in 1805. If it were not for the entry about William (see item 8, below), these Macon data would permit JM to have drawn his sketch as early as 1808, but not before that year.

4. Nelly (1760–1802) married Isaac Hite (1758–1836) in 1783. JM notes "1 son. 1 daugr." The son died in 1791.

5. Francis (1753–1800) married Susanna Bell in 1772. JM seems to record that they had "five sons & fi[ve daugr?]." Perhaps he was correct but, if so, two sons remain unidentified.

6. Ambrose (1755–1793) married Mary Willis Lee (d. 1798) about 1780. JM states that they had two daughters. This may be true, but only one is known.

7. Catlett (1758). JM appears to write "not mar[rie]d." Catlett died in the year of his birth.

8. William (1762–1843) married Frances Throckmorton (1765–1832) in 1783[?]. JM notes "6 sons 4 living[;] 4 daugr: 3 livg." This comment again raises the question about the date when JM made his sketch. The first death among the four daughters was on 28 December 1813. Hence, the chart could not have been produced before that date. Furthermore, there were probably seven sons rather than six. Four were living in 1813, but only three after 16 September 1819. Therefore, JM seems to have prepared this "family tree" at some time between 1813 and 1819.

9. Reuben (1771–1775).

10. A "child" stillborn in 1770. There also was a son who lived only one day in 1766.

Petition of Orange County Planters to the Virginia House of Delegates

RC (Virginia State Library). Not in JM's hand.

[*ca.* 5 December 1777]

To the Honourable the Speaker and House of Delegates of the Common-Wealth of Virginia

The Petition of the Inhabitants of the County of Orange Hum[b]ly Sheweth That your Petitioners having nothing so much at heart as the Liberty and Independance of their Country are Extreamly Anxious to See every regulation take place that may be Conducive to their Final Establishment. That convinced of the Expediency at all times and the indispensible Necessity at Present of improving our internal resources for Defence Against hostile invasions, Your Petitioners Wish and pray that the Cultivation of Tobacco may be Restrained and greater Leisure and Obligation thereby given to the raising and Manufacturing of those Articles which are Necessary for the accomodation of our Army and the Prosecution of the War. Your Petitioners living in a part of the Country Where Tobacco has been the Staple Commodity, and being themselves Planters have an Oppertunity of forming a good Judgment of the impressions Such a Measure Would make and are persuaded it Would be no Less Agreeable to the People than it would be beneficial to the Public. They have heard the Subject frequently canvassed and have met with few persons even among those most devoted by interest and use to the planting Business Who are not Sensible of the propriety of restraining it and Would not chearfully Acquise in Such restriction, provided it Were general and enforced by Law Your Petitioners Would not Undertake to prescribe the exact limitation That Would be best in this Case, but are of Opinion that Four Thousand plants per poll Ought not to be exceeded. They would also leave to your Wisdom and Discretion the particular indulgence requisite for the poor, Who having none to labour but themselves may With more reason Claim and With less inconveniency be Allowed to employ themselves in any Way that Will best enable Them to bear their share of the public Burdens

And your Petitioners as in duty bound Shall ever pray &c.[1]

213

1 The names of the 105 signers, including JM and his father, are omitted here. After the petition was read to the Virginia House of Delegates on 5 December 1777, a motion to refer it to a committee failed to pass by a voice vote (*Journal of the House of Delegates*, October 1777, p. 58). This action was equivalent to a refusal to consider the measure asked for by the petitioners.

Session of Virginia Council of State

MS (Virginia State Library).

EDITORIAL NOTE

The eleventh article of Virginia's Form of Government (Hening, *Statutes*, IX, 116) provided for a Privy Council, or Council of State, of eight members to be chosen by the legislature. Every three years the two houses of the legislature, by joint ballot, removed two of the councilors and thereupon, by the same method, chose two persons in their stead. The two thus displaced must wait at least three years to be eligible for re-election to the council. The president of the Privy Council, chosen annually by its membership, was also the lieutenant governor of the commonwealth. Official action by the council required at least four members to be present at its session. A lesser number sometimes met to discuss public business, but, in order to become effective, decisions had to be approved at the first subsequent meeting when a quorum was present.

From the minutes taken by the clerk at each session and signed by each councilor who was present, the clerk then prepared the finished journal and appended the signatures to it in his own hand. JM's attendance is therefore a matter of record. The journal also notes when a councilor was in Williamsburg but could not come to a meeting by reason of illness or other cause. On the other hand, the loss of the minutes for the period between 6 April 1779 and 12 May 1780 makes JM's final eight months of service as a councilor almost a blank. In 1779, however, he probably followed his custom of spending the "sickly season," from about mid-July to early November, at Montpelier.

Neither the council nor the governor had any significant constitutional authority except when they worked together. According to the Form of Government (Art. 9), the governor should "with the advice of a Council of State, exercise the executive powers of government according to the laws of this commonwealth; and shall not, under any pretence, exercise any power or prerogative by virtue of any law, statute, or custom, of *England*." More specifically, the constitution enabled the governor, on advice of council, to grant reprieves and pardons in most instances; to "embody" and direct the militia, and commission or suspend its officers; to name *ad interim* administrative and judicial officials, when the legislature was not in session; and to appoint justices of the peace, sheriffs, and coroners upon nomination by the court of the county in which they were to serve (*ibid.*, IX, 115–19).

Although these were the only definite duties assigned by the constitution

to the governor acting in conjunction with the Council of State, the legislature delegated many special powers to them, both before and while JM
was a councilor. These added responsibilities, which were often of an emergency nature occasioned by the Revolution, included a great extension of
the powers to appoint state employees; to issue financial warrants; to direct
recruiting, training, equipping, provisioning, and utilization of troops and
seamen; to erect fortifications, barracks, and military hospitals; to apprehend
traitors and take their forfeited property into custody; to suppress domestic
insurrections, Indian uprisings, counterfeiting, and the engrossment of essential war commodities; to prevent the exportation of foods and other articles
needed by the troops; to maintain fair prices; and to supervise the commonwealth's lead mines, land office, and navy (*ibid.*, IX, 178–592; X, 15–217,
passim).

In view of this impressive variety of important duties, membership on the
council was no sinecure. Reflecting the rapid inflation, the total salary which
the eight members were to divide annually among themselves, in proportion to the frequency with which each of them appeared at the council
meetings, rose from £2,400 to £20,000 (*ibid.*, IX, 435, 521; X, 118, 219).
JM took his seat at the council table on 14 January 1778. He had been chosen
by the members of the General Assembly on 12 November 1777, when sixty-
one votes were cast for him against forty-two others given in favor of his
closest competitor, Meriwether Smith. Three days later the Senate confirmed
the outcome of this joint ballot (*Journal of the House of Delegates*, October
1777, pp. 25, 29; Brant, *Madison*, I, 313–15). The seat to which JM was elected
had been vacant for nearly five months. The extant minutes of the council
bear witness that JM attended 177 of its sessions. Of these, 170 date in 1778,
while the remaining 7 are the only ones during the next year of which any
official record survives. With the exception of a week's illness in May and
one day in June, he shared in every session of the council from 14 January
to 13 July 1778. Thereafter, until 7 November of that year, he was at Montpelier. Loss of the minutes leaves in doubt the day of his final service as a
councilor. In all likelihood it was shortly after 14 December 1779 when the
legislature chose him to go to the Continental Congress as one of the delegates from Virginia. (See Credentials as a Delegate to Continental Congress,
14 December 1779, and JM to Benjamin Harrison, 16 [December] 1779.)

Although two letters of Edward Coles, written some thirty years after
Jefferson's death, state that Jefferson had told him of JM's service to Governor Patrick Henry as an amanuensis and as the only member of Virginia's
executive branch who understood French, this recollection is too general and
was recorded too long after the alleged facts to be relied upon in the absence
of contemporary evidence (Edward Coles to Hugh B. Grigsby, 23 December
1854, Virginia Historical Society; Edward Coles to William C. Rives, 26
March 1858, LC: William C. Rives Papers). In no instance, insofar as any
contemporary manuscript is concerned, can JM's service as a councilor be
isolated from that of his fellow members. For this reason, the editors have
limited their publication of the council minutes, and of letters from the Gov-

ernor in Council, to samples illustrative of its problems and procedures on days when JM was in attendance and hence presumably contributed his advice. An edition of the *Journals of the Council of the State of Virginia,* for the period of JM's service, was carefully edited by H. R. McIlwaine and published by the Virginia State Library at Richmond in 1932.

Wednesday January 14th 1778

present

His Excellency[1]

Dudley Digges	Nathaniel Harrison &
John Blair	David Jameson

Esquires[2]

James Madison jun. Esquire, who hath been duly elected a Member of the Privy Council, appeared, and the Oath of Office being administered to him, he took his Seat at the Board accordingly[3]

Present James Madison jr. Esqr.

A Warrant was issued by the Governor, with the Advice of the Council, upon the public Treasurer for one thousand pounds payable to Benjamin Putney for the use of Mr John Pierce upon Account as purchasing Commissary of provisions.[4]

The Governor having communicated to the Board a Letter from a Commee of Congress, of the 31st December last, representing the alarming Accounts of the Distresses of the American Army for the Want of provisions, insomuch that it is hinted to Congress, by General Washington, that the Troops, unless an immediate supply is sent, must either *"Starve Disolve* or *Disperse"* and asking the advice of the Council thereupon—they do advise his Excellency to give Directions to Colonel Aylett the Continental Commissary, forthwith to send off an active intelligent & proper person to the Northwestern parts of this State in order to buy up all the pork Beef & Bacon that can be procured, & to forward it with all possible Dispatch to Head Quarters, & to procure Waggons for conveying such Salt & other necessaries as his Excellency may think can best be supplyed from hence. All which the Governor orders accordingly And he also with the Advice of Council sent ye said Letter to the Assembly.[5]

His Excellency informed the Council that he had prevailed on Colonel David Rogers of the Senate, to Convey to the Governor of New Orleans by way of the Missisipi, a Letter which he was anxious to send & laying the same before them it was read approved of & ordered to be recorded.[6] His Excellency then laid before the Council the following Instructions to Colonel Rogers which were also approved of viz.

COLONEL ROGERS

You are to proceed with out Loss of time to engage a Lieutenant, Ensign & twenty eight men on double pay & with them you are to go to New Orleans with Despatches to the Governor of that place. I expect some Goods are to be sent from thence for this State which you will take under your Care & safely convey home with Answers to my Letters. General Hand will be desired to give you Assistance as to the Boats &c necessary for the Trip.[7]

I desire to know the Strength of the English possessions on Missisippi & whether they supply the West Indies with any & what articles. The present State, Temper & Condition of these people must be gathered by such means as will not endanger Discovery. You are to consider of a proper place to fix a post at for facilitating & securing the Trade to New Orleans & Consult the Spanish Governor on it.[8]

Describe to that Gentleman the real Strength & situation of Virginia the progress of the War & whatever else he may wish to know of the American Confederacy.

You are to convey my Instructions to Colonel Clark[9] by which he is directed to escort you homeward & you are to correspond with me & let me know the upshot of this Business soon as possible.

Adjourned till tomorrow 10 oClock

Signed   DUDLEY DIGGES
         JOHN BLAIR
         NATHL HARRISON
         DAVID JAMESON
         JAMES MADISON JR

---

[1] Patrick Henry, governor of Virginia, 5 July 1776 to 1 July 1779, and 30 November 1784 to 30 November 1786.

[2] John Blair (1732–1800), a lawyer of Williamsburg, had been a burgess during most of the years 1766–1771, and a member of the Convention of 1776. For a decade after 1778 he held several high judicial offices in his state. He was the rector of the College of William and Mary in 1781, a member of the Constitutional Convention of 1787, and an associate justice of the United States Supreme Court from 1789 to 1796. Nathaniel Harrison (ca. 1708–1786) served on the Council of State from October 1776 to December 1778. From the latter date until his death he was in the state Senate and served as its speaker in the session of October 1779 (Earl G. Swem and John W. Williams, eds., Register of the General Assembly, pp. 10–23; Charles P. Keith and Henry H. Wilson, The Ancestry of Benjamin Harrison [Harrisburg, Va., 1932]). David Jameson (1757–1793), later a correspondent of JM, was a Yorktown merchant-patriot who became lieutenant governor of Virginia in 1781, after four years on the Council of State. In 1783 he was a member of the state Senate.

[3] The oath prescribed by law (Hening, Statutes, IX, 120) and administered by Governor Henry was as follows:

"I [James Madison, Jr.] elected one of the privy council of Virginia by the representatives thereof, do solemnly promise and swear, that I will, to the best of my skill and judgment, execute the said office diligently and faithfully according to law, without favour, affection, or partiality; and that I will be faithful to the commonwealth of Virginia, and will support and defend the same, according to the constitution thereof, to the utmost of my power; and that I will keep secret such proceedings and orders of the privy council as the board shall direct to be concealed, unless when the same shall be called for by either house of assembly. So help me God."

4 Benjamin Putney (*ca.* 1746–post-1819), a tobacco merchant, an ensign, and later a second lieutenant of Surry County militia, was a state tobacco inspector and a member of the House of Delegates in 1778. He moved to North Carolina sometime after 1790 (*Journal of the Senate of the United States,* 15th Cong., 2d sess. [Washington, 1818], p. 211; John D. Boddie, *Colonial Surry* [Richmond, 1948], pp. 161, 171). John Pierce, Sr. (*ca.* 1736–*ca.* 1819), of James City County was named purchasing commissary of provisions on 17 October 1777. After serving as assistant commissary general for Virginia from December 1780 to September 1781, he was commissary general until his resignation on 12 January 1782. In April 1785 he became the sheriff of his county. He was a member of the House of Delegates from 1787 to 1798 (H. R. McIlwaine *et al.,* eds., *Journals of the Council of the State of Virginia* [Richmond, 1931——], II, 11; III, 431; *Calendar of Virginia State Papers,* II, 424, 663; III, 18).

5 See below, Henry to Virginia Delegates, 20 January 1778 and nn. 2, 3. Washington's grim comment about the fate of his army is in his letter of 23 December 1777, which was referred to the Board of War on 29 December (*Journals of the Continental Congress,* IX, 1065; Fitzpatrick, *Writings of Washington,* X, 192).

6 Henry asked Bernardo de Gálvez (*ca.* 1746–1786), governor of Louisiana since 1777 and later the captor of Baton Rouge and Natchez (1779), Mobile (1780), and Pensacola (1781), to assist Rogers in moving supplies from New Orleans to Fort Pitt, and to loan money to Virginia. Henry also suggested to Gálvez that it would be in Spain's interest to unite West Florida to the United States, for thereby he would stop the rivalry with Spain of the English settlement in that area of Florida (H. R. McIlwaine, ed., *Official Letters of Virginia Governors,* I, 227–29). Irish-born David Rogers (d. 1779) was a major in the militia of Ohio County and briefly its first county lieutenant in 1777. On 20 January 1778, the Council of State approved a warrant of £625 to defray his expenses and those of the thirty men accompanying him. By mid-August 1779, he was at Kaskaskia with two boatloads of goods from New Orleans. On 4 October 1779, near the mouth of the Licking River in Kentucky, Indians killed Rogers and fifty-six persons with him (*ibid.,* I, 104 n.; *Journals of the Council of State,* I, 358, 444; II, 69; III, 312; James Alton James, ed., *George Rogers Clark Papers, 1771–1781* [Springfield, Ill., 1912], pp. 38 n., 356; Ross B. Johnston, ed., *West Virginians in the American Revolution* [Parkersburg, W. Va., 1959], p. 239).

7 Brigadier General Edward Hand (1744–1802) of Pennsylvania, who became adjutant general of the Continental Army, 1781–1783, and a member of Congress, 1784–1785, was ordered by Congress on 10 April 1777 to go to Fort Pitt to "take measures for the defence of the western frontiers." Congress relieved him of his onerous assignment in May 1778 (*Journals of the Continental Congress,* VII, 252; XI, 417). Henry's letter to him, describing Rogers' mission, is in H. R. McIlwaine, ed., *Official Letters of Virginia Governors,* I, 230.

8 In his letter to Gálvez, Henry proposed to construct "a fort at some place at the mouth of the Ohio," but added that whether this should or should not be

erected would hinge upon "what Your Excellency considers it advisable to reply to me."

9 George Rogers Clark (1752–1818), who would capture Kaskaskia and Vincennes from the British in the summer of 1778, reinforced Rogers with about forty men a year later. Most of the forty shared Rogers' own fate (above, n. 6).

Patrick Henry in Council to Virginia Delegates in Congress

RC (NA: PCC, No. 71, I, 131–34). During the session of 14 January 1778, JM's first day on the Council of State, the subject of this letter was one of the principal matters discussed. The council heard and approved the letter on 20 January (*Journals of the Council of State*, II, 64, 69).

WMSBURG VIRGA Jany 20th. 1778.

GENTLEMEN,

Francis Lightfoot Lee Esquirs[1] Letter for the Committee on the Subject of provisions filled me with Concern & astonishment.[2] I applied to the Deputy Commissary General to furnish some Active persons for throwing an instant Supply of Provisions to the Army to answer the present Exigency.[3] I was told by him that he could get none such immediately but he would write to his Deputy to do the Business.

I thought this plan by no means satisfactory. For in the Northwestern parts of this State in that Deputy's Quarter, I found upon Enquiry that Eight or ten thousand Hogs & several thousand fine Beeves might have been had very lately in a few Counties convenient to the Camp. In order therefore to avoid blending my Transactions with the Commissary's & to give Despatch & Efficacy to the Measure, I employ'd Abraham Hite, Thomas Hite, & James Barbour, Esqrs. Gentlemen of Character to purchase instantly Beef, or Pork, if Beef could not be had, to the Amount of ten thousand pounds & drive it to Camp in the most Expeditious Manner, and advanced them the Cash. I have also directed Colonel Simpson to seize two thousand Bushels Salt on the Eastern Shore & send it to the Head of Elk for the grand Army & to reserve a thousand more to answer further Orders that may become necessary.[4]

A Galley is also ordered to carry 600 Bushels along the Western Shore to Elk for the same purposes. In the Article of Flour I have not meddled, thinking from Mr. Lees Letter that it was not wanting. By these several Steps, the best which in the sudden Exigency could be taken, I hope a temporary Supply may be obtained.

But Gentlemen I cannot forbear some Reflections on this Occasion, which I beg you will please to lay before Congress as the Sentiments of the Executive Body of this State. It is with the deepest Concern that the Business of supplying provisions for the grand Army, is seen fall into a State of uncertainty & Confusion. And while that Executive hath been more than once called upon to make up for Deficiency's in that Department, no Reform is seen to take place. Altho a great Abundance of provisions might have been procured from Virginia, yet no Animadversions that I know of, have been made upon the Conduct of those whose Business it was to forward it to the Army. In this Situation of things Intelligence is given to *me* that from this State it is expected most of the Supplies must be drawn. What may be inferred from this, I do not well Know. If any kind of Superintendance or Controul over the Commissariate is meant, Congress will please to recollect that the Gentlemen in that office are not amenable to me. If it is expected that friendly Assistance should be given, I am happy in saying this has been anticipated. Large Loans of Flour, Meat, & Salt have been made from Time to Time to great amount, nor will they be withheld but from the most absolute necessity. But I earnestly desire that it may be understood & remembered once for all that the Executive power here has nothing to do with the Comissarys Business.[5] That it hold itself guiltless of all the Mischief which in future may arise from Delinquency in that Office.

It will indeed be unworthy the Character of a Zealous American to entrench himself within the Strict line of official Duty, & there quietly behold the starving & dispersion of the American Army. The Genius of this Country is not of that Cast.

I do not wish to avoid any Labour which may serve the general Interest and which cannot be executed better by others. But I have the Mortification to know, that the present Business I have directed, will be executed with great Loss to the Public. The pressing occasion puts the price of Meat &c in the power of wicked avaricious & disaffected Men. The Value of Money will be more & more lessened, the means of supporting public Credit counteracted & defeated I will not enumerate further the Evils which must follow from suffering Business of this vast import to remain in the Channel where it is now going. Let it suffice to say that this Country abounds with the provisions for which the Army is said to be almost starving particularly that part of it nearest the Camp.

The Executive has no Authority over or Commission with the Commissariate. The Temporary supply ordered to Camp concludes the Interference which is made in that Business & is kept as a distinct & separate Transaction. But if in the Course of future Events it should become at any Time necessary that the Commissariate should receive any aid within the Line of the Executive power of this State it will be afforded with the greatest pleasure—yet in such a Case it is much to be wished that as early Notice as possible may be given of such Necessity.

The pain which Government feels on this occasion, & which is generally diffused throughout this State, for the melancholy, the perilous Situation of the American Army will be relieved when a Reform takes Place in that Department from mismanagement in which have flowed Evils threatening the Existence of american Liberty.[6]

I beg leave Gentlemen to apologize for the Freedom of this Letter. Congress will please to be assured of the most perfect Regard of every Member of the Executive of Virginia But that Body would be wanting in the Duty they owe to the great Council of America & to their Country, if they concealed any of their Sentiments on a Subject so alarming as the present. The Honour & Credit of that great Council are conceived to be deeply concerned in rectifying what is wrong in these Matters: And nothing but the highest Regard, & most anxious Care to preserve that honor from aspersion should extort the painful observation from me. I pray for the prosperity & Happiness of Congress as the Guardians of America & with the greatest Esteem

I am, Gentlemen, Your very Humble & most obedt. Servant

P. HENRY

[1] After serving as a burgess from Loudoun County before the Revolution, Francis Lightfoot Lee (1734–1797) established his home at Menokin, a plantation in Richmond County. While in Congress between 1775 and 1779, as a delegate from Virginia, he signed the Declaration of Independence. He was a member of the Virginia Senate from 1780 to 1782 (Cazenove G. Lee, Jr., *Lee Chronicle*, pp. 73–74).

[2] Lee's letter to Governor Henry was probably dated 31 December 1777. On that day Congress made available to the delegates of Virginia $50,000 "for the purpose of paying for goods collected and seized for the continental army, . . . the said state to be accountable" (*Journals of the Continental Congress*, IX, 1070). On 24 November Congress had chosen Elbridge Gerry (Mass.) to be the chairman of a committee of five members, not including Lee, "to devise ways and means for providing a sufficient supply of provisions for the army," but the action of 31 December was more directly a result of Washington's letters of the 22d and 23d of that month, which warned Congress that the army at Valley Forge would "Starve, dissolve, or disperse" unless furnished speedily with "subsistence" (*ibid.*, IX, 962, 976–78, 1054, 1065; Fitzpatrick, *Writings of Washington*, X, 183–88, 192–98).

[3] This action by Governor Henry squared with the advice given to him by the Council of State. See above, Session of Council, 14 January 1778. A month earlier, Henry had written to Aylett, the deputy commissary general of purchases, "reprehending him for his neglect" (*Journals of the Council of State*, II, 53).

[4] Governor Henry's revised method of procedure, including the choice of the three men named in this paragraph, was the outcome of his deliberations with the Council of State on 15 January. Five days earlier, the House of Delegates adopted a measure to enable the "public contractors" to assemble provisions for "the ensuing campaign." This law also prohibited the exportation of beef, pork, and bacon, an example which Congress, about a month later, strongly urged North Carolina to follow (*Journal of the House of Delegates*, October 1777, p. 112; Hening, *Statutes*, IX, 385–87; *Journals of the Continental Congress*, X, 156). After Governor Henry submitted Lee's letter to the General Assembly, that body enacted on 24 January an emergency law "for authorising the seizure of Salt, in the same manner as provisions for the use of the army" (*Journal of the House of Delegates*, October 1777, p. 136; Hening, *Statutes*, IX, 381). Abraham Hite (1729–1790) of Hampshire County was a militia captain and a veteran of the Battle of Point Pleasant. He was a burgess from 1769 to 1771, a member of the Virginia Convention of May 1776, and a member of the House of Delegates in 1776–1779 and 1782–1783. Thomas Hite (1750–1779) of Berkeley County was a burgess in 1772–1774, and a delegate to the General Assembly in 1776–1779 (Earl G. Swem and John W. Williams, eds., *Register of the General Assembly*, pp. 1–8). James Barbour (*ca.* 1734–1783) was a burgess from Culpeper County, 1761 to 1765, and its county lieutenant for several years. Southy Simpson (*ca.* 1725–1779) of Accomack County had been a burgess from 1761 to 1774. The Convention of May 1776, of which he was a member, named him to manage the saltworks on the eastern shore (Ralph T. Whitelaw, *Virginia's Eastern Shore: A History of Northampton and Accomack Counties* [2 vols.; Richmond, 1951], II, 1083, 1085, 1088; Hening, *Statutes*, IX, 125). "Head of Elk" is now Elkton, Md., where the Elk River flows into a northern arm of Chesapeake Bay.

[5] The commissary general of purchases and his deputies were elected by Congress and responsible to it alone (*Journals of the Continental Congress*, VIII, 433–48).

[6] Henry's letter was read in Congress on 2 February 1778 (*ibid.*, X, 110). More than two weeks earlier, it had named a committee "to report such alterations" in "the commissariate system" as "they shall deem best calculated to answer the end of its institution." The committee's report of 23 February, after frequent debate and amendment by Congress, was adopted on 13 March. This reform, by no means thoroughgoing, probably pleased Governor Henry to the extent that it prevented deputy commissary generals from overbidding prices fixed by state law for articles of food needed by the Continental Army (*ibid.*, X, 51, 192, 248–52).

To James Madison, Sr.

RC (LC: Madison Papers). The address sheet makes it clear that this letter was carried to its destination by Major William Moore. Long after the letter was written, William Cabell Rives bracketed the first, fifth, and sixth sentences, and the second paragraph of the postscript, thus indicating the portions selected by him for publication in Madison, *Letters* (Cong. ed.), I, 30–31.

WILLIAMSBURG Jany. 23d. 1778

HOND SIR

I got safe to this place on Tuesday following the day I left home,[1] and at the earnest invitation of my Kinsman Mr. Madison have taken my lodgings in a Room of the Presidents house, which is a much better accom[mo]dation than I could have promised myself.[2] It would be very agreeable to me if I were enabled by such rarities as our part of the Country furnishes, particularly dried fruit &tc which Mr. Madison is very fond of to make some little returns for the Culinary favours I receive. Should any opportunity for this purpose offer I hope they will be sent. You will see by the inclosed Acct. of Sales what money you have in Mr. Lee's hands, and if you chuse to draw for it, you can transmit me your Bills for Sale.[3] You will be informed in due time by Advertisement from the Governor what is proper to be done with the Shoes &tc. collected for the Army.[4] You will be able to obtain so circumstantial an Acct. of public affairs from Majr. Moore that I may spare myself the trouble of anticipating it. Majr. Moore also has for my Mother 4 Oz. of Bark.[5] The other Articles wanted by the family are not at present to be had. Whenever I meet with them I shall provide and transmit them. I hope you will not forget my parting request that I might hear frequently from home and whenever my brother returns from the Army[6] I desire he may be informed I shall expect he will make up by letter the loss of intelligence I sustain by my removal out of his way. With the sincerest affection for yourself & all others whom I ought particularly to remember on this occasion,

I am Dear Sir Your Affecte. son

JAMES MADISON JNR.

I find on enquiry that Mr. Benjamin Winslow is discontinued in the military appointment given him by the Governour & Council.[7] I promised to let him know this by letter but my being as yet unprovided with paper makes it necessary to leave this information for him with you.

J. M JR.

Although I well know how inconvenient and disagreeable it is to you to continue to act as Lieutenant of the County I can not help informing you that a resignation at this juncture is here supposed to have a very unfriendly aspect on the execution of the Draught and consequently to betray at least a want of patriotism and pe[r]severence. This is so much the case that a recommendation of Conty Lt. this day received by the Govr., to supply the place of one who had resigned to the Court, produced a private verbal message to the old Lt. to continue to act at least as long as the present measures were in execution.[8]

J M JR

[1] JM was sworn into office on the Virginia Council of State on 14 January, the day after his arrival in Williamsburg.

2 Reverend James Madison (1749–1812), an Anglican minister who was JM's second cousin, served as professor of natural and moral philosophy at the College of William and Mary, and as its president from 1777 until his death. The American Philosophical Society recognized his interest in science by admitting him to membership in 1780. Ten years later, the Archbishop of Canterbury consecrated him as Bishop of the Episcopal Church in Virginia. Except during JM's membership in the Council of State, he and his kinsman were not closely associated. JM, however, always held him in high regard for his "intellectual power and diversified learning," his "benevolence," "courtesy," and devotion to "our Revolution, and to the purest principles of a Government founded on the rights of man" (JM to Robert Walsh, 22 August 1831, in Madison, *Letters* [Cong. ed.], IV, 194).

3 Inclosure not found. William Lee (1739–1795), a younger brother of Arthur and Richard Henry Lee, acted as business agent of many Virginia planters while engaged in mercantile pursuits in Europe from 1768 to 1783. During the Revolution he was also the commercial representative of Virginia and the United States at Nantes, France, and U.S. commissioner at the courts of Prussia and the Holy Roman Empire (Cazenove G. Lee, Jr., *Lee Chronicle*, pp. 194–203, 230–35).

4 On 13 December 1777, in accordance with a resolution of the Assembly of Virginia late in November, Governor Patrick Henry asked "the Lieutenant or Commanding Officer of the Militia of each County . . . to request of the Inhabitants of their County one pair of Shoes, Stockings, Gloves or Mittens for each Soldier raised by the County & now serving in the Continental Army" (H. R. McIlwaine, ed., *Official Letters of Virginia Governors*, I, 217–18). This was the Valley Forge winter, when Washington's army suffered greatly from lack of sufficient clothing. The governor's "advertisement" did not state how the articles collected were to be forwarded.

5 Cinchona (quinine) bark, or a local substitute, efficacious as a remedy for malaria.

6 Ambrose Madison.

7 Benjamin Winslow (*ca.* 1737–1826), Orange County planter, and several other men were relieved of their captaincies on 17 December 1777 because they had "failed to recruit anything near their Quotas" for a state regiment of artillery, then in process of formation (John McGill, ed., *The Beverley Family of Virginia: Descendants of Major Robert Beverley, 1641–1687, and Allied Families* [Columbia, S.C., 1956], p. 821; *Journals of the Council of State*, II, 49).

8 The "old Lt." has not been identified. Possibly because of the increasing difficulties in recruiting soldiers, JM's father yielded his position as county lieutenant to Zachariah Burnley before the close of 1778 (Brant, *Madison*, I, 323–24; W. W. Scott, *History of Orange County*, p. 72).

Session of Virginia Council of State

MS (Virginia State Library).

Friday January 23d 1778

present
His Excellency;

John Page[1]	Nathaniel Harrison
Dudley Digges	David Jameson &
John Blair	James Madison

Esquires

The Governor with the Advice of the Council, issued the following Warrants upon the Treasurer for the Bounty of the Draughts to be made in the Several Counties agreeable to Act of Assembly for filling up the fifteen Virginia Regiments.[2]

. . . .

A Warrant for one hundred & three pounds ten Shillings payable to William Moore Esquire on account of Orange Draughts.[3]

. . . .

The General Assembly having empowered the Governor with the Advice of the Privy Council, to appoint two Brigadiers General, if the numbers of Voluntiers who may enlist agreeable to the Directions of the Act entituled An Act for Speedily recruiting the Virginia Regiments on the Continental Establishment & for raising additional Troops of Voluntiers[4] shall make it necessary to appoint them the Board, being of opinion that it might greatly encourage that Service to let it be known what Gentlemen are likely to be appointed, advise his Excellency the Governor as soon as the Enlistments shall give him a Right to do so, to appoint Thomas Nelson jr & Alexander Spotswood Esquires Brigadiers General to Command the said Troops.[5] And the Governor with the Advice of the Council, was pleased to appoint Monday the 23d Day of February next for the nomination of the Field officers of the several Battalions & to direct public Notice thereof to be given in the Virginia Gazettes[6] to the Intent that all persons willing to offer their services to their Country on this occasion may have an opportunity of doing so, in any way the most convenient to themselves.

Adjourned till Tomorrow 10 oClock

Signed JOHN PAGE
DUDLEY DIGGES
JOHN BLAIR
NATHL HARRISON
DAVID JAMESON
JAMES MADISON

[1] John Page (1743–1808) of Gloucester County was lieutenant governor of Virginia. Other major offices which he held were those of United States representative from 1789 to 1797 and governor from 1802 to 1805.

[2] Hening, *Statutes*, IX, 588–92.

[3] Issuing warrants, especially to militia officers, was one of the most frequent tasks of the Council of State during JM's tenure. At this session sixteen other warrants were authorized, besides the sample given here. William Moore carried home a letter from JM to his father (*q.v.*) on the same day that this warrant was issued.

[4] Printed in Hening, *Statutes*, IX, 337–49.

[5] Thomas Nelson, Jr. (1738–1789), frequently a member of the Virginia House of Burgesses and House of Delegates and twice a member of the Continental Congress,

reached his political apogee on 12 June 1781, when he was chosen to succeed Governor Thomas Jefferson. In August and September 1777 he was a brigadier general in command of all Virginia militia called out to defend the state against a short-lived British invasion (*Journals of the Council of State*, I, 470, 499). In 1781, while governor, he helped in besieging the British in Yorktown, the village of his residence. Alexander Spotswood (1751–1818) had been a colonel of the 2d Virginia Regiment until his resignation in October 1777. In March 1781 he was appointed commander of a special legion to defend the state against invasion. His unit, however, never took the field (Clayton Torrence, "A Cloud-Capped Legion," *William and Mary Quarterly*, 2d ser., I [1921], 137–41). Apparently enlistments in 1778 were insufficient to justify the appointment of Nelson and Spotswood.

6 *Virginia Gazette* (Williamsburg, Purdie; and Dixon and Hunter). This public notice is not available, since the pertinent issues for January and February 1778 have not survived.

Session of Virginia Council of State

MS (Virginia State Library).

Thursday February 12th 1778.

present

Dudley Digges   David Jameson &   ⎫
John Blair   James Madison jr   ⎬ Esquires
                                             ⎭

The Express sent with a Letter written by the Board Yesterday to the president of the Council at Rosewell being returned & unable to Cross York river by the Wind; and sundry other Matters of Importance presenting for the Consideration of the Council, a Letter was written to the Governor by Express informing him thereof and pressing his immediate attendance[1] and then the Members present

  Adjourned till Tomorrow

Signed DUDLEY DIGGES
JOHN BLAIR
DAVID JAMESON
JAMES MADISON

[1] This session highlights a problem which frequently disturbed the council during JM's tenure. For a quorum, four members of the council, not counting the lieutenant governor if the governor did not attend, had to be present. On 11 February the four councilors present sent an emergency summons to President John Page, who was at his estate of Rosewell, across the York River only eight miles from Williamsburg. Governor Henry had been gone since 28 January, when he "informed the Board that his absence from this City for some time, was necessary, and that he had nothing particular at this time for their Consideration; He therefore advised their adjourning over till a distant Day; but that if in the interim any thing urgent should demand their attendance, the Lieutenant Governor should be advised thereof And desired

to attend. The Board accordingly adjourned till the 18. Next Month" (*Journals of the Council of State*, II, 77). Page's departure after the 5 February session broke the quorum until Nathaniel Harrison's reappearance eight days later. During Page's absence, Dudley Digges, the ranking member of the council under Page, acted as lieutenant governor to convene the council. Page finally returned on 17 February, and Governor Henry two days later.

Session of Virginia Council of State

MS (Virginia State Library).

Friday February 13th 1778

present

Dudley Digges Esquire Lieutenant Governor
John Blair   David Jameson &
Nathaniel Harrison   James Madison jr

Esquires

A Warrant was issued by the Lieutenant Governor with the Advice of the Council, for one hundred pounds payable to Colonel Thomas Marshall upon Account for forwarding the recruiting his Regiment of State Artillery[1]

The Lieutenant Governor having in the absence of the Governor received a Letter to his Excellency from the Treasury Board mentioning that on account of the great Demands from all Quarters on the Continental Treasury it had become necessary to draw on their Loan Office in this State for thirty five thousand Dollars payable to Alexander Rose Esquire for the purchase of Supplies for the Army; and desiring that the said Mr Rose might receive out of the Treasury of this State so much as he might not be able to negotiate at the said Loan Office the Commissioner thereof giving Certificates for the amount of the money so advanced, to be kept until he can exchange the same. The Board duly weighing the importance of this Business & the necessity of Complying with this request, advise the Lieutenant Governor notwithstanding the weak Condition of our own Treasury at present, to give a Warrant on the Treasury for Six thousand one hundred & eighty pounds eighteen Shillings equal to twenty thousand six hundred & three Dollars, & a Draught on Maurice Symonds Esquire Agent for the State at Charles Town for ten thousand Dollars more payable to said Mr Rose or order, which Sums together with what he has received at the Loan Office, amount to the thirty five thousand Dollars drawn for.[2] But the Board at the same time advise the Lieutenant Governor or his

Excellency the Governor if he should return in time, to write the Treasury Board, that there being a Loan Office here for the purpose of borrowing Money for the use of this State it can by no means consist with our Circumstances to lend Money till the Continental Loan office here may be enabled to repay it, which from appearances will not happen in any short time and that the Loan is made in complyance with the urgency of the occasion, and in full confidence that the Continental Treasury Board will in some short time repay the Money lent, either by remitting the same to the Treasury of this State, or by honouring the Governors Draught for the amount as soon as it shall become necessary to make it.[3] The Lieutenant Governor accordingly issued his Warrant on the Treasurer in favor of Mr Rose for Six thousand one hundred & eighty pounds eighteen Shillings & a Draught on Maurice Symonds Esquire at Charles Town for ten thousand Dollars. a Letter was written Mr Symonds advising him thereof.

On considering the petition of Major Thomas Smith of Gloucester County the Board advise the Lieutenant Governor to grant him leave to apply to the Commanding Officer either at York or Hampton for a flag of Truce attending with a proper officer to go on Board any of the Ships of War belonging to the Enemy lying convenient to these Stations respectively to make application for thirteen Slaves which he has lost, and are said to be on board some of the said Ships.[4]

On Considering the petition of Colonel Littleton Savage of Northampton County, in behalf of himself & others who have lost Slaves, which are supposed to be on board some of ye Enemy's Ships; the Lieutenant Governor is advised to empower the County Lieutenant of the said County (no Troops being stationed at this time on that Shore) to send a proper officer of his Militia, to go with a Flag of Truce, attended by the owners of Such Slaves, in order to make application to have them returned.[5]

Adjourned till tomorrow 10. oClock

Signed   DUDLEY DIGGES
JOHN BLAIR
NATHL HARRISON
DAVID JAMESON
JAMES MADISON JR

[1] Colonel Thomas Marshall (1730–1802), the father of Chief Justice John Marshall, was chosen by the Assembly in November 1777 to command a proposed regiment of artillery (*Journal of the House of Delegates,* October 1777, pp. 27, 30). He had been a burgess from Fauquier County for five terms in the 1760's and early 1770's, and attended the conventions of 1774, 1775, and 1776. From 1783, when he moved

to Kentucky, until his death, he was prominent in its political and economic life (Albert J. Beveridge, *The Life of John Marshall* [4 vols.; Boston, 1916–19], I and II, *passim*).

2 On 3 October 1776, Congress ordered the creation of loan offices in each state to forward the money which its citizens were willing to loan at interest to the central government. The current request of the Board of Treasury was made on 26 January 1778 (*Journals of the Continental Congress*, V, 845–46; X, 90–91). Colonel Maurice Simons (1744–1785), a prominent resident of Charleston, S.C., commanded the militia of that city during much of the war (*Journals of the Council of State*, III, 11, 33; *South Carolina Historical and Genealogical Magazine*, XXXVII [1936], 144, 150 n.). Alexander Rose (*ca.* 1738–1807) was a well-known Charleston merchant. He was in business at least from 1768 to 1799 (*ibid.*, XVII [1916], 8, 10 n., 40; XXIV [1923], 181; XXX [1929], 238–39; XXXII [1931], 80; L [1949], 2, 147 n.).

3 On 9 March a warrant for $30,603 was authorized by Congress for the reimbursement of "the governor and council of the State of Virginia" (NA: PCC, No. 136, II, 139, 211; *Journals of the Continental Congress*, X, 234). The money reached the state treasury on 17 April (H. R. McIlwaine, ed., *Official Letters of Virginia Governors*, I, 266).

4 Major Thomas Smith (d. *ca.* 1807), a militia soldier, planter, and merchant of Gloucester County and (after 1791, when Mathews County was formed) of Mathews County. He was a justice of the peace in both counties, agent for state trade and director of military stores from 1777 to 1779, a delegate to the General Assembly from 1780 to 1790 and 1793 to 1796, and a delegate to the Virginia Convention of 1788, which ratified the Federal Constitution (*ibid.*, I, 67 n.; Polly Cary Mason, comp., *Records of Gloucester County, Virginia* [2 vols.; Newport News, 1946–48], I, 121; Earl G. Swem and John W. Williams, eds., *Register of the General Assembly*, pp. 11–33, 40–46, 244). The expression "flag of truce" had several connotations during the war. In this instance, after arranging in advance with the British commander, a patriot under such a "flag" could safely enter the enemy lines on a matter of legitimate business. Sometimes the term refers to a ship engaged in the exchange of prisoners of war, or carrying materials for their support (Session of Council of State, 29 March 1779).

5 Littleton Savage (*ca.* 1740–1805) was a member of the Northampton County Committee of Safety in 1774–1776, a county justice in 1792, and a colonel of militia. He is sometimes identified with the neighboring county of Accomack because of his landed property there (*Journals of the Council of State*, I, 334; III, 385, 390; *William and Mary Quarterly*, 1st ser., XVI [1907–8], 104; Lyon G. Tyler, ed., *Encyclopedia of Virginia Biography*, I, 319). John Burton (*ca.* 1746–1786) was the Northampton County lieutenant. From 1769 to 1774 he had been a burgess from that county, and he was a member of its Committee of Safety and a delegate to the Revolutionary Convention of March 1775 (*Journals of the Council of State*, I, 334; William G. and Mary Newton Stanard, comps., *The Colonial Virginia Register*, pp. 184–96, *passim*, 202).

Session of Virginia Council of State

MS (Virginia State Library).

Friday February 27th 1778

present

His Excellency;

Dudley Digges   James Madison jr
John Blair   And
David Jameson   Bolling Stark[1]

Esquires

On Considering the proceedings of a general Court Martial of Militia Officers held in Louisa County on Richard Anderson Esquire County Lieutenant: the Board approve the Sentence of the Court Martial & advise His Excellency to discontinue the said Richard Anderson as County Lieutenant agreeable to the said Sentence.[2]

The proceedings of a general Court Martial on the trial of Lieutenants Walker Richardson of the second Regiment of State Troops for fighting a Duel with Lieutenant Triplett of the same Regiment[3] Contrary to the Articles of War section 7th & Article Second, being laid by the Governor before the Board for their Opinion thereupon and it appearing that the said Richardson was Sentenced by the said Court to be cashiered for a Breach of the said Article, but that inasmuch as he had conducted himself as a Gentleman & Officer it was recommended that he be reinstated to his former Rank: The Council taking the same into Consideration are unanimously of Opinion that the said Sentence be Confirmed, & to shew their abhorrence of the practice of Duelling notwithstanding the Recommendation of the Court advised his Excellency to let him remain Cashiered; which the Governor orders accordingly.[4]

The County Lieutenant of Loudoin[5] having complained to the Governor that the Draught of Militia which was appointed to be made in that County on the 16th of this month agreeable to a late Act of Assembly was prevented by the violent & riotous behaviour of the people, in Consequence of which the 11th of March was appointed for Compleating that necessary Business, but that without some exertions of Government there was little reason to expect a more successful Issue than before and the Governor asking the opinion of the Board thereupon they advised his Excellency to give Orders that in case of another Opposition to the Draught the County Lieutenant transmit to him the names of the ring leaders on that occasion, & that he farther desire the Attorney General to prosecute such offenders in the General Court, with the utmost rigour of the Law.[6]

Adjourned till tomorrow 10 oClock

Signed DUDLEY DIGGES

JOHN BLAIR

DAVID JAMESON

JAMES MADISON

BOLLING STARK

[1] Bolling Stark (1733–1788) was named to the Council of State on 24 January 1778 and took his seat on 18 February. He had been a burgess and delegate from Dinwiddie County, and a member of the Convention of May 1776. He would be the state auditor from 1781 to 1783 (*Journal of the House of Delegates*, October 1777, pp. 131, 134; *Journals of the Council of State*, II, 84; Lyon G. Tyler, ed., *Encyclopedia of Virginia Biography*, I, 330).

[2] Early in 1777, Colonel Richard Anderson (1735–1819) had been acquitted by a court-martial of improperly performing his duties as county lieutenant. On 28 October 1777 he was again suspended, this time for "Mal-Conduct" in forming the militia of Louisa "into Divisions for raising the Quota of Men required to be sent from the said County (by the Lieutenant Governor) to this City (Williamsburg) when an Invasion was apprehended." Two months before, the lieutenant governor had ordered Anderson to send two companies "forthwith" to the capital. Perhaps he took the "forthwith" too literally and rushed makeshift companies to Williamsburg without regard for his rotation rosters and without making provisions for replacements, as was ordered in "An act for providing against Invasions & Insurrections," passed on 28 June 1777 (*Journals of the Council of State*, I, 266–67, 351, 467; II, 18; Hening, *Statutes*, IX, 291–97). Despite his conviction by court-martial in 1778, Anderson was elected to the House of Delegates in 1780–1781. He had also been a burgess from 1765 to 1774, a member of his county's Committee of Safety in 1775, and several times a justice of the county court (Earl G. Swem and John W. Williams, eds., *Register of the General Assembly*, p. 11; William G. and Mary Newton Stanard, comps., *The Colonial Virginia Register*, pp. 170–96; Malcolm H. Harris, *History of Louisa County*, pp. 18, 21, 23, 52, 54).

[3] According to John H. Gwathmey, *Historical Register of Virginians in the Revolution*, p. 662, Walker Richardson (d. *ca.* 1783) of James City County became a second lieutenant in the 1st Continental Artillery on 4 March 1778, after serving with the same rank in the state line from 22 April 1777 until he was cashiered ten months later (*Journals of the Council of State*, I, 395, 495). His opponent in the duel must have been Roger Triplett (d. post-1791), a lieutenant in the 2d Virginia Regiment. Triplett was court-martialed in May 1779 for "ungentleman-like behaviour in drinking and carousing with the common soldiers." The verdict cleared him of the charges of being ungentlemanly and a carouser, but he was reprimanded for drinking with the rank and file. On 22 August 1779 he was cashiered for appearing drunk on the parade ground. He is said, however, to have participated in the siege of Yorktown about two years later. After the Revolution he moved to Edgefield County, S.C. (John Gwathmey, *Historical Register of Virginians in the Revolution*, p. 782; Fitzpatrick, *Writings of Washington*, XV, 69; XVI, 150; Katherine Baughman Hocker, comp., genealogical chart of the Triplett family [1945], in Virginia State Library; *Heads of Families: South Carolina* [Washington, 1908], p. 61).

⁴ Section XI of the Articles of War adopted by the Virginia Convention of July 1775 provided for punishment "at the discretion of a general court-martial" of any officer or soldier convicted of abetting or participating in a duel (Hening, *Statutes*, IX, 38). The Articles of War adopted by Congress on 20 September 1776 directed a court-martial at its discretion to cashier any officer of the army of the United States who permitted, abetted, or shared in a duel (*Journals of the Continental Congress*, V, 793).

⁵ Francis Peyton (1748–*ca.* 1814) was three times county lieutenant between 1774 and 1790. He also served as a burgess from 1769 to 1775, a member of the county Committee of Safety from 1774 to 1775, a member of all the state Revolutionary conventions of 1775 and 1776, a trustee for the towns of Colchester, Alexandria, and Middleburg, a delegate to the General Assembly three times between 1776 and 1787, and state senator from 1791 to 1811 (Loudoun County Court Records, Order Book F, p. 497, microfilm in Virginia State Library; William G. and Mary Newton Stanard, comps., *The Colonial Virginia Register*, pp. 180–99 and 201–9, *passim*; Horace E. Hayden, *Virginia Genealogies*, p. 506; Earl G. Swem and John W. Williams, eds., *Register of the General Assembly*, pp. 1–24, 36–80, *passim*).

⁶ The discipline of the Virginia militia had so far deteriorated by 1778 that on 1 June the General Assembly strengthened the control of commanding officers (*Journal of the House of Delegates*, May 1778, p. 35). The need for such legislation had become obvious when an attempted draft of military eligibles in Loudoun County led to rioting on 2 and 3 February. Not until 12 May did the local authorities have the situation sufficiently in hand to bring the nine alleged ringleaders into court for a jury trial. Two of the accused were acquitted. The others were sentenced to punishment ranging from a fine of £3 to a fine of £50 and twenty days in prison. Upon confession by the convicted men of "sorrow and Contrition of heart," the fines were suspended and the terms of imprisonment remitted (Loudoun County Court Records, Order Book G, p. 93, microfilm in Virginia State Library).

To James Madison, Sr.

RC (LC: Madison Papers).

WILLIAMSBG March 6th. 78

HOND SIR

Since I wrote to you by Mr. Cave¹ I have taken the freedom to give an order on Mr. Lee² who is at present at Nants for the money due to you in favour of the Revd. Mr. Madison³ who wanted to procure from Europe a few literary curiosities by means of a French Gentleman just setting out on public Business for this State,⁴ addressed to the management of Mr. Lee. I take the opportunity by Mr: Harrison from Culpeper⁵ of giving you the earliest notice of this circumstance that you may not dispose of your Bills to any other person. As some little return for the favours I am daily receiving from Mr. Madison I shall not charge him more than the legal rate of exchange for the money. I have sent for a few Books also on my own account and Mr. Lee is requested to transmit whatever late publications relate to G. B. or the present state of European Politics. If any Balance should remain after these purposes are provided for Capt. le Maire the french Gentln. alluded to has engaged to lay it out for us in linnen &c.

We have no news here that can be depended on. It is said by Mr. King[6] who is just from Petersbg that a Gentleman was at that place who informed that sundry persons had arrived at Edenton from Providence Island[7] who affirmed that they saw in Providence a London Paper giving an account that Burgoyne's disaster had produced the most violent fermentation in England that the Parliant. has refused to grant the supplies for carrying on the war and that a motion for acknowledging our independ[ence] was overruled by a small majority only. The People who bring this news to Edenton, as the story goes, were Prisoners w[ith] the Enemy at[8] Providence, where they were released by a New-England privateer who suddenly landed her men took possession of the small for[t] that commanded the Harbour and secured several Ves[sels] that lay in it one of which was given up to these men to bring them to the Continent. I leave you to form your own Judgment as to the credibility of this report. I wish it carried stronger marks of truth.[9]

The Govr has just recd a letter from the Capt. of french frigate[10] I mentioned in my last[11] informing him of his safe arrival in N. C. with a rich Cargo of various useful and important Articles, which will be offered for sale to us. The frigate belongs to a Company at Nants in France. We also hear but in a less authentic manner that 7000 Tents have arrived at Martinique on their way from France to the Grand Army[.][12] Salt at South. Quay sells at £3.10 [per bushel?] and is falling.[13] A letter from York-Town [this] moment read informs us that an Exchange of Prisoners is at last agreed on between W. & H.[14]

I wish much to hear from you, and shall continue to write by every opportunity.

I am Dr. Sir with my constant good wishes & &c Yr Affecte. Son

JAMES MADISON JR.

[1] Letter not found. Possibly Belfield Cave (*ca.* 1756–1811), who rose from second lieutenant to colonel in the Orange County militia between 1779 and 1799 and held many local political offices during the last twenty years of his life. He was also a mill owner and farmer. He is frequently mentioned in the Orange County Minute Books, Nos. 2, 3, and 4.

[2] William Lee.

[3] Reverend James Madison.

[4] Captain Jacques Le Maire (*ca.* 1740–1791), after being in Virginia for a few

months, was engaged by the state on 18 March 1778 to return to Europe to purchase artillery and other military stores. Having fulfilled this mission with considerable success, he was commissioned a brevet lieutenant colonel of the Virginia Dragoons and was on active service until after Cornwallis' surrender in October 1781. Thereafter he experienced considerable difficulty in securing the salary and land bounty promised by Virginia (*Calendar of Virginia State Papers*, IV, 13–14; *Journals of the Council of State*, III, 418, 455; Boyd, *Papers of Jefferson*, VII, 430; H. R. McIlwaine, ed., *Official Letters of Virginia Governors*, I, 250–51, 262–63).

⁵ Probably Reverend Thomas Harrison (1750–1814), then of Bromfield Parish, Culpeper County, and Dettingen Parish, Prince William County (*Virginia Magazine of History and Biography*, XXIV [1916], 212). On the address sheet of this letter JM wrote, "favd. by Mr. Harrison."

⁶ This could well have been Miles King (1747–1814), a merchant of Hampton and a member of the House of Delegates in 1777–1778 and continuously from 1784 to 1799. As the captain of a minuteman company in the Revolution he was frequently on patrol duty along Virginia's southeast coast. Late in life he served twice as mayor of Norfolk (*William and Mary Quarterly*, 1st. ser., XVI [1907–8], 108–10; Lyon G. Tyler, ed., *Encyclopedia of Virginia Biography*, II, 363–64).

⁷ Edenton, N.C., is near the mouth of the Chowan River, which flows into Albemarle Sound. Following the word "Edenton" in the manuscript, the words "which he was travelling from" are inclosed in brackets and struck out—whether by JM or someone else cannot be known. New Providence Island is one of the Bahamas.

⁸ Following "at" in the manuscript, the words "Jamaica from whence they got to" are crossed out.

⁹ Late in January 1778, Captain John P. Rathburne, commanding the continental sloop "Providence," hailing from Rhode Island, performed the feat summarized here by JM. No one was killed during the raid. Rathburne released thirty American prisoners (Gardner W. Allen, *A Naval History of the American Revolution* [2 vols.; Boston, 1913], I, 292–95). One of the enemy craft captured by Rathburne probably had been sailed to Edenton. Although the news of the surrender at Saratoga on 17 October 1777 of John Burgoyne (1722–1792), reaching England early in December, caused a prolonged attack in Parliament upon the ministry of Lord North, the opposition failed by a wide margin to muster enough votes to effect a change of administration (William Cobbett, ed., *Parliamentary History of England from the Earliest Period to the Year 1803*, XIX, 414–1255, *passim*).

¹⁰ This is probably the ship mentioned below in Session of Council of State, 12 June 1778, and in Henry to Laurens, 18 June 1778.

¹¹ Letter not found.

¹² Washington's troops, then encamped at Valley Forge. The preceding paragraph, as well as this paragraph down to "Grand Army," are inclosed in brackets. So, too, is the final sentence of this paragraph. These brackets, added many years later by William C. Rives, marked the portions of this manuscript to be printed in Madison, *Letters* (Cong. ed.), I, 31–32.

¹³ A blot on the manuscript obscures the quantity to be had for that price, but it undoubtedly was a bushel. South Quay was in Nansemond County on the Blackwater River, close to its junction with the Nottoway River. With British ships often in control of Chesapeake Bay during the Revolution, South Quay was an important Virginia entrepot because of its easy access by water to Albemarle Sound and thence to the ocean (Rogers Dey Whichard, *The History of Lower Tidewater Virginia* [2 vols.; New York, 1959], II, 148).

¹⁴ By "York-Town" JM most likely meant York, Pa. There Congress met from 30 September 1777 to 27 June 1778, because of the British occupancy of Philadelphia. The agreement between Washington and General William Howe (1729–1814) to exchange prisoners was reached on 10 February 1778 (Fitzpatrick, *Writings of*

Washington, X, 444–46; *Journals of the Continental Congress*, X, 179, 194, 197–98). Word of this agreement had likely been sent to Governor Patrick Henry by one of the delegates of Virginia in Congress.

To William Bradford

RC (Historical Society of Pennsylvania). Accompanying this letter is an address sheet on which there appears, in JM's hand, "To Col. William Bradford Junr Philadelphia." Possibly this sheet has been mistakenly filed with this letter because JM must have known that Philadelphia was in British hands and that his old friend Bradford, then deputy commissary general of musters of the Continental Army, was probably at Valley Forge.

WILLIAMSBG March 23th. 78

DEAR SIR

An Express being just setting off for Head Quarters,[1] I cannot help imparting to you some very agreeable intelligence just recd. A Capt. of a Letter of Marke Vessel from thi[s] State,[2] writes to the Govr. from Cheasepeak Bay that he left Martinique on the 23 Ult. that Letters had been recd. there from France as lat[e] as 1st. from sundry respectable Merchts. relating that the French Court had actually recognized Docr. Franklin as Embassador for the Independent States of America in the most public and authentic manner and that the Docr. had formed an alliance for 30 years[3] That the King of Prussia had notified his intention of sending several ships loaded with Stores to America and had threatened in case of their being interrupted by the British Ship of War to invade Hanover with a formidable Army and that he had declared Empden a free Port.[4] This account also says that the Queen of Portugal had opened her ports to the United States.[5] Some parts of this News carry the face of great improbability, but there are several circumstances that encourage us to hope that the substance of it may not be entirely groundless. It comes through two other oral channels, one in particular by Capt. Bush[6] an intelligent and honest man from this State who left Martinique as lately as the 10th. instt. and affirms that the News respectg Dr. Franklin & the King of Prussia was recd. by the Govr. of M. in dispatches fr[om] France and that 13 rounds were fired from their Canon in reference of the 13 independent States of America.[7] The Express has been detained for the purpose of sealing these few and I can only add that I am as I ought to be

Yrs. &c

J M JR

1 At Valley Forge.

2 That is, a privateer operating under a letter of marque issued by the government of Virginia. The vessel in question has not been identified.

3 Contrary to the statement in this letter, there was no time limit specified in the treaty of alliance. It and a treaty of amity and commerce were concluded between France and the United States on 6 February 1778. King Louis XVI did not grant a formal audience to the American commissioners, Benjamin Franklin, Silas Deane, and Arthur Lee, until 20 March. Congress first announced the news of the alliance on 2 May (*Journals of the Continental Congress*, XI, 418; Wharton, *Revolutionary Diplomatic Correspondence*, II, 490–91, 517).

4 King Frederick the Great of Prussia did not open the ports of his country to U.S. merchants and trading ships until 17 February 1779. Emden is a North Sea port at the mouth of the Ems River. King George III of England was also the Elector of Hanover. In the winter and early spring of 1778, in spite of William Lee's word to Congress that Frederick the Great would acknowledge the independence of the United States as soon as King Louis XVI did so, the Prussian Monarch was too concerned about having the support of England in the Bavarian succession crisis to offend her by exhibiting marked friendliness toward the American rebels (Wharton, *Revolutionary Diplomatic Correspondence*, II, 213, 343, 406, 447, 489, 510–11, 516–17; III, 66; Doniol, *Histoire*, III, 112–16).

5 This report was false. A decree of 4 July 1776 was still effectively barring American vessels from entering Portuguese harbors. And yet, by early 1778, the government of Queen Maria I was exhibiting restlessness against the longstanding commercial entente with England. Rumors were afloat that the Portuguese court would soon attune its commercial policy with that of the United States and France (Wharton, *Revolutionary Diplomatic Correspondence*, II, 161, 188, 207, 491).

6 Probably Goodrich Boush (*ca.* 1738–1782) of Norfolk County, captain of the "Congress," an armed vessel of Virginia's navy (Robert Armistead Stewart, *The History of Virginia's Navy of the Revolution* [Richmond, 1934], pp. 16, 43–44, 153).

7 On a date not ascertained but probably later than reported here, the governor of Martinique, assisted by William Bingham, the American agent at Saint Pierre, feted the alliance between France and the United States (C[abuzell] A. Banbuck, *Histoire politique, économique et sociale de la Martinique sous l'ancien régime, 1635–1789* [Paris, 1935], p. 149, n. 22).

Session of Virginia Council of State

MS (Virginia State Library).

Tuesday April 7th 1778

present
His Excellency

Dudley Digges   James Madison &
David Jameson   Bolling Stark

Esquires

. . . .

The Board taking into Consideration the Cases of the several Criminals Sentenced by the general court to be executed & it appearing from the unanimous recommendation of the Judges, the grounds of which were explained to the Board by the Honourable John Blair[1] one of the Judges, that Frederick Rampendall & Elizabeth Orphan[2] are proper objects of Mercy the Board do advise the Governor to grant them his pardon And his Excellency orders pardons to be made out accordingly.

. . . .

The Board being credibly informed that his Excellency General Washington has been unsupplied for some time past with many articles of Living which Custom & the great fatigues to which he is constantly exposed must make necessary to the preservation of his health; and considering that it may be impossible to provide these Articles in the exhausted part of America where the Army is at present fixed, do advise the Governor to direct the Commissary of Stores to procure a Stock of good rum, wine, Sugar & such other Articles as his Excellency may think needful & send them on to head Quarters, to be charged either to the Continent, or to be considered as a present from this State, to the General, as the assembly may hereafter direct; & the Governor is advised to inform them at their next meeting of his proceedings herein.[3]

Adjourned till tomorrow 10 oClock

Signed   DUDLEY DIGGES
DAVID JAMESON
JAMES MADISON
BOLLING STARK

[1] John Blair became judge of the General Court on 23 January 1778, even though he remained on the Council of State until 28 February. Later he was the court's chief justice.

[2] The editors have been unable to learn more about Rampendall, Orphan, and their crime. Their conviction must have occurred between 2 and 28 March (Hening, *Statutes*, IX, 402).

[3] On 16 May 1778 Washington thanked "the Governor and Council for their agreeable present." He added: "It is now on its way from the head of Elk; When it arrives I make no doubt, but it will find us in a humour to do it all manner of justice" (Fitzpatrick, *Writings of Washington*, XI, 394). Who paid for the "agreeable present" is not clear. It goes unmentioned both in the journal of the House of Delegates and in the journal of the Council of State.

Session of Virginia Council of State

MS (Virginia State Library).

Thursday April 30th 1778.

present

His Excellency the Governor;

John Page	David Jameson &
Dudley Digges	James Madison jr

Esquires

The Business hitherto done without a regular Board was this day laid before them and was approved of.[1]

. . . .

Adjourned till Tomorrow 10 oClock

Signed   JOHN PAGE
DUDLEY DIGGES
DAVID JAMESON
JAMES MADISON

[1] This action demonstrates the council's method of procedure relating to earlier business done by too few members of that body to constitute a quorum. Thus, at seven meetings between 16 and 29 April, JM and two or three other councilors had reached numerous decisions "subject to the future Controul of the Board" (*Journals of the Council of State*, II, 121–25).

Session of Virginia Council of State

MS (Virginia State Library).

Friday May 1st 1778.

present
His Excellency;

John Page	James Madison &
David Jameson	Bolling Stark

Esquires

. . . .

The Governor laid before the Board a Letter from Colonel Muter[1] informing him that Phillips the noted Traitor has again made an Insurection in Princess Anne County at the head of fifty men;[2] Whereupon they do Advise his Excellency to order one hundred men from

the Militia of Nansemond to act in Conjunction with the party which
Colonel Thomas R. Walker[3] may raise for quelling these Insurgents—to
offer a Reward of five hundred Dollars for apprehending Phillips the
Ringleader dead or alive & to direct that the Booty taken from the said
Insurgents be divided amongst the Captors thereof. His Excellency
having written Letters to the County Lieutenant of Nansemond,[4] Colo.
Thomas R. Walker & Colonel John Wilson[5] on the Subject the same
were read approved of & ordered to be recorded.
  Adjourned till tomorrow 10 oClock

                                         Signed   JOHN PAGE
                                                  DAVID JAMESON
                                                  JAMES MADISON
                                                  BOLLING STARK

[1] After serving for over a year as captain of the "Hero" galley, George Muter
(d. 1811), a merchant of Scottish birth, was appointed on 18 November 1777 a lieutenant colonel of a newly recruited regiment of state artillery. Later he was commander of the state garrison regiment and commissioner of the state war office. In
1785 he became a judge in the district of Kentucky and also served as judge of the
Appellate Court of Kentucky from 1792 until his retirement as Chief Justice in
1806 (Louis A. Burgess, ed., *Virginia Soldiers of 1776*, II, 685; *Journal of the House
of Delegates*, October 1777, pp. 28, 30; *Journals of the Council of State*, I, 53, 118,
393, 456; III, 449; *Register of the Kentucky State Historical Society*, XXVII [1929],
468; *Journal of the House of Representatives of the Commonwealth of Kentucky*
[Frankfort, 1806], p. 134; Kentucky Records Research Committee, *Kentucky Ceme-
tery Records*, I [Lexington, 1960], 376).

[2] Josiah Philips or Phillips (d. 1778), a former laborer of Princess Anne County
who led a band of robbers which terrorized the southeastern corner of Virginia,
had been in prison as recently as January 1778, when the council granted a reward
to his captors (*Journals of the Council of State*, II, 58). Although Philips claimed
to be acting under a commission from Dunmore—and thus to be a prisoner of war
rather than a common bandit—Thomas Jefferson described him as "a mere robber,
who availing himself of the troubles of the times, collected a banditti, retired to the
Dismal swamp, and from thence sallied forth, plundering and maltreating the neighboring inhabitants, and covering himself, without authority, under the name of a
British subject." Shortly after Muter's complaint, Jefferson drew up a bill to attaint
Philips and his principal confederates "unless they render themselves to justice
within a certain time." This, the only bill of attainder passed by the Virginia legislature during the Revolutionary War, was introduced on 28 May and became a law
three days later (Paul Leicester Ford, ed., *The Works of Thomas Jefferson* [12 vols.;
New York, 1904–5], XI, 405–6; *Journal of the House of Delegates*, May 1778, pp.
22–24, 28, 35; October 1778, p. 39; Hening, *Statutes*, VIII, 463–64; W. P. Trent, "The
Case of Josiah Philips," *American Historical Review*, I [1895–96], 444–54).
  Philips and four of his companions were captured on 16 June and lodged in jail,
but the council did not grant its promised reward to the "Voluntier Company"
which captured them until nearly five months later (*Virginia Gazette* [Williams-
burg, Purdie], 19 June 1778; *Journals of the Council of State*, II, 210). The dread

with which his neighbors regarded Philips is shown by the "Petition signed by a number of Inhabitants of the Counties of Princess Anne & Norfolk praying that a strong & sufficient Guard may be kept over Philips & the rest of the Prisoners of his daring Party of Robbers lately taken & sent to the Public Jail in Williamsburg." The council responded by increasing the number of sentries at the jail and directing the jailer to keep "a strict watch over the said Prisoners" (*Journals of the Council of State*, II, 169). The *Virginia Gazette* (Purdie) of 30 October 1778 reported: "On Friday the 16th commenced, and continued to the 21st, the trial of sundry prisoners from the publick jail, when Josiah Philips, James Hodges, Robert Hodges, and Henry M'Clellan, from Princess Anne for robbing the publick waggons (and who were accused of murder, treason, and sundry other outrages) were capitally convicted." They were hanged on 23 November (*Virginia Gazette* [Williamsburg, Dixon and Hunter], 4 December 1778).

³ Thomas Reynolds Walker (d. 1788) served as an officer (captain to colonel) of Princess Anne County minutemen or militia from 1776 to 1779. He also held many other local offices, being a member of the Committeee of Safety in 1774 and 1776, county escheator in 1779, and a vestryman of Lynnhaven Parish for many years. In 1777 he was commissioned to oversee the removal of Princess Anne and Norfolk residents who were considered enemies of America (*Journals of the Council of State*, I, 127, 200, 350, 481; John H. Gwathmey, *Historical Register of Virginians in the Revolution*, p. 801; *Lower Norfolk County Virginia Antiquary*, I [1895–96], 9, 46, 64; V [1904–5], 31; *Virginia Magazine of History and Biography*, XV [1907–8], 191; XVI [1908–9], 173).

⁴ Willis Riddick (1725–1800) was county lieutenant of Nansemond County. His inept defense of Suffolk against a British incursion in May 1779 brought him into public disfavor for several years (Jos[eph] B. Dunn, *The History of Nansemond County, Virginia* [n.p., 1907], pp. 43–44). Riddick was a burgess from 1757 to 1771; a member of the state Revolutionary conventions of March 1775 and May 1776; a delegate to the General Assembly from 1776 to 1779 and from 1784 to 1800; and a delegate to the Virginia Convention of 1788 to consider the Federal Constitution (William G. and Mary Newton Stanard, comps., *The Colonial Virginia Register*, pp. 141–88, *passim*, 202, 209; Earl G. Swem and John W. Williams, eds., *Register of the General Assembly*, pp. 1–8 and 20–56, *passim*, 244).

⁵ John Wilson (1730–1779) was Norfolk County lieutenant in 1777–1778, a burgess in 1769–1771, and a delegate to the General Assembly in 1776–1778. A bounty was first put on Philips' head as a result of Wilson's letter in June 1777 to the Governor in Council, stating that "sundry evil disposed persons, to the number of ten, or twelve, have conspired together, to foment a Dangerous Insurrection in the said County, and at present are lurking in secret places threatening and doing actual mischief to the peaceable and well affected Inhabitants of this Commonwealth; and that Livy Sykes, Josiah Phillips and John Ashley are the principles who govern and direct the said party in their atrocious actions." The council then offered $150 to any person or persons who should capture any of the three (Earl G. Swem and John W. Williams, eds., *Register of the General Assembly*, pp. 1–6; *Journals of the Council of State*, I, 435–36).

Session of Virginia Council of State

MS (Virginia State Library).

Monday May 25th 1778.

present

His Excellency;

John Page	Nathaniel Harrison
Dudley Digges	David Jameson &
Thomas Walker	James Madison jr

Esquires

. . . .

The Board being informed that the Barracks at York Town were lately burnt by some unknown accident & it being absolutely necessary that the same should be rebuilt as speedily as possible they do advise the Governor to empower & direct Mr James Taylor to purchase Timber & Materials upon the best Terms they can be had, for rebuilding the said Barracks so soon as proper persons shall be employed for that purpose.[1]

Report being made by the assistant Engineer respecting the Situation of York & the additional Fortifications necessary for that place as a protection to our Allies; and the Board taking the same under their consideration they do advise the Governor to direct Colonel Marshall to consult with Captain Fourneer the assistant Engineer[2] & take the proper Steps for extending the Works at that place & for fortifying the Gloster Shore so as to cooperate with York, and to encrease the number of Labourers for the purpose upon the best Terms possible. And the Governor is also advised to desire the Navy Board to direct that two Gun Boats be immediately built according to a plan to be furnished by Captain Fourneer.

Adjourned till tomorrow 10 oClock

Signed   JOHN PAGE
DUDLEY DIGGES
THOMAS WALKER[3]
NATHANIEL HARRISON
DAVID JAMESON
JAMES MADISON

---

[1] The barracks at Yorktown could barely have been completed before they were burned. Barracks sufficient to hold 250 men had been ordered by the Council of State on 25 July 1777, but two months later no progress had been made because no

241

contractor wanted to undertake the project. On 22 August, Charles Minnis offered "his Service, as far as he is able," but he died six months later, and on 3 March his commission was transferred to James Taylor (*Journals of the Council of State*, I, 457, 462, 472–73; II, 96). Taylor may have been the James Taylor (*ca.* 1731–1786) who was a carpenter-joiner and moved his business from Yorktown to Surry County by 1758. In 1759 he was a constable in that county (*Virginia Gazette* [Williamsburg, Hunter], 17 April 1752; Surry County Court Records, Order Book, 1757–1763, p. 175; Order Book, 1775–1785, p. 395; Order Book, 1786–1789, pp. 86, 137; and Surry County Will Book, No. 12, pp. 142–43, all on microfilm in the Virginia State Library).

2 Colonel Thomas Marshall. J. F. (F. I.) Fournier (Fourneer, Fornier), a self-styled teacher of mathematics and military science, was appointed on 18 October 1777 as assistant engineer for Virginia. Shortly after beginning work on the Yorktown fortifications, he was promoted in consideration of his "Abilities & Services" to "Second Engineer for this State with the Rank & pay of Major." The purpose of the defensive works had been described two weeks earlier by Governor Henry. They were "for protecting against a Superior Fleet of our Enemy, any Ships of War as well as Merchantmen belonging to our Allies that may have occasion to come to this State." The council then asked the inspector general and Fournier to report on the advisability of locating these fortifications at Yorktown, "which is supposed to be preferable to any other Place in the Country" (*Journals of the Council of State*, II, 12, 132, 147; *Virginia Gazette* [Williamsburg, Purdie], 22 August 1777).

3 Thomas Walker (1715–1794) of Castle Hill, Albemarle County. For a summary of his notable career as a physician, soldier, explorer, land speculator, commissioner to make treaties with Indians and to extend westward the boundary line between North Carolina and Virginia, and as a burgess, member of the House of Delegates, and privy councilor, see Thomas Perkins Abernethy's article in the *Dictionary of American Biography*, XIX, 360–61.

Election to Virginia House of Delegates Voided

Printed text (*Journal of the House of Delegates*, May 1778, p. 20).

WEDNESDAY, May 27, 1778.

Resolved, That James Madison, jun. Esq. who at the last election[1] for the county of Orange, was elected and returned one of the delegates to serve in General Assembly, being at the time of election a member of the Council of State, was incapable of being elected a member of this House;[2]

Ordered, That the Speaker be desired to issue a writ for the election of a delegate for the county of Orange, in the room of the said James Madison, jun. Esq.[3]

1 Among the Election Returns, House of Delegates, 1776–1782, MSS in the Virginia State Library, is the following certificate:

Orange &ct.

This is to certify that, on thursday the 23rd. of this Month (April, being Court day[)] Wm. Moore & James Madison Junior Esqrs. were duly elected Delegates for the said County to serve in General Assembly for one year next following
given under my hand & seal this
23rd. day of April 1778

FRANCIS MOORE, S.O.C.
[Sheriff, Orange County]

2 This was in accordance with Article XI of the Form of Government of Virginia (Hening, *Statutes*, IX, 116).

3 No one was able to serve in JM's stead at that session, since it adjourned on 1 June 1778. On 18 June 1778, however, Francis Moore certified to the election that day of Charles Porter "in the room of James Madison the Younger" (Election Returns, House of Delegates, 1776–1782, MSS in the Virginia State Library).

Session of Virginia Council of State

MS (Virginia State Library).

Friday June 12th 1778
present
John Page Esquire Lieutenant Governor;

| Dudley Digges | Nathaniel Harrison & |
| Thomas Walker | James Madison jr |

Esquires

It appearing from satisfactory Information respecting the Case of Toby a negro man Slave belonging to Benjamin Wilkins,[1] now under Sentence of Death by the Court of Prince George County for Burglary that the said Toby is a proper object of Mercy the Board do advise the Lieutenant Governor to grant a pardon in the said Toby's favour And a pardon issued accordingly.

The Board being of Opinion that a Serjeant & Eight Men will be a sufficient Guard over the public powder in Hanover they do advise the Lieutenant Governor to give orders for the present guard to be reduced to that number & orders were given accordingly.

The Board having purchased a large Cargo of Goods in compliance with a late Resolution of the general assembly,[2] it is become indispensably necessary, not only for the Reception of the said Cargo, but to prevent the Confusion that would arise from its being sold by the Commissary of Stores, to appoint some able & discreet person to take charge & dispose of such Articles as are to be sold to the Inhabitants at large & Robert Prentis esquire of this City[3] offering his Services on this occasion & to furnish four Storehouses for the Reception & safe keeping of the said Cargo & other Cargoes that may be purchased under the said Resolution the Board do agree in consideration of the abilities of the said Robert Prentis & the convenience & fitness of the Storehouses aforesaid to employ him in the said business giving him as a full allowance for his trouble therein at the rate of thirty five pounds per Month & fifteen pounds per Month as rent for his Houses so long as they shall be used by the public; engaging to give him three Months notice before they discontinue the use of them. (Bond executed)

Adjourned till Thursday next 10 oClock.

Signed   JOHN PAGE
            DUDLEY DIGGES
            THOMAS WALKER
            NATHL HARRISON
            JAMES MADISON

[1] Little is known about Benjamin Wilkins (d. *ca.* 1798) except that he owned fourteen slaves and 583 acres in Prince George County in 1782 (Prince George County Land Tax Book, 1782, p. 15, in Virginia State Library).

[2] On 30 May 1778 the following resolution was passed:

"Whereas, it is represented, that certain cargoes of goods, containing many articles necessary for the army, and others, which are not necessary for them, are offered for sale to the Governor and Council, who doubt whether a purchase of the whole, including such unnecessary articles, may be approved,

"*Resolved*, That they be empowered and advised to purchase the same, or any other cargoes of a like nature, if to be done on terms which they think reasonable; that such parts thereof as shall be necessary for the use of the troops raised by this Commonwealth, be disposed of for their use, as by law heretofore directed, and such others as are unnecessary and improper for them, be sold in such parts of the country, and on such terms, as the Governor and Council may think most for the general good, not giving a preference to any person in the sale thereof" (*Journal of the House of Delegates,* May 1778, pp. 29, 33).

The cargo in question is described more fully below in Henry to Laurens, 18 June 1778 and n. 5.

[3] Robert Prentis, a member of a prominent Williamsburg mercantile family, had sold guns and supplies to the army in 1776. He had been the clerk of Receiver General Richard Corbin in 1775 and later was one of the commissioners appointed to rent or sell Lord Dunmore's estate. In 1778 he was a delegate from York County in the General Assembly. His life dates have not been found, but he was still living in Williamsburg in 1805 (*Journal of the House of Delegates,* October 1777, p. 116; May 1778, pp. 5, 33, 52–53, 63, 66; *Journals of the Council of State,* I, 281; III, 343; *Virginia Magazine of History and Biography,* XIII [1905–6], 424; XXVIII [1920], 63; XXXII [1924], 250–51; Rutherfoord Goodwin, *A Brief & True Report Concerning Williamsburg in Virginia* [3d ed.; Richmond, 1940], p. 270; William Armstrong Crozier, ed., *Williamsburg Wills* [*Virginia County Records,* Vol. III, New York, 1906], p. 29).

Patrick Henry in Council to Henry Laurens

RC (NA: PCC, No. 71, I, 153–54). Entirely in Henry's hand.
Read in Congress on 26 June, according to the docket.

Wms.burgh June 18th. 1778

SIR.[1]

General Washington sent me an Account of the Drafted Soldiers that have joined the Army from this State; & it appears that not one half of the Number voted by the Assembly have got to Camp. Truth obliges me to add that very few more of the Drafts will ever be got into the Service. I lament this capital Deficiency in our Quota of Troops; but no Efforts of the Executive have been sufficient to prevent it.[2] The Assembly at their late sitting, have directed three hundred & fifty Cavalry & two thousand Infantry to be forthwith raised & to join the grand Army.[3] Some of the former will be raised, but from every Appearance I am sorry to say there is but too little Reason to expect any Success in getting the Infantry. I can only assure you Sir that I shall pay due Regard to the Requisition you are pleased to make for compleating our Quota of men by exerting myself to the utmost altho' I fear it will be in vain.[4]

The honble Dudley Digges Esqr. lately wrote you a Letter on the Subject of furnishing Congress with a large Quantity of Goods lately purchased by this State. I wish to be favord with an Answer to that proposition quickly as possible because the Goods cannot be disposed of 'til it arrives, & their laying long on Hand will produce some capital Inconveniences.[5] Tobaco in payment will be greatly prefer'd to Cash of which we have a superabundance producing Evils of the most alarming Nature.[6]

With the highest Regard I have the Honor to be Sir
Your most obedient & very humble Servant,

P. HENRY

The honble
Mr. Laurens

---

[1] Henry Laurens (1724–1792), a South Carolina delegate in Congress in 1777–1779 and 1784–1785, was at this time president of Congress. In 1780 he was captured by the British while en route to the Netherlands to negotiate a loan.

[2] George Washington wrote Henry on 23 May 1778 to complain that Virginia's reinforcements for the army were far short of expectations. Only 716 draftees and substitutes had joined the army, not counting 41 left on the road and 42 deserters

(Fitzpatrick, *Writings of Washington*, XI, 438–39). These men were raised under "An Act for speedily recruiting the Virginia Regiments on the continental establishment, and for raising additional troops of Volunteers" (Hening, *Statutes*, IX, 337–49).

3 "An act for raising Volunteers to join the Grand Army" and "An act for raising a regiment of Horse" were both signed into law on 1 June 1778 (*ibid.*, IX, 445–51; *Journal of the House of Delegates*, May 1778, p. 35).

4 On 10 June 1778 Congress approved a letter to the Virginia executive stating that:

"In duty, therefore, to their constituents, Congress earnestly call upon you, sir, and your State, to adopt the most effectual and vigorous measures for speedily reinforcing the continental army with your quota of troops. . . .

"The urgent necessity for the provisions with which your State is to furnish the army, induces Congress to press upon you, sir, immediate and constant attention to this important business, and the present absence of the enemy's ships from the bay of Chesapeake may be improved by seizing the opportunity of water conveyance to the Head of Elk" (*Journals of the Continental Congress*, XI, 583–84; see also Henry to Virginia Delegates, 20 January 1778, n. 4).

5 Digges's letter has not been found, but it was probably written on 8 June 1778. On that day, in the absence of Governor Henry and Lieutenant Governor Page, Digges presided over the council meeting which decided that:

"The Commissary of Stores for this State is impowered & directed to purchase of Peter Francis Chevallie such of the Goods & Merchandizes as remain unsold or are not particularly excepted of the Cargo on board the Fier Rodorique belonging to the said Mr Chevallie allowing for the same Six Shillings Virginia Money for every Levie [the Spanish real] of the first Cost in France & engaging in part of payment therefor to deliver alongside of the said Ship at York fifteen hundred Hogsheads of Tobacco & five hundred Hogsheads alongside any other Ship Mr Chevallie may send to Alexandria the remainder of the Debt to be deposited by Mr Chevallie in the Hands of the Treasurer bearing Interest at the Rate of Six per Centum per Annum as long as it shall there remain or be laid out for him in Tobacco for which he is to pay the Cost & all expences incurred by ye Agent in Providing it" (*Journals of the Council of State*, II, 146).

The French merchant ship "Fier Roderique" arrived in Hampton Roads, Va., around 28 May, having been sent to America by Pierre Augustin Caron de Beaumarchais. On 10 June Congress requested Governor Henry to purchase, "as cheap as he can," a long list of goods consisting mainly of clothing, powder, bullets, and wine. On 9 July Congress decided to buy "such part of the *Roderique's* cargo, purchased by the State of Virginia, as they shall think wanting for continental use" (*Journals of the Continental Congress*, XI, 576, 584, 678; *Journal of the House of Delegates*, October 1779, pp. 80–81).

6 Why the governor requested tobacco rather than the depreciated paper currency is suggested by the quotation in n. 5. Unlike tobacco, the paper had almost no value abroad in purchasing military supplies.

Session of Virginia Council of State

MS (Virginia State Library).

Thursday July 2d 1778.

present
His Excellency

Dudley Digges	David Jameson &
Nathaniel Harrison	James Madison jun.

Esquires

. . . .

It being represented to the Board that Doubts have arisen concerning the extent of the privilege granted to the Officers and Soldiers raised in this State of being supplied with Goods from the public Stores at the reduced prices—They do advise the Governor to direct the Commissary of Stores in this City[1] and the Agent appointed to issue Necessaries to Virginia's Quota of Troops in the grand army,[2] not to furnish Goods at the said prices to Commissaries Contractors or Waggon-Masters or any others retaining to the Army whose Salaries are not Limited or ascertained by Law, it being presumed that such persons have provided an adequate reward for their Services in their respective Contracts and consequently do not come within the intention of the Law.

And the Board considering the great confusion and abuses that might result from the Commissary of Stores selling Goods at ye reduced prices to the Troops without any regulation as to the Time of applying and the quantity to be taken, do Advise the Governor to Instruct Mr Armistead not to issue any Goods to the Officers or Soldiers unless their Wants be certified in a Necessary Roll, specifying the name and wants of each Individual, by the Commander in chief of the State Troops for the time being, at each Station, which Roll the Governor is further advised to direct the Commanders in chief aforesaid to provide once a Month as soon as may be after the Day on which the Troops receive their Monthly pay And his Excellency orders accordingly.[3]

Adjourned till tomorrow 10 oClock

Signed   DUDLEY DIGGES
NATHL HARRISON
DAVID JAMESON
JAMES MADISON JUN

1 William Armistead, Jr. (1754–1793), of New Kent County resigned from the Court of Admiralty in August 1776, and on 3 December 1777 he became Virginia's commissary of stores. He held this office until 18 February 1782. His duties were "to receive all Goods & other Necessaries that may be imported or purchased for the use of this State and to purchase all such other Articles as may be wanted from time to time & to deliver them out in such manner as shall be found Necessary, & to do every thing in his power for preserving the Stores that may come into his possession." Armistead was one of the representatives of his county in the House of Delegates from 1784 to 1786 (*Journals of the Council of State*, I, 122; II, 40, 359; III, 47; Earl G. Swem and John W. Williams, eds., *Register of the General Assembly*, pp. 20, 22; C. G. Chamberlayne, ed., *The Vestry Book and Register of St. Peter's Parish, New Kent and James City Counties, Virginia* [Richmond, 1937], p. 557).

2 Colonel Richard Morris (*ca.* 1746–1821), first of Hanover and later of Louisa County, was a planter and merchant. In 1776 he was a state treasury official and a state commissary and paymaster. On 3 June 1778 he was named in place of John Hawkins as purchaser of provisions for the Continental Army. His public career appears to have closed following his service as state co-ordinator of the specific grain tax, 1781–1782, and as a member from Louisa County in the House of Delegates in 1788 (John H. Gwathmey, *Historical Register of Virginians in the Revolution*, p. 566; *Journals of the Council of State*, II, 143; *Calendar of Virginia State Papers*, II, 397, 491; Louisa County Records, Will Book No. 6, p. 270, microfilm in Virginia State Library).

3 This order was apparently not strong enough to solve the problem of supplies for the soldiers, for on 26 October 1778, when JM was still at Montpelier, the Council of State took the following action:

"It being represented to the Board that great abuses are practised by the Soldiers in their Dealings at the public Store whereby they obtain more Goods than are necessary for their own use making Sale of the overplus and that the former Regulations directing that necessary Rolls from each Station signed by the Commanding Officer to be sent to the Commissary of Stores monthly, specifying the Goods wanted for each Officer & Soldier is neglected: The Governor is advised to issue Orders to the Commissary of Stores to refuse delivering the Goods to the Officers & Soldiers of this State unless the Names of the Officers & Soldiers be mentioned & the several Articles be specified in such Rolls from each Station aforesaid; & to direct the Clerk to transmit a Copy of this Order to the Commanding Officer at each Garrison Which his Excellency Orders accordingly" (*Journals of the Council of State*, II, 203–4).

Patrick Henry in Council to Henry Laurens

RC (NA: PCC, No. 71, I, 165–67). In the hand of a clerk, except for the complimentary close, signature, and postscript.

WMSBURG July 8th 1778

SIR

Some Resolutions of Congress & proceedings of the Board of War,[1] have been lately transmitted to me, by which it appears that an Expedition against Fort Detroit is resolved on. In order to effect the purposes of it 2000 of the Militia together with Amunition, provisions, Horses, military Stores, Cloathing &c. &c. are requested to be furnished by this State: I should most chearfully exert myself in accomplishing the Desires of the Board of War & to provide without Delay whatever this Country could afford for the Expedition, agreeable to the Resolution of Congress, did not Reasons of the greatest Importance arrest me in the first Step. I entreat for the Candour and attention of Congress while I submit to their Consideration some of the Reasons which have induced me to think the Expedition to Detroit as announced to me by the Board of War, utterly impracticable at this Season of the year, & under our present Circumstances. In the first place it is impossible to procure Flour in Time. I observe it is proposed to be purchased in the County of Goochland. Neither that, or the adjacent Counties, or adjacent Country can afford the Quantity wanted. Suppose the Contrary, the transportation of it, is absolutely impossible by the Time required.

The Horses may possibly be got but I will venture to say that the immediate purchase of 5000 & upwards which are required will raise the price to four Times the Estimate, and amount I think to near half a million of pounds.[2]

Indeed I am satisfied upon a view of the Articles wanted for this Expedition, that the preparations ought to have begun early in the Winter, & that those now making cannot be compleated before next Spring. 5000 pack Saddles, tight seasoned Casks for carrying the powder, collecting the Cattle together, transporting 30,000 lb. Lead from the Mines, fabricating 1000 horse Belts 400 felling Axes 3000 Hatchets, Kettles made of rolled Iron, procuring Tents, Knapsacks, Haversacks, complete Suits of Clothes for the Regulars, the recruiting, Arming, accoutring & Disciplining them; forming Magazines of provisions & military Stores, finding the means of transportation thro that Country: These and a vast Variety of other particulars which I do not enumerate, cannot be accomplished of a Sudden: On the contrary, from a Scarcity of Workmen & materials, from the want of Waggons, from the exhausted State of this Country, as to several Articles called for, and the distressed Situation of our people, Resources & Supplies, I think the next Spring, is as soon as the march proposed can be thought of.

My perfect Reliance on the Wisdom of Congress makes me wish by no means to touch upon any matter that lays within their province to determine. And I should not say anything now touching the general

Expence of this Expedition, did not the advanced price of most Articles in this Country, joined to the nature of the proposed Service & the plan for effecting it make it my Duty to hint, that in my Opinion the amount will far exceed the Ideas of Congress; & perhaps approach to a Comparison with the Sum which the grand Army of Infantry costs the united States for the same length of Time. All I request is that Congress will be pleased to review the Estimate of Expences the nature of the Business and the Time for executing it; And if they shall be pleased to persist in the first plan, I shall think it my Duty to forward to the utmost what they direct.

In the mean Time, Lieutenant Colonel Campbell[3] who brings me the Despatches on this Subject, is now here, having the Stores of the State thrown open to him, & is desired to select such Articles of Clothes as the Troops to be raised, may want & can be found in them. Orders to the Leadmines will also be sent to forward some Lead towards Fort Randolph[4] or Pittsburgh.

The Miseries of the people of Virginia who live exposed to the Assaults of the Savages, affect me most Sensibly. And in my anxiety to See something doing for their protection, I hope for Excuse from Congress when I suggest, that if an Expedition is directed against the Hostile Tribes nearest our Frontiers, very good Consequences might result. Such a Step seems to be free from the Objections which are hinted against the Attack of Detroit, where a post will be difficult to maintain while the great intermediate Country is occupied by Hostile Indians, & from which it seems easy for the enemy to retreat with all their Stores while they are Superior upon the adjacent Waters[5]

Our Frontier people wish for offensive Measures against the Indian Towns & will enlist freely for that purpose. But I cannot help doubting whether the apparent Difficulties of succeeding against Detroit at present, will not be an Obstacle with them against engaging in the Service.

I beg to be favoured with the Decisions of Congress upon this matter quickly as possible; that necessary Measures may not be delayed, or useless purchases or Expenditures for preparations be made by the several Agents who are already engaged in their respective Departments.[6]

The Sentiments contained in this Letter come from a full Board of Council as well as from me.[7]

I beg to be informed whether it is necessary to push forward the Cavalry & Infantry voted by the last Assembly here. They are to serve but a Short Time & if they are not wanted, much Expence will be Saved by knowing it in Time & preventing their Inlistments which will be made upon a most expensive plan & which nothing but a supposed necessity induced the Legislature to adopt.[8]

    With great Regard I have the Honor to be Sir
    your most obedient & very humble Servant

P. Henry

P.S. The Express has Orders to wait for an Answer to this, & indeed the State of affairs seems to require it speedily

The honble Henry Laurens Esqr.
President of Congress

    [1] On 11 June 1778 Congress accepted the Board of War's recommendation that a defensive war would be an insufficient protection against the western Indians and resolved that "an expedition be immediately undertaken, whose object shall be, to reduce, if practicable, the garrison of Detroit, and to compel to terms of peace such of the Indian nations now in arms against these states as lie on, or contiguous to, the route betwixt Fort Pitt and Detroit." The governor and council of Virginia were requested "to call forth such a body of their militia, (not exceeding 2,500 men,) as shall be judged necessary to complete" the force of three thousand men which was to participate in the campaign (*Journals of the Continental Congress*, XI, 588–89).

    [2] Congress had estimated the cost of the Detroit expedition as "about £97,990 equal to Dollars 261,306" (*ibid.*, XI, 590).

    [3] Richard Campbell (d. 1781), sheriff of Shenandoah County in 1774, became lieutenant colonel of the 13th Virginia Regiment on 20 February 1778. He served at Pittsburgh and in the McIntosh expedition against the Indians of the Ohio region (below, n. 5). As a lieutenant colonel of the 4th Virginia Regiment, he was wounded at Camden on 25 April 1781 and killed at Eutaw Springs on 8 September 1781 (Fitzpatrick, *Writings of Washington*, VIII, 71 n.; IX, 285 n.; F. B. Heitman, *Historical Register of Officers of the Continental Army*, p. 114; Lyon G. Tyler, ed., *Encyclopedia of Virginia Biography*, II, 245–46; John W. Wayland, *A History of Shenandoah County, Virginia* [Strasburg, Va., 1927], p. 110).

    [4] Fort Randolph, at the junction of the Great Kanawha and Ohio rivers, was named for Peyton Randolph in 1776. Its former name was Fort Pleasant (H. R. McIlwaine, ed., *Official Letters of Virginia Governors*, I, 39).

    [5] On 25 July 1778 when Congress abandoned the expedition against Detroit, it ordered General Lachlan McIntosh to assemble fifteen hundred troops at Fort Pitt to "destroy such towns of the hostile tribes of Indians as he, in his discretion, shall think will most effectually tend to chastise and terrify the savages, and to check their ravages on the frontiers of these states." Henry was asked to send militia to join McIntosh (*Journals of the Continental Congress*, XI, 720–21). On 6 August the officers of fourteen western counties were ordered by Henry and the Council of State to provide as many militiamen "as General Mackintosh may demand" (*Journals of the Council of State*, II, 174, 220–21; below, Session of Council, 10 November 1778, n. 1; and Henry to Laurens, 23 November 1778).

    [6] The decision of Congress to give up the Detroit campaign "for the present" was announced to the Council of State on 6 August (*Journals of the Council of State*, II, 174).

[7] On 7 July the Council of State, "considering the advanced Season of the year, the extensive preparations called for & the exhausted State of this Country as to most of the particulars which are to compose them, with the dispersed Situation of the Militia & the distance of the Object, are of Opinion that the Expedition is utterly impracticable within the present Campaign And Advise his Excellency to write to Congress submitting to their Consideration the cogent objections which support such an Opinion giving Congress Notice at the same time, that the Executive power of this State will give every requisite Aid to the persons employed in procuring the Articles necessary for the Enterprize until their ultimate decision in this matter be known." The next day the council "read approved of & ordered to be recorded" Henry's letter of 8 July (*ibid.,* II, 161–62).

[8] The men to be recruited under "An act for raising Volunteers to join the Grand Army" and "An act for raising a regiment of Horse" were to serve only until the end of 1778 (Hening, *Statutes,* IX, 445, 450). On 25 July Congress resolved that a change in circumstances had rendered the "services of those troops at present inexpedient" and asked that Henry cease their enlistment. However, he was asked to send to General McIntosh at Fort Pitt "such of the infantry as are already raised, and are in the vicinity of the frontiers, together with a troop of cavalry, not exceeding fifty men, under the command of an intelligent and active officer" (*Journals of the Continental Congress,* XI, 721).

Patrick Henry in Council to Henry Laurens

RC (NA: PCC, No. 71, I, 169).

WMS.BURGH July 10th. 1778

SIR.

Just after sending away my Letter to you of the 8th. on the Subject of the Expedition to Detroit, the inclosed Letter from Mr. Lockhart came to my Hands.[1] As it [is] impossible to furnish him with the capital Articles he wants, & as the Beef Cattle cannot be taken from the Monopolizers he mentions, I think additional Reasons appear for postponing the Expedition.[2] However refering to my last & to Mr. Lockharts the whole Business is submitted to the Decision of Congress whose Resolves I shall ever take pleasure in Executing to the utmost.

With great Regard I have the Honor to be Sir Yr. most obedient & very humble Servant

P. HENRY

[1] Patrick Lockhart (*ca.* 1749–*ca.* 1810) was a merchant of Fincastle, Botetourt County, as early as 1772. In 1773 and frequently thereafter for twenty years he was a justice of the peace. He served in the Virginia Convention of May 1776, in the House of Delegates in 1776–1778, and as sheriff of Botetourt County in 1784. His militia service advanced him to the rank of major before the close of the Revolution and to colonel in 1788. In 1782, Governor Harrison appointed him commissioner of public stores in Botetourt and three adjoining counties. He was appointed by Con-

gress on 11 June 1778 "to procure...necessaries" for the expedition against Detroit (Earl G. Swem and John W. Williams, eds., *Register of the General Assembly*, pp. 1, 3, 5, 242; Botetourt County Court Records, Order Book, 1788–1793, pp. 23, 29, microfilm in Virginia State Library; *Bulletin of the Virginia State Library*, XIV [1921], 122; *Journals of the Continental Congress*, XI, 589). Lockhart wrote to Henry on 7 July 1778, telling of his difficulties in obtaining necessary supplies and asking assistance from the state government. He especially complained about the difficulty of obtaining beef and suggested that it might necessarily have to be impressed (NA: PCC, No. 71, I, 173–75). On 9 July the council advised the governor "as the only Method of saving much useless expence to the public, to recommend to Capt. Lockhart to desist from his purchases till the result of the last application to Congress on that Subject shall be known" (*Journals of the Council of State*, II, 163).

2 For the outcome, see Henry to Laurens, 8 July 1778, nn. 5 and 6.

From Samuel Stanhope Smith

RC (LC: Madison Papers). Addressed to "The Honble; James Madison Junr; Orange." Probably in his old age, JM docketed this letter "Smith Sam: S. (Revd.) Sepr. 15. 1778." William C. Rives wrote "Discussion of *Liberty & Necessity*" after this note.

HAMPDEN-SIDNEY Septr. 15th. 1778

DEAR SIR,

I have read over your *theoretical* objections against the doctrine of moral liberty; for *practically* you seem to be one of its disciples.[1] I remember the manner in which you have formerly expressed yourself upon that intricate subject. And indeed they express the difficulties that occured to me in attempting to resolve it. I reasoned without hopes that the solution I have given it is at least as clear, & as free from material defects as any I had seen, otherwise I should not have submitted it to your discernment. It was with a view to avoid the objections with which you press me, that I made a distinction betwixt *desire*, & *volition;* & supposed that the latter solely regards our *actions*, & not merely the *objects* themselves that excite desires the immediate motives of volition. I conceive it to be a faulty mode of expression to say that the *will* determines itself. The will is only a faculty of the soul. Its self determinations would be indeed blind & undistinguishing. But perhaps the same objection does not lie against the mind determining her own volitions, after fair examination of the different motives that allure her. She will in that case chuse & act in a manner the most agreable to herself: & yet she has power to suspend her choice still longer, & consider more attentively the motives before her: she has even the power by intense application, by pursuing a certain train of ideas with frequency, by leaving out some branches in the train & cultivating others, to render an object originally less agreable, at length the most pleasing. This seems to be a happy mechanism of nature to make neither good nor evil necessary, by puting it in our power to cultivate the virtuous in opposition to the vicious motive. I am aware of the question that presses this part of the theory. What determines her to suspend her immediate volition, or to push the inquiry & comparison among her motives any farther? I have endeavoured to answer it in my dissertation, by finding certain habitual motives of *duty*, & *self-interest*, whose perpetual presence in the mind appears to be designed by nature to guard her from the danger to which she would be exposed from the force of other motives without this seasonable check in the co[n]stitution. You will say if the sentiments of duty are more plea[s]ing than others they will have their necessary effect; otherwise, they will make but a vain opposition against their fatal antagonists. I say that these sentiments of duty, independent of any pleasure that may attend them, ca[rr]y an *authority*, & an *interest* with them that fits them to ballance any, or all other motives, unless it be in the case of inveterate habits which indeed seem to induce a species of necessity in action. When I say fits them to ballance &.c I do not mean to affirm that they have just an equal mechanical momentum, or force of attraction. I would wish rather to exclude, as far as possible, all mechanical ideas out of moral subjects. But only that they have such an influence as to prevent any necessary & irresistible effect of their antagonists. The *mechanism* of the idea is the objection which I make to your illustration of a motive deficient *by* $\frac{1}{3}$ of the force necessary to produce an action—which then would not be commensurate to the effect, & would require some supplement to make up the deficiency. It appears to me impossible that there should be such deficiency of motion in the proportion of $\frac{1}{3}$ or any other quantity. Every motive is an adequate *occasion*, I would rather say than *cause*, of volition. For suppose there is one motive possessed of its full power, without any defect. This would be an adequate cause in the mechanical phrase; but then suppose it to be opposed by a thousand others of equal force; then if the first were only possessed of a power adequate to the effect, before the others interposed their influence; all being mutually opposed by all would produce an utter incapacity in the will to move. And if pursuing this hypothesis we suppose each of the others somewhat less in power than the first, then they would diminish a proportionable

part of its influence; being but barely sufficient in the beginning, otherwise there would be no room to suppose a deficiency of $\frac{1}{3}$, it would
be incapable to produce any effect; contrary to experience where we
hourly percei[ve] volitions to arise in the midst of a thousand contending motives. From whence I conclude that there is no deficiency
of mot[ive] in any common case; but every motive may be a sufficient
occasion of action. *Occasion* I call it because to me the influen[ce] of
motives appears to consist rather in rousing & disposing the mind for
action than in any absolute *causality*, to use an extremely metaphisic[al]
term, which they enjoy. Human nature is a compages[2] of sen[ses?],
passions, &c. besides the power of understanding & reason whose business is to compare together their impressions and emotions, & to determine betwixt them. The former affected by their proper objects
produce sensations either pleasing or painful, which raising desire of
some species become the motives of action. By a crowd of these we
are constantly solicited; the understanding as it were situated in the
midst of a large prospect, from whence it has a commanding view of
a great extent & all the motives comprehended within it, perceives that
happiness may flow to her from many different quarters (I omit on
purpose the consideration of the motives that may be derived from
pain). It is impossible to grasp every pleasure that occurs to the imagination at the same time. And yet if all motives enjoyed an absolutely
necessary causal influence, we should unavoidably endeavour to reach
them all at once; or remain fixed & immovable in the midst of their
contrary attractions. But since the understanding contemplates them
without any such constraint following, we must be possessed of some
innate vigour & force of soul, to fix the choice upon one, & to pass
another by after having passed a judgment upon this previous contemplation. To preserve the liberty of these elections one happy expedient of nature is the consciousness that no single object or class of
objects is absolutely, & alone necessary for our happiness. A thousand
others may serve the purpose equally well. Or if they are less pleasing
at first, we know that by turning our attention to them, habit will
supply the place of original nature. This habitual recollection often
prevents the violence with which the mind would be apt to rush towards a particular end, & seems not a little favourable to the exercise
of our moral freedom. This sentiment derives the greater probability
from the common observation that habit induces a species of necessity;
for this reason perhaps, that the habitual indulgence of one appetite
&c gives it such strength, & so turns the attention of the mind from

every other object, that she comes at length to regard it as almost her only happiness. How that innate vigour & force of soul is exerted in determining her elections I confess I cannot explain. Yet is not this[3] any valid objection against the truth. It is no more than occurs in every speculative subject. It is at least as easy to explain as the necessary force of motives upon a mind conscious of her own liberty. In every common phenomenon of nature we must be contented with some inexplicable circumstance. It is well if we can investigate the general process & economy of nature. Can we explain how the colour of green is formed? can we even explain what green is, unless by appealing to a common sensation of mankind? Altho we are not able to explain the idea of *moral liberty*, & that innate *energy* of mind that is involved in it, so as to be exempt from all questioning & doubt, yet we have as clear a sentiment of nature to appeal to, as in the case of colour.[4]

If the existence of human liberty may be demonstrated; if the mechanism of nature that contributes to it may be unfolded; if the aids in our own constitution, & in the system of things that are subservient to it can be investigated; we are not to reject the idea of liberty as fallacious because we cannot pry deeper into this subject than is practicable in all other subjects in nature. We have a *power* to chuse among a variety of motives. we chuse *freely*. Do you ask me to explain that *power*, & the precise *manner* in which it acts? I cannot in language more than I can the *nature* & *sensation* of colour, but I refer you to an obvious experiment—make a choice betwixt two opposite motives, & you may have as precise an idea as any words can convey in any case. It is the only definition that can be given of simple ideas. By this process we find out, with as much certainty as is competent to the human mind in any science, that obscure & inexplicable part of this subject after which we inquire. You ask, might we not have had the same feeling in acting under an absolute & irresistible inspiration from Heaven? And if so, no valid argument can be derived from thence in favour of moral freedom. What might have been possible with the Deity I will not dispute. But we are to be guided in our reasoning upon the present system of things, by the present appearances they exhibit. To say the least, we are in possession of a very plausible argument. It lies upon the fatalists to prove that it is *actually* false.

The habitual motives of duty & interest, which I have introduced into my dissertation, I designed to be the ultimate stage to which a fatalist could drive me; & not merely a new link in the endless chain of Arminian suspensions & self-determination[s.] If this doctrine be not vindicable without seizing an end of that chain, then I confess it is not vindicable at all.

But I have been drawn much farther into this subject agai[n] than I designed when I first sat down to write. I take my leave of it; I care not if it be for ever. I was led into it merely as a subject of curious amusement. Every thing is amusing that affords employment to the powers of reason. I have no conception, like the bigot[s] of all parties, that the existence of religion, or the salvation of men depends upon the solution of this question. When all parties are afraid lest the opinions of their antagonists are destructive of religion, it is a proof that none of them are so. Such doubty[5] champions are true knight-errants in philosophy, & like Don Quixote when they cannot find real adventures have an admirable talent at inventing imaginary ones. As I have no inclination to contest about questions merely of a speculative nature, as essential to good morals, I have still less ambition to distinguish myself as a sectary. I pretend not to the talents that would intitle me to be a leader if that were an honourable station; & I am not willing to be implicitly led. Sects in philosophy have been injurious to the progress of knowlege; & in religion, to the cultivation of charity & good morals. I mean *zealous & implicit partizans;* for as the world goes, it has become almost necessary to assume some name, & to class yourself even with those you despise. In the *present situation* of ecclesiastical affairs there seems to be a favourable opportunity to unite some of our religious parties, if their leaders were sufficiently catholic.[6] I should be ready to concur in such a design. I have a mind benevolent & diffusive enough to wish for an event that might extinguish reserve, suspicion, & animosity, & proud enough to scorn to beg it. I would be glad to know what turn religious politics are likely to take in the legislature?[7] what maxims of penal law are about to be adopted?[8] upon *what principles the clergy are denied the common privileges of citizenship,*[9] when they are not intitled to be a distinct body in the state, nor to receive any extraordinary support from the laws?[10]

The parents of some of the students have requested that their sons might be exempted from learning the greek. Your Brother[11] I believe thought it a privilege, & perhaps that was one reason for his desiring at present to enter upon the study of French. I can translate with considerable ease out of that language; the pronunciation I am convinced I am by no means perfect in, tho I had a native of France living in my house above a month; & in speaking the tongue I must unavoidably be greatly deficient for want of a habit in it. I do not chuse to teach what I am so little master of.

I hope to have the pleasure of your letters whenever your more serious avocations will afford you leisure. And be assured that they will always afford the greatest gratification to

Sir,   Yrs &c.

SAML S SMITH

[1] JM's reply to Smith's letter of November 1777–August 1778 (*q.v.*) is lost, but at least part of what he must have written is implicit, and occasionally explicit, in the present answer.

[2] A system or structure of many parts united.

[3] "Yet this is not" makes the meaning clearer.

[4] Smith inadvertently repeated "in." From Smith's rebuttal it would appear that JM had countered Smith's distinction between desire and volition by advancing a staple argument of the opponents of freedom of the will to the effect that desire and volition are both conditioned by a chain of antecedent forces necessarily determining any given choice. Another important thread of JM's argument seems to have been an effort to confound Smith's derivation of moral liberty from the multitude of desires, passions, interests, etc., which press upon human beings. JM apparently tried to show by a specific percentage analysis of the contending motives that even the interplay of forces from which Smith derived moral liberty might well be a part of the great chain of events predetermining every course of action. As in his previous letter, Smith returns in the end to a reliance on certain inexplicable forces in human nature which must be responsible for man's consciousness of moral liberty. The existence of these forces is demonstrated by the common experience of mankind.

[5] Doughty.

[6] The Anglican establishment, heretofore closely bound to the mother church in England, had naturally been weakened in Virginia by the Revolution. At the same time, however, the various dissenting sects found it difficult to agree upon a common platform concerning the proper relationship between religion and government.

[7] On 19 December 1776 the Virginia General Assembly, in harmony with the guarantee of religious liberty in the state constitution, had exempted dissenters from paying taxes for the support of the Anglican Church. But it was unwilling to face up to the broader issue of whether the state government should levy a general assessment for the benefit of all Christian denominations. This question was still much discussed at the time that Smith wrote and would not be answered until 1785 (Charles R. Lingley, *The Transition in Virginia*, p. 201).

[8] Jefferson was the chairman and moving spirit of a committee appointed by the Assembly on 5 November 1776 to propose a revision of the laws of Virginia, including the statutes dealing with crime. The committee's elaborate report, embracing 126 bills, was sent to the June 1779 session of the legislature, and was largely enacted into law by 1786 (Hening, *Statutes*, IX, 175–77; Boyd, *Papers of Jefferson*, II, 301 ff., esp. 663–64).

[9] The state constitution of 1776 declared "all ministers of the Gospel of every denomination ... incapable of being elected members of either House of assembly or the Privy Council" (Hening, *Statutes*, IX, 117).

[10] Although in 1778 the Presbyterians, for whom Smith was a leading spokesman, apparently favored state financial support for all religious denominations, they would abandon this position a few years later (Charles R. Lingley, *The Transition in Virginia*, pp. 204–5).

11 William Madison probably transferred from the preparatory school of the College of New Jersey to Hampden-Sydney Academy at about the time Smith began to teach there in 1776. How long William remained in Hampden-Sydney is unknown, although Smith's statement seems to imply that the boy was then at Montpelier but might come back to the academy if he could be tutored in French. JM's letter of 8 December 1779 to his father (*q.v.*) may be interpreted to mean that his brother had so returned for at least a part of that year but had left once again, possibly when Smith resigned on 28 October 1779 to rejoin the faculty of the College of New Jersey.

Session of Virginia Council of State

MS (Virginia State Library).

Tuesday November 10th 1778.

present

His Excellency;

John Page	David Jameson
Dudley Digges	James Madison
Thomas Walker	And
Nathaniel Harrison	Bolling Stark
Esquires.	

. . . .

The Board taking into consideration the perilous Situation of the People of Monongalia County,[1] Advised the Governor that orders be given to convey 130 Rifles belonging to the public at Fredericksburg, to that County addressed to the Care of the County Lieutenant[2] with Directions to sell them for their value to such of the Inhabitants who from their particular Situation & Circumstances are most in want of Arms & who are most likely to make proper use of them: That he pay to John Pierce DuVall Esquire[3] two hundred & forty pounds for transporting the said Arms & one thousand pounds powder out of the money arising from the Sale of the said Arms according to contract entered into with Colonel Gaddis of Monongalia,[4] & it was accordingly Ordered by the Governor.

Adjourned till tomorrow 10 oClock

Signed   JOHN PAGE
          DUDLEY DIGGES
          THOS WALKER
          NATHL HARRISON
          DAVID JAMESON
          JAMES MADISON
          BOLLING STARK

1 Indian incursions were frequent in Monongalia County during the Revolutionary War. In the summer of 1778, a large body of Indians penetrated to Cobun's Creek and burned a fort near Morgantown. Another raid later, near Statler's Fort on the Monongahela River, left eighteen dead (Samuel T. Wiley, *History of Monongalia County, West Virginia* . . . [Kingwood, W.Va., 1883], pp. 55–71, *passim*, esp. pp. 59–62). Immediately following a treaty made at Fort Pitt in September 1778 with the Delaware tribe of Indians, General Lachlan McIntosh led troops through their territory in order to build and garrison Fort McIntosh, thirty miles below Fort Pitt, and Fort Laurens on the Tuscarawas River in hostile Indian country (below, Henry to Laurens, 23 Nov. 1778, n. 7; Max Savelle, *George Morgan: Colony Builder* [New York, 1932], pp. 157–59).

2 The acting county lieutenant of Monongalia was Colonel Daniel McFarland (1731–1817). He was born in Worcester, Mass., spent much of the prime of his life in fighting Indians on the Virginia frontier, and died in Washington County, Pa. (Ross B. Johnston, ed., *West Virginians in the American Revolution*, p. 189).

3 John Pierce DuVall (*ca.* 1751–1792) was a member of the House of Delegates from Monongalia County between 1777 and 1779, and a state senator from his district between 1780 and 1791. He also served for several years as a state commissary of provisions, as county lieutenant of Monongalia and Harrison counties, successively, and as a trustee of Randolph Academy (*Journals of the Council of State*, III, 6, 335, 355, 470; *Calendar of Virginia State Papers*, IV, 177, 410; V, 414; Hening, *Statutes*, XII, 639).

4 Militia of Monongalia County, led by Colonel Thomas Gaddis (1742–1834), garrisoned Fort Liberty (the present town of West Liberty, Ohio County, W. Va.) during the last four months of 1776, and shared in the McIntosh and William Crawford campaigns against the western Indians in 1778 and 1782, respectively. Gaddis, a resident of Uniontown, lived in a portion of Monongalia County which, in 1784, would be relinquished by Virginia to Pennsylvania and become a part of its Westmoreland County. In 1794, as a distiller, Gaddis participated in the Whiskey Rebellion (*Journals of the Council of State*, I, 348; John H. Gwathmey, *Historical Register of Virginians in the Revolution*, p. 293; H. R. McIlwaine, ed., *Official Letters of Virginia Governors*, I, 109 n.).

Patrick Henry in Council to Virginia Delegates in Congress

RC (NA: PCC, No. 71, I, 189–91). According to the docket sheet, this letter was read in Congress on 27 November.

WMSBURG Novr. 14th. 1778.

GENTLEMEN,

The Executive power of this State having been impressed with a strong apprehension of incursions on their Frontier Settlements from the Savages situated about the Illinois & supposing the Danger would be greatly obviated by an enterprize against the English Forts & possessions in that Country which were well known to inspire the Savages with their bloody purposes against us, sent a Detachment of Militia consisting of one hundred & seventy or eighty men commanded by Col. George Rogers Clarke on that Service sometime last Spring.[1] By Despatches which I have just received from Col. Clarke[2] it appears that his Success has equalled the most sanguine expectations. He has not only reduced Fort Chartres & its dependencies but has struck such a Terror into the Indian Tribes between that Settlement & the Lakes that no less than five of them viz. the Puans, Sacks, Renards, Powtowantanies & Miamies[3] who had received the Hatchet from the English Emissaries have submitted to our Arms[, surrendered?][4] all their English presents & bound themselves by Treaties and promises to be peaceable in future.

The Great Blackbird a Choppowaw chief[5] has also sent a Belt of peace to Col. Clarke influenced he supposes by the Dread of Detroits being reduced by the American Arms. This latter place according to Col. Clarkes representation is at present defended by so inconsiderable a Garrison & so scantily furnished with provisions for which they must be still more distressed by the loss of Supplies from the Illinois, that it might be reduced by any number of Men above five hundred. The Governor of that place Mr. Hamilton[6] was exerting himself to engage the Savages to assist him in retaking the Places that had fallen into our Hands, but the favourable impressions made on the Indians in general in that Quarter the influence of the French on them & the reinforcement of their Militia Col Clarke expected flattered him that there was little danger to be apprehended. Included in the Despatches is a Letter from Captn. Helm who commands a party posted by Col Clarke at St. Vincents.[7] according to this information The Wabash & upper Indians consisting of the Piankeshaws Tawaws Peorias Delawares Pikakishaws Masketans & some of the Shawanese Chiefs[8] had also given up all their tokens of attachment to our Enemies & pledged their fidelity to the united States. Captn. Helm adds that he was on the point of setting out with the assistance of part of the Inhabitants of St Vincent & some of the principal Wabash Chiefs with a View to retake a quantity of Merchandize seized by the English from Detroit, belonging to the people at St Vincents & on its way to them. The Captain speaks with Confidence of Success in this enterprize & extends his hopes even to the destruction of Detroit if joined on his way by the expected number of Indians & Volunteers.[9] My reason for troubling Congress with these particulars is, that they may avail themselves of the Light they throw on the State of things in the Western Country. If the party under Col. Clarke can cooperate in any respect with the

Measures Congress are pursuing or have in view I shall with pleasure give him the necessary orders.[10] In order to improve & secure the advantages gained by Col. Clarke I propose to support him with a reinforcement of Militia. But this will depend on the pleasure of the Assembly to whose consideration the measure is submitted.[11]

The french Inhabitants have manifested great Zeal & Attachment to our Cause, & insist on Garrisons remaining with them under Colo. Clarke. This I am induced to agree to, because the Safety of our own Frontiers, as well as that of these people demands a Compliance with the Request. Were it possible to secure the St. Lawrence & prevent the English Attempts, up that River by seizing some post on it, peace with the Indians would seem to me to be secured.

With great Regard I have the Honor to be Gentn. your most obedient Servant

P. Henry

P. S. Great Inconveniences are felt here for want of Letters of Marque.[12]

honble Virga. Delegates

[1] In January 1778 Governor Patrick Henry, acting with the advice of the Council of State and the authorization of the General Assembly, directed Lieutenant Colonel George Rogers Clark to raise a force of 350 men to capture Kaskaskia and other British posts in the Illinois country, north of the Ohio River (Hening, *Statutes*, IX, 433; James A. James, ed., *George Rogers Clark Papers*, pp. 33–34). By midsummer, leading about one half the number of troops authorized, Clark was in possession of Kaskaskia, Cahokia, Prairie du Rocher, St. Philippe, Fort Chartres, and Vincennes. The first four of these posts were on or near the Mississippi River in what is now southwestern Illinois; Cahokia was on the Illinois bank of that river, directly south of St. Louis; and Vincennes was on the Wabash River in what is now Knox County, Ind.

[2] Not found. Having read these dispatches, the House of Delegates on 23 November 1778 adopted a resolution thanking Clark and his command (*Journal of the House of Delegates*, October 1778, p. 79).

[3] The Puan (Winnebago), Sac, and Renard (Fox) Indians lived along the Mississippi and Rock rivers in the northwestern part of what is now the state of Illinois; the Potawatomis in the north and northeastern area of that state; and the Miamis in what is now west-central and southwestern Ohio.

[4] Blank in the manuscript.

[5] The Chippewas occupied the southern portion of the present state of Michigan. For Black Bird, see James A. James, ed., *George Rogers Clark Papers*, pp. 252–55.

[6] The British Lieutenant Governor Henry ("Hair Buyer") Hamilton (d. 1796), whom Clark would capture when he retook Vincennes on 25 February 1779. Held prisoner until 1781, Hamilton then returned to England but was again in North America in 1782 as lieutenant governor of Quebec.

[7] Letter not found. Leonard Helm (*ca.* 1720–1782) of Prince William County was a friend of Clark who had fought beside him in Lord Dunmore's War. In December

1777 Clark commissioned Helm to raise a company for service in the West, and appointed him to command at Vincennes in August 1778. On 17 December of that year, he became a prisoner of the British when Lieutenant Governor Hamilton recaptured Vincennes. Helm regained his freedom when Vincennes again fell to Clark in February 1779. Still under Clark's command, Helm was stationed late in the Revolution at Fort Jefferson near Louisville, where he acted as superintendent of Indian affairs (*ibid.*, pp. lxv, lxxii, 27, 280, 297, 601; Louis A. Burgess, ed., *Virginia Soldiers of 1776*, II, 889).

8 The Piankashaws and Pekakishaws lived along the Wabash River and appear to have been one group of Indians rather than two. The Tawaws (Ottawas) dwelt along Lake Michigan; the Peorias along the Illinois River; the Masketons along the upper reaches of the Wabash River; and the Delawares along the Muskingum River and, with the Shawnees, along the Ohio River, east of the mouth of the Wabash River.

9 Helm, of course, did not capture Detroit. However, his expedition in February and March 1779 was successful in gaining the friendship, or at least the neutrality, of many Indians north of Vincennes and in taking forty British prisoners, along with seven boats loaded with provisions and trading goods (James A. James, ed., *George Rogers Clark Papers*, pp. lxxxv–lxxxvi, 259–60).

10 Congress did nothing during 1779 to extend Clark an opportunity to "cooperate," and it even delayed until 8 July of that year before congratulating him upon capturing Vincennes and Lieutenant Governor Hamilton (*Journals of the Continental Congress*, XIV, 809–10).

11 On 12 December 1778 Governor Henry wrote to Clark that the General Assembly had authorized the recruitment of five more companies of militia to be added to his command (H. R. McIlwaine, ed., *Official Letters of Virginia Governors*, I, 338).

12 Apparently no letters of marque were supplied by Congress to the governor of Virginia until the summer of 1779 (*ibid.*, II, 14).

Session of Virginia Council of State

MS (Virginia State Library).

Tuesday November 17th 1778.

present
His Excellency;

Dudley Digges	David Jameson
Thomas Walker	James Madison
Nathaniel Harrison	Bolling Stark &
Joseph Prentis Esquires[1]	

. . . .

Walter Batwell[2] esquire a British Subject & formerly an Officer in the British Service having been for some years in this State and hitherto been unable to remove himself & family to Britain & having set forth his Distressed Situation to this Board & praying an allowance of

Rations for the Support of himself & Family until next April by which Time he has reason to apprehend he shall be able to remove to some part of Europe; And as this Board consider the said Walter Batwell as a Prisoner of War, They advised his Excellency to Order that two Rations a Day be allowed by the Commissary at this Station unto the said Batwell until the first Day of May next taking his Draught upon the British Commissary General of Prisoners for the amount of such Rations; And his Excellency ordered accordingly.

To this Measure Bolling Stark Esquire Dissented,[3] It not appearing to him that the said Walter Batwell can, with propriety, be considered as a prisoner of War, for altho' he was a half pay Officer under the British King at the time of his comming to this State, as is set forth yet from his own confession it appears also that he some time ago resigned or sold the said Commission, consequently must stand in the same predicament with other British Subjects now residing in this State who have refused to take the oath of fidelity thereto. That the said Batwell is an object of Charity the Dissentient is fully convinced of; yet the proper mode to adopt for relieving him, as the Dissentient humbly conceives, is not by Rations out of the public Stock of provisions, but by private Contributions: Add to this that establishing such a precedent may possibly be attended with bad consequences at this juncture in as much as every person in a distressed Situation hath an equal claim on the public fund of provisions. Upon these principles & for these Reasons he entered his Dissent.

. . . .

Adjourned till tomorrow 10 oClock

Signed   DUDLEY DIGGES
THOS WALKER
NATHL HARRISON
DAVID JAMESON
JAS MADISON
BOLLING STARK
JOS. PRENTIS

[1] Joseph Prentis (1754–1809) of Williamsburg was elected to the Council of State on 30 May 1778 but did not take his seat until 7 July (*Journal of the House of Delegates*, May 1778, pp. 26, 33; *Journals of the Council of State*, II, 161). He was frequently a member of the House of Delegates between 1777 and 1788, and was its speaker during his last year in that body. Thereafter he served as a judge of the General Court until his death (Lyon G. Tyler, ed., *Encyclopedia of Virginia Biography*, II, 31).

[2] Walter Battwell and his family, living in Williamsburg in 1774 and 1775, planned to leave Virginia during the summer of the following year, if by then he could pay

his creditors. Evidently he either was unable to clear his debts or found no means of leaving the state (*William and Mary Quarterly*, 1st ser., I [1892–93], 16; *Virginia Gazette* [Williamsburg, Dixon and Nicolson], 18 May and 14 September 1776; *Virginia Gazette* [Williamsburg, Purdie], 13 December 1776).

[3] The *Journals of the Council of State* record no other dissent during JM's tenure. This is negative evidence that he either approved of all decisions made by the council or at least was never sufficiently adamant in his disagreement to ask that it be noted in the journal.

Patrick Henry in Council to Henry Laurens

RC (NA: PCC, No. 71, I, 193–97). The docket states that it was "Recd 2d. Decem Read 5d. Referred to the marine Comee."

WMSBURG Novr. 23d. 1778.

SIR

I am Honoured with the Receipt of your Favour of the 14th. instant covering two Acts of Congress viz. one of the 10th. instant for obtaining from this State & Maryland, Gallies to attack East Florida.[1] another of the 11th for requesting permission to export from Petersburg in Virginia a Quantity of Flour & Bread for the use of his most Christian Majesty.[2]

No Time has been lost in giving Efficacy & Despatch to both these Measures. Orders are issued to the Naval Office to permit the Exportation of the Flour & Bread as requested.[3] I only wish that the French Gentlemen might be informed, that the Quality of our Flour this year is by no means equal to what it is in common Harvests, owing to the Weavil & other Accidents.

In the Deliberation which was had on the Subject of furnishing the requisite Aid to attack Florida, the Council with myself ever anxious to forward the Views of Congress, were not a little embarrassed. We have two Vessels called Ship Gallies drawing eight or nine feet water carrying about eighteen 3 or 4 Pounders & one of them formed to use two heavy Guns in the Bow in Still Water with Men, & about Six smaller Gallies, calculated for Service in the Bay or rivers. The latter it is thought cannot without great Danger of Sinking, be sent to Sea. The former are therefore pitched upon to go on the Service required, if Congress think them fit.[4] In the mean time Orders are given for them to be got in readiness which I'm informed may be in three Weeks; and they will proceed to Charles Town unless they are countermanded by Congress.

Besides these two Vessels there is the Ship Caswell belonging to this State Stationed in North Carolina to protect the Trade. She carrys about Guns 12, 9, & 6 pounders & 135 men & draws about 5 feet Water.[5] I write to Day to Governor Caswell[6] to know if she can be spared, & if possible to get her added to the other two above described, for the expedition. When Congress were pleased to call for Vessels fitted for this particular Service, their Designs might have been answered if the Service had been explained. Not being favor'd with any such Explanation I have been obliged to proceed in uncertainty.

When General McIntosh[7] was directed to begin his Operations on the Frontiers against the Indians I gave orders to 14 Counties beyond the Mountains to furnish him with any number of Militia he should call for. His Requisitions were sent to such of them as he chose long since. The number of Men sent to him, I know not. But a few Days ago three County Lieutenants appeared before the Council Board & informed that their Counties & two others adjacent, were called upon by the General to send him 1,000 men immediately. These Gentlemen easily convinced the Executive, that it was impossible to comply with this Demand, because it would be the 20th December before the men could be assembled at some rendezvous to begin the march, & that no Tents, Kettles, Horses, provisions or Necessaries were to be had for the Service: And because many of the Troops would have 400 Miles to proceed thro' a Country chiefly Desart, & utterly unfurnished with those Things which are essential to the Support of human Life at that inclement Season when the Snows are several Feet Deep on the great Ridges of Mountains, many of which Lay in their Rout. Knowing therefore the utter impossibility of the Measure, the Council unanimously concurred with me in judging it necessary to countermand General McIntosh's orders, & I have accordingly done so.[8] The General shall be apprized of it as soon as possible, & will take his measures accordingly.

I did myself the honor to inform you by Letter which I doubt from yours has not reached your Hands, of several Matters respecting the marching of the Militia from this State to Charles Town, which was requested by Congress.[9] When the requisition arrived here the Assembly was sitting. It became necessary to lay the matter before them as the Law gave the power of marching the Militia to a Sister State only in cases of actual Invasion. An Act was thereupon passed to enable the Executive to send out the Militia when *certain Intelligence* of an *intended* Invasion should be received.[10] Just in the Instant when orders were going to be sent to put the Men in Motion for Charles Town, a Letter from Governor Johnston arrived, by which it was apparent the Enemy had no Designs on that place but it was said, meditated a Descent on the Eastern Shore. Upon this the Council thought with me it was proper to suspend the Matter, & it has remained in that Suspense 'till the present Time.[11]

I send inclosed a List of sundry Acts of Congress received Since Septr. last,[12] most or all of which I thought I had acknowledged the Receipt of by particular addresses which I had the honor of sending you.

The Variety of Matter which the present occasion calls on me to mention will I hope plead my Excuse for the Length of this Letter.

I beg to be presented to Congress in the most acceptable manner & in Terms expressive of that high Regard with which I have the Honour to be

Sir Yr. Mo. obedt. & very hble Servt.

P. HENRY

P.S. I am looking out for a Messenger to carry your Despatches to Govr. Caswell

---

[1] The retained copy of Laurens' letter of 14 November is in NA: PCC, No. 13, fols. 162–63. On 2 November, Congress resolved that if the enemy did not invade South Carolina and Georgia as expected, the considerable patriot army gathered there under General Benjamin Lincoln should "endeavour to reduce the province of East Florida." Believing that the capture of St. Augustine would require a land and sea operation of considerable size, Congress on 10 November authorized Lincoln to recruit more soldiers in the south and called upon Maryland and Virginia to dispatch "armed galleys" there, at continental expense, as quickly as possible (*Journals of the Continental Congress*, XII, 1091, 1116–21).

[2] Having purchased in the name of Louis XVI the cargoes of the ships "Gentille" and "Adventurer," Conrad Alexandre Gérard, French minister to the United States, requested Congress on 11 November "to give the necessary orders" for them to sail. Congress acceded on that day by authorizing Laurens to write Governor Henry explaining "the nature of this transaction, and the necessity of the vessels immediate departure" (*ibid.*, XII, 1122). In his letter asking Henry to permit them to sail, Laurens assured Henry that the breadstuffs were for French military use, "wholly unconnected with private trade." On 17 November 1778 the General Assembly of Virginia passed an "Act to enable the Governour and Council to supply the armies and navies of the United States, and of their allies, with grain and flour" (Hening, *Statutes*, IX, 584–85; *Journal of the House of Delegates*, October 1778, p. 66).

[3] On 23 November the Council of State "advised his Excellency to grant permits to the two Vessels" and to inform Congress of his action (*Journals of the Council of State*, II, 222).

[4] The Council of State on 23 November advised Henry "to request the Commissioners of the Navy Board to give directions for the Dragon & Tartar Ships of war (there being no Gallies fit for the Service) to be got in readiness for the Ex-

pedition" (*loc. cit.*). In December 1776, "for the protection of *Chesapeake* Bay and the adjacent cape and coasts," Virginia was building "four gallies of eighty odd feet keel" and taking steps to construct as many more "much larger" ones (*Journal of the House of Delegates*, October 1776, p. 102). Owing to the fall of Savannah to the British on 29 December 1778, the "Dragon" and "Tartar" did not leave Virginia.

[5] The "Caswell" was stationed in Ocracoke Inlet, an arm of the sea giving ready access through Pamlico and Albemarle sounds into the Blackwater River in southeastern Virginia. Evidently the ship was hardly seaworthy, because in June 1779 Jefferson reported that "her bottom is eaten out" and she had "sunk at her station" (Boyd, *Papers of Jefferson*, III, 20).

[6] Richard Caswell (1729–1789), prominent in the civil and military life of his state for thirty-five years before his death, delegate to the First Continental Congress and to the Constitutional Convention of 1787, served as governor of North Carolina in 1777–1779 and 1784–1786. Henry's letter to him is in H. R. McIlwaine, ed., *Official Letters of Virginia Governors*, I, 327–28.

[7] Brigadier General Lachlan McIntosh (1725–1806) was named on 25 July 1778 to lead an expedition that autumn against the western Indians. See above, Henry to Laurens, 8 July 1778, and notes. Hampered by a shortage of men and equipment, McIntosh was unable to launch his expedition until October. By the end of the year he had reached the junction of the Muskingum and Tuscarawas rivers in the Ohio country. After building and garrisoning Fort Laurens there, he withdrew with the remainder of his force to Fort Pitt (Fitzpatrick, *Writings of Washington*, XIII, 79–80, 499–502).

[8] On 20 November 1778 the Council of State advised Governor Henry to countermand McIntosh's demand for two hundred militia from each of the counties of Washington, Montgomery, Botetourt, Greenbrier, and Rockbridge (*Journals of the Council of State*, II, 220–21).

[9] Henry's letter of 9 November on this subject was read in Congress on 18 November 1778 (*Journals of the Continental Congress*, XII, 1140).

[10] This act empowered the governor, if "he shall receive certain information" of the enemy's intention to invade another state, to send a maximum of three thousand Virginia militiamen to its aid (Hening, *Statutes*, IX, 477).

[11] On 31 October 1778, while the governor and the Council of State were conferring about dispatching one thousand militia to Charleston, the letter from Governor Thomas Johnson (1732–1819) of Maryland arrived, naming Boston as the likely target of the enemy fleet which had left New York on the 17th. Johnson apparently did not mention "the Eastern Shore" (H. R. McIlwaine, ed., *Official Letters of Virginia Governors*, I, 319–20). Sixteen ships under Vice Admiral John Byron, hampered by a storm, made an unsuccessful attempt to blockade in Boston harbor the French ships under Vice Admiral Charles Henri Hector, Comte d'Estaing. See Fitzpatrick, *Writings of Washington*, XIII, 259–60.

[12] Inclosure not found.

Session of Virginia Council of State

MS (Virginia State Library).

Friday November 27th 1778

present
His Excellency;

John Page	Nathaniel Harrison
Dudley Digges	David Jameson
Thomas Walker	James Madison &

Joseph Prentis Esquires.

The Governor having communicated to the Board a Letter, which he had received from Colonel Muter,[1] giving an Account that a British Ship of War (the Swift) in chace of the Rattlesnake privateer, run aground near Cape Henry, & that the Crew to the number of 91 had surrendered themselves prisoners of War to Colonel Thomas Reynolds Walker, of Princess Anne,[2] And asking the advice of the Board what was best to be done with the said Prisoners: They advised his Excellency to order Colonel Muter to send the officers to this place by Water, & the rest of the Crew, under a strong guard of Norfolk Militia, to Surry County, from thence to be conveyed by a guard of that Militia to Cumberland old Courthouse now in Powhatan County[3] there to remain as Prisoners of War 'til further orders They also advised his Excellency to issue his Warrant upon the Treasurer for one hundred & fifty pounds payable to Lieutenant John Lightfoot[4] & to be conveyed by him to Colonel Muter for defraying the Expences of the aforenamed prisoners on their march to Powhatan.

Adjourned till tomorrow 10 oClock

Signed   JOHN PAGE
DUDLEY DIGGES
THOMAS WALKER
NATHL HARRISON
DAVID JAMESON
JAS. MADISON
JOS. PRENTIS

[1] George Muter.

[2] The *Virginia Gazette* (Williamsburg, Dixon and Hunter) of 27 November 1778, reported: "Last Monday the Swift, a British 20 gun ship, being in chase of the Rattlesnake privateer, run ashore on the Middle Ground. The crew of the Swift threw over her guns, but finding it impossible to get her off, set fire to her, and delivered

themselves up to the commanding officer at Portsmouth. The Rattlesnake was drove ashore, and burnt also." The "Rattlesnake," commanded by Stephen Seymour, had earlier been commissioned to protect the port of Charleston, S.C. (Charles Oscar Paullin, *The Navy of the American Revolution* [Chicago, 1906], pp. 426–27).

3 Powhatan County was created from parts of Cumberland and Chesterfield counties on 28 June 1777 (*Journal of the House of Delegates*, May 1777, p. 112).

4 Probably John Lightfoot (*ca.* 1744–1807) of Brunswick County who enlisted as an ensign in the militia in 1777 and was a captain in the 1st Virginia Regiment, continental line, before the end of the war (*William and Mary Quarterly*, 1st ser., XXIV [1915–16], 103; Brunswick County Court Records, Will Book, No. 7, p. 204, microfilm in Virginia State Library).

Patrick Henry in Council to Henry Laurens

RC (NA: PCC, No. 71, I, 201–3). The docket states that it was "Read Decr. 8. 1778 Referred to Marine Commee."

WMSBURG Novr. 28th 1778.

SIR,

Your favor of the 16th. inst. is come to hand together with the Acts of Congress of the 26th. of August for establishing provision for Soldiers & Seamen maimed or disabl'd in the public Service—of the 26th September for organizing the Treasury, a proclamation for a General Thanksgiving, & three Copies of the Alliance between his most Christian Majesty & these united States.[1]

I lost no time in laying your Letter before the privy Council & in deliberating with them on the Subject of sending 1,000 Militia to Charles Town So. Carolina.[2] I beg leave to assure Congress of the great Zeal of every Member of the Executive here, to give full Efficacy to their Designs on every occasion. But on the present, I am very sorry to Observe, that Obstacles great & I fear unsurmountable, are opposed to the immediate march of the Men. Upon Requisition to the Deputy Quarter Master General in this Department for Tents, Kettles Blankets & Waggons, He informs they cannot be had. The Season when the March must begin will be severe & inclement, & without the forementioned necessaries impracticable to men indifferently Clad & equipped as they are in the present general scarcity of Clothes.[3]

The Council as well as myself are not a little perplexed, on comparing this Requisition to defend South Carolina & Georgia from the Assaults of the Enemy with that made a few Days past for Gallies to conquer East Florida. The Gallies have orders to rendezvous at Charles Town, which I was taught to consider as a place of acknowledged

Safety; And I beg leave to observe that there seems some Degree of Inconsistency in marching Militia such a Distance in the Depth of Winter under the Want of Necessaries to defend a place which the former measure seemed to declare safe.

The Act of Assembly whereby it is made lawful to order their march confines the Operations to measures merely Defensive to a Sister State & of whose Danger there is certain Information recd.[4]

However as Congress have not been pleased to explain the matters herein alluded to, & altho a good deal of perplexity remains with me on the Subject, I have by advice of the privy Council given orders for 1,000 Men to be instantly got into Readiness to march to Charles Town, and they will march as soon as they are furnished with Tents, Kettles and Waggons In the mean Time if Intelligence is received, that their march is essential to the preservation of either the states of So. Carolina or Georgia the men will encounter every difficulty & have Orders to proceed in the best way they can without waiting to be supplied with those necessaries commonly afforded to Troops even on a Summers march.[5]

I have to beg that Congress will please to remember the State of Embarrassment in which I must necessarily remain with Respect to the ordering Gallies to Charles Town in their way to invade Florida,[6] while the Militia are getting ready to defend the States bordering on it, & that they will please to favor me with the earliest Intelligences of every Circumstance that is to influence the measures either offensive or Defensive.

I have the Honor to be Sir Yr. mo: obed. & very Hble Servant

P. HENRY

P.S. The Despatches to Govr. Caswell[7] are sent by a safe hand

1 The retained copy of President Henry Laurens' letter of 16 November is in NA: PCC, No. 13, fols. 174–76. The papers mentioned are missing, but copies of them are in the *Journals of the Continental Congress*, XI, 448–55, 838; XII, 953–54, 956–61, 1138–39. The proclamation, adopted on 17 November, named 30 December as the day of "general Thanksgiving."

2 In his letter, Laurens supported his urgent request for the dispatch of militia by mentioning that the Creek Indians, at the instigation of the British, were harassing Georgia and were expected to raid into South Carolina, and that a British fleet carrying about 2,500 troops was ready to sail from New York, with St. Augustine, Fla., or the coast of Georgia as its probable destination. Laurens again emphasized that East Florida should be subdued, "if possible" (above, Henry to Laurens, 23 November 1778, n. 1). The expeditionary force left New York on 27 November, reached Tybee Island near Savannah on 23 December, and occupied the town six days later.

3 Considering "the impossibility of furnishing such Militia with sufficient Tents

Kettles &c. without which it is almost impracticable for them to march at this in-clement Season," the Council of State on 28 November advised the governor not to dispatch the troops to South Carolina but merely to hold them in readiness to march. He was also requested to explain to Congress the reasons for the delay (*Journals of the Council of State*, II, 226–27).

4 Above, Henry to Laurens, 23 November 1778, n. 10.

5 *Ibid.*, n. 11.

6 *Ibid.*, n. 4.

7 Governor Richard Caswell of North Carolina.

Patrick Henry in Council to Virginia Delegates in Congress

RC (NA: PCC, No. 71, I, 205–7). The docket sheet shows that Congress heard this letter on 15 December and referred it to the Marine Committee.

WMSBURG December 4th 1778

GENTLEMEN,

The great distress our Trade has of late and does at present suffer from the Ships & privatiers of the Enemy which infest our Coast has given the Executive power inexpressible uneasiness.[1] A great number of Captures have been made not only of Vessels belonging to this State but of those belonging to our Allies and the other States. And as the long nights and windy Season during which it is well known European Merchantmen embarking in the American Trade adventure with most confidence have now taken place, it may be expected the Vigilance of the Enemy and consequently our losses will daily increase. The depar-ture of the French Fleet from the American Coasts[2] is another Circum-stance that will embolden them in their depredations & enable them to shut up our ports with a force so inconsiderable as to be easily spared from other Services. In this situation of Things, having no armed Ves-sels of our own of sufficient Strength to oppose even privateers except two which have been found on trial too slow to be of use against them & which are besides soon to be sent against East Florida on the requisi-tion of Congress,[3] The Council have advised me to request your ap-plication to Congress for some naval Assistance from them. As I am a total stranger to the Naval Affairs of the Continent it is impossible for me to determine what degree of aid can be afforded or ought to be asked. A single Frigate or even a single Ship of less force would render very essential service. But unless the Continental Ships are engaged in some very critical enterprize I cannot help suggesting that the duty owing to our Allies who trade chiefly into Chesapeek Bay & the Interest Maryland & Pennsylvania and in some degree North Carolina as well as Virginia have in the protection of Trade through that Channel evidently claim all the Assistance Congress can possibly give us. Certain it is that on no other Station within the united States the remains of their Fleet can be of such extensive benefit or so easily & plentifully supplied with provisions, or if their destination be to distress the Trade of the Enemy it may with the greatest probability be presumed they would on our Coast save from the depredations of the Enemy ten Vessels for one that would be captured by offensive Cruises; not to mention the security of the former and the danger of the latter services. I have only to add that it is the earnest wish of the Council as well as myself that this measure may be pressed on Congress in the most cogent terms[4] & yt.

I am Gentn. with great Respect Yr. most obedt. & Hble Servant

P. HENRY

[1] On 11 September 1778, Lieutenant Governor John Page and the Council of State directed the Navy Board of Virginia to have the "Tartar, Dragon & Northampton Ships of War" cruise off Cape Charles, "using their utmost diligence to capture the Enemys Cruisers." At that time some "Continental Frigates" were expected to join in this patrol (*Journals of the Council of State*, II, 186). Evidently it was ineffective, especially against the marauding ships of the Tory John Goodrich and his sons of Isle of Wight and Nansemond counties.

[2] Comte d'Estaing and his ships had left Boston for the French West Indies on 4 November (above, Henry to Laurens, 23 November 1778, n. 11).

[3] *Ibid.*, n. 2.

[4] On 15 January 1779 Congress directed its president to notify Governor Henry that "measures have been taken to protect the trade of Chesapeake Bay, and that Congress flatter themselves a speedy end will be put to the depredations of Godridge [Goodrich] and his associates" (*Journals of the Continental Congress*, XIII, 69). The only action which seems to have been taken to justify this optimism was a letter of 9 January from the Marine Committee to the Commissioners of the Navy Board of the Eastern Department, stating that "Effectual measures must be immediately taken to prevent their [the Goodriches'] depredations; The Committee are in daily hopes of hearing that a Sufficient force is cruizing on that Coast" (Charles Oscar Paullin, ed., *Out-Letters of the Continental Marine Committee and Board of Admiralty* [2 vols.; New York, 1914], II, 37). The optimism of Congress was unjustified, for the Goodriches long continued to harry American shipping (Jameson to JM, 4 November 1780, n. 4).

Patrick Henry in Council to
George Rogers Clark

FC (Virginia State Library).

[12 December 1778]

To COLONEL GEORGE ROGERS CLARKE Commander in Chief of the Virginia Troops in the County of Illinois.

You are to retain the Command of the Troops now at the several Posts in the Country of Illinois and on the Wabash[1] which fall within the Limits of the County now erected & called Illinois County[2] which Troops marched out with & have been embodied by you. You are also to take the Command of five other Companies raised under the Act of Assembly[3] which I send herewith, & which if compleated as I hope they will speedily, will have orders to join you without Loss of Time & are likewise to be under your command. With your whole force you are to protect the Inhabitants of the Country & as occasions may serve, annoy the Enemy. It is thought that the Indian Nation may be over-awed & inclined to peace with us by the Adoption of proper Measures with you. Or if that cannot be effected, that such of them as send out Parties towards our Frontiers on this Side of Ohio, may be chastized by Detachments from your Quarter. For this purpose it will behove you to watch their Motions, & to consider, that one great Advantage expected from your Situation is, to prevent the Indians from warring on this side of Ohio.

In order more effectually to prevent this, you are to establish such posts in different parts of the Country as you judge best for your Troops to occupy.

I consider your further Successes as depending upon the good will & friendship of the Frenchmen & Indians who inhabit your part of the Commonwealth. With their concurrence, great Things may be accomplished. But their Animosity, will spoil the fair prospect which your past Successes have opened. You will therefore spare no pains to conciliate the affections of the French & Indians. Let them see & feel the Advantages of being fellow Citizens & free men. Guard most carefully against every Infringement of their property, particularly with Respect to Land, as our Enemies have alarmed them as to that. Strict & even severe Discipline with your Soldiers may be essential to preserve from Injury those whom they were sent to protect & conciliate. This is a great & capital Matter, & I confide that you will never lose Sight of it or suffer your Troops to injure any person without feeling the punishment due to the offence. The Honor & Interest of the State are deeply concerned in this & the Attachment of the French & Indians depends upon a due observance of it.

John Todd Esquire being appointed County Lieutenant according to Law during pleasure, with ample powers chiefly confined to the Civil Department will have Directions to act in concert with you where it can be done. On your part, you will omit no opportunity to give him the necessary Cooperation of the Troops where the Case necessarily requires it. Much will depend upon the Mutual Assistances you may occasionally afford each other in your respective Departments. And I trust that a sincere Cordiality will subsist between you. The Contrary will prove highly detrimental.[4]

Some Measures will be fallen on for carrying on a Trade to supply Goods for the Inhabitants of your County. You will afford the Agents such aid or protection from Time to Time as affairs require & your Circumstances will permit.

I send you herewith some Copies of the Act of Government & Bill of Rights,[5] together with the french Alliance. These will serve to shew our new friends, the Ground upon which they are to stand & the Support to be expected from their Countrymen of France. Equal Liberty & Happiness are the objects, to a participation of which we invite them. Upon a fair presumption that the people about Detroit have similar Inclinations with those at Illinois & Wabash, I think it possible, that they may be brought to expell their British Masters & become fellow Citizens of a free State. I recommend this to your Serious Consideration, & to consult with some confidential persons on the Subject. perhaps Mr. Gibault the Priest[6] (to whom this Country owes many Thanks for his Zeal & Services) may promote this affair. But I refer it to you to Select the proper persons to advise with & to act as Occasion offers. But you are to push at any favourable Occurrences which Fortune may present to you. For our peace & Safety are not secure while the Enemy are so near as Detroit.

I wish you to testify to all the Subjects of Spain upon every occasion, the high Regard, & sincere friendship of this Commonwealth towards them. And I hope it will soon be manifest that mutual Advantages will derive from the Neighbourhood of the Virginians & the Subjects of his Catholic Majesty.[7]

I must observe to you, that your Situation is critical[.] Far detached from the Body of your Country, placed among French Spaniards & Indian Nations strangers to our people, anxiously watching your Actions & Behaviour, & ready to receive Impressions favourable, or not so, of our Commonwealth & its Government, which Impressions will be hard to remove & will produce lasting good or ill Effects to your Country, These Considerations will make you cautious & Circumspect. I feel the Delicacy & Difficulty of your Situation, but I doubt not your Virtue will accomplish the arduous Work with Honour to yours[elf] and Advantage to the Commonwealth. The Advice & Assistance of discreet good men will be highly necessary. For at the Distance of your County, I cannot be consulted. General Discretionary powers therefore are given you to act for the best in all Cases where these Instructions are silent, & the Law has made no provisions.

I desire Your particular attention to Mrs. Rocheblare & her Children, & that you suffer them to want for Nothing. Let Mr. Rochblare's property which was taken be restored to his Lady so far as it can be done. You have the Sum of Sixty pounds sent for her use, in case you can't find her husbands Effects to restore.[8]

Prudence requires that provisions be laid in to subsist the Troops you have & those to be expected to arrive with you. Colonel Bowman[9] has contracted to deliver 35,000lb Bear Bacon at Kentucky, But Bread must be had at Illinois. You will provide it if possible before the arrival of the Troops, or the necessity to buy it becomes general known, as perhaps Advantages may be taken by raising the price. Lay up also a good Stock of pow[der] & Lead.

There is a Cargoe of Goods at a Spanish post near you[10] belonging either to the Continent or this State. Rather than let your Troops be naked, you are to take a Supply for them out of these Goods. But this is not to be done but in Case of absolute Necessity. Let an exact account be kept of what is used & let me receive it.

In your Negotiations or Treatys with the Indians, you will be assisted by Mr Todd. Let the Treatys be confined to the Subject of Amity & peace with our people & not to touch the Subject of Lands. You may accept of any Services they offer, for Expelling the English from Detroit or elsewhere. In case you find presents to the Savag[es] necessary, make them sparingly as possible, letting them know our Stock of Goods is small at present, but by means of our Trade with the french & other Nations we expect plenty of Goods before it is long.

Lieutenant Colonel Montgomery[11] will convey to you ten thousand pounds for payment of the Troops & for other Matters requiring

Money. In the Distribution of the Money you will be careful to keep exact Accounts from time to time & take Security where it is proper.

[1] Above, Henry to Virginia Delegates, 14 November 1778, n. 1.

[2] The county of Illinois was created by an act of the General Assembly on 18 December 1778 (*Journal of the House of Delegates*, October 1778, p. 122). This statute, limited in its duration to one year, provided a "temporary form of government" headed by "a county lieutenant or commandant in chief," appointed by the governor with the advice of his council, who was to serve at his "pleasure" (Hening, *Statutes*, IX, 552–55).

[3] The statute creating the county of Illinois authorized the governor, with the advice of the Council of State, "forthwith to order, raise, and levy, either by voluntary enlistments, or detachments from the militia, five hundred men, ... to march immediately into the said county" to garrison the posts and establish liaison with "the Spanish settlements" on the Mississippi River. On 12 December the Council of State instructed Lieutenant Colonel John Montgomery of Kentucky County to start the necessary recruiting "with all possible Expedition" and send on to Clark at least one hundred men at a time (*Journals of the Council of State*, II, 239–40).

[4] Governor Henry on 12 December appointed Clark's close friend, John Todd (1750–1782), a colonel of the militia of the county of Kentucky, as the first county lieutenant of Illinois and directed him to co-operate with Clark and "to inculcate upon the [French] people the Value of Liberty, & the difference between the State of free Citizens of this Commonwealth, & that Slavery to which Illinois was destined" (*ibid.*, II, 233–36). Todd arrived at Kaskaskia and inaugurated the new government in May 1779. In a letter of 18 August 1779 to William Fleming, Todd remarked: "Mr. Madison sent me an army commission I wd rather he had kept it, as it is of no use to me" (Clarence Walworth Alvord, ed., *Kaskaskia Records, 1778–1790* [Springfield, Ill., 1909], p. 110).

[5] That is, the Virginia Constitution of 1776, together with its Declaration of Rights (Hening, *Statutes*, IX, 109–19).

[6] Father Pierre Gibault (1737–1804), the Catholic vicar-general of the Illinois country. Both at Kaskaskia, where he lived, and as far east as Vincennes, he rendered great service to the Americans by encouraging the French settlers to help Clark in many ways (James A. James, ed., *George Rogers Clark Papers*, pp. 121–22, 237, 239).

[7] At New Orleans the Spanish governor, Bernardo de Gálvez, aided the merchant, Oliver Pollock, commercial agent of the United States and Virginia there, to procure and forward essential supplies and munitions to Clark (*ibid.*, pp. lxvi, xcvi, 38 n.).

[8] Phillippe de Rastel, Chevalier de Rocheblave, the British commandant at Kaskaskia, was captured by Clark when he took that post on 4 July 1778. Rocheblave's slaves and other property were confiscated and he was taken as a prisoner to Williamsburg. He escaped in 1780 and managed to return to Canada (*ibid.*, pp. lxii–lxiv, 67, 86, 203, 240; Edward G. Mason, ed., *Early Chicago and Illinois* [Chicago, 1890], pp. 360–81).

[9] Colonel John Bowman (1752–1782) of Harrodsburg in Kentucky County.

[10] Probably Ste Genevieve, on the west bank of the Mississippi River, about forty-five miles south of St. Louis.

[11] Lieutenant Colonel John Montgomery (*ca.* 1742–1794) succeeded George Rogers Clark in command in Illinois, when Clark left in 1781. A native of Botetourt County, Va., he had been a "long hunter" since 1771 and was widely experienced in Indian warfare. Later he was killed by the Indians in Kentucky (James A. James, ed., *George Rogers Clark Papers*, p. 431; Clarence Walworth Alvord, ed., *Cahokia Records, 1778–1790* [Springfield, Ill., 1907], pp. xcv, cxix).

Session of Virginia Council of State

MS (Virginia State Library).

Wednesday December 23d 1778.

present
His Excellency;

Dudley Digges James Madison &
Thomas Walker Benjamin Waller[1]
Esquires

. . . .

The General Assembly having passed a Resolution empowering the Governor with the Advice of Council, to raise a Regiment of Voluntiers to consist of Six hundred Men rank & file, with proper officers to command them, for the particular purpose of guarding the British Prisoners which are now, or may hereafter be stationed in this Commonwealth, &, until such Regiment be raised, to call out Detachments of the Militia for the purpose aforesaid;[2] and it being represented that upwards of 4000 prisoners are on their March to Charlottesville in Albemarle County—The Board advised his Excellency to give Orders to the County Lieutenants of Amherst, Buckingham, Louisa, Orange, Culpeper & Goochland to march one hundred of their respective Militias to guard the said Prisoners when Colonel Charles Lewis of Albemarle[3] shall give them Notice, & to desire the said Lieutenants respectively in conjunction with two of their field officers immediately to appoint two Captains two Lieutenants & two Ensigns & to direct them forthwith to raise two Companies of Voluntiers to relieve the Militia in the Duty of guarding the said prisoners; And the Board also advised that Charles Lewis Esqr. be appointed the Colonel, Francis Taylor the Lieutenant Colonel,[4] & William Fountaine the Major[5] to command the said Regiment, when raised; And that a Letter be written to Colonel Lewis informing him of what has been done and desiring that he would represent to the Officer who commands the Escorte to the prisoners[6] the necessity of his staying 'til a regular Guard is inlisted, by shewing the Danger of committing the Business to raw Militia ill armed, half Clad, ignorant of Discipline, & of every thing requisite to prevent the Mischiefs which may be done by the prisoners, many of whom as well Of-

278

ficers as privates may be ill disposed & watchful to take every Advantage which Ignorance or Inattention may give them.

Adjourned till tomorrow 10 oClock.

Signed DUDLEY DIGGES
THOMAS WALKER
JAMES MADISON
BENJA WALLER

¹ Benjamin Waller (1710–1786) was elected to the Council of State on 19 December 1778 to replace Nathaniel Harrison, who had resigned. He took his seat on 22 December. He was a Williamsburg attorney who served also as clerk of the council, a burgess for James City County, admiralty judge, and a judge of the General Court (Lyon G. Tyler, ed., *Encyclopedia of Virginia Biography*, I, 351; *Journal of the House of Delegates*, October 1778, p. 127).

² On 19 December 1778 the General Assembly declared:

"Whereas, it will be exceedingly burthensome and inconvenient to the inhabitants of this Commonwealth to keep so large a body of militia on constant duty, as will be necessary to guard the British prisoners which now are, or hereafter may be stationed in this Commonwealth:

"*Resolved*, That the Governor, with the advice of the Council, shall be, and he is hereby empowered, to raise as soon as possible, by voluntary enlistments, a regiment of soldiers, to consist of six hundred men, rank and file, with proper officers to command them, for the particular purpose of guarding the British prisoners aforesaid; and that he is empowered to offer a bounty not exceeding thirty dollars to each man to be so enlisted; and this Assembly will make good the expense of raising, maintaining, clothing and paying the said regiment; and that until such regiment be raised, the Governor is hereby empowered, with the advice of the Council, to call out detachments of militia for the purpose of guarding the said prisoners" (*Journal of the Senate*, October 1778 [Richmond, 1828], pp. 81–82).

The "British prisoners" were, of course, the troops surrendered by General John Burgoyne by the Convention of Saratoga, 16 October 1777. They were held in Massachusetts until October 1778, when Congress "*Resolved*, That General Washington be directed ... to take the necessary steps for removing, with all convenient speed, all the prisoners of the convention of Saratoga to the town of Charlotteville, in the county of Albemarle, in the State of Virginia." The Board of War was directed to "apply to the governor and council of Virginia, for a sufficient force of militia to guard the said prisoners" (*Journals of the Continental Congress*, XII, 1016–17). The prisoners began their march to Virginia early in November 1778. They were kept in Albemarle County for nearly two years, when most of them were moved into Maryland to prevent their recapture by Major General Alexander Leslie. See Jones to JM, 10 November 1780, n. 4.

³ Charles Lewis (*ca*. 1740–1779) of North Garden was a colonel of the 14th Virginia Regiment from 12 November 1776 to 28 March 1778. He had led a force against the Cherokee Indians in 1776 (*Journals of the Council of State*, I, 104, 339; Fitzpatrick, *Writings of Washington*, XIV, 57; *Virginia Magazine of History and Biography*, XVI [1908], 170–71; XX [1912], 279).

[4] Francis Taylor had recently become a supernumerary officer after serving in Virginia's continental line since 1775. He was appointed colonel of the Convention Guards in January 1779, upon the death of Colonel Charles Lewis. He held this position until the force was disbanded in June 1781, when the prisoners were moved north from Winchester (*Tyler's Quarterly Historical and Genealogical Magazine*, II [1920–21], 335–37).

[5] William Fontaine (1754–1810) of Hanover County served as lieutenant colonel of the Convention Guards from June 1779 to June 1781. He had been a student at the College of William and Mary. From 1775 to 1778 he was an officer in the 2d Virginia Regiment (*Journals of the Council of State*, I, 475; John H. Gwathmey, *Historical Register of Virginians in the Revolution*, p. 280; *Virginia Magazine of History and Biography*, XX [1912], 368).

[6] Theodorick Bland (below, Session of Council of State, 29 March 1779).

Session of Virginia Council of State

MS (Virginia State Library).

EDITORIAL NOTE

The official manuscript "Journal of the Council of State of Virginia," from which the earlier samples of the minutes of this body were taken for reproduction in the present volume, is missing for this session. The minutes given below reproduce those entered in rough form by the secretary of the council in the "Council Minute Book."

Monday March 29th 1779

present Jno Page Esqr. Lieut Govr
D Digges D Jameson Jas Madison Jos. Prentis & B Waller Esqrs.

. . . .

Colo. Theoderick Bland having been apptd by Genl Washington to command at ye barracks of ye Convention Troops in Albemarle,[1] & having made application to this board for Instructions & assistance—the board were of opinion that a small party of Light horse to pursue Deserters & be ready for emergencies & such Supplies for a Table as will maintain ye dignity & importance of his Station are things necessary; but as ye Superintendence of that business has been expressly disclaimed by them,[2] they could do no more than recomd it to ye Col to send for 15 Dragoons f'm his own Regt[3] to serve at ye barracks, & to certify to Congress as their opn that a Table is necessary;[4] which ye Lieut Govr. was requested to do by Lr. a Lr. was accordgly written & ordd. to be recorded. (Copy filed).

A Lr. from Majr. Genl. Lincoln[5] referring to Majr. Meade[6] for an acct of Affairs to ye Southard was read; & Majr. Meade attending & having related ye Distressed Situation of Genl Lincoln for want of

Troops the Board advised that Colo. Mason[7] be written to, to March off so many Militia ordered for ye Expedition as he may be able to collect, without delay, by ye shortest Rout to join the Genl & a Lr. was written & recorded.

The Board, taking under their consideration sevl Letters f'm Colo Muter[8] relative to ye procuring Boats for ye reception of ye Stores f'm on board ye Flags of Truce, & finding such Interruptions to their Delibe[r]ations by having their attention called off so often to ye affairs of ye Convention Troops;[9] advised that Colo Muter be requested & empowerd to take under his direction entirely ye management of every thing relative to ye Business of ye Flags of Truce & to hire such Vessel, as may be necessary for ye more Expeditious Dispatch of ye sd Flags And a Letter was written to Colo Muter accordgly. A Copy filed.

Adjd. till Friday next ten oClock

JOHN PAGE
DUDLEY DIGGES
DAVID JAMESON
10
J. PRENTIS
BEN: WALLER

[1] Theodorick Bland (1742–1790) was appointed on 5 November 1778 to "regulate and conduct" the convention troops on their journey from Massachusetts to Virginia. Bland left on this service the next day (Fitzpatrick, *Writings of Washington*, XIII, 207–8). Later he was in Congress with JM from 1780 to 1783, served in the Virginia legislature, and opposed the ratification of the Federal Constitution in the Convention of 1788. Nevertheless, he was the only member of the Virginia delegation in the first United States Congress who supported Hamilton's proposal to have the federal government assume the states' debts.

[2] The Council of State's disclaimer has not been found, but on 14 December 1778 the House of Delegates resolved that the governor "despatch an express immediately to the honorable the president of Congress, and the board of war . . . informing them of the difficulties attending the guarding of the said prisoners with draughts from the militia, and the danger of an escape from such a guard, and to request Congress will order a sufficient corps of continental troops for that purpose, and to inform them that in the mean time every step will be taken to secure the prisoners till the arrival of such troops, which is to be as soon as possible" (*Journal of the House of Delegates*, October 1778, pp. 112–13). This was rejected by the Senate.

[3] Bland was colonel of the 1st Continental Dragoons (F. B. Heitman, *Historical Register of Officers of the Continental Army*, p. 89).

[4] Meaning that Bland should receive supplies enabling him to entertain in a manner appropriate to his rank.

[5] Major General Benjamin Lincoln (1733–1810) had been commander of the southern department since September 1778. At this time he and his troops were in the Savannah neighborhood. In May 1780 he was captured with his army at Charleston but was exchanged in time to participate in the Yorktown campaign. He was

Secretary at War from 1781 to 1783, commander of the force that suppressed Shays's Rebellion, and lieutenant governor of Massachusetts in 1788.

6 Major Everard Meade (1746–1802) of Amelia County was a captain in the 2d Virginia Regiment in 1776. On 7 May 1777 he was appointed an aide-de-camp to Major General Lincoln (*Journals of the Council of State*, I, 21; Fitzpatrick, *Writings of Washington*, VIII, 23). Meade rose to the rank of colonel, and commanded Spotswood's 2d Legion at least until August 1782 (*Journals of the Council of State*, III, 112, 133). He served in the Virginia Senate from 1795 to 1797 and was a trustee of Hampden-Sydney College (John H. Gwathmey, *Historical Register of Virginians in the Revolution*, p. 540; P. Hamilton Baskervill, *Andrew Meade of Ireland and Virginia: His Ancestors and Some of His Descendants and Their Connections* [Richmond, 1921], p. 42).

7 David Mason (1733–1792) had resigned his commission as a colonel of the 15th Virginia Regiment on 31 July 1778 because of his wife's illness. In May 1779 he commanded a Virginia militia regiment in North Carolina. He represented Sussex County in the House of Burgesses from 1758 to 1775, in all but one of the Revolutionary conventions of 1775 and 1776, and in the House of Delegates in 1780 and 1781. He also held many local offices (Fitzpatrick, *Writings of Washington*, XI, 423; *Journals of the Council of State*, I, 455, 500; III, 366; Writers' Program, Virginia, *Sussex County: A Tale of Three Centuries* [Richmond, Va., 1942], pp. 43, 44, 54; *Virginia Magazine of History and Biography*, XVI [1908], 180).

8 George Muter.

9 See Session of Council of State, 13 February 1778, n. 4.

10 Although JM is recorded as present at the sessions of 29 and 31 March, he did not sign his name to their minutes. The fact that in each instance a space was left for his signature probably indicates that he was not present when the original minutes were signed.

Patrick Henry in Council to John Jay

RC (NA: PCC, No. 71, I, 225–27). The docket shows that it was read on 21 May and referred to the Board of War.

WILLIAMSBURG 11th. May 1779.

SIR,

On Saturday last[1] in the Evening a British Fleet amounting to about thirty Sail consisting of one 64 Gun Ship (supposed by some to be the Saint Albans, and fifteen or Sixteen large Ships, some of them either Frigates or armed Vessels it is not known certainly which, and the others Vessels of lesser Size) came into the Bay of Chesapeak, and the next day proceeded to Hampton Roads, where they anchored, and remained quiet until Yesterday about Noon, when several of the Ships got under way, and proceeded towards Portsmouth, which place I have no doubt they intend to attack by Water or by Land, or by both, as they have many flatt bottomed Boats with them for the purpose of landing their Troops.[2] As I too well know the weakness of that Garrison[3] I am in great Pain for the Consequences, there being great Quantities of Merchandize, the property of French Merchants and others in this State, at that Place as well as considerable Quantities of Military Stores which tho' Measures some time since were taken to remove, may nevertheless fall into the Enemys Hands. Whether they may hereafter intend to fortify and maintain this Post is at present unknown to me, but the Consequences which will result to this State and to the united States finally if such a measure should be adopted, must be obvious.[4] Whether it may be in the power of Congress to adopt any measures which can in any manner counteract the Design of the Enemy is submitted to their Wisdom.[5] At present I cannot avoid intimating that I have the greatest Reason to think that many Vessels from France, with public and private merchandize may unfortunately arrive while the Enemy remain in perfect Possession of the Bay of Chesapeak, and fall Victims unexpectedly.[6]

Every Precaution will be taken to order Look out Boats on the Sea Coast to furnish proper Intelligence but the Success attending the execution of this necessary Measure, will be precarious in the present Situation of Things.

It is not in my Power to be more explicit at this Time, but the Weightiness of this affair has induced me not to defer sending the best Information I cou'd obtain by Express.

You may depend that so soon as further particulars respecting the Designs of the Enemy, shall come to my Knowledge, they shall be communicated without Delay to Congress.

With great Regard I have the Honor to be Sir your most obedient Servant

P. HENRY

The Honble. John Jay President of Congress Philadelphia[7]

---

[1] 8 May.

[2] The British fleet under Commodore Sir George Collier consisted of the sixty-four-gun "Raisonnable," the forty-four-gun "Rainbow," and "the Otter, Diligent and Haerlem, sloops, and Cornwallis galley, together with several private ships of war and twenty-two transports" carrying about two thousand troops (Gardner W. Allen, *A Naval History of the American Revolution*, II, 395). Collier's goal, as General Clinton described it, was to retard "the levy of 2000 men whom Virginia was at that time collecting to send to Mr. Washington's army, and to destroy some considerable magazines formed there . . . and a quantity of naval stores which that province had provided for supplying a French fleet [Estaing's] they were in expectation of. There were also some ships of force that they were building and fitting out there, which I wished to deprive of the power of doing us a mischief" (William B. Willcox, ed., *The American Rebellion: Sir Henry Clinton's Narrative of His Campaigns, 1775-1782* [New Haven, Conn., 1954], pp. 122-23). This mission was accomplished between 10 and 24 May. On the latter date Collier reluctantly

obeyed Clinton's order to re-embark the troops and return to New York (*ibid.*, pp. 406–7; below, n. 4).

[3] In April 1778 the garrison had been weakened by smallpox. The following October, a special guard had been authorized for the "Continental Ship Yard at Portsmouth" (*Journals of the Council of State*, II, 123, 192).

[4] The British evacuated Portsmouth late in May, but not before destroying "many vessels there," capturing and burning part of Suffolk, and, in the words of Governor Henry, committing "horrid ravages and depredations, such as plundering and burning houses, killing and carrying away stock of all sorts, and exercising other abominable cruelties and barbarities" (proclamation of 15 May, in H. R. McIlwaine, ed., *Official Letters of Virginia Governors*, I, 370). Admiral Collier described his activities as follows: "The fort was raz'd, the season'd timber for ship building burnt, the buildings and storehouses of the finest yard on this continent underwent the same fate; the sufferings of individuals I endeavoured to prevent all in my power and in general happily succeeded, and by it I hope have procured many friends to the royal cause" (Gardner W. Allen, *A Naval History of the American Revolution*, II, 396).

[5] On 21 May Congress resolved that Henry's letters on the British operations in Chesapeake Bay should be sent to General Washington and the "Minister Plenipotentiary of France," Conrad Alexandre Gérard (*Journals of the Continental Congress*, XIV, 623). On 25 June the captain of the frigate "Deane" was "directed to proceed in company with the Frigate Boston from the Capes of Delaware into Chesapeake Bay and on your arrival there, at Hampton or any Other way, endeavour to Obtain the best intelligence if any of the enemies Ships of war or Privateers are in the Bay, and if you find there are and of such force as you are able to encounter, you are to proceed up and attack them, . . . taking or destroying as many of the said Vessels as may be in your power." By then all of the larger British ships had departed, but smaller ships and privateers continued to operate in the bay and at least two of them were captured (Gardner W. Allen, *A Naval History of the American Revolution*, II, 398).

[6] Perhaps the reference was to the expected arrival of Admiral d'Estaing's fleet, convoying merchant ships bearing war supplies from France especially for the use of the patriot army in Georgia and South Carolina. This fleet, however, did not arrive off the Georgia coast until 1 September 1779 (*Journals of the Continental Congress*, XV, 1108; JM to Bradford, 30 October–5 November 1779, n. 3).

[7] On 10 December 1778, the day after Henry Laurens resigned as president of Congress, John Jay was elected to that position (*Journals of the Continental Congress*, XII, 1202, 1206).

From Philip Mazzei

RC (LC: Madison Papers). On the cover the address reads "Honble: Js: Maddison Esqre. Counsellor of State Williamsburg."

Hob's Hole,[1] June 13th. 1779.

Dear Sir,

There was in the copy of the Cipher you gave me[2] twice *8*. It may perhaps be so in my original. I have converted one of the 2 in 81. I have likewise added the *j* besides the *v*, & so completed the Alphabet consisting of 26 letters, & not of 24. I wish therefore that you will keep the inclosed, & destroy the other, to avoid misunderstanding.

I have put my papers with a 4 pounds ball in a bag to be thrown overboard, if prudence should require it; but I have first made an extract, & have interlined it in old papers of private accounts &c, which I don't think would be taken from me, as both figures & words are masked in a manner as to give no suspicion; & it will be necessary the assistance of my memory to recollect myself the originals they represent. In case I should sink the papers & escape, the said memorandum will enable me to act while I am waiting for the copies of my Commissions & Instructions, the sending of which I hope you will not neglect.[3] These, I suppose, could be amended & improved in proportion to the amendment & improvement of your *venerable* board.[4] If such a thing was to happen (which I ardently wish for the public good) pray, have my observations upon them considered, & that use made of them which you think they deserve. I hope you will believe me when I tell you, that the greatest inducement for a Sovereign to grant a loan of good [gold?] & silver will be the prospect of great part of the money remaining in his Dominions. Success in this scheme will afford us a great & sudden relief. Therefore all proper means ought to be used to promote it. Among the steps, which could be taken to defeat the scheme, I cannot think of one more effectual, than that of sending out 2. Agents, one to a place to borrow the money, & one to spend it in another. However well disposed the Gran-duke,[5] or the Genoese might be to lend us money, I am confident that as soon as they know, that part of it is to be drawn in favour of another part of Europe to pay for things, which could have been bought in their Country, they would withdraw highly, & in my opinion justly, disgusted. I told you already, that I ought to have been furnished with a copy of the invoice given to Mr. Smith,[6] with a power to purchase on equal terms ('though at this juncture it would have been proper, in order to obtain our end, not to stand upon trifles) & if such articles, as we are in want of, are not to be got there,[7] our intention would produce a good effect, & I could then with propriety say that such things must be purchased elsewhere immediately, & untill they could be manufactured in their Country. The late Governor, Mr. Page,[8] & you agreed in January last, that, in good policy as well as gratitude, as much money as it was necessary to employ in goods, was to be layed out in the country of the Lender, or Lenders. If prudence & common sense are to be given up, & the interest of the Country sacrificed to gratify the humour & spleen of narrow-minded & ill-disposed men,[9] we are in a really bad condition. It is a melancholy reflection, that the men, who have caused obstacles to be put in the way, are those better acquainted than others with the difficulty of borrowing money, & the disposition of men to trust thousands in goods rather than £50. in cash. A Sovereign has a much greater interest to find market for the manufacturies of his Country, & especially where they are almost on the ground for want of a market. Pray, remove the obstacles, rather help me, & instruct me about a banker to keep your money, & accept & pay your bills' in case I should succeed. I told you, that if I should not, I will publish a factum,[10] in which no circumstance shall be omitted, & the Actors shall be justly described. I really think, that both my honour & regard to my Friends would require it, & I feel that my personal resentment would have a small share in it in comparison to the sensibility for the public good. I don't doubt but I should make some impression, as I am confident that I shall have in my power to render, exclusive of that, essential services to the Country. I leave to your prudence to make a proper use of this letter, but as to Mr. Jefferson & Mr. Page I wish they will take the trouble to read it, & consult with you on *quid agendum*.[11] I refer y[ou] to Mr. Page for an information abt. Capn. Wood[ford']s[12] fate. Remember me to our Friends, & believe me most sincerely,

dr. Sir, Your most Obliged & Obedt. Servt.

PH. MAZZEI

17. do. NEAR URBANA.[13]

We are here stopped, & probably shall be obliged to go back. It is reported that several privateers are in the bay, & have done a great deal of mischief, which cannot be avoided as long as your men of war are most usefully, honorably, & patriotically employed in fishing oisters. The season is so advanced, that I am much uneasy abt. the cloathing for the army, & I think it will be prudent, as soon as I get to Paris, to persuade my acquaintances to become adventurers[14] by sending on the terms proposed the articles you want for it, least it should be too late when I get to Tuscany.

---

[1] Even though Hobb's Hole in Essex County on the Rappahannock River had been renamed Tappahannock by the General Assembly of Virginia in 1705 (Hening, *Statutes*, III, 417), the old designation of this official port of entry was commonly used during the Revolution.

2 Philip Mazzei (1730–1816) of Florence, Italy, after seventeen years in England as an importer of wines, emigrated to Virginia in 1773. There he was helped by leading planters, and above all by Jefferson, to acquire a property (Colle) neighboring Monticello, for the purpose of growing grapes and making wine. His eagerness to aid the patriot cause resulted in the collapse of his promising experiments in viniculture. On 8 January 1779 Governor Patrick Henry and the council, of which JM was a member, commissioned Mazzei to go to his native Tuscany to negotiate a loan of not over £900,000 specie, and to use at least a portion of it, together with tobacco shipped from Virginia, to purchase needed military supplies, including cloth, for the troops of that commonwealth. JM appears to have favored this arrangement and may have drafted Mazzei's commission and instructions (E[ugenio] C. Branchi, trans., "Memoirs of Philip Mazzei," *William and Mary Quarterly*, 2d ser., IX [1929], 251–52). Now, six months later, Mazzei was impatiently waiting aboard the brigantine "Johnston Smith" to set out upon his mission (Richard Cecil Garlick, Jr., *Philip Mazzei, Friend of Jefferson: His Life and Letters* [Baltimore, 1933], pp. 9, 22, 26–52, *passim*, 163; Howard R. Marraro, ed., *Philip Mazzei, Virginia's Agent in Europe: The Story of His Mission as Related in His Own Dispatches and Other Documents* [New York, 1935], p. 9; Reverend James Madison to JM, 3 August 1780, n. 7; Jameson to JM, 20 September 1780, n. 6).

3 These precautions proved to be well advised. On 20 June 1779, when the "Johnston Smith" was about to be captured by a British privateer off the Virginia capes, Mazzei threw overboard the "bag" containing, among other papers, his commission and instructions. After being held prisoner in the New York City area for the rest of the summer, he was given free transportation by the British to Cork, Ireland. He finally reached Nantes in November 1779, Paris in February 1780, and Italy in the summer of that year (Richard C. Garlick, Jr., *Philip Mazzei*, pp. 59–69).

4 Of the eight members of the Governor's Council only two—Joseph Prentis (1754–1809) and David Jameson (1757–1793)—were younger than Madison. The average age of the other five was fifty-five years. If by "venerable," Mazzei meant "esteemed" rather than "aged," his underlining of the word probably signified that he used it ironically.

5 Leopold I (1747–1792), Grand Duke of Tuscany, 1765–1790, and, as Leopold II, Emperor of the Holy Roman Empire for the two years preceding his death.

6 By "invoice," Mazzei likely meant both a list of desired articles and the maximum price authorized to be paid for each of them. "Mr. Smith" was Thomas Smith, Virginia's agent for trade from 1777 to 1779.

7 Northern Italy.

8 That is, Governor Patrick Henry and John Page, a member of the Governor's Council. See above, n. 2.

9 No doubt JM knew to whom Mazzei referred, but these men cannot now be identified with certainty.

10 A statement of facts.

11 What should be done.

12 Probably Thomas Woodford (b. 1736 and d. "soon after the Revolution"), captain of a merchant ship and a brother of Brigadier General William Woodford, Jr., of Caroline County. Privateers captured Captain Woodford and his vessel in May or June 1779 (*Virginia Magazine of History and Biography*, XXXIII [1925], 34; Mazzei to JM, 19 June 1779).

13 Urbanna in Middlesex County, on the Rappahannock below Hobb's Hole and about seventeen miles from Chesapeake Bay.

14 That is, risking their money to send to Virginia on credit the articles needed.

Order of Virginia Council of State Placing
Henry Hamilton and Others in Irons

Broadside (NA: PCC, No. 71, I, 245). "Williamsburg: Printed by John Dixon and Thomas Nicolson" at foot of text. Inclosed in Governor Jefferson's letter of 19 June 1779 to John Jay, in which he declared, "I thought it my duty to lay it before Congress as early as possible, with the reasons supporting it; nothing doubting but it will meet with their approbation; it's justice seems to have been confirmed by the general sense of the people here" (Boyd, *Papers of Jefferson*, III, 4–5).

In COUNCIL, *June* 16, 1779.

The Board proceeded to the consideration of the letters of Colonel Clarke,[1] and other papers relating to Henry Hamilton, Esq; who has acted some years past as Lieutenant Governour of the settlement at and about Detroit, and commandant of the British garrison there, under Sir Guy Carleton as Governour in Chief; Philip Dejean, Justice of the Peace for Detroit,[2] and William Lamothe, Captain of volunteers,[3] prisoners of war, taken in the county of Illinois.

They find that Governour Hamilton has executed the task of inciting the Indians to perpetrate their accustomed cruelties on the citizens of these states, without distinction of age, sex, or condition, with an eagerness and activity which evince that the general nature of his charge harmonized with his particular disposition; they should have been satisfied from the other testimony adduced that these enormities were committed by savages acting under his commission, but the number of proclamations which, at different times were left in houses, the inhabitants of which were killed or carried away by the Indians, one of which proclamations,[4] under the hand and seal of Governour Hamilton, is in possession of the Board, puts this fact beyond doubt. At the time of his captivity it appears, that he had sent considerable detachments of Indians against the frontier settlements of the[5] states, and had actually appointed a great council of Indians to meet him at the mouth of the Tanissee,[6] to concert the operations of this present campaign. They find that his treatment of our citizens and soldiers, captivated and carried within the limits of his command, has been cruel and inhumane;[7] that in the case of John Dodge, a citizen of these states, which has been particularly stated to this Board,[8] he loaded him with irons, threw him into a dungeon, without bedding, without straw,

288

without fire, in the dead of winter and severe climate of Detroit; that in that state he harrassed and wasted him, with incessant expectations of death; that when the rigours of his situation had brought him so low that death seemed likely to withdraw him from their power, he was taken out and attended to till somewhat mended, and then again, before he had recovered abilities to walk, was returned to his dungeon, in which a hole was cut seven inches square only, for the admission of air, and the same load of irons again put on him; that appearing again to be in imminent danger of being lost to them, he was a second time taken from his dungeon, in which he had lain from January to June, with the intermission before-mentioned of a few weeks only; that Governour Hamilton gave standing rewards for scalps, but offered none for prisoners, which induced the Indians, after making their captives carry their baggage into the neighbourhood of the fort, there to put them to death, and carry in their scalps to the Governour, who welcomed their return and successes by a discharge of cannon; that when a prisoner brought alive, and destined to death by the Indians, the fire already kindled, and himself bound to the stake, was dexterously withdrawn and secreted from them by the humanity of a fellow prisoner; a large reward was offered for the discovery of the victim, which having tempted a servant to betray his concealment, the present prisoner Dejean being sent with a party of soldiers, surrounded the house, took and threw into jail the unhappy victim, and his deliverer, where the former soon expired under the perpetual assurances of Dejean, that he was to be again restored into the hands of the savages, and the latter when enlarged was bitterly and illiberally reprimanded and threatened by Governour Hamilton.

It appears to them that the prisoner Dejean, was on all occasions the willing and cordial instrument of Governour Hamilton, acting both as judge and keeper of the jail, and instigating and urging him by malicious insinuations and untruths, to increase rather than relax his severities, heightening the cruelty of his orders by the manner of executing them; offering at one time a reward to one prisoner to be the hangman of another, threatening his life on refusal, and taking from his prisoners the little property their opportunities enabled them to acquire.

It appears that the prisoner Lamothe, was a Captain of the volunteer scalping parties of Indians and whites, wh[o] went out, from time to time, under general orders, to spare neither men, women, nor children.

From this detail of circumstances which arose in a few cases only,

coming accidentally to the knowledge of the Board, they think themselves authorized to presume by fair deduction what would be the
horrid history of the sufferings of the many who have expired under
their miseries (which therefore will remain for ever untold) or who
have[9] escaped from them, are yet too remote and too much dispersed to bring together their well grounded accusations against these
prisoners.

They have seen that the conduct of the British officers, civil and
military, has in its general tenor, through the whole course of this war,
been savage and unprecedented among civilized nations; that our officers and soldiers taken by them have been loaded with irons, con-
signed to loathsome and crouded jails, dungeons, and prison ships;
supplied often with no food, generally with too little for the sustenance
of nature, and that little sometimes unsound and unwholesome, whereby so many of them have perished that captivity and miserable death
have with them been almost synonimous; that they have been trans-
ported beyond seas where their fate is out of the reach of our enquiry,
have been compelled to take arms against their country, and by a new
refinement in cruelty to become the murtherers of their own brethren.

Their prisoners with us have, on the other hand, been treated with
moderation and humanity; they have been fed on all occasions with
wholesome and plentiful food, lodged comfortably, suffered to go at
large within extensive tracts of country, treated with liberal hos-
pital[ity], permitted to live in the families of our citizens, to labour
for themsel[ves], to acquire and to enjoy property, and finally to participate of the principal benefits of society while privileged from all
its burthens.

Reviewing this contrast which cannot be denied by our enemies
themselves in a single point, which has now been kept up during four
years of unremitted war, a term long enough to produce well founded
despair that our moderation may ever lead them into the practice of
humanity, called on by that justice which we owe to those who are
fighting the battles of their country, to deal out at length miseries to
their enemies, measure for measure, and to distress the feelings of
mankind by exhibiting to them spectacles of severe retaliation, where
we had long and vainly endeavoured to introduce an emulation in
kindness; happily possessed by the fortune of war of some of those
very individuals, who having distinguished themselves personally in
this line of cruel conduct, are fit subjects to begin on with the work
of retaliation, this Board has resolved to advise the Governour that

the said Henry Hamilton, Philip Dejean, and William Lamothe, prisoners of war, be put into irons, confined in the dungeon of the publick jail, debarred the use of pen, ink, and paper, and excluded all converse except with their keeper.[10] And the Governour orders accordingly.

(A Copy)

Attest

ARCHIBALD BLAIR, C. C.[11]

[1] This refers particularly to George Rogers Clark's letter of 29 April 1779 to Patrick Henry (Boyd, *Papers of Jefferson*, II, 256–60), in which he told of the capture of Henry Hamilton. An extract from the letter was sent to Congress (NA: PCC, No. 71, I, 251–53). The "other papers" probably included a statement from John Dodge (below, n. 8).

[2] Sir Guy Carleton (1724–1808), later Baron Dorchester, was governor of Quebec, 1767–1778, 1786–1796. Philip Dejean, described by Clark as "Grand Judge of Detroit," had been justice of the peace at Detroit at least since 1777. He was paroled in October 1779, and in April 1780 he returned to Vincennes (James Alton James, ed., *George Rogers Clark Papers*, pp. 145, 203; Clarence W. Alvord, ed., *Kaskaskia Records*, pp. 16, 168–69).

[3] Guillaume La Mothe (d. 1799) had been a trader at Detroit since 1767. Early in the Revolution he became a captain of militia there. He was at Vincennes with Hamilton when the town was captured. He was paroled in October 1779 and exchanged in 1781 (*ibid.*, p. 104 n.).

[4] "An Address to the inhabitants of Illinois, by Henry Hamilton, Lieutenant Governour of Detroit and its dependencies, &c., &c., found among Mr. Hamilton's papers" (printed in *Virginia Gazette* [Williamsburg, Dixon and Hunter], 26 June 1779). It relates Hamilton's plan "to expel the rebels" with many Indian raids. See also John D. Barnhart, ed., *Henry Hamilton and George Rogers Clark in the American Revolution* (Crawfordsville, Ind., 1951).

[5] Corrected in an unknown hand to "these."

[6] The Tennessee River.

[7] Corrected in an unknown hand to "inhuman."

[8] John Dodge was a trader from Connecticut who was imprisoned by the British at the outbreak of the Revolutionary War because of his obvious sympathies for the Americans. After being held at Detroit, he was taken to Quebec, whence he escaped in 1779. In Virginia he won the friendship of Governor Jefferson and was appointed the state's Indian agent for the county of Illinois, serving until he was removed in 1781 (Clarence Walworth Alvord, ed., *Cahokia Records, 1778–1790*, p. xcv n.). The accusations which Dodge made to the Virginia Council of State were probably similar to the fanciful and lurid charges in his pamphlet, *Treatment of John Dodge, by the English at Detroit: Written by Himself* (Philadelphia, 1779). His attitude toward the British prisoners is shown by this comment in a letter of 13 July 1779: "I am going to Williamsburg in a few days to prosecute Hamilton and that Rascal Dejean Lamotte, likewise Hominay Hay. They will all be hanged without redemption, and the Lord have mercy on their Souls" (Clarence W. Alvord, ed., *Kaskaskia Records*, pp. 104–5). During Dodge's brief service as Indian agent many accusations of malfeasance were made against him (*ibid., passim*). "Hominay" Hay was probably Major Jehu Hay, who was captured with Hamilton at Vincennes. After Hay was paroled by Virginia in 1781, he became the British lieutenant governor of Detroit (*ibid.*, 105 n.).

9 Changed in an unknown hand to "having."

10 On 29 September, after receiving General Washington's admonition of 6 August that "Mr. Hamilton could not according to the usage of War after his Capitulation, even in the manner it was made, be subjected to any uncommon severity," the Council of State ordered the three prisoners released from their irons and close confinement. At first Washington had approved the treatment of Hamilton, but this suggestion came after "more mature consideration" (Boyd, *Papers of Jefferson*, III, 30, 61, 94–95, 97). In Hamilton's report of his captivity he tells that he was "honored" with the largest fetters, "which weighed eighteen pounds eight ounces" (James A. James, ed., *George Rogers Clark Papers*, p. 197).

11 Archibald Blair (1753–1824) was clerk of the Council of State throughout the Revolutionary War.

From Philip Mazzei

RC (LC: Madison Papers). Although the address sheet is missing and the letter is unsigned, it was written beyond any doubt by Mazzei, and almost as certainly to Madison.

URBANA,[1] June 18th. 1779.

DEAR SIR,

With a disturbed mind I am now going to write to you on topics not very agreable. Mr. Penet[2] told me, that although the Capn.[3] was a scotchman, all the crew were Americans. Perhaps it was so at that time, but at present we have no more than 2. Americans on board, one of which is the cabbin-boy. We have an Italian[4] & a Spaniard (who came on board on my account) & a frenchman; all the rest are british. The Capn. has been left by 2. mates since he came in the river, the last of whom with another young fellow (both americans) went away since I came on board, & I heared him tell the Capn. that no other will do for him but a scotchman. He has no mate now, & says he wants none. I think he will go without, which you know how imprudent it will be. In time of the invasion[5] he sent away 4. saylors. Mr. Penet did not like so strange an economy when saylors are so difficult to be replaced, & while they rise dayley in their demands. Probably they were Americans. The Capn. told me at Port-Royal,[6] that he wanted only 2. men; I knew he wanted 4, or 5; he lost 2. since, as I said above; & now Giovanni tells me that he refused to take a Genoese good saylor, saying that he had men enough, when he had just in my presence done his utmost, but without purpose, to get a scotchman. The prospect is really gloomy. I assure you, that I do not like my present situation. I am however obliged to appear satisfied, & trust to chance, as thare is no other vessel for me to go.[7] The fellow knows it too well, & has made his terms accordingly. He has obliged me to put on board a prodigious quantity of provisions, besides other very costly conveniencies, & to give him a bill for 60 ghineas payable in France for 2 square yards room. Since I came up, besides the currancy I brought with me, which I thought would have sufficed, I have been obliged to part with many ghineas, & to draw at last on Mr. Blair for £.615.[8] In comparison to this neighburhood every thing is for nothing in Williamsburg. To give you a specimen of the expences in this part of the world I need only to tell you, that for 6 *small* hams I have been obliged to pay £.60:15. If we should stay here 8, or 10 days longer the Capn. will buy more provisions, & probably charge £.300. more for my share. These heavy expences, joined to what I already observed to you, induce me to wish, that as a lover of justice you would propose what you think right as soon as you have a majority capable of deciding on disinterested principles. I did, & do now, agree with you, that it was better to say nothing of this when I was in Williamsburg, but I don't think it would be prudent to delay too long.[9] I will be extremely obliged to you, my dear Sir, if you will contrive to spare me the unpleasant business. It is noble to offer, & very disagreable to ask. I was appointed the 8th. of January.[10] My expences from that time to April deserve some consideration, as I was at your orders, sometimes going about to look for a passage, & other times waiting after having prejudiced my interest in hurrying the settlement of my affairs to get in readiness;[11] but since that time I find that I am above £3000. out of pocket already, exclusive of the £615. drawn on Mr. Blair, & the hard money. I abhor the very idea of venality, but the other extreme is not always a merit. I did, you know, refuse the Governor's offer of paying me for my services; I confined my own salary myself to what will hardly bear my expences, considering the travels; & I wish for nothing more; but on the other hand I would be treated as a gentleman, & cannot bear advantages to be taken of me by people endowed with jewish principles. I wish you may not consider my expressions as complaints of an old woman. I only mean to open my bosom to you, & hope you will make use of my hints in proper time as a sensible unprejudiced friend. If my salary is to begin at the time of my appointment I am satisfied with discharging all expenses without making an Apothecary's account.[12] But let it be as it will, I must beg the favour of you to let me know as soon as possible what I am to depend upon.

I will likewise observe to you, that Mr. Jameson[13] seemed to hint that the £7000. currency were left in my hands in lieu of the 700. st;[14] to which I could not decently object, because he did not express himself fully. I proposed to accept of currency to facilitate matters. It would be really strange that I should take it at an exchange different from what I could have for the stirling I can command in Europe, & with which I must now maintain myself. I have been offered 15 at Port-Royal & Fredericksburg; but 12. was the exchange at the time I recd. the money I had left in Richmond, & that ought to be the exchange in equity for both parties. The gold I have expended here, & what I am to pay the Capn. in France, will oblige me to borrow money of Penet & Co; which I know I can have on my own credit, but I shall be obliged to return it as soon as I arrive in Tuscany, where perhaps I am not now worth a penny, if all my effects were put on board Woodford's vessel,[15] as I had directed. It is true, that my Friends will not let me in want, but would it not be prudent [and] more honorable, that I should be supplied from hence? Abt. or rather above the half of my first year's salary will be gone by the time I get to France, & the ballance due me for the year is £.116:13:6 St. Whether you pay me my expences till then, or my year begins at the time of my appointment, there can be no objection to give me credit immediately for £5, or 600. St. on Penet & Co: And I can tell you that there is no doubt of a refusal, if I can get there, & acquaint Da Costa[16] with what Penet thought proper to confide to me, & would not trust to writing. I hope you will not neglect to remit tobacco as often as you can, which you must continue to do for the credit of our Country even after having obtained the loan.

There being a probability of going out, & the pilot leaving us here at the mouth of Rapahanack, I must seal. Adieu.

Mr. Joseph Warwick of Hob's Hole is the Pilot,[17] who has promised me to send this in a parcel to the Governor by a safe hand. Please to let me know the receit by first opportunity.

[1] Urbanna.

[2] Late in December 1775 the Continental Congress encouraged J. Pierre Penet in his plan to collect munitions in France for shipment to the United States. In October 1776 Congress, at Washington's suggestion, appointed Penet "aide de camp" by brevet to Washington's staff. On 2 January 1779 Congress agreed to Penet's proposal to bring over European master workmen and establish an arms manufactory in the United States. During these years Penet had a series of associates in his merchant and shipping firm at Nantes, France. Thus his firm was, at one time, Penet and de Plearne (Emanuel de Plearne); at another, Penet, de Wendel

(Windel) et Cie; at still another, Penet et Couloux (Coulaux la Vigne); and, by June 1779, Penet, d'Acosta Frères et Cie. As late as April 1781, Vigne was its agent in the United States (NA: PCC, No. 41, VIII, 60–63; Fitzpatrick, *Writings of Washington*, IV, 159; VI, 174; *Journals of the Continental Congress*, III, 466; IV, 16; VI, 869–70; XIII, 16–17, 82, 170–72, 303–5; XIV, 776; XVIII, 890; XIX, 401; XX, 719). Penet's company owned the "Johnston Smith" on which Mazzei was sailing. In 1780–1781 Penet's "Le Comité," bringing military supplies from France to Virginia, was to cause JM and Governor Jefferson much concern (Nightingale to Virginia Delegates, 6 December 1780, n. 4; Jefferson to Virginia Delegates, 18 December 1780).

3 Andrew Paton (Peyton). He may have been secretly in the pay of the British (Howard R. Marraro, ed., *Philip Mazzei*, pp. 67, 70, 87).

4 In view of his reference to "Giovanni" later in this letter, Mazzei probably did not mean his valet, Francesco del Maglio. The "Italian" must have been a member of the crew. Mazzei's stepdaughter and wife also accompanied him.

5 Between 8 and 28 May 1779 the British raided the Hampton Roads neighborhood, capturing Portsmouth and Norfolk, burning Suffolk, and destroying shipping and military stores (above, Henry to Jay, 11 May 1779 and notes).

6 In Caroline County on the Rappahannock.

7 Mazzei had originally planned to go "in a large and strong French vessell," loading at Portsmouth, but this ship was burned by the British in May (Howard R. Marraro, ed., *Philip Mazzei*, p. 86).

8 Archibald Blair.

9 When Mazzei left Williamsburg, Governor Henry gave him £7,000 in Virginia currency, and a letter of credit for 300 louis d'ors on the Penet company in Nantes (*ibid.*, pp. 85–86).

10 See Mazzei to JM, 13 June 1779, n. 2.

11 Through Jefferson's influence, Mazzei's home, Colle, had been rented in February 1779 to the captured British Major General Friedrich Adolph, Baron von Riedesel, his wife, and three daughters (William Leete Stone, trans., *Memoirs, and Letters and Journals, of Major General Riedesel, during his Residence in America* [2 vols.; Albany, 1868], II, 69–70, 239–40).

12 Probable meaning: a detailed and accurate record of expenses.

13 David Jameson, a member of the Council of State with JM.

14 Although in February 1779 the official depreciation rate of Virginia currency in relation to specie had been 10 for 1, by June it was 20 for 1 (Henry Phillips, *Historical Sketches of the Paper Currency of the American Colonies, Prior to the Adoption of the Federal Constitution*, 1st ser. [Roxbury, Mass., 1865], p. 202).

15 Thomas Woodford.

16 His given name is not known but he was one of two or more brothers. In the primary sources their surname is variously de la Costa, de Costa, du Costa, d'Acosta, or with the "d" capitalized in each instance. He and at least one brother were Penet's partners in the trading company at Nantes. Mazzei's faith in Costa was destined to be rudely shaken (Boyd, *Papers of Jefferson*, III, 299–301).

17 Warwick of Hobb's Hole (Tappahannock) on the Rappahannock had been pilot's mate on the Virginia State brig "Mosquito" in 1779. Little more is known of him than that he apparently became a deserter in 1781, was captured, and later escaped (*Calendar of Virginia State Papers*, II, 430).

From Philip Mazzei

RC (LC: Madison Papers). Possibly this page, lacking a salutation, is the final sheet of a longer letter. It was not Mazzei's custom to write so briefly. The address sheet is missing, but Madison was in Williamsburg as a member of the Privy Council.

June 19th. 1779.

After a Tour of about 400. miles by land & water, since I left you, I am at last safely arrived, at York.[1] And as my next stage will be, in the opinion of every one, at New-York,[2] I beg you will do me the favour to ride here to morrow-morning with Dr. Mc.Clurg[3] to consult, or rather to advise me upon an Idea of mine, which I cannot communicate by letter.[4] Pray, give yourself this trouble; the business is of consequence, & I may perhaps go to-morrow-night. The Dr. is to come to see old Mrs. Goosley.[5] In the parcel to the Governor, which I had given yesterday to Jo: Warwick of Hob's hole, & which now comes by Mr. Goosley's[6] boy, there are letters for you, Mr. Blair,[7] Mr. Page,[8] Mr. Fitzhugh[9] &c. I wish you will go immediately for yours, & that you will tell the Govr:[10] & Mr. Blair where I am. I wish to Know some news of Mrs: Bellini, & if Mr. Bellini[11] is returned. I am with my respects to Mr. & Mrs. Maddison,

Dr. Sr. Yours &c. &.

PH. MAZZEI

York Town   *Turn over*.[12]

As I refer you all to Mr. Page abt. Woodford,[13] & now I consider that Mr. Page will not receive my letter probably before monday, I acquaint you, that he was taken by 2. privateers in his passage from Leghorn, & carried to New-York abt. 7 weeks ago. You will see the copy of his letter to his brother, the General.[14]

---

[1] Mazzei had probably visited the Madisons at Montpelier, since it was not far from his own home (Colle) in Albemarle County. But where else he had been in order to stretch to four hundred miles the distance from there to Yorktown, near the entrance of Chesapeake Bay, is unknown (Richard C. Garlick, Jr., *Philip Mazzei*, p. 53).

[2] Mazzei means that the ship in which he is about to sail for France might be taken by an enemy vessel outside the capes and he would be carried to New York as a prisoner. This was exactly what happened.

[3] James McClurg (1746–1823), a European-trained physician who was professor

of anatomy and medicine at the College of William and Mary and head surgeon of the Virginia military forces during much of the Revolution. After the war he served for ten years on the Privy Council, attended the Constitutional Convention of 1787 as a delegate from Virginia, and was mayor of Richmond frequently in the period from 1797 to 1804.

4 What Mazzei's "Idea" was and whether JM or Dr. McClurg went to Yorktown are unknown.

5 Mrs. Martha Gooseley (d. 1780), the widow of a Yorktown metal worker and gunsmith, took in lodgers and nursed the sick in that town (Frances Norton Mason, ed., *John Norton & Sons: Merchants of London and Virginia: Being the Papers from Their Counting House for the Years 1750 to 1795* [Richmond, 1937], pp. 75, 102, 319–21; *William and Mary Quarterly*, 1st ser., VII [1898–99], 136; XII [1903–4], 83; XIV [1905–6], 129).

6 Mr. Gooseley was probably Martha Gooseley's son William (1748–1809), a captain of York County minutemen. As a Yorktown merchant, he had met Mazzei in London in 1770. After the war, Gooseley held numerous political offices in his county, including the shrievalty for several years in the early 1790's (*Journals of the Council of State*, I, 182, 250; Frances N. Mason, ed., *John Norton & Sons*, p. 128; *Tyler's Quarterly Historical and Genealogical Magazine*, VII [1925–26], 113; IX [1927–28], 95–96; *Virginia Magazine of History and Biography*, XXVII [1919], 342; *Calendar of Virginia State Papers*, III, 360–61; VI, 138).

7 Archibald Blair. The letter for JM was probably Mazzei's of 18 June to him (*q.v.*).

8 John Page.

9 William Fitzhugh (1741–1809), a planter of King George County and later of Stafford County. Between 1775 and 1788 he held many political offices, including membership in both houses of the Virginia Assembly, and, for a few months in 1779, in the Continental Congress.

10 Patrick Henry.

11 Carlo (Charles) Bellini (d. 1804) came from Tuscany in 1774 to assist Mazzei with his viniculture at Colle. By the close of 1778, Bellini's linguistic ability had earned him the post of "Clerk of Foreign Languages" for the state of Virginia and a professorship at the College of William and Mary. Bellini was a close friend of Jefferson. Mazzei's inquiry about Mrs. Bellini may have been prompted by her ill health. She was a helpless cripple for at least three years before her death in 1787 (Howard R. Marraro, trans., *Memoirs of the Life and Peregrinations of the Florentine, Philip Mazzei, 1730–1816* [New York, 1942], pp. 199–200; *William and Mary Quarterly*, 2d ser., V [1925], 1–29; 3d ser., IV [1947], 350–55; *Journals of the Council of State*, II, 109, 157).

12 This injunction is appropriate to the manuscript but not to a copy of it.

13 Thomas Woodford.

14 William Woodford, Jr. (1734–1780), was appointed colonel of a Virginia regiment of the continental line and promoted to the rank of brigadier general on 21 February 1777. Captured when Charleston fell to the British in May 1780, he died a prisoner of war in New York City on 13 November of that year (*Virginia Magazine of History and Biography*, XXXIII [1925], 34).

To James Madison, Sr.

RC (LC: Madison Papers).

WILLIAMSBG June 25th. 1779

HOND SIR

I have recd. from Mr. Hunter[1] £2000. I shall not put it into the loan office as it is does not appear that Certificates will be taken in payment for land.[2] I have applied to Col Zane[3] on the subject of Iron, but can not get a positive promise. He has taken a Mem. and says he will write to you immediately on his return home. I was sorry to find the Horse you sent me in such meagre plight. The dry weather has so much injured the pasturage that I am obliged to be at some little expence in forage. This with the sickliness of the place and season will induce me to come up as soon as possible. I can not yet determine the time, but suppose it will be between the 10 & last of next Month. I send by Majr Moore[4] the last Newspapers & refer you to him for an acct. of the public proceedings.

With great affection I remain Yr. Dutiful son

JAMES MADISON JUNR

[1] Most probably James Hunter, Jr. (1746–1788), a Fredericksburg merchant with whom the Madisons had many business dealings (R. Walter Coakley, "The Two James Hunters of Fredericksburg, Patriots among the Virginia Scotch Merchants," *Virginia Magazine of History and Biography*, LVI [1948], 3–21).

[2] The Assembly of Virginia established a loan office in Williamsburg in June 1777. Any citizen might lend $200 or more through this office to the Continental Congress and receive in return a loan certificate bearing 6 per cent annual interest and maturing after three years (*Journal of the House of Delegates*, May 1777, p. 112; Hening, *Statutes*, IX, 283–85). By an act of 6 December 1779, the loan certificates, which were to mature on 1 March 1780, were made acceptable in payment for such public lands of Virginia as were for sale (*Journal of the House of Delegates*, October 1779, p. 80; Hening, *Statutes*, X, 148).

[3] Isaac Zane, Jr.

[4] The Virginia Assembly adjourned on 26 June 1779. William Moore, a member of the House of Delegates, was evidently returning to his home in Orange County.

Thomas Jefferson in Council to Thomas Whiting

RC (Henry E. Huntington Library). The letter and its inclosed memorandum are in JM's hand rather than in that of
Archibald Blair, the clerk of the Council of State. JM addressed the cover sheet and also noted on it: "Requisition of
sundry Articles from the Executive for the Directors of the
Works at Richmond June 26. 1779."

IN COUNCIL June 26th. 1779

SIR[1]

At the request of the directors of the public Buildings in Richmond,[2]
I am to desire that you will provide for them[3] locks of different kinds
fit for house doors, hinges for do., window glass, putty, lathing nails
and shells. For the quantities I must refer you to the Directors themselves. I am Sir Your Humble Servant,

TH: JEFFERSON[4]

Memod. for the Board of Trade.

800 feet of Glass—10 by 12.
300 lb Putty
500 lb of white lead in Kegs ground.
50 Gallons Linseed oil
250000 4d. Nails for lathing
25000 Floaring 20d. brads:
25,000 20d. Nails.
50,000 6d. do.
20,000 10d. do.
Six large strong locks—12 pr. strong HL hinges—12 good locks
for inside doors—
Iron plates.[5]

---

[1] Thomas Whiting (ca. 1712–1781), a wealthy merchant of Gloucester County,
was a member of the Board of Trade of Virginia. Jacquelin Ambler was its chairman and Duncan Rose, a Petersburg merchant, was its other member. Why Jefferson addressed his note to Whiting rather than to Ambler or Rose is not clear.
Perhaps Whiting was either the only one of the three conveniently at hand or,
as a merchant, had been awarded the contract for supplying the articles mentioned
in the memorandum. The Board of Trade had been created by the Assembly in
May 1779. Serving as the executive agency of the Governor in Council, the board
directed a wide range of activities, including the importation and allocation of
military goods of all kinds, the manufacture of them within Virginia insofar as
possible, and the providing of civilian necessities such as salt, cottons, and woolens

at reasonable prices (*Journal of the House of Delegates,* May 1779, pp. 13, 17, 53, 54; Hening, *Statutes,* X, 15–16).

[2] On 18 June 1779 the Assembly decided to move the "seat of government" from Williamsburg to Richmond. This action was designed to keep the capital upon a navigable stream but in a more central location, less exposed to "insults and injuries of the publick enemy" (*ibid.,* X, 85–86). On 24 June, by joint ballot of the two houses of the Assembly, Turner Southall of Richmond was elected the chairman; and Archibald Cary and Robert Goode of Chesterfield County, James Buchanan of Richmond, and Robert Carter Nicholas of Hanover County were chosen to be the other members of the board of directors of the public buildings of the state at Richmond (*Journal of the House of Delegates,* May 1779, pp. 64–65).

[3] Because of the exigencies of the war, the scarcity of materials, and the high price of labor, the directors were ordered to provide only "temporary buildings for the sitting of the general assembly, the courts of justice, and the several boards" (Hening, *Statutes,* X, 88).

[4] On 1 June 1779 the legislature elected Jefferson to succeed Patrick Henry as governor.

[5] At the end of the memorandum, Archibald Cary, presiding officer of the state Senate as well as one of the directors of public buildings, wrote: "These the board of Trade is to send for, on Acct. of the Directors for removeing seat of Goverment Archd Cary June 26th. 1779."

To William Bradford

RC (Historical Society of Pennsylvania).

WMSBG. July 17th. 1779

MY DEAR FRIEND

I had the pleasure of receiving yours of the 29th.[?] Ulto.[1] by yesterday's post, and agreeable to your request take this immediate opportunity of acknowledging it.

The Inhabitants of this City roused by the extortions of the times and the example of your State are instituting regulations similar to those you mention. Whether they will have the necessary prudenc[e,] firmness & perseverence, or whether the other parts of the State will concur in the undertaking time only can shew.[2] The Specific Tax adopted here[3] and the plentiful crops in prospect in the middle States it is to be hoped will facilitate the execution of it.

The Govr. has recd. authentic information from the Southward that Gen Lincoln[4] on the 20th. of last Month made a regular attack on the Enemy's lines on the mainland opposite the Island abt. 20 Miles from C. Town where our main body lay. The assault continued 56 Minutes. A party of Highlanders which sallied out were driven back with great slaughter. The result was however that the Genl. finding the place more impregnable than he expected & reinforcements from the Island having arrived during the engagement withdrew his troops with all his wounded & Artillery. Our loss is represented as inconsiderable and that of the Enemy as probably material.[5] Govr. Rutledge adds that our Army was greatly animated with the experiment and were satisfied that had the Enemy quitted their lines, that in a fair & open combat, they should have beat them.[6]

The General Washington a Ship belonging to this State and just arrived from France, left Brest in company with a fleet consisting of 1-80 Gun Ship[,] 5-74[,] 2[?] Frigates[,] 24-20 Gun Ships with 60 Transports containing 10,000 troops destined for the W. Indies. She parted with the Fleet on the 1st. of June off Madeira.[7]

I mentioned to you in my last that upon the receipt of it it would be necessary to change the direction of your Letters from this City to Orange. I propose to set of[f] about the last of next week.

Adieu

JM Jr.

---

[1] Not found.

[2] Bradford had probably mentioned a meeting on 25 May 1779 in which prominent citizens of Philadelphia, under his father's chairmanship, adopted and urged others to agree to measures designed to hold down prices and to penalize those who failed to co-operate, in order to prevent a further depreciation of the currency. Their "Address of the Committee of the City and Liberties of Philadelphia, to Their Fellow Citizens throughout the United States" appeared in the *Virginia Gazette* (Williamsburg, Dixon and Nicolson) of 7 August 1779. On 15 and 16 July, however, "respectable citizens and freemen" of Williamsburg, meeting in the courthouse, had blamed the "alarming depreciation of our paper currency" largely upon "monopolizers, forestallers, and engrossers," and appointed a standing committee (*a*) to maintain for basic commodities a monthly schedule of prices; (*b*) to prevent these commodities from being removed from the town to more profitable markets; (*c*) to brand transgressors as hostile "to the rights and liberties of America"; and (*d*) to urge other communities to do likewise, including an acceptance of approximately the Williamsburg price schedule (*ibid.*, 24 July 1779).

[3] On 26 June 1779 the Assembly provided by law that annually for the next four years there must be furnished, without charge to the state, one bushel of wheat or its equivalent value in other grains, hemp, or tobacco, for every able-bodied man and "every woman slave" over sixteen years of age (*Journal of the House of Delegates*, May 1779, p. 70; Hening, *Statutes*, X, 79).

[4] Major General Benjamin Lincoln.

[5] Early in June 1779 the British Major General Augustine Prevost and his force of about 2,500 troops occupied a strongly fortified position on John's Island and especially on the nearby mainland at Stono Ferry on the Stono River. Between 16 and 19 June, however, he and all except about nine hundred of his men left by sea for Savannah. On the 20th, some twelve hundred patriot soldiers led by Lincoln assaulted the enemy redoubts at Stono Ferry. After a hard-fought battle, having failed to attain their objective before British reinforcements began to arrive

from John's Island, they retreated in good order back to Charleston. Apparently their loss amounted to 146 men killed or wounded and 155 missing; that of the British to 129 killed or wounded and one missing. Shortly after the battle the remainder of the enemy troops left for Port Royal Island on their way to Savannah (Christopher Ward, *The War of the Revolution*, ed. by John Richard Alden [2 vols.; New York, 1952], II, 685–88).

6 Probably the "authentic information" mentioned at the beginning of this paragraph had come to Governor Thomas Jefferson from Governor John Rutledge (1739–1800) of South Carolina. Rutledge would be a member of the Constitutional Convention of 1787, an Associate Justice of the Supreme Court of the United States, 1789–1791, and briefly in 1795 its acting Chief Justice.

7 The "General Washington" was apparently an armed schooner which returned to Alexandria, Va., in June from a nine-month voyage, mainly spent in and near the Bay of Biscay. On its return passage the "General Washington" captured a British privateer off Cape Henry. Toussaint Guillaume, Comte de La Motte-Picquet de la Vinoyère, commanded the French fleet, which was composed of five ships of the line, three frigates, and sixty transports (Doniol, *Histoire*, IV, 252 n.).

Money

Printed text (Philip Freneau's *National Gazette* [Philadelphia], 19 and 22 December 1791). The original manuscript of the essay is not known to be extant. In the Tracy W. McGregor Library, University of Virginia, is a transcript of about the first one-third of the article, which John C. Payne probably copied from the newspaper version of it.

[September 1779–March 1780]

MONEY.

Observations written posterior to the circular Address of Congress in Sept. 1779, and prior to their Act of March, 1780.[1]

It has been taken for an axiom in all our reasonings on the subject of finance, that supposing the quantity and demand of things vendible in a country to remain the same, their price will vary according to the variation in the quantity of the circulating medium; in other words, that the value of money will be regulated by its quantity. I shall submit to the judgment of the public some considerations which determine mine to reject the proposition as founded in error. Should they be deemed not absolutely conclusive, they seem at least to shew that it is liable to too many exceptions and restrictions to be taken for granted as a fundamental truth.

If the circulating medium be of universal value as specie, a local increase or decrease of its quantity, will not, whilst a communication subsists with other countries, produce a correspondent rise or fall in its value. The reason is obvious. When a redundancy of universal money prevails in any one country, the holders of it know their interest too well to waste it in extravagant prices, when it would be worth so much more to them elsewhere. When a deficiency happens, those who hold commodities, rather than part with them at an undervalue in one country, would carry them to another. The variation of prices in these cases, cannot therefore exceed the expence and insurance of transportation.

Suppose a country totally unconnected with Europe, or with any other country, to possess specie in the same proportion to circulating property that Europe does; prices there would correspond with those in Europe. Suppose that so much specie were thrown into circulation as to make the quantity exceed the proportion of Europe tenfold, without any change in commodities, or in the demand for them: as soon as such an augmentation had produced its effect, prices would rise tenfold; or which is the same thing, money would be depreciated tenfold. In this state of things, suppose again, that a free and ready communication were opened between this country and Europe, and that the inhabitants of the former, were made sensible of the value of their money in the latter; would not its value among themselves immediately cease to be regulated by its quantity, and assimilate itself to the foreign value?

Mr. Hume in his discourse on the balance of trade supposes, "that if four fifths of all the money in Britain were annihilated in one night, and the nation reduced to the same condition, in this particular, as in the reigns of the Harrys and Edwards, that the price of all labour and commodities would sink in proportion, and every thing be sold as cheap as in those ages: That, again, if all the money in Britain were multiplied fivefold in one night, a contrary effect would follow." This very ingenious writer seems not to have considered that in the reigns of the Harrys and Edwards, the state of prices in the circumjacent nations corresponded with that of Britain; whereas in both of his suppositions, it would be no less than four fifths different. Imagine that such a difference really existed, and remark the consequence. Trade is at present carried on between Britain and the rest of Europe, at a profit of 15 or 20 per cent. Were that profit raised to 400 per cent. would not their home market, in case of such a fall of prices, be so exhausted by exportation—and in case of such a rise of prices, be so overstocked with foreign commodities, as immediately to restore the general equilibrium? Now, to borrow the language of the same author, "the same causes which would redress the inequality were it to happen, must forever prevent it, without some violent external operation."[2]

The situation of a country connected by commercial intercourse with other countries, may be compared to a single town or province whose intercourse with other towns and provinces results from political connection. Will it be pretended that if the national currency were to be accumulated in a single town or province, so as to exceed its due proportion five or tenfold, a correspondent depreciation would ensue, and every thing be sold five or ten times as dear as in a neighboring town or province?

If the circulating medium be a municipal one, as paper currency, still its value does not depend on its quantity. It depends on the credit of the state issuing it, and on the time of its redemption; and is no otherwise affected by the quantity, than as the quantity may be supposed to *endanger* or *postpone* the redemption.

That it depends in part on the credit of the issuer, no one will deny. If the credit of the issuer, therefore be perfectly unsuspected, the time of redemption alone will regulate its value.

To support what is here advanced, it is sufficient to appeal to the nature of paper money. It consists of bills or notes of obligation payable in specie to the bearer, either on demand or at a future day. Of the first kind is the paper currency of Britain, and hence its equivalence to specie. Of the latter kind is the paper currency of the United States, and hence its inferiority to specie. But if its being redeemable not on demand but at a future day, be the cause of its inferiority, the distance of that day, and not its quantity, ought to be the measure of that inferiority.

It has been shewn that the value of specie does not fluctuate according to local fluctuations in its quantity. Great Britain, in which there is such an immensity of circulating paper, shews that the value of paper depends as little on its quantity as that of specie, when the paper represents specie payable on demand. Let us suppose that the circulating notes of Great Britain, instead of being payable on demand, were to be redeemed at a future day, at the end of one year for example, and that no interest was due on them. If the same assurance prevailed that at the end of the year they would be equivalent to specie, as now prevails that they are every moment equivalent, would any other effect result from such a change, except that the notes would suffer a depreciation equal to one year's interest? They would in that case represent, not the nominal sum expressed on the face of them, but the sum remaining after a deduction of one year's interest. But if when they represent the full nominal sum of specie, their circulation contributes no more to depreciate them, than the circulation of the specie itself would do; does it not follow, that if they represented a sum of specie less than the nominal inscription, their circulation ought to depreciate them no more than so much specie, if substituted, would depreciate itself? We may extend the time from one, to five, or to twenty years; but we shall find no other rule of depreciation than the loss of the intermediate interest.

What has been here supposed with respect to Great Britain has actually taken place in the United States. Being engaged in a necessary war without specie to defray the expence, or to support paper emissions for that purpose redeemable on demand, and being at the same time unable to borrow, no resource was left, but to emit bills of credit to be redeemed in future. The inferiority of these bills to specie was therefore incident to the very nature of them. If they had been exchangeable on demand for specie, they would have been equivalent to it; as they were not exchangeable on demand, they were inferior to it. The degree of their inferiority must consequently be estimated by the time of their becoming exchangeable for specie, that is the time of their redemption.

To make it still more palpable that the value of our currency does not depend on its quantity, let us put the case, that Congress had, during the first year of the war, emitted five millions of dollars to be redeemed at the end of ten years; that, during the second year of the war, they had emitted ten millions more, but with due security that the whole fifteen millions should be redeemed in five years; that, during the two succeeding years, they had augmented the emissions to one hundred millions, but from the discovery of some extraordinary sources of wealth, had been able to engage for the redemption of the whole sum in one year: it is asked, whether the depreciation, under these circumstances, would have increased as the quantity of money increased —or whether on the contrary, the money would not have risen in value, at every accession to its quantity?[3]

It has indeed happened, that a progressive depreciation of our currency has accompanied its growing quantity; and to this is probably owing in a great measure the prevalence of the doctrine here opposed. When the fact however is explained, it will be found to coincide perfectly with what has been said. Every one must have taken notice that, in the emissions of Congress, no precise time has been stipulated for their redemption, nor any specific provision made for that purpose. A general promise entitling the bearer to so many dollars of metal as the paper bills express, has been the only basis of their credit. Every one therefore has been left to his own conjectures as to the time the redemption would be fulfilled; and as every addition made to the quantity in circulation, would naturally be supposed to remove to a proportionally greater distance the redemption of the whole mass, it could not happen otherwise than that every additional emission would be followed by a further depreciation.

In like manner has the effect of a distrust of public credit, the other source of depreciation, been erroneously imputed to the quantity of money. The circumstances under which our early emissions were made, could not but strongly concur, with the futurity of their redemption, to debase their value. The situation of the United States resembled that of an individual engaged in an expensive undertaking, carried on, for want of cash, with bonds and notes secured on an estate to which his title was disputed; and who had besides, a combination of enemies employing every artifice to disparage that security. A train of sinister events during the early stages of the war likewise contributed to increase the distrust of the public ability to fulfil their engagements. Before the depreciation arising from this cause was removed by the success of our arms, and our alliance with France, it had drawn so large a quantity into circulation, that the quantity itself soon after begat a distrust of the *public disposition* to fulfil their engagements; as well as new doubts, in timid minds, concerning the issue of the contest. From that period, this cause of depreciation has been incessantly operating. It has first conduced to swell the amount of necessary emissions, and from that very amount has derived new force and efficacy to itself. Thus, a further discredit of our money has necessarily followed the augmentation of its quantity; but every one must perceive, that it has not been the effect of the quantity, considered in itself, but considered as an omen of public bankruptcy.*[4]

* As the depreciation of our money has been ascribed to a wrong cause, so, it may be remarked, have effects been ascribed to the depreciation, which result from other causes. Money is the instrument by which men's wants are supplied, and many who possess it will part with it for that purpose, who would not gratify themselves at the expence of their visible property. Many also may acquire it, who have no visible property. By increasing the quantity of money therefore, you both increase the means of spending, and stimulate the desire to spend; and if the objects desired do not increase in proportion, their price must rise from the influence of the greater demand for them. Should the objects in demand happen, at the same juncture, as in the United States, to become scarcer, their prices must rise in a double proportion.

It is by this influence of an augmentation of money on demand, that we ought to account for that proportional level of money, in all countries, which Mr. Hume attributes to its direct influence on prices. When an augmentation of the national coin takes place, it may be supposed either, 1. not to augment demand at all; or, 2. to augment it so gradually that a proportional increase of industry will supply

Whether the money of a country, then, be gold and silver, or paper currency, it appears that its value is not regulated by its quantity. If it be the former, its value depends on the general proportion of gold and silver, to circulating property throughout all countries having free inter communication. If the latter, it depend[s] on the credit of the state issuing it, and the time at which it is to become equal to gold and silver.

Every circumstance which has been found to accelerate the depreciation of our currency naturally resolves itself into these general principles. The spirit of monopoly hath affected it in no other way than by creating an artificial scarcity of commodities wanted for public use, the consequence of which has been an increase of their price, and of the necessary emissions. Now it is this increase of emissions which has been shewn to lengthen the supposed period of their redemption, and to foster suspicions of public credit. Monopolies destroy the natural relation between money and commodities; but it is by raising the value of the latter, not by debasing that of the former. Had our money been gold or silver, the same prevalence of monopoly would have had the same effect on prices and expenditures; but these would not have had the same effect on the value of money.

---

the objects of it; or, 3. to augment it so rapidly that the domestic market may prove inadequate, whilst the taste for distinction natural to wealth, inspires, at the same time, a preference for foreign luxuries. The first case can seldom happen. Were it to happen, no change in prices, nor any efflux of money, would ensue; unless indeed, it should be employed or loaned abroad. The superfluous portion would be either hoarded or turned into plate. The second case can occur only where the augmentation of money advances with a very slow and equable pace; and would be attended neither with a rise of prices, nor with a superfluity of money. The third is the only case, in which the plenty of money would occasion it to overflow into other countries. The insufficiency of the home market to satisfy the demand would be supplied from such countries as might afford the articles in demand; and the money would thus be drained off, till that and the demand excited by it, should fall to a proper level, and a balance be thereby restored between exports and imports.

The principle on which Mr. Hume's theory, and that of Montesquieu's before him, is founded, is manifestly erroneous. He considers the money in every country as the representative of the whole circulating property and industry in the country; and thence concludes, that every variation in its quantity must increase or lessen the portion which represents the same portion of property and labor. The error lies in supposing, that because money serves to measure the value of all things, it represents and is equal in value to all things. The circulating property in every country, according to its market rate, far exceeds the amount of its money. At Athens oxen, at Rome sheep, were once used as a measure of the value of other things. It will hardly be supposed, they were therefore equal in value to all other things.

The depreciation of our money has been charged on misconduct in the purchasing departments: but this misconduct must have operated in the same manner as the spirit of monopoly. By unnecessarily raising the price of articles required for public use, it has swelled the amount of necessary emissions, on which has depended the general opinion concerning the time and the probability of their redemption.

The same remark may be applied to the deficiency of imported commodities. The deficiency of these commodities has raised the price of them; the rise of their price has increased the emissions for purchasing them; and with the increase of emissions, have increased suspicions concerning their redemption.

Those who consider the quantity of money as the criterion of its value, compute the intrinsic depreciation of our currency by dividing the whole mass by the supposed necessary medium of circulation. Thus supposing the medium necessary for the United States to be 30,000,000 dollars, and the circulating emissions to be 200,000,000 the intrinsic difference between paper and specie will be nearly as 7 for 1. If its value depends on the time of its redemption, as hath been above maintained, the real difference will be found to be considerably less. Suppose the period necessary for its redemption to be 18 years, as seems to be understood by Congress; 100 dollars of paper 18 years hence will be equal in value to 100 dollars of specie; for at the end of that term, 100 dollars of specie may be demanded for them. They must consequently at this time be equal to as much specie as, with compound interest, will amount, in that number of years, to 100 dollars. If the interest of money be rated at 5 per cent. this present sum of specie will be about 41 1-2 dollars. Admit, however the use of money to be worth 6 per cent. about 35 dollars will then amount in 18 years to 100. 35 dollars of specie therefore is at this time equal to 100 of paper; that is, the man who would exchange his specie for paper at this discount, and lock it in his desk for 18 years, would get 6 per cent. for his money. The proportion of 100 to 35 is less than 3 to 1. The intrinsic depreciation of our money therefore, according to this rule of computation, is less than 3 to 1; instead of 7 to 1, according to the rule espoused in the circular address,[5] or 30 or 40 to 1, according to its currency in the market.

I shall conclude with observing, that if the preceding principles and reasoning be just, the plan on which our domestic loans have been obtained, must have operated in a manner directly contrary to what was intended. A loan-office certificate differs in nothing from a common bill of credit, except in its higher denomination, and in the interest allowed on it; and the interest is allowed, merely as a compensation to the lender, for exchanging a number of small bills, which being easily transferable, are most convenient, for a single one so large as not to be transferable in ordinary transactions. As the certificates, however, do circulate in many of the more considerable transactions, it may justly be questioned, even on the supposition that the value of money depended on its quantity, whether the advantage to the public from the exchange, would justify the terms of it. But dismissing this consideration, I ask whether such loans do in any shape, lessen the public debt, and thereby render the discharge of it less suspected or less remote? Do they give any new assurance that a paper dollar will be one day equal to a silver dollar, or do they shorten the distance of that day? Far from it: The certificates constitute a part of the public debt no less than the bills of credit exchanged for them, and have an equal claim to redemption within the general period; nay, are to be paid off long before the expiration of that period, with bills of credit, which will thus return into the general mass, to be redeemed along with it. Were these bills, therefore, not to be taken out of circulation at all, by means of the certificates, not only the expence of offices for exchanging, reexchanging, and annually paying the interest, would be avoided; but the whole sum of interest would be saved, which must make a formidable addition to the public emissions, protract the period of their redemption, and proportionally increase their depreciation. No expedient could perhaps have been devised more preposterous and unlucky. In order to relieve public credit sinking under the weight of an enormous debt, we invent new expenditures. In order to raise the value of our money, which depends on the time of its redemption, we have recourse to a measure which removes its redemption to a more distant day. Instead of paying off the capital to the public creditors, we give them an enormous interest to change the name of the bit of paper which expresses the sum due to them; and think it a piece of dexterity in finance, by *emitting loan-office certificates,* to elude the necessity of *emitting bills of credit.*

---

1 Pledging on 1 September 1779 not to increase its $160,000,000 of outstanding bills of credit by more than 25 per cent, and that only in case of a dire emergency, the Continental Congress had John Jay draft a "Circular Address" to the states (adopted 13 September) exhorting them to supply enough soldiers, money, and matériel to restore public credit and advance the common cause. And yet, by 18 March 1780, the gloomy situation obliged Congress to authorize the states to issue new bills of credit and declare that the old continental issues would be redeemed at only one-fortieth of their face value (*Journals of the Continental*

Congress, XV, 1052–62; XVI, 262–67). Although in the prefatory note JM declared that he wrote his essay during the six months intervening between these two actions by Congress, he probably could have narrowed the time to the period from late in December 1779 to early in March of the next year.

In his brief third-person autobiography, written long afterward, JM mentioned his election to Congress on 14 December 1779, and then added: "To prepare himself for this service, he employed an unavoidable detention from it in making himself acquainted with the state of Continental affairs, and particularly that of the finances which, owing to the depreciation of the paper currency, was truly deplorable. The view he was led to take of the evil, and its causes, was put on paper, now to be found in several periodical publications, particularly Freneau's National Gazette No.   ." By "unavoidable detention" he most likely referred to his necessary preparations at Montpelier for his residence in Philadelphia, and the heavy snow which delayed his departure for that city until 6 March 1780, or for some days after he had planned to begin the trip. The essay was printed as the fourth in JM's series of seventeen politically tinged articles appearing in Freneau's newspaper late in President Washington's first term. Even though JM may have revised his original manuscript before releasing it for publication, it deals with a problem which was much less acute by 1791 than when he wrote the essay nearly twelve years earlier.

² JM accurately reflects the thought, but does not always quote the exact words, of David Hume in his *Political Discourses* (Edinburgh, 1752), pp. 82–83.

³ The portion of the essay in the issue of the *National Gazette* for 19 December 1791 ends here. The remainder is in the issue of 22 December 1791.

⁴ This entire footnote is in italics in the *National Gazette*. In the last paragraph of the footnote, JM refers to Book XXII of Montesquieu's *De l'esprit des lois*, first published in Geneva in 1748 and soon thereafter translated into English. JM's daring in challenging the correctness of this redoubtable authority is noted by Paul Merrill Spurlin in his *Montesquieu in America, 1760–1801* (Baton Rouge, La., 1940), pp. 175–76.

⁵ Above, n. 1.

Advertisement for Missing Horse

Printed text (*Virginia Gazette* [Williamsburg, Dixon and Hunter], 30 October 1779, p. 3, col. 2).

WILLIAMSBURG, *October* 25, 1779.

Strayed or stolen from the common of this city,¹ a sorrel horse, about 12 years old, and upward of 14 hands high, with a hanging mane and switch tail; he is of a strong make, his hind feet are white and he has a few saddle spots. He formerly was owned by Mr. *Edwin Fleet* of *King & Queen*, deceased.² Whoever will deliver the said horse to me in *Williamsburg*, or to Col. *James Madison* in *Orange*, shall be paid one hundred dollars.

JAMES MADISON, JUN.³

¹ The particular "common" has not been located. The act of the provincial assembly of Virginia on 7 June 1699, "Directing the Building the Capitol and the City of Williamsburgh," designated several parcels of land which should be left "in comon" at the "Discretion of the Directors" (Rutherfoord Goodwin, *A Brief & True Report Concerning Williamsburg in Virginia,* pp. 335, 342). Since JM calls it "the common of this city," it was more likely the Palace Green, whch adjoined the governor's "Palace," than the 150-acre "pasture" of the College of William and Mary, where JM lived in the home of its president, Reverend James Madison.

² Edwin Fleet (1729–1778) of King and Queen County also had large land holdings in Orange County and thus was probably known by the Madisons. His will indicates that he was either a bachelor or a childless widower (Beverley Fleet, comp., "Virginia Colonial Abstracts" [mimeographed], XIV, 36, 37).

³ In a conversation on 25 April 1827 with Jared Sparks, JM apparently failed to recall the lost horse but he did tell about having his hat stolen while he was a member of the Council of State. As Sparks reported JM's anecdote: "He [JM] sent out for a new hat, but none could be found in all the shops of Williamsburgh, and he was actually obliged to keep within doors for two days for the want of a hat. At last he obtained a second-hand one from a tailor, for which he paid an enormous price, and which gave him such an appearance when on his head, as to make him the amusement of his friends during the whole session" (Herbert B. Adams, *The Life and Writings of Jared Sparks* [2 vols.; Boston, 1893], II, 36).

To William Bradford

RC (Historical Society of Pennsylvania). Large portions are torn from the top of the first two pages and the bottom of the third page. The cover sheet, date, salutation, complimentary close, and signature are missing. The handwriting is JM's, while the content of the letter and its presence in the Bradford papers combine to identify the addressee.

[WILLIAMSBURG, 30 October–5 November 1779]¹

satisfaction, a visit from
I must own as your not
any beneficial affects fro[m]
a satisfaction should be
your health, than that
the waters have been as
I flatter myself they have
for a confirmation of it to
future season when it may be convenient for you to extend your ride as far as Orange; where I may generally be found in those months in which the Springs are most used.²

The abrupt arrival of the French on the Coast of Georgia will have reached you long before this.[3] Reports already begin to prevail that the British Army is in part if not wholly captivated. It will be a great disappointment to me I confess if many of them escape. This fortunate event will thoroughly cure them of their rapacious zeal for the rich & flourishing Metropolis of S. Carolina. The people in that quarter have been sorely infested with them for the greatest part of a year, and will no doubt cooperate, by the most decisive exertions[4]

                             rate of Articles best [?]
                             Every days experience
                             [ex]pedients can extricate
                             [reme?]dial Tax imposed in
                             tly the demand for Money
                             no reliance on foreign loan[s][5]
                             [ev]er afforded any sensible
relief, nor ca[n] any [relief be expected?] as long as our money is in a course of depreciation. The sale of confiscated estates or of unappr[opr]iated lands can have little influence I fear on an evil of such magnitude. The most natural & extensive remedy we can apply seems to be taxation & Congress seem to have stretched it as far as they thought they could prudently venture. Their requisition from the States as well as I recollect, for the current year amounts to no less than 60 Million of Dollars. Most people supposed when it was made, that it wd. be at lea[s]t equal to this years expenditures, and when aided with other resources would produce a favourable revolution in the State of our Finances. I own I was myself of this number. But the present state of things threaten a total disappointmt. of their expectations. And from the Journals of Congress a copy of which has lately fallen into my hands, I find that on the 4th. of June last the emissions of the present year amounted to rather more than 35 Million of Dollars; which, as the last 2 or 3 emissions appear to have been double the preceeding ones, & the [n]ecessity of a progressive enlargement in the remaing seven Months will con[ti]nue[,] will probably swell them by end of the year to 100 Million. Should this be the case the Continental debt instead of being aided by the taxes of this year, will be higher by 40 Million of Drs. than at the beginning of it.[6] Is it not manifest then that untill some measures are generally taken to prevent the further emission of money whilst the redemption of that already emitted is going on that the public credit must every day grow worse & worse? What [bett?]er views Congress may have I am a total stra[nger to.]

I am somewhat astonished as they must be fu[ll]y sensible of the

evil and have been a[p]prized of the remedy adopted here[7] that they hav[e not] recommended it to the other States. It promises I think certain relief, and the people in general as far as I can find are so much of the same
was ever less unaccepta[ble]
    I have dwelt so
room to add
off on my return to
always give me infin[ite]
unalterable friendship.

[1] JM's loss of his horse in Williamsburg late in October (see above, advertisement in *Virginia Gazette*, 25 October 1779) makes it almost certain that he was still there, attending the Council of State, when he wrote this letter. Its missing date is suggested by the nature of JM's remarks about the military operations in Georgia. His mention of reports that the British army, or some part of it, had been "captivated" appears to reflect his reading of the sanguine account in the 30 October 1779 issue of the *Virginia Gazette* (Williamsburg, Clarkson and Davis). On the other hand he probably had not seen this paper for 6 November, with its much less cheering word about the military situation in Georgia. In the second paragraph of the letter JM's statement that the British army had infested South Carolina "for the greatest part of a year" also helps a little to solve the problem of the date. Having captured Savannah on 29 December 1778, General Augustine Prevost and his troops were raiding along the South Carolina coast early in January 1779 to within seventy miles of Charleston and, after a number of reverses, to the outskirts of that city by early May (JM to Bradford, 17 July 1779, n. 5).

[2] In this much mutilated section, JM is apparently suggesting that since his friend was still in poor health, he should try "the waters" in Virginia and visit Montpelier during the trip. Because of illness, Bradford had resigned his commission as lieutenant colonel in the Pennsylvania continental line on 1 April 1779.

[3] Beginning early in September 1779, a French fleet and landing force under Admiral Charles Henri Hector, Comte d'Estaing, together with American troops commanded by General Benjamin Lincoln, surrounded General Prevost's troops in Savannah. An assault upon them by land and by sea failed on 9 October 1779. About ten days later the French fleet sailed away and Lincoln's army withdrew to Charleston (Christopher Ward, *War of the Revolution*, II, 688–94).

[4] Following "exertions," a section of the letter, perhaps comprising seven lines of text, is missing.

[5] During 1779 Congress borrowed 2,407,800 livres (approximately $24,078,000 in specie) from France (*Journals of the Continental Congress*, XV, 1442).

[6] During 1779 Congress emitted bills of credit totaling $65,141,120. Of this amount $35,000,680 had been issued up to 4 June. Therefore JM's prediction of $100,000,000 to be issued during 1779 was much too gloomy. Congress attempted to back its paper money issues by requisitioning $60,000,000 from the states (Virginia's share, $9,600,000) in that year. If they all had paid their quotas in full, the national debt, exclusive of foreign loans, would have increased by only $5,141,260 during the year, rather than the $40,000,000 anticipated by JM. On 1 September 1779 Congress resolved that the bills of credit to be issued during that calendar year, when added to those outstanding from earlier emissions, should not exceeed $200,000,000. This ceiling was reached by the close of 1779 (*Journals of the Continental Con-*

gress, XIII, 28; XIV, 626, 1013–14; XV, 1324–25). JM's interest in the financial situation, manifested in this letter, led him to prepare an essay on "Money" sometime late in 1779 or early in 1780 (*q.v.*).

7 By "remedy adopted here" JM may allude to the actions mentioned in nn. 2 and 3 to his letter to Bradford of 17 July 1779 (*q.v.*).

Proclamation Ordering Embargo

Newspaper clipping (NA: PCC, No. 71, I, 305). This proclamation was printed in the *Virginia Gazette* (Williamsburg, Dixon and Nicolson), 11 December 1779. It was forwarded to Congress in Jefferson's letter of 30 December 1779 to President Samuel Huntington (Boyd, *Papers of Jefferson*, III, 249–51).

[30 November 1779]

By His Excellency THOMAS JEFFERSON, *Esq; Governour or Chief Magistrate of the commonwealth of* VIRGINIA:

A PROCLAMATION.

WHEREAS the exportation of provisions from this state will be attended with manifest injury to the United States, by supplying the enemy, and by rendering it difficult for the publick agents and contractors to procure supplies for the *American* troops, and will moreover give encouragement to engrossers and monopolizers to prosecute their baneful practices, I have therefore thought fit, by and with the advice and consent of the Council of State, to issue this my proclamation for laying an embargo on provisions; and I do hereby lay an embargo on provisions, *viz.* On all beef, pork, bacon, wheat, *Indian* corn, pease or other grain, or flour or meal made of the same; to continue until the first day of *May* next.[1] And I do hereby strictly prohibit all mariners, masters, and commanders of vessels, and all other persons whatsoever within this state, from loading on board any vessel for exportation, and from exporting all or any of the above species of provisions, by land or water, from the date hereof, during the term aforesaid, under pain of incurring the penalties inflicted by the act of Assembly intitled *An act to empower the Governour and Council to lay an embargo for a limited time*, except as in the said act is excepted.[2] And I do hereby strictly charge and command all naval officers and others, in their respective departments, to exert their best endeavours to the end that this embargo be strictly observed.

GIVEN under my hand this 30th day of November, 1779

THOMAS JEFFERSON.

1 The embargo proclamation was reissued on 17 May and 17 July 1780 and on 19 January 1781. On 15 December 1779 Congress renewed its request of 21 August 1779 that the states continue or levy an embargo on "wheat, flour, rye, Indian corn, rice, bread, beef, pork, bacon and live stock" (Boyd, *Papers of Jefferson*, III, 209 n.; *Journals of the Continental Congress*, XIV, 986; XV, 1383).

2 "An act to empower the Governour and Council to lay an Embargo for a limited time" passed the House of Delegates on 29 October, and the amendments submitted by the Senate were accepted the next day. Forfeiture of ship and cargo was the stipulated penalty for violating the embargo. It, however, did not apply to ships laden with material for the military forces of the United States or its allies. Furthermore, with the permission of the governor and council, and after posting a bond equal to double the value of its cargo, a ship could carry supplies to "inhabitants of any of the United States . . . in real distress for want of provisions" (*Journal of the House of Delegates*, October 1778, pp. 32, 36; Hening, *Statutes*, IX, 530–32).

To James Madison, Sr.

RC (LC: Madison Papers). The recipient used a portion of the cover sheet to add three columns of figures.

WILLIAMSBURG Decr. 8th. 1779

HOND SIR

Having an opportunity by Mr. Collins I add a few lines to those I sent by Col. Burnley on the Subject of your's by him.[1] The Assembly have not yet concluded their plan for complying with the requisitions from Congress.[2] It may be relied on that that can not be done without very heavy taxes on every species of property. Indeed it is thought questionable whether it will not be found absolutely impossible. No exertions however ought to be omitted to testify our zeal to support Congress in the prosecution of the War. It is also proposed to procure a large sum on loan by stipulating to pay the Interest in Tobo. A tax on This Article necessary for that purpose is to be collected.[3] Being very imperfectly acquainted with the proceedings of the Assembly on this matter I must refer you for the particulars to the return of Majr. Moore,[4] or some future opportunity. The law for escheats & forfeitures will be repealed as it respects Orphans &.[5] The effects of the measures taken by the Assembly on the credit of our money & the prices of things cannot be predicted. If our expectations had not been so invariably disappointed they ought to be supposed very considerable. But from the rapid progress of depreciation at present and the universal struggle among seller[s] to bring up prices, I can not flatter myself with the hope of any great reformation. Corn is already at £20 & rising.[6] Tobo. is also rising. Pork will probably command any price. Imported goods exceed every thing else many hundreds PerCt.

I am much at a loss how to dispose of Willey.[7] I can not think it would be expedient in the present state of things to send him out of the State. From a New Arrangement of the College here nothing is in future to be taught but the higher & rarer branches of Science.[8] The preliminary studies must therefore be pursued in private Schools or Academies. If the Academy at Prince Edward[9] is so far dissolved that you think his return thither improper, I would recommend his being put under the instruction of Mr. Maury[10] rather than suffer him to be idle at home. The languages including English, Geography, & Arithmetic ought to be his employmen[t] till he is prepared to receive a finish to his Education at this place.

By the late change also in the College, the former custom of furnishing the table for the President & professors is to be discontinued. I am induced by this consideration to renew my request for the Flour mentioned to you. It will perhaps be the only opportunity I may have of requiting received & singular favours, and for the reason just assigned will be extremely convenient.[11] I wish to know without any loss of time how far this supply may be reckoned & 5 or 600 lb. at least, I persuade myself may be spared from your Stock withou[t] encroaching on your own consumption. Perhaps Mr. R. Burnley[12] would receive & store it for me. Capt. Wm. Anderson[13] I believe also lives at that place and would probably do any favour of that sort. I am desired by a Gentleman here to procure for him 2 Bear Skins to cover the foot of his Chariot. If they can be bought any where in your Neighborhood I beg you or Ambrose will take the trouble to enquire for them & send them to Capt. Anderson at Hanover Town.[14] If the flour should come down the same opportunity will serve for them. Capt. Anderson may be informed that they are for Mr. Norton.[15] If they can be got without too much trouble I should be glad of suceeding as he will rely on my promise to procure them for him.

Having nothing to add under the head of News I subscribe myself Yr. dutiful Son

JAMES MADISON JNR.

PS. I have got the Warrant on S. Young's[16] Claim, but do not think fit to trust it to the present conveyance. There is one fine [sh]irt among mine with your mark but I believ[e it among the?] number transferred to me by my moth[er.]

1 William Collins (*ca.* 1746–1816) of Orange County was a planter and neighbor of Zachariah Burnley. The letters to and from JM, mentioned in this sentence, have not been found.

2 On 7 October 1779 the Continental Congress decided to requisition $15,000,000 from the states during 1780. Of this total, the quota assigned to Virginia was $2,500,000 or 16⅔ per cent (*Journals of the Continental Congress,* XV, 1150; Jefferson to JM, 26 July 1780, n. 2).

3 On 24 December 1779 the General Assembly enacted a law, to be in force for twelve years, imposing a tax of thirty pounds of tobacco, first payable by 1 August 1780, on almost every male, free or slave, of twenty-one years of age or over. The state government planned to use the tobacco as security for a bond issue (Hening, *Statutes,* X, 182–88; JM to Bradford, 17 July 1779, n. 3).

4 William Moore.

5 On 13 December 1779 the General Assembly amended two earlier statutes in order to assure Virginia-born orphans, wives, and widows (or wives and widows of Virginia-born husbands), who were or recently had been overseas for no unpatriotic reason, that they might recover their escheated or confiscated property, or its equivalent value (Hening, *Statutes,* X, 153–56).

6 That is, per bushel.

7 See Smith to JM, 15 September 1778 and n. 11. If William was at the grammar school of William and Mary College, JM's need to "dispose" of him is probably explained in the next footnote, as well as by JM's expected election to Congress. If the boy was there, Reverend James Madison's memory failed when he wrote JM on 18 January 1781 (*q.v.*) that "Your Brother has not returned since ye first Invasion." This was in May 1779.

8 On 4 December 1779 the Board of Visitors of the college decided to reduce its organization to five college-level schools or departments by abolishing its grammar school and two divinity schools (Lyon G. Tyler, *The College of William and Mary in Virginia: Its History and Work, 1693–1907* [Richmond, 1907], p. 60). "Science," of course, meant any systematized knowledge.

9 Hampden-Sydney Academy.

10 Walker Maury (1752–1788), graduate of the College of William and Mary and an able classical scholar, was at this time the head of a grammar school near Barboursville in Orange County. In 1780 he established a similar school in Williamsburg. Six years later, having been ordained an Episcopal minister, he moved to Norfolk to become headmaster of its academy (W. W. Scott, *History of Orange County,* p. 127; *Lower Norfolk County Virginia Antiquary,* I [1895–96], 25).

11 JM probably was the more eager to express his appreciation for Reverend James Madison's hospitality because he would likely return home soon. Less than a week after he wrote this letter, he was elected by the General Assembly to be a delegate from Virginia in the Continental Congress.

12 Richard Burnley (*ca.* 1726–*ca.* 1782), a merchant of Hanover County and a brother of Zachariah Burnley (Emma Dicken, comp., *Our Burnley Ancestors,* pp. 13, 18–19).

13 Anderson (d. 1796), senior partner in the firm of Anderson and Company of Hanover County, was a large landowner in several counties and an officer in the militia. He had been a commissioner for the sequestration of British property. He was to serve as a justice of the peace and, from 1783 to 1785, as a member of the General Assembly from Louisa County. Sometime after 1785 he became a merchant in London, England (W. P. Anderson, *Anderson Family Records* [Cincinnati, 1936], p. 11).

[14] A thriving settlement, extinct now for more than a century, on the Pamunkey River about thirty miles northeast of Richmond (Joseph Martin, ed., *A New and Comprehensive Gazetteer of Virginia* [Charlottesville, Va., 1835], p. 187; Henry Howe, *Historical Collections of Virginia* . . . [Charleston, S.C., 1845], pp. 292–93). A "chariot" was a light four-wheeled carriage.

[15] John Hatley Norton (1745–1797), junior partner in the mercantile firm of John Norton and Sons of Norfolk (Frances N. Mason, ed., *John Norton & Sons,* p. 516).

[16] Probably Samuel Young (1747–*ca.* 1837), a freeholder of Culpeper County and a private in the Virginia state line (Raleigh T. Green, comp., *Genealogical and Historical Notes on Culpeper County, Virginia,* p. 129). The nature of the warrant is unknown but was presumably for land.

Credentials as a Delegate to Continental Congress

MS (NA: PCC, Credentials of Virginia Delegates, fol. 45).

IN THE HOUSE OF DELEGATES.
the 14th: December 1779

Resolved that James Henry, Joseph Jones, James Madison jn. and John Walker Esquires, be appointed Delegates to represent this Commonwealth in Congress untill the first Monday in November next, in the room of the Gentlemen who have resigned; they having been so elected by joint ballot of both Houses of Assembly.[1]

Teste.

December 14th: 1779.   JOHN BECKLEY C. h. d.

Agreed to by the Senate   A Copy
     WILL: DREW; C. S   JOHN BECKLEY C. h. d.[2]

[1] JM submitted these credentials to Congress on the first day of his attendance, 20 March 1780 (*Journals of the Continental Congress,* XVI, 268). James Henry (1731–1804) of Accomack County served in Congress only until July 1780. He was a judge of the Virginia Court of Admiralty from 1782 to 1788 and of Virginia's General Court from 1788 to 1800. Joseph Jones (1727–1805) of King William County was a member of Congress (1777–1778, 1780–1783) and of the House of Delegates (1776–1777, 1780–1781, 1783–1785). He served also as a member of the Virginia Convention of 1788 to consider the Federal Constitution. John Walker (1744–1809) of Albemarle County attended Congress only from May to November 1780. Briefly in 1790 he served in the United States Senate (Edmund C. Burnett, ed., *Letters of Members of the Continental Congress* [8 vols.; Washington, 1921–36], V, lxiv.

[2] These initials stand, respectively, for clerk of the Senate and clerk of the House of Delegates. William Drew (*ca.* 1747–1785) of Berkeley County became clerk of the Virginia Senate in June 1779, succeeding Beckley, and retained the

office through 1784. He had been a member of the commission to dispose of Lord Dunmore's Berkeley County estate and clerk of various state and county committees (*Journal of the House of Delegates*, May 1779, p. 55; October 1780, p. 78). John Beckley (1757–1807) was the clerk of one public agency or another for the greater part of his life. He became clerk of the Henrico County Committee of Safety in 1774 and held eight other clerkships, including that of the Virginia Senate (1777–1779), the Virginia House of Delegates (1779–1789), and the U.S. House of Representatives (1789–1797, 1801–1807). He was first Librarian of Congress and an active participant in the founding of the Jeffersonian Republican party (*Journals of the Council of State*, I, 232, 295, 298, 445; III, 469, 578; Noble E. Cunningham, Jr., "John Beckley: An Early American Party Manager," *William and Mary Quarterly*, 3d ser., XIII [1956], 40–52).

To Benjamin Harrison

RC (LC: Madison Papers). The cover sheet bears the notation, "Letter James Madison Ordered to lay on the Clerks table."

WILLIAMSBURG Novr. [December][1] 16th. 1779

SIR[2]

Being notified that the General Assembly have honoured me with a delegation to serve this commonwealth in general Congress, I beg the favour of you Sir to communicate to them my acceptance thereof,[3] and my assurances that as far as fidelity and zeal can supply the place of abilities the interests of my Country shall be punctually promoted. I have the honor to be with great respect Yr. Most Obt Servt.

JAMES MADISON JUNR.

[1] Madison inadvertently wrote "Novr." The clerk correctly docketed the letter, "Decemr: 16th: 1779." Pages 397–98 of the manuscript journal of the House of Delegates in the Virginia State Library note on that date: "The Speaker laid before the House a Letter from John Walker Esqr. a member of the Privy Council or Council of State containing his acceptance of the appointment of a Delegates [*sic*] to represent this Commonwealth to Congress: also a Letter from James Madison junior Esqr. a member of the Privy Council or Council of State to the same effect: which were read and ordered to lie on the table."

[2] Speaker of the House of Delegates.

[3] Why JM, who had declined to have his name put in nomination for appointment as a delegate to Congress in June 1779 (*Journal of the House of Delegates*, May 1779, p. 51), was willing to accept six months later is unknown.

Thomas Jefferson in Council
to Samuel Huntington

RC (NA: PCC, No. 71, I, 307–9). In the hand of a clerk, except for Jefferson's signature.

WMSBURG Decr. 16. 1779.

SIR[1]

We have information from our Delegates in congress that the detention of some continental arms by the executive of this State during the course of the last summer has given considerable umbrage to congress.[2] I beg leave therefore, thro' you Sir, to lay before that honorable body facts, simply as they occurred, hoping that these will satisfy them that, the arms being justly due to this State, necessity alone dictated the measure, and that no sentiment of disrespect to congress entered into the transaction. This State in an early part of the present contest raised at first two, and soon Afterwards seven Battalions for its particular defence, finding however that the dangers of our being invaded became less, our legislature made a tender of these Battalions for the continental Service. the tender was accepted of by congress only on condition that We would permit them to carry their Arms with them.[3] They were accordingly marched to the grand army, time after time,[4] as we could get them armed. I think this condition was dispensed with as to two Battalions only which congress, induced by their increasing wants of men, permitted to march on with out their arms. This is one of the Articles of Debit in our Account of Arms against the continent, which I State particularly, in order to bring it into recollection with some of your honorable members; and because, being recollected, it will go far in our justification as to the number of arms retained with us. Since this however, at different times, and for different corps, many Smaller parcels of arms have been Sent to congress by us.[5] It is a fact, which we are to lament, that, in the earlier part of our Struggles, we were so wholly occupied by the great Object of establishing our rights, that we Attended not at all to those little circumstances of taking receipts, and vouchers, keeping regular accounts, and preparing subjects for future disputes with our friends. if we could have supported the whole continent, I believe we should have done it, and never dishonored our exertions by producing accounts; sincerely assured that, in no circumstances of future necessity or distress, a like free application of any thing theirs would have been thought hardly of or would have rendered Necessary an appeal to Accounts. hence it has happened that, in the present case, the collection of vouchers for the arms furnished by this State has become tedious and difficult. Our board of War has been Attending to this business a considerable time, but have as yet authenticated the loan of only 5664 Stand of Arms and 580 rifles. they seem however to believe that (exclusive of considerable numbers delivered where no receipts were taken and the Officers to whom delivered are dead or not to be found which of course we shall lose) they will be able to establish a right to 10,000 Stand. These arms were most of them of the very best quality, imported from Great Britain, by the State, for its own use. After the loan of so many to the continent, the loss of a considerable number put into the hands of the militia during the Short invasion of the last Spring,[6] many of which we were never able to recover, and a very recent Loan of 1000 Stand, to be sent on, at the request of congress, to South Carolina,[7] we were reduc[ed] to not more than 3000 Stand in all our Magazines. Rumors were Spread of an intended invasion by the enemy for the purpose of rescuing the convention Troops; that body of men were in the heart of our Country under a guard not able to furnish centinel[s] for ordinary duty; congress had just recommended to us to prepare for the most immediate and most vigorous operations, and to have our militia ready to march at the Shortest warning;[8] the knolege of the low State of our magazines had by some means got abroad, and Spread a general alarm among our people: in this Situation of things a vessel, loaded with arms, seemed to be guided by the hand of providence into one of our harbours.[9] they were it's true the property of our friends, but of friends indebted to us for those very articles. they were for the common defence too, and we were a part of the Body to be defended. an Officer came for the purpose of removing them out of the State. would circumstances have permitted a previous application to congress, tho' not present myself I so thoroughly know the respect which the executive bears for Congress, that I am safe in affirming that such an Application would most certainly have been made. But had they awaited that ceremony, the arms would have been gone: the continent of course would have been at the expence, & the arms exposed to the injury, and risk, of a double transportation: for I cannot but take for granted that congress would on such an Application, in the case of a State So reduced in her magazines, and reduced by Loans to them, have ordered the arms to be replaced.[10] time however did not Admit of this ceremony; the executive therefore retained 5000 Stand. We shall not draw examples of similar liberties taken by other States; we shall never recapitulate aids granted to, or taken by our brethren, from the common Stock, because we wish it to be freely used for their service, and to draw nothing from it for ourselves unless our distresses should at any time be such as to point us out to them as objects needing the common Aid. But we will observe in general, that, between congress and this State, similar freedoms in other articles, had been repeatedly and mutually taken, on many former occasions and never had been the cause of discontent to either party. This precedent then, Strengthened by the existence of an actual Debt, seemed to give a Double sanction to the executive for what they did: nor did any instance occur to them of unreadiness at any time to spare freely on continental requisition any articles within their possession or power, which might expose them to experience in turn the disregard of congress. I flatter myself therefore that that honorable Body whenever this matter shall be the subject of their deliberations will be of opinion that the proceedings of the Lieutenant Governor and council were substantially justifiable. they hope that no want of ceremony, or other smaller circumstance, may have been matter of Offence to congress. if in this they should be mistaken, feeling the most real respect for that body, impressed with the Idea that its authority can never be wounded without injury to the present union, they are to lament the misapprehension & wish to remove it by assuring you, as they may with truth, that no sentiment of theirs, either on this, or any other occasion, has justified it. A motive of duty and respect to the collective council of our union has led me into this detail to remove all ground of discontent from among us, and to Assure you Sir at the same time that I shall consider as occasions of manifesting my zeal for our sacred cause, those which shall occur of proving how sincerely

I am Sir their and your most Obedient and most humble Servant

TH: JEFFERSON[11]

---

[1] Samuel Huntington (1731–1796) was a member of the Continental Congress from 1776 to 1784, and its president in 1779–1781 and 1783. He was governor of Connecticut from 1786 to 1796.

[2] After the Continental Board of War wrote to claim the weapons, Lieutenant Governor John Page replied on 28 August 1779 that the Council of State had directed the Virginia Board of War to "retain 5000 Stand of the said Arms, and place them to the Credit of the United States in part of the Arms so furnished." This was justified by "the defenceless Condition of our Country, the want of the Arms, with which the united States have been furnished by this Common

Wealth" (H. R. McIlwaine, ed., *Official Letters of Virginia Governors*, II, 37). After deliberating upon this letter, a committee of Congress urged that body to declare that Virginia "had no right to detain the Arms imported on account and for the use of the United States, as thereby the safety and welfare of these States may be essentially endangered." The committee further recommended that Congress make known to the governor and council of Virginia that their action, if acquiesced in, would establish "a precedent that might hereafter operate to the manifest injury of the United States." Nevertheless, the committee tempered its report by suggesting that "the 5000 stand of Arms detained by the Board of War of the State of Virginia by order and direction of the Lt. Govr. and council of the said State be permitted to remain in said State and that the State of Virginia be charged therewith." Read in Congress on 20 October, this report was then recommitted and apparently no further action was ever taken on it (*Journals of the Continental Congress*, XV, 1190–91). The Virginia delegates in Congress probably informed Jefferson of the tenor of the report shortly after it was submitted. Evidently he delayed his reply until the state's Board of War had collected the data needed to defend the council's action.

3 The condition imposed by Congress on the state was reflected in this resolution of 25 March 1776: "*Resolved*, That the three colonial battalions of Virginia be also on the pay and at the expence of the continent, as soon as they shall be armed fit for service, and accordingly mustered" (*ibid.*, IV, 235).

4 Meaning "from time to time."

5 As recently as 13 April 1779 Congress had requested and received the loan of one thousand arms from Virginia. Arms had also been asked of the state on 13 March 1777 (*ibid.*, VII, 173; XIII, 444; XIV, 623).

6 See above, Henry to Jay, 11 May 1779 and notes.

7 See above, n. 5.

8 On 29 September 1779 Congress had recommended that the Virginia executive "superintend the stationing and safe keeping of the convention troops, in case any invasion shall be made on that State" (*Journals of the Continental Congress*, XV, 1126).

9 Possibly it was the privateer "General Washington," which arrived at Alexandria from Brest with a British privateer sloop captured off the coast of North Carolina. In the *Virginia Gazette* (Williamsburg, Dixon and Nicolson) of 24 July 1779, the cargo of the "General Washington" was advertised for sale (*Virginia Magazine of History and Biography*, XVI [1908], 176–77; Boyd, *Papers of Jefferson*, III, 37).

10 In the report complaining of Virginia's action in keeping the arms, the committee declared that the proper course for the state to follow was "to apply to Congress for the Arms they wanted for the use of that State, And whether there had or had not been Arms due from the United States to the State of Virginia, yet Congress, from the disposition they have ever manifested to render every assistance to the several States in the Union, would have been willing on the present occasion to gratify the State of Virginia. Provided such request could have been complied with, without manifest injury to the U. S." (*Journals of the Continental Congress*, XV, 1191).

11 This letter was read in Congress on 13 January 1780 but apparently was never answered (*ibid.*, XVI, 54).

INDEX

"Swift," 269
Swift, Jonathan, 92, 93 n.
Sykes, Livy, 240 n.
Syme, John, Jr., 49 n., 142 n.
Syme, Sarah Hoops (Mrs. John, Jr.), 49 n.
Synod; *see* Presbyterian Church, synod of

Tabb, John, 163, **164 n.**
Tabb, Martha (Giles, Mrs. William B.), 164 n.
Tacitus, 5, 21–22, 30 nn., 31 n.
Taliaferro, Lawrence, 147, **148 n.**
Tappahannock, Va., 284, 286 n., 287 n., 294, 295 n., 296
"Tartar," 267–68 n., 273 n.
Taxes, 258 n., 300, 301 n., 312, 315
Taylor, Francis, 124, **125 n.**, 147, 278, 280 n.
Taylor, George, 3 n.
Taylor, James (of Orange Co., Va.), 124, **125 n.**, 147
Taylor, James (of Surry Co., Va.), 241, **242 n.**
Taylor, Rachel Gibson (Mrs. George), 3 n.
Taylor, Richard Squire, 166–67, **168 n.**
Tazewell, John, 186, 188, **189 n.**
Temple, Benjamin, 166, **168 n.**
Terence, 10, 25 n.
Thanksgiving, Proclamation of, 270
Thomas, Rowland, 147, **148 n.**
Thompson, James, 45, **47 n.**, 160
Thucydides, 5
Thyatira, N.C., 67 n.
Timanthes, 140 n.
Tobacco, 185 n., 213, 245, 246 nn., 287 n., 301 n., 315, 317 n.
Toby; *see* Slaves
Todd, Dolley Payne; *see* Madison, Dolley Payne Todd
Todd, John, 275, 276, **277 n.**
Todd, John Payne, xvi, xx–xxii
Tories: in N.Y., 141; in Pa., 99 n., 111 n., 149; in Va., 69 n., 135, 141, 147 n., 151–52, 153 n., 161, 169 n., 189 n., 190–91, 215, 238–39, 263–64, 273 n., 295 n.; mention of, 65
Townshend Acts, 46 n.
Trade; *see* Commerce
Treasury Board; *see* Continental Congress, structure of, Board of Treasury
Treat, Richard, 91, **93 n.**
Treaty of Camp Charlotte, 116 n., 122 n., 129, 137 n.
Trenton, N.J., 47 n., 60 n.
Triplett, Roger, 230, **231 n.**
Troilus; *see* Slaves
Troops; *see* Army; Virginia troops
Tucker, George, xxiii
Tucker, Josiah, 115, **117 n.**, 160
Tureman, George, 182–83 n.
Tureman, Ignatius, 181, **182–83 n.**
Turkey, 56, 118, 120 n.
Tuscany, 187 nn., 294, 297 n.
Tyrtaeus, 126, **128 n.**

Uniontown, Pa., 260 n.
United States Supreme Court, 48 n., 217 n., 302 n.
University of Chicago, xxv–xxvi
University of Pennsylvania; *see* College of Philadelphia
University of Virginia, xxv–xxvi, 70, 302
Urbanna, Va., 286, 287 n., 292

Valley Forge, Pa., 221 n., 224 n., 234 n., 235, 236 n.
Van Schreeven, Wiliam J., xxv
Vattel, Emeric de, 126, 127 n.
Vincennes, NW. Terr., 219 n., 261, 262–63 nn., 277 n., 291 nn.
Virgil, 5, 18, 27 n., 29 n., 93 n., 152
Virginia: Board of Trade, 299 and n., 300 nn.; Board of Treasury and treasurer, 176, 188, 246 n., 248 n.; Board of War, 239 n., 321, 322 n.; commissary of provisions, 216, 218 n., 219, 223, 224 n., 227, 248 n., 260 n., 264, 314; commissary of stores, 168 n., 189 n., 229 n., 237, 243, 246 n., 247, 248 n., 252 n., 314; Committee of Safety, 164 n., 182 n., 190 n.; Court of Admiralty, 318 n.; Declaration of Rights, 166, 170–78, 178–79 nn., 184 n., 275; delegates in Continental Congress (*see* Continental Congress; Continental Congress, First); foreign agents of, 224 n., 229 n., 232–33, 277 n., 284–86, 292–94, 296; Form of Government, 165–66, 170, 171, 174–78, 178–79 nn., 184 and n., 186, 214–15, 243 n., 258 nn., 275,

PRINTED IN U.S.A.

The Papers of James Madison

DESIGNED BY JOHN B. GOETZ
COMPOSED BY THE UNIVERSITY OF CHICAGO PRESS
IN LINOTYPE JANSON WITH DISPLAY LINES IN
MONOTYPE JANSON AND CASLON OLD STYLE
PRINTED BY THE UNIVERSITY OF CHICAGO PRESS
ON WARREN'S UNIVERSITY TEXT, A PAPER WATERMARKED
WITH JAMES MADISON'S SIGNATURE AND MADE EXPRESSLY
FOR THE VOLUMES OF THIS SET
PLATES PRINTED BY MERIDEN GRAVURE COMPANY
COLOR FRONTISPIECE PRINTED BY PHOTOPRESS, INCORPORATED
MAPS DRAWN BY FRANZ ALTSCHULER
BOUND BY BROCK AND RANKIN IN COLUMBIA BAYSIDE LINEN
AND STAMPED IN GENUINE GOLD